THE WISDEN GUIDE TO
INTERNATIONAL CRICKET 2014

The definitive player-by-player guide

EDITED BY STEVEN LYNCH

First published in the UK in 2013 by
John Wisden & Co
An imprint of Bloomsbury Publishing Plc
50 Bedford Square, London WC1B 3DP
www.wisden.com
www.bloomsbury.com

Copyright © John Wisden & Co 2013

ISBN: 978 1 4081 9473 7

All rights reserved. No part of this publication may be reproduced
in any form or by any means – graphic, electronic or mechanical,
including photocopying, recording, taping or information storage
and retrieval systems – without the prior permission in writing
of the publishers.

Cover by Steve Leard
Inside photographs © Getty Images

A CIP catalogue record for this book is available from the British Library.

This book is produced using paper that is made from wood
grown in managed, sustainable forests. It is natural, renewable and
recyclable. The logging and manufacturing processes conform to the
environmental regulations of the country of origin.

Typeset in Mendoza Roman and Frutiger
by Saxon Graphics Ltd, Derby

Printed and bound in Great Britain by CPI Group (UK) Ltd, Croydon CR0 4YY

INTRODUCTION

Welcome to the **Wisden Guide to International Cricket 2014**, which includes – in words and pictures, facts and figures – details of 200 leading players from the ten Test teams, telling you *how* they play as well as where they come from. You will also find a rundown on the players from the leading non-Test nations, and a handy guide to upcoming international fixtures. To help you identify everyone on the field or in the dressing-room, there are also photographs and short descriptions of the international umpires, coaches and referees. Finally there is a section containing records for all international matches – Tests, one-dayers and Twenty20s – with a country-by-country breakdown too.

Many of the profiles in the book are edited versions from ESPN Cricinfo's player pages, used with their kind permission. We have tried to include every player likely to appear in Test cricket in 2014 – but, like all selectors, we will undoubtedly have left out someone who should have been included. Details of anyone who managed to escape our selectorial net can be found on www.cricinfo.com.

The statistics have been updated to **September 17, 2013**, the end of the international season in England. The abbreviation 'S/R' in the batting tables denotes runs per 100 balls; in the bowling it shows the balls required to take each wicket. A dash (–) in the records usually indicates that full statistics are not available (such as details of fours and sixes, or balls faced, in all domestic matches).

Thanks are due to Christopher Lane of Wisden, Charlotte Atyeo and Nick Humphrey at Bloomsbury, Rob Brown and the typesetters at Saxon, Steve Leard who designed the new cover, and Cricinfo's technical wizards Robin Abrahams and Travis Basevi.

Finally, I couldn't have managed without the support of my wife Karina, who puts up with this annual intervention into our lives with amazing patience, and our sons Daniel and Mark.

Steven Lynch
September 2013

CONTENTS

4	Player Index	214	The Netherlands
6	**Player profiles A-Z**	216	Scotland
206	Afghanistan	218	Officials
208	Canada	226	Overall records
210	Ireland	232	Country-by-country records
212	Kenya	272	International schedule 2013–14

PLAYER INDEX

AUSTRALIA
Agar, Ashton 11
Bailey, George 18
Bird, Jackson 22
Clarke, Michael 39
Cowan, Ed 41
Cummins, Pat 42
Faulkner, James 55
Fawad Ahmed 56
Finch, Aaron 57
Haddin, Brad 65
Harris, Ryan 68
Hughes, Phillip 70
Johnson, Mitchell 76
Khawaja, Usman 84
Lyon, Nathan 91
Marsh, Shaun 98
Pattinson, James 123
Rogers, Chris 141
Siddle, Peter 164
Smith, Steven 168
Starc, Mitchell 171
Wade, Matthew 193
Warner, David 196
Watson, Shane 198

BANGLADESH
Abdur Razzak 7
Abul Hasan 9
Elias Sunny 51
Enamul Haque 52
Jahurul Islam 74
Junaid Siddique 78
Mahmudullah 96
Mashrafe Mortaza 101
Mushfiqur Rahim 114
Nasir Hossain 117
Rubel Hossain 144
Shafiul Islam 155
Shahadat Hossain 156
Shahriar Nafees 158
Shakib Al Hasan 159
Sohag Gazi 169
Tamim Iqbal 174

ENGLAND
Anderson, James 14
Bairstow, Jonny 19
Bell, Ian 20
Bopara, Ravi 23
Bresnan, Tim 28
Broad, Stuart 29
Buttler, Jos 31
Carberry, Michael 32
Cook, Alastair 40
Finn, Steven 58
Hales, Alex 66
Morgan, Eoin 112
Onions, Graham 120
Panesar, Monty 121
Pietersen, Kevin 128
Prior, Matt 132
Rankin, Boyd 139
Root, Joe 143
Swann, Graeme 173
Taylor, James 176
Tredwell, James 181
Tremlett, Chris 182
Trott, Jonathan 183
Woakes, Chris 202

INDIA
Ashwin, Ravichandran 16
Dhawan, Shikhar 45
Dhoni, Mahendra Singh 46
Gambhir, Gautam 62
Harbhajan Singh 67
Jadeja, Ravindra 73
Karthik, Dinesh 81
Khan, Zaheer 83
Kohli, Virat 87
Kumar, Bhuvneshwar 89
Mishra, Amit 109
Ojha, Pragyan 119
Pathan, Irfan 122
Pujara, Cheteshwar 133
Raina, Suresh 135
Sehwag, Virender 154
Sharma, Ishant 160
Sharma, Rohit 161
Tendulkar, Sachin 178
Vijay, Murali 189
Vinay Kumar 190
Yadav, Umesh 203
Yuvraj Singh 205

NEW ZEALAND
Boult, Trent 24
Bracewell, Doug 25
Brownlie, Dean 30
Franklin, James 59
Fulton, Peter 60
Guptill, Martin 64
McClenaghan, Mitchell 92
McCullum, Brendon 93
McCullum, Nathan 94
Mills, Kyle 107
Ronchi, Luke 142
Rutherford, Hamish 147
Ryder, Jesse 148
Southee, Tim 170
Taylor, Ross 177
Vettori, Daniel 188
Wagner, Neil 194

PLAYER INDEX

Watling, B-J 197
Williamson, Kane 201

PAKISTAN
Abdur Rehman 8
Adnan Akmal 10
Ahmed Shehzad 12
Asad Shafiq 15
Azhar Ali 17
Faisal Iqbal 54
Junaid Khan 77
Kamran Akmal 80
Khurram Manzoor 85
Misbah-ul-Haq 108
Mohammad Hafeez 110
Mohammad Irfan 111
Nasir Jamshed 118
Rahat Ali 134
Saeed Ajmal 149
Shahid Afridi 157
Umar Akmal 185
Umar Gul 186
Younis Khan 204

SOUTH AFRICA
Abbott, Kyle 6
Amla, Hashim 13
de Villiers, AB 44
Duminy, J-P 48
du Plessis, Faf 49
Elgar, Dean 50
Imran Tahir 71
Ingram, Colin 72
Kallis, Jacques 79
Kleinveldt, Rory 86
McLaren, Ryan 95
Miller, David 106
Morkel, Morne 113
Petersen, Alviro 125
Peterson, Robin 126
Philander, Vernon 127
Rudolph, Jacques 145
Smith, Graeme 167
Steyn, Dale 172
Tsotsobe, Lonwabo 184

SRI LANKA
Chandimal, Dinesh 35
Dilshan, Tillekeratne 47
Eranga, Shaminda 53
Herath, Rangana 69
Jayawardene, Mahela 75
Karunaratne, Dimuth 82
Kulasekara, Nuwan 88
Lakmal, Suranga 90
Malinga, Lasith 97
Mathews, Angelo 102

Mendis, Ajantha 104
Mendis, Jeevan 105
Perera, Thisara 124
Pradeep, Nuwan 131
Randiv, Suraj 138
Sangakkara, Kumar 152
Tharanga, Upul 179
Thirimanne, Lahiru 180
Vithanage, Kithuruwan 191
Welagedara, Chanaka 199

WEST INDIES
Best, Tino 21
Bravo, Darren 26
Bravo, Dwayne 27
Chanderpaul, Shivnarine 34
Charles, Johnson 36
Deonarine, Narsingh 43
Gabriel, Shannon 61
Gayle, Chris 63
Narine, Sunil 116
Pollard, Kieron 129
Powell, Kieran 130
Ramdin, Denesh 136
Rampaul, Ravi 137
Roach, Kemar 140
Russell, Andre 146
Sammy, Darren 150
Samuels, Marlon 151
Sarwan, Ramnaresh 153
Shillingford, Shane 162
Simmons, Lendl 166

ZIMBABWE
Chakabva, Regis 33
Chatara, Tendai 37
Chigumbura, Elton 38
Masakadza, Hamilton 99
Masakadza, Shingi 100
Mawoyo, Tino 103
Mutumbami, Richmond 115
Sibanda, Vusi 163
Sikandar Raza 165
Taylor, Brendan 175
Utseya, Prosper 187
Vitori, Brian 192
Waller, Malcolm 195
Williams, Sean 200

OTHER COUNTRIES
Afghanistan 206
Canada 208
Ireland 210
Kenya 212
Netherlands 214
Scotland 216

KYLE **ABBOTT**

SOUTH AFRICA

Full name	**Kyle John Abbott**
Born	**June 18, 1987, Empangeni, KwaZulu-Natal**
Teams	**Dolphins**
Style	**Right-hand bat, right-arm fast-medium bowler**
Test debut	**South Africa v Pakistan at Centurion 2012-13**
ODI debut	**South Africa v Pakistan at Bloemfontein 2012-13**
T20I debut	**South Africa v Pakistan at Centurion 2012-13**

THE PROFILE Kyle Abbott was added to South Africa's squad for the Centurion Test against Pakistan in 2012-13 as a precaution after Morne Morkel injured a hamstring. He was expected to carry the drinks and get a sniff of the international atmosphere, but it turned out rather differently: Jacques Kallis tweaked a calf muscle at an optional practice session the day before the match, and Abbott was in. Tall, and specialising in probing, back-of-a-length seam and swing bowling at a decent if not deadly speed, he was nervous to start with: when he got up to bat, he fell down the side of the chair and badly grazed his leg. But it didn't stop him bowling ... and how. Called up for the 18th over, he dismissed Mohammad Hafeez with his sixth ball, and Misbah-ul-Haq shortly afterwards. Then, following a breather, he mopped up with five for five in 22 balls, finishing with 7 for 29 – the best figures on debut for South Africa behind 8 for 64 in 1996-97 by Lance Klusener ... who just happens to be his coach. "He has really helped me on the mental side of things and with being slightly more aggressive," said Abbott. "He has given me the push I needed." Abbott is also a useful batsman: he made 80 against Titans in January 2011, then took 5 for 53. He made his first-class debut for KwaZulu-Natal in February 2009, and progressed to the South Africa A side in 2011. But he made his case for full selection in 2012-13, ending up as the leading wicket-taker in the country with 65, including 12 in the match against Cape Cobras shortly before his remarkable Test baptism.

THE FACTS Abbott took 7 for 29 in his first Test, the ninth-best debut figures overall and the second-best for South Africa behind Lance Klusener's 8 for 64 against India at Kolkata in 1996-97... Abbott took 8 for 45 (12 for 96 in the match) for Dolphins v Cape Cobras at Cape Town in January 2013 ... In December 2000 Abbott made 116* for KwaZulu-Natal v Zimbabwe Under-13s ...

THE FIGURES *to 17.09.13* ESPNcricinfo.com

Batting & Fielding	M	Inns	NO	Runs	HS	Avge	S/R	100	50	4s	6s	Ct	St
Tests	1	1	0	13	13	13.00	46.42	0	0	1	0	0	0
ODIs	2	1	0	5	5	5.00	125.00	0	0	1	0	2	0
T20Is	1	1	0	2	2	2.00	100.00	0	0	0	0	0	0
First-class	40	58	10	908	80	18.91	43.13	0	4	127	6	11	0

Bowling	M	Balls	Runs	Wkts	BB	Avge	RpO	S/R	5i	10m
Tests	1	172	68	9	7–29	7.55	2.37	19.11	1	0
ODIs	2	86	66	1	1–35	66.00	4.60	86.00	0	0
T20Is	1	24	41	1	1–41	41.00	10.25	24.00	0	0
First-class	40	7310	3330	156	8–45	21.34	2.73	46.85	8	1

ABDUR RAZZAK

BANGLADESH

Full name **Khan Abdur Razzak**
Born **June 15, 1982, Khulna**
Teams **Khulna**
Style **Left-hand bat, slow left-arm orthodox spinner**
Test debut **Bangladesh v Australia at Chittagong 2005-06**
ODI debut **Bangladesh v Hong Kong at Colombo 2004**
T20I debut **Bangladesh v Zimbabwe at Khulna 2006-07**

THE PROFILE Another of Bangladesh's seemingly never-ending supply of left-arm spinners, Abdur Razzak first made his mark when he helped unheralded Khulna to their first-ever National Cricket League title in 2001-02. Quite tall, with a high action, "Raj" played for the A team against Zimbabwe early in 2004, and made the most of his opportunity with 15 wickets, including 7 for 17 in the third encounter on the batting paradise of Dhaka's old Bangabandhu National Stadium. He has an uncanny ability to pin batsmen down, although his action has often been questioned, most recently late in 2008, when he was suspended by the ICC after tests showed he sometimes flexed his elbow by almost twice the permitted 15 degrees. After remedial work, he was cleared to resume playing in March 2009. He was immediately hurried back, playing in the World Twenty20 in England then taking seven wickets in Bangladesh's rare one-day clean sweep against a depleted West Indies side in the Caribbean in July. Razzak had played his first Test in April 2006, against Australia on a turning track at Chittagong (even the Aussies played three spinners), but failed to take a wicket, and has continued to struggle for penetration in Tests, although he took 15 wickets in a domestic first-class game in 2011-12, and a career-best 9 for 84 the following season. But he has become an automatic one-day selection, maintaining a miserly economy-rate, and currently tops his country's wicket-taking lists in ODIs and Twenty20s. He was the only Bangladeshi signed up for the first year of the Indian Premier League in 2008, although he did not return for the second season.

THE FACTS Abdur Razzak took 5 for 29 in an ODI against Zimbabwe at Mirpur in December 2009 ... He took a hat-trick – Bangladesh's second in ODIs, after one by Shahadat Hossain in 2006 – against Zimbabwe at Mirpur in December 2010 ... Razzak's best first-class figures are 9 for 84 for Khulna v Chittagong at Bogra in November 2012 ... He took 7 for 11 (10 for 62 in the match) for Khulna at Sylhet in 2003-04 ...

THE FIGURES to 17.09.13   espncricinfo.com

Batting & Fielding	M	Inns	NO	Runs	HS	Avge	S/R	100	50	4s	6s	Ct	St
Tests	9	17	5	214	43	17.83	65.64	0	0	30	4	3	0
ODIs	144	91	35	742	53*	13.25	76.02	0	1	50	21	30	0
T20Is	27	18	10	41	9	5.12	56.94	0	0	1	0	9	0
First-class	63	104	14	1721	83	19.12	62.35	0	8	–	–	25	0

Bowling	M	Balls	Runs	Wkts	BB	Avge	RpO	S/R	5i	10m
Tests	9	2133	1185	18	3–93	65.83	3.33	118.50	0	0
ODIs	144	7491	5591	201	5–29	27.81	4.47	37.26	4	0
T20Is	27	624	720	38	4–16	18.94	6.92	16.42	0	0
First-class	63	15068	6973	251	9–84	27.78	2.77	60.03	11	4

ABDUR REHMAN

Full name	**Abdur Rehman**
Born	**March 1, 1980, Sialkot, Punjab**
Teams	**Sialkot, Habib Bank**
Style	**Left-hand bat, slow left-arm orthodox spinner**
Test debut	**Pakistan v South Africa at Karachi 2007-08**
ODI debut	**Pakistan v West Indies at Faisalabad 2006-07**
T20I debut	**Pakistan v South Africa at Johannesburg 2006-07**

THE PROFILE Abdur Rehman made his international debut late in 2006 at the ripe old age of 26 (elderly considering the usual subcontinental trait of ruthlessly exposing youth to the world's best), and immediately did well, with two wickets in each of his first three one-dayers against West Indies. He's not a huge turner of the ball, but is accurate and consistent, and can exploit the rough well. For years other spinners, usually better batsmen, were preferred – but Rehman kept himself in contention with good domestic performances: in 2006-07 he was the leading bowler as Habib Bank won the Pentangular Cup, with 11 in an important victory over Sind. With Pakistan looking for variety, Rehman got a Test chance against South Africa at home at the end of 2007, and took eight wickets on his debut – unusually, he took 4 for 105 in each innings – and finished the short series with 11 victims. After three years out of the Test side he returned in 2010-11, and grabbed his chance with 29 wickets in six Tests, including six West Indian scalps on a Basseterre "bunsen" which he said he'd like to roll up and carry around with him. He formed a potent spin partnership with Saeed Ajmal. Rehman took 6 for 25 and 5 for 40 in successive innings as England were whitewashed at the start of 2012, although he found Sri Lanka's batsmen a tougher proposition later on. A successful county stint with Somerset was marred when he tested positive for cannabis. He was banned for 12 weeks, but the county still wanted him back in 2013 – but international commitments, including a one-day recall for the Champions Trophy in England in June, got in the way.

THE FACTS Abdur Rehman had identical figures of 4 for 105 in each innings of his Test debut, the first instance of this since Willie Bates took 2 for 43 twice for England v Australia at Melbourne in 1881-82 ... Rehman took 6 for 25 against England in Abu Dhabi in January 2012 ... He took 9 for 65 (14 for 101 in the match) for Somerset v Worcestershire at Taunton in September 2012 ... Rehman made 96 for Habib Bank v National Bank in January 2006 ...

THE FIGURES to 17.09.13

Batting & Fielding	M	Inns	NO	Runs	HS	Avge	S/R	100	50	4s	6s	Ct	St
Tests	19	26	3	321	60	13.95	40.68	0	1	39	8	7	0
ODIs	28	20	6	111	31	7.92	52.85	0	0	9	1	7	0
T20Is	7	4	2	15	7	7.50	88.23	0	0	0	0	6	0
First-class	129	176	19	2645	96	16.84	–	0	12	–	–	57	0

Bowling	M	Balls	Runs	Wkts	BB	Avge	RpO	S/R	5i	10m
Tests	19	5833	2480	90	6–25	27.55	2.55	64.81	2	0
ODIs	28	1510	1056	29	4–48	36.41	4.19	52.06	0	0
T20Is	7	150	174	11	2–7	15.81	6.96	13.63	0	0
First-class	129	28571	12396	479	9–65	25.87	2.60	59.64	23	5

ABUL HASAN

Full name	**Mohammad Abul Hasan**
Born	**August 5, 1992, Kulaura**
Teams	**Sylhet**
Style	**Left-hand bat, right-arm fast-medium bowler**
Test debut	**Bangladesh v West Indies at Khulna 2012-13**
ODI debut	**Bangladesh v West Indies at Khulna 2012-13**
T20I debut	**Bangladesh v Ireland at Belfast 2012**

THE PROFILE Abul Hasan shot to fame late in 2012 when he became only the fourth No. 10 to score a Test century, and the first to do it on debut for more than 110 years. An aggressive left-hander, Abul started belligerently, zooming to 50 with four and six from successive deliveries from Darren Sammy, and only slowed down when in sight of three figures, which he eventually reached just before the end of the first day, from 106 balls. He came down to earth after that: after scoring 113 with the bat, he conceded 113 when he bowled, without taking a wicket. And he had been selected as a fast bowler, even if his previous performances had hardly set the world alight: six previous frst-class matches had produced only eight wickets. Abul had worked his way through the age-group teams, first playing as a batsman for the Sylhet Under-15s. Minhazul Abedin, a former national captain, convinced him to take up quick bowling seriously after watching a promising spell, and was rewarded a few years later when Abul claimed 34 wickets in 11 Dhaka Premier League one-day games. He was on the fringe of national selection for a while before being called up to tour Ireland in mid-2012. Abul was retained for the World Twenty20 in Sri Lanka in September, and took the only two wickets to fall in defeat by Pakistan at Pallekele. That set him up for what became a historic Test debut – but lack of penetration started to count against him, and he missed the tour of Zimbabwe in 2013 after managing only three wickets in two Tests in Sri Lanka earlier in the year.

THE FACTS Abul Hasan hit 113 on Test debut against West Indies at Khulna in November 2012, only the fourth No. 10 to score a Test century, and the second on debut after Reggie Duff (a specialist batsman going in down the order for tactical reasons) for Australia v England at Melbourne in 1901-02 ... Abul had taken only eight wickets in six first-class matches before his Test debut ... He took 5 for 26 against Zimbabwe and 5 for 50 v Pakistan in under-19 one-day internationals ...

THE FIGURES to 17.09.13   **cricinfo.com**

Batting & Fielding	M	Inns	NO	Runs	HS	Avge	S/R	100	50	4s	6s	Ct	St
Tests	3	5	3	165	113	82.50	59.35	1	0	17	5	3	0
ODIs	3	1	0	3	3	3.00	50.00	0	0	0	0	0	0
T20Is	4	1	0	9	9	9.00	112.50	0	0	1	0	0	0
First-class	12	16	3	355	113	27.30	65.61	1	1	41	13	5	0

Bowling	M	Balls	Runs	Wkts	BB	Avge	RpO	S/R	5i	10m
Tests	3	528	371	3	2–80	123.66	4.21	176.00	0	0
ODIs	3	84	106	0	–	–	7.57	–	0	0
T20Is	4	66	108	2	2–33	54.00	9.81	33.00	0	0
First-class	12	1465	903	11	2–38	82.09	3.69	133.18	0	0

ADNAN AKMAL

Full name **Adnan Akmal**
Born **March 13, 1985, Lahore**
Teams **Lahore Ravi, Sui Northern Gas**
Style **Right-hand bat, wicketkeeper**
Test debut **Pakistan v South Africa at Dubai 2010-11**
ODI debut **Pakistan v Zimbabwe at Bulawayo 2011**
T20I debut **No T20Is yet**

THE PROFILE One of three brothers to play – and keep wicket – for Pakistan, Adnan Akmal is usually considered the best pure keeper of the trio. He replaced his elder brother Kamran behind the stumps in October 2010, and took eight catches in his fourth Test, in New Zealand: it was a surprise when Mohammad Salman and Sarfraz Ahmed were both given a run with the gloves as well after the 2011 World Cup, in which Kamran had had a chequered time behind the stumps. Adnan, though, was back in favour by the time of the Zimbabwe tour in September 2011, and gave a polished performance as Pakistan won the only Test. He then produced an important innings in what was his first one-day international, briefly batting alongside his other brother, Umar. After more chopping and changing, Adnan was recalled for another Test tour of Zimbabwe in September 2013, with Kamran keeping in the limited-overs games. But for a miscommunication back in 2004, Adnan might have played for Pakistan much earlier. By mistake, both he and Kamran were called up for a national camp before a one-day tournament and, after much confusion over who was actually wanted, Kamran was the one retained – even though Bob Woolmer, Pakistan's coach at the time, apparently thought Adnan was the country's best keeper. He kept plugging away on the domestic scene, improving his batting – he made two first-class hundreds early in 2013, to double his tally – and the continuing errors of Kamran kept him in the frame. Eventually, with Kamran out of favour, Adnan received the summons to join the national squad. While he was travelling to the Gulf his brother Umar stepped in as Pakistan's wicketkeeper in a one-day international.

THE FACTS Adnan Akmal followed his brothers Kamran and Umar in keeping wicket in international matches for Pakistan ... Adnan took seven catches in an innings (11 in the match) for Lahore Blues v Karachi Blues at Karachi in December 2004 ... He scored 149* for Lahore Ravi v Hyderabad at Islamabad in February 2013 ...

THE FIGURES to 17.09.13 espncricinfo.com

Batting & Fielding	M	Inns	NO	Runs	HS	Avge	S/R	100	50	4s	6s	Ct	St
Tests	18	25	5	548	64	27.40	44.01	0	3	67	0	55	8
ODIs	5	4	1	62	27	20.66	69.66	0	0	3	0	3	0
T20Is	0	0	–	–	–	–	–	–	–	–	–	–	–
First-class	107	162	18	3823	149*	26.54	–	4	17	–	–	363	15

Bowling	M	Balls	Runs	Wkts	BB	Avge	RpO	S/R	5i	10m
Tests	18	0	–	–	–	–	–	–	–	–
ODIs	5	0	–	–	–	–	–	–	–	–
T20Is	0	0	–	–	–	–	–	–	–	–
First-class	107	0	–	–	–	–	–	–	–	–

ASHTON **AGAR**

Full name **Ashton Charles Agar**
Born **October 14, 1993, Melbourne, Victoria**
Teams **Western Australia**
Style **Left-hand bat, slow left-arm orthodox spinner**
Test debut **Australia v England at Nottingham 2013**
ODI debut **No ODIs yet**
T20I debut **No T20Is yet**

THE PROFILE Test debuts are meant to be stressful, worrying occasions – but you wouldn't have known, from Ashton Agar's relaxed demeanour, that he was winning his first cap in the 2013 Ashes series opener. You wouldn't have known it from his batting, either: strolling in with Australia in tatters at 117 for 9, the 19-year-old Agar stroked an enchanting 98 – the highest Test score by a No. 11 ever, let alone by a debutant – in a record last-wicket stand with Phillip Hughes which turned what had looked like a sizeable deficit into a lead of 65. He hit 12 fours and two sixes, and departed after narrowly missing his hundred not with a scowl but a resigned smile. "A lot of young players are very mechanical," said Justin Langer, "but he's the opposite." The oddity is that Agar was selected for his bowling – respectable slow left-arm from an easy action that makes the most of his height – ahead of Nathan Lyon, who had seemingly been inked in as the frontline spinner. In that department Agar took only two wickets, and none in the next Test at Lord's, where he was hindered by a hip injury. He sat out the rest of the series, but is sure to feature again soon. Agar, whose mother is Sri Lankan, was raised in Melbourne but was snapped up by Western Australia after doing well in the 2012 Under-19 World Cup. He made his first-class debut in January 2013, took 22 wickets in his first six Sheffield Shield matches, and was attached to the Test team for the Indian tour as part of the learning process: some good performances there landed him a spot in the Ashes squad.

THE FACTS Agar made 98 on his debut against England at Trent Bridge in July 2013: it was the highest score by a No. 11 in Tests, beating Tino Best's 95 at Edgbaston in 2012 ... He and Phillip Hughes added 163 at Trent Bridge, a new Test record for the tenth wicket, beating two instances of 151 ... Agar was, at 19 in 2013, the youngest Australian spin bowler to take a Test wicket ... He took 5 for 65 for Western Australia v South Australia at Adelaide in March 2013 ...

THE FIGURES to 17.09.13   espncricinfo.com

Batting & Fielding	M	Inns	NO	Runs	HS	Avge	S/R	100	50	4s	6s	Ct	St
Tests	2	4	0	130	98	32.50	63.10	0	1	18	2	0	0
ODIs	0	0	–	–	–	–	–	–	–	–	–	–	–
T20Is	0	0	–	–	–	–	–	–	–	–	–	–	–
First-class	13	21	7	474	98	33.85	52.66	0	4	60	6	4	0

Bowling	M	Balls	Runs	Wkts	BB	Avge	RpO	S/R	5i	10m
Tests	2	504	248	2	2–82	124.00	2.95	252.00	0	0
ODIs	0	0	–	–	–	–	–	–	–	–
T20Is	0	0	–	–	–	–	–	–	–	–
First-class	13	2306	1225	34	5–65	36.02	3.18	67.82	1	0

AHMED SHEHZAD

Full name **Ahmed Shehzad**
Born **November 23, 1991, Lahore**
Teams **Lahore Ravi, Habib Bank**
Style **Right-hand bat, occasional legspinner**
Test debut **No Tests yet**
ODI debut **Australia v Pakistan at Dubai 2008-09**
T20I debut **Australia v Pakistan at Dubai 2008-09**

PAKISTAN

THE PROFILE Ahmed Shehzad originally based his game on that of Ricky Ponting – not a bad role model – and had some success with this aggressive style in his early international outings. A solidly built right-hander with the ability to hit over the top, Shehzad was still only 19 when he made 115 in a one-day international against New Zealand in February 2011, and added another hundred against West Indies in St Lucia a couple of months later – but in between he endured a disappointing World Cup, his top score from five innings being just 13. He had made his first-class debut in January 2007, just two months after his 15th birthday, and in August 2007 he made 167 as Pakistan Under-19s chased down 342 to beat England at Derby (the home attack included Steven Finn and Chris Woakes). Shehzad followed that with some impressive performances at home as Australia's Under-19s were thrashed 5-0. Another century followed in a youth Test against Bangladesh, and he carried that form into a triangular tournament in Sri Lanka, which Pakistan won. Early in 2009 he made the Test squad for the home series against Sri Lanka, although he didn't actually play, then played his first one-day international in Dubai shortly afterwards. Since then he's been confined to the shorter formats, despite consistent runs at first-class level at home – in 2010-11 he averaged 102.71 from six matches with three centuries (one a double), and the following season made 970 runs at 44. In 2013 he followed a doughty 64 in an ODI in the West Indies by slamming 70 and 98 not out in the Twenty20 internationals in Zimbabwe in August.

THE FACTS Ahmed Shehzad was 19 when he scored 115 against New Zealand at Hamilton in February 2011: only Shahid Afridi, Imran Nazir and Salim Elahi have scored centuries at a younger age for Pakistan in ODIs ... Shehzad's 98* against Zimbabwe at Harare in August 2013 is Pakistan's highest score in T20Is ... He scored 254 for Habib Bank at Faisalabad in October 2010, and shortly afterwards made 123 and 109* for them at Sialkot ...

THE FIGURES to 17.09.13   **ESPNcricinfo.com**

Batting & Fielding	M	Inns	NO	Runs	HS	Avge	S/R	100	50	4s	6s	Ct	St
Tests	0	0	–	–	–	–	–	–	–	–	–	–	–
ODIs	27	27	1	679	115	26.11	64.66	2	2	72	7	9	0
T20Is	15	15	1	442	98*	31.57	121.42	0	3	47	14	5	0
First-class	50	86	3	3407	254	41.04	61.84	7	19	489	23	54	0

Bowling	M	Balls	Runs	Wkts	BB	Avge	RpO	S/R	5i	10m
Tests	0	0	–	–	–	–	–	–	–	–
ODIs	27	15	20	0	–	–	8.00	–	0	0
T20Is	15	0	–	–	–	–	–	–	–	–
First-class	50	1073	740	14	4-7	52.85	4.13	76.64	0	0

HASHIM **AMLA**

Full name	**Hashim Mahomed Amla**
Born	**March 31, 1983, Durban, Natal**
Teams	**Dolphins, Surrey**
Style	**Right-hand bat, occasional right-arm medium-pacer**
Test debut	**South Africa v India at Kolkata 2004-05**
ODI debut	**South Africa v Bangladesh at Chittagong 2007-08**
T20I debut	**South Africa v Australia at Brisbane 2008-09**

SOUTH AFRICA

THE PROFILE An elegant, wristy right-hander with a fine temperament, Hashim Amla was the first South African of Indian descent to reach the Test team. His elevation was hardly a surprise after he reeled off four centuries in his first eight innings in 2004-05, after captaining the Dolphins (formerly Natal) at the tender age of 21. He made his Test debut against India late in 2004, but was not an instant success, with serious questions emerging about his technique as he mustered only 36 runs in four innings against England shortly afterwards, struggling with an ungainly crouched stance and a bat coming down from somewhere in the region of gully. But he made his second chance count, with 149 against New Zealand at Cape Town in April 2006, followed by big hundreds against New Zealand (again) and India in 2007-08, before a fine undefeated 104 helped save the 2008 Lord's Test. He came into his own in India early in 2010 with a monumental 253 not out to set up victory at Nagpur, following by valiant twin centuries in defeat at Kolkata. He was dominant in England in 2012, stroking South Africa's first triple-century at The Oval and adding another important hundred in the win at Lord's that guaranteed top spot in the ICC's Test rankings. He then made 150 in an ODI at Southampton. Not originally seen as a one-day player, after slamming 140 against Bangladesh late in 2008 he made 80 not out and 97 in consecutive victories over Australia to make his place safe, then flourished to the extent that by September 2013 he had the highest average of anyone with 2000 ODI runs. Amla is a devout Muslim, whose beard is probably the most impressive in the game today.

THE FACTS Amla made 311*, South Africa's first Test triple-century, against England at The Oval in 2012 ... He scored 253* at Nagpur, and 114 and 123* at Kolkata in the two-Test series in India in February 2010: his series average of 490 has been exceeded only by England's Wally Hammond (563.00 v New Zealand in 1932-33) ... Amla's older brother Ahmed also played for the Dolphins ...

THE FIGURES *to 17.09.13*   **cricinfo.com**

Batting & Fielding	M	Inns	NO	Runs	HS	Avge	S/R	100	50	4s	6s	Ct	St
Tests	70	121	10	5785	311*	52.11	52.61	19	27	719	8	58	0
ODIs	76	73	6	3675	150	54.85	91.19	11	21	367	18	29	0
T20Is	15	15	2	269	47*	20.69	118.50	0	0	32	4	4	0
First-class	162	268	25	12582	311*	51.77	–	39	62	–	–	123	0

Bowling	M	Balls	Runs	Wkts	BB	Avge	RpO	S/R	5i	10m
Tests	70	54	37	0	–	–	4.11	–	0	0
ODIs	76	0	–	–	–	–	–	–	–	–
T20Is	15	0	–	–	–	–	–	–	–	–
First-class	162	357	253	1	1–10	253.00	4.25	357.00	0	0

JAMES **ANDERSON**

ENGLAND

Full name	**James Michael Anderson**
Born	**July 30, 1982, Burnley, Lancashire**
Teams	**Lancashire**
Style	**Left-hand bat, right-arm fast-medium bowler**
Test debut	**England v Zimbabwe at Lord's 2003**
ODI debut	**England v Australia at Melbourne 2002-03**
T20I debut	**England v Australia at Sydney 2006-07**

THE PROFILE When the force is with him, James Anderson is capable of irresistible spells, seemingly able to swing the ball round corners at an impressive speed. New Zealand were blown away at Nottingham in 2008 (Anderson 7 for 43); the following May the West Indians looked clueless in Durham, while back at Trent Bridge in 2010 Pakistan's inexperienced batsmen could hardly lay a bat on him (5 for 54 and 6 for 17). He followed that with 24 wickets in the 2010-11 Ashes triumph, and 22 in the 2013 series, despite not quite hitting his best form after taking ten in the first Test. By then he had become England's leading wicket-taker in all formats. There is still the odd bad day, when the ball isn't coming out quite right and refuses to swing: he can then sometimes look downcast. Anderson had played only occasionally for Lancashire when he was hurried into England's one-day squad in Australia in 2002-03 as cover for Andy Caddick. He didn't have a number – or even a name – on his shirt, but ten overs for 12 runs in century heat at Adelaide earned him a World Cup spot. There was a five-for in his debut Test, against Zimbabwe in 2003, and a one-day hat-trick against Pakistan ... but then a stress fracture sidelined him for most of 2006. By the end of the following year, though, Anderson looked the part of pack leader again. His batting also steadily improved: he went 54 Test innings before collecting a duck, an unlikely England record, and at Cardiff in 2009 he survived for 69 nail-chewing minutes to help stave off defeat by Australia. He is also a superb fielder.

THE FACTS Anderson was the first man to take an ODI hat-trick for England, against Pakistan at The Oval in 2003 ... In 2013 he overtook Ian Botham (528) as England's leading wicket-taker in all formats ... Anderson went 54 Test innings before being out for a duck in 2009, an English record; only AB de Villiers (78), Aravinda de Silva (75) and Clive Lloyd (58) have started with more duckless innings in Tests ...

THE FIGURES to 17.09.13   **ESPN**cricinfo.com

Batting & Fielding	M	Inns	NO	Runs	HS	Avge	S/R	100	50	4s	6s	Ct	St
Tests	87	117	42	787	34	10.49	39.07	0	0	100	2	49	0
ODIs	174	69	37	237	28	7.40	46.37	0	0	19	0	47	0
T20Is	19	4	3	1	1*	1.00	50.00	0	0	0	0	3	0
First-class	156	190	70	1189	37*	9.90	–	0	0	–	–	83	0

Bowling	M	Balls	Runs	Wkts	BB	Avge	RpO	S/R	5i	10m
Tests	87	19207	9907	329	7–43	30.11	3.09	58.37	15	2
ODIs	174	8609	7132	245	5–23	29.11	4.97	35.13	2	0
T20Is	19	422	552	18	3–23	30.66	7.84	23.44	0	0
First-class	156	31097	16132	589	7–43	27.38	3.11	52.79	25	3

ASAD SHAFIQ

Full name	**Asad Shafiq**
Born	**January 28, 1986, Karachi**
Teams	**Karachi, Pakistan International Airlines**
Style	**Right-hand bat, occasional legspinner**
Test debut	**Pakistan v South Africa at Abu Dhabi 2010-11**
ODI debut	**Pakistan v Bangladesh at Dambulla 2010**
T20I debut	**Pakistan v New Zealand at Hamilton 2010-11**

THE PROFILE A solid right-hander with a compact technique reminiscent of Javed Miandad, arguably Pakistan's finest batsman, Asad Shafiq is a product of the Karachi tape-ball circuit. He made a fine start in first-class cricket, scoring a double-century in only his seventh match and falling just short of 1000 runs in his debut summer of 2007-08, making 926 at 57.87. Second-season syndrome kicked in, and his average dipped to 21 the following year – although he performed better in one-day games – but he roared back in 2009-10 to put his name firmly in the selectors' sights: 1244 runs at a fraction under 50, with four more hundreds. He played his first one-day internationals during the Asia Cup in Sri Lanka in mid-2010, and although he missed the Tests in England that followed he played in the one-day games which rounded off that fractious tour, looking good in scoring 50 at Headingley and 40 at The Oval. A Test debut followed on a placid pitch in Abu Dhabi: Shafiq made an unhurried 61, and added 83 in his next Test, to help Pakistan to a ten-wicket victory over New Zealand at Hamilton. He sat out the first few matches of the 2011 World Cup before finally getting a game and hitting 78 not out against Zimbabwe; 46 followed against Australia, then 30 in the semi-final defeat by India to show that his earlier omission was a mistake. Shafiq nailed down a Test place in 2012, following a maiden century against Bangladesh late the previous year with some solid displays against England, then an impressive double of 75 and 100 not out against Sri Lanka at Pallekele in July. But 2013 was a letdown: apart from a five-hour Test century against South Africa at Cape Town early on, his only score of note was 84 in a one-dayer against Ireland.

THE FACTS Asad Shafiq scored 223 in only his seventh first-class match, for Karachi Whites at Faisalabad in December 2007 ... He made 181, and put on 431 for the second wicket with Yasir Hameed – who scored 300 – for North West Frontier Province against Baluchistan at Peshawar in March 2008 ...

THE FIGURES to 17.09.13   cricinfo.com

Batting & Fielding	M	Inns	NO	Runs	HS	Avge	S/R	100	50	4s	6s	Ct	St
Tests	21	34	3	1136	111	36.64	42.24	3	7	138	6	17	0
ODIs	43	42	3	1083	84	27.76	70.14	0	8	94	4	10	0
T20Is	10	10	0	192	38	19.20	103.78	0	0	19	2	3	0
First-class	66	115	9	4022	223	37.94	49.22	11	16	516	17	54	0

Bowling	M	Balls	Runs	Wkts	BB	Avge	RpO	S/R	5i	10m
Tests	21	0	–	–	–	–	–	–	–	–
ODIs	43	0	–	–	–	–	–	–	–	–
T20Is	10	0	–	–	–	–	–	–	–	–
First-class	66	158	117	1	1-14	117.00	4.44	158.00	0	0

RAVICHANDRAN **ASHWIN**

Full name **Ravichandran Ashwin**
Born **September 17, 1986, Madras (now Chennai)**
Teams **Tamil Nadu, Chennai Super Kings**
Style **Right-hand bat, offspinner**
Test debut **India v West Indies at Delhi 2011-12**
ODI debut **India v Sri Lanka at Harare 2010**
T20I debut **India v Zimbabwe at Harare 2010**

THE PROFILE A tall offspinner with a high action, Ravichandran Ashwin made a superb start in international cricket. From the word go his stats have been eye-catching: in his maiden first-class season, 2006-07, he took 31 wickets at less than 20. He showed promise with the bat as well the following season, although he was restricted by injury, and made his maiden first-class hundred in 2009-10. He was signed by Chennai Super Kings for the first IPL in 2008, and by the third instalment in 2010 proved to be the most economical regular bowler on view, often taking the new ball, and going for 6.1 an over, miserly in Twenty20 terms. Ashwin continued to perform consistently for Tamil Nadu, and captained them to the domestic one-day title in 2008-09. He was awarded a central contract that season but, with Harbhajan Singh the offspinner in possession, it was a long time before the selectors gave him a chance, particularly in Tests – even after some crafty one-day displays. But when Ashwin did get into the five-day side, against West Indies late in 2011, he immediately made it count, taking nine wickets in his first match, then adding nine more – and a century – in his third. He reached 50 wickets in only his ninth Test, an Indian record, and was making Harbhajan look like yesterday's man. He has an impressive range of variations, including his own patent version of the "Carrom" ball, which spits out of the front of the hand. England's batsmen got on top of him at the end of 2012 – but Ashwin bounced back with 29 wickets, including 12 in the Chennai Test, as Australia were whitewashed 4-0 early in 2013.

THE FACTS Ashwin took 12 for 85 against New Zealand at Hyderabad in August 2012 and 12 for 198 v Australia at Chennai in February 2013 ... He took 6 for 47 in his first Test, and made 103 in his third, both against West Indies in 2011-12 ... Ashwin took 5 for 65 and 6 for 64 for Tamil Nadu v Baroda in January 2007, in only his fourth first-class match ... He took a wicket (Tatenda Taibu of Zimbabwe) with his third ball in Twenty20 internationals ...

THE FIGURES to 17.09.13   ESPNcricinfo.com

Batting & Fielding	M	Inns	NO	Runs	HS	Avge	S/R	100	50	4s	6s	Ct	St
Tests	16	22	5	616	103	36.23	62.79	1	3	74	5	3	0
ODIs	58	34	12	376	38	17.09	83.37	0	0	31	2	15	0
T20Is	18	5	3	53	17*	26.50	120.45	0	0	6	1	3	0
First-class	51	67	17	1786	107*	35.72	58.49	3	10	251	6	18	0

Bowling	M	Balls	Runs	Wkts	BB	Avge	RpO	S/R	5i	10m
Tests	16	5433	2625	92	7-103	28.53	2.89	59.05	9	2
ODIs	58	3079	2467	80	3-24	30.83	4.80	38.48	0	0
T20Is	18	425	530	14	2-16	48.00	7.48	30.35	0	0
First-class	51	13927	6394	226	7-103	28.29	2.75	61.62	20	5

AZHAR ALI

Full name	**Azhar Ali**
Born	**February 19, 1985, Lahore**
Teams	**Lahore, Khan Research Laboratories**
Style	**Right-hand bat, legspinner**
Test debut	**Pakistan v Australia at Lord's 2010**
ODI debut	**Pakistan v Ireland at Belfast 2011**
T20I debut	**No T20Is yet**

THE PROFILE Azhar Ali made steady progress in domestic cricket after a stuttering start in which he played only eight first-class matches in five seasons after his 2001-02 debut. Promotion to open paid off, though, and he made 409 runs at 68 in 2006-07 – with his first two hundreds – and improved on that in each of his next two seasons, good going in a country where opening has long been difficult. Azhar has a compact and correct technique, and although he initially had a few problems against the shorter ball he seemed to have addressed them by the end of the 2010 England tour, during which he was unlucky to miss a maiden Test century at The Oval, stranded on 92 after more than four hours' batting. Azhar started that long trip batting at No. 3, after the selectors decided they could do without Younis Khan and Mohammad Yousuf (although Yousuf was eventually called up), and although his inexperience showed at first he played two important innings – 30 and 51 – as Pakistan beat Australia in the second Test at Headingley. Once the dust settled from a fractious tour, Azhar continued to do well in Tests, although he was still not seen as a one-day player. He finally cracked the three-figure barrier against Sri Lanka in October 2011, and secured his place the following year with 157 against England in February. He added 157 and 136 in Sri Lanka later in the year, not long after improving his one-day stats with 96 and 81 not out against them. In 2013, after a brief one-day return, he struggled in the Tests in South Africa before unsurprisingly having more success in Zimbabwe.

THE FACTS Azhar Ali scored 157 against England at Dubai in February 2012 – and 157 v Sri Lanka in Colombo in June ... After not making a century in his first nine first-class matches, spread over five seasons, he scored nine in his next 17 games ... Azhar took 14 for 128 for Lahore Greens v Azad Jammu & Kashmir in a non-first-class match in October 2000 ...

THE FIGURES to 17.09.13   cricinfo.com

Batting & Fielding	M	Inns	NO	Runs	HS	Avge	S/R	100	50	4s	6s	Ct	St
Tests	29	54	4	2029	157	40.58	38.94	4	15	209	3	22	0
ODIs	14	14	3	452	96	41.09	64.84	0	4	39	1	2	0
T20Is	0	0	–	–	–	–	–	–	–	–	–	–	–
First-class	99	168	16	5502	157	36.19	–	16	26	–	–	82	0

Bowling	M	Balls	Runs	Wkts	BB	Avge	RpO	S/R	5i	10m
Tests	29	102	67	1	1-4	67.00	3.94	102.00	0	0
ODIs	14	48	41	0	–	–	5.12	–	0	0
T20Is	0	0	–	–	–	–	–	–	–	–
First-class	99	1371	893	26	4-34	34.34	3.90	52.73	1	0

GEORGE **BAILEY**

Full name **George John Bailey**
Born **September 7, 1982, Launceston**
Teams **Tasmania, Hampshire**
Style **Right-hand bat**
Test debut **No Tests yet**
ODI debut **Australia v West Indies at Kingstown 2011-12**
T20I debut **Australia v India at Sydney 2011-12**

THE PROFILE George Bailey caused a stir – and a footnote in history – when he was named as Australia's Twenty20 captain early in 2012. He hadn't played international cricket before, so became the first man to skipper the full Australian side on debut since Dave Gregory back in the very first Test of all in 1877. Bailey got the job after some adroit leadership of Tasmania, where he took the reins in 2009-10 after three years as Daniel Marsh's deputy. Tasmania won the one-day FR Cup in Bailey's first year in charge, when he was second in the runscoring lists with 538 at 60 – he was called up for the Australian one-day squad to play the Chappell-Hadlee series against New Zealand, but didn't make the starting XI – and in 2010-11 they won the Sheffield Shield too. His early international results were encouraging, although there were, almost inevitably, murmurs from some who doubted his right to be in the side. Bailey had been a consistent performer in the Tasmanian middle order for some years: he made 673 Shield runs in 2008-09, after 734 the previous season. After his Twenty20 international baptism he was included in the ODI side too, and made some useful contributions throughout 2012 – including 65 against England at The Oval, then an important unbeaten 57 as Pakistan were downed in Sharjah at the end of August. Early the following year Bailey made his first ODI century – an unbeaten 125 against West Indies at Perth – and remained a short-format regular, captaining in Twenty20s, and in the 50-overs Champions Trophy in England in June as Michael Clarke's back was playing up. But a Test cap remained elusive.

THE FACTS Bailey was only the second man, after Dave Gregory in the first-ever Test in 1877, to captain Australia in his first international match ... He made 160* for Tasmania v Victoria at Hobart in February 2011 ... Bailey has played for Scotland, and scored 123* against Warwickshire at Edgbaston in 2010 ... His great-great-great-grandfather (also George) was part of the Australian team which toured England in 1878 without playing a Test ...

THE FIGURES *to 17.09.13*   **cricinfo.com**

Batting & Fielding	M	Inns	NO	Runs	HS	Avge	S/R	100	50	4s	6s	Ct	St
Tests	0	0	–	–	–	–	–	–	–	–	–	–	–
ODIs	29	27	4	1061	125*	46.13	84.54	1	8	77	21	19	0
T20Is	18	15	3	298	63	24.83	134.23	0	1	24	10	8	0
First-class	96	170	15	5936	160*	38.29	55.06	14	30	–	–	86	0

Bowling	M	Balls	Runs	Wkts	BB	Avge	RpO	S/R	5i	10m
Tests	0	0	–	–	–	–	–	–	–	–
ODIs	29	0	–	–	–	–	–	–	–	–
T20Is	18	0	–	–	–	–	–	–	–	–
First-class	96	84	46	0	–	–	3.28	–	0	0

JONNY **BAIRSTOW**

Full name	**Jonathan Marc Bairstow**
Born	**September 26, 1989, Bradford**
Teams	**Yorkshire**
Style	**Right-hand bat, wicketkeeper**
Test debut	**England v West Indies at Lord's 2012**
ODI debut	**England v India at Cardiff 2011**
T20I debut	**England v West Indies at The Oval 2011**

THE PROFILE A star was born – or so it seemed – in the closing stages of the 2011 season. England looked up against it, needing 75 from 50 balls to win the final ODI against India at Cardiff, when the coathanger-shouldered debutant Jonny Bairstow strolled in. Seemingly unfazed, he clouted 41 from 21 balls, including three sixes. The second one, off the medium-pacer Vinay Kumar, disappeared into the River Taff, and third sailed out of the ground too. "I think we've just found a player," said Alastair Cook. In 2012 Bairstow made his Test debut, and encountered a few problems against West Indian bouncers – but, recalled against South Africa when Kevin Pietersen was dropped, he lit up Lord's with two fine knocks of 95 and 54, full of his trademark whipped on-drives. His progress stalled a little in 2013, with seven innings between 14 and 67 in his maiden Ashes series. The son of the former England player David Bairstow, Jonny is also a red-haired wicketkeeper, though good enough to play solely as a batsman. He was the inaugural *Wisden* Schools Cricketer of the Year in 2007, and signed a full-time contract with Yorkshire two years later. He made an immediate impression with 82 on first-class debut against Somerset in June, and added five more fifties that season. He went close to 1000 first-class runs in 2010, but a century still eluded him – something he put right in fine style against Nottinghamshire in May 2011, converting his maiden ton into 205. His stirring international debut soon followed: the only sadness was that his father wasn't there to see it. David Bairstow took his own life early in 1998, when Jonny was just eight.

THE FACTS Bairstow made 205 for Yorkshire v Nottinghamshire at Trent Bridge in May 2005 ... He scored 41* from 21 balls in his first Twenty20 international, against India at Cardiff in September 2011 ... Bairstow made 205, his maiden first-class century, for Yorkshire v Nottinghamshire at Trent Bridge in May 2011 ... His late father David played four Tests and 21 ODIs for England between 1979 and 1984 ...

THE FIGURES to 17.09.13   **ESPNcricinfo.com**

Batting & Fielding	M	Inns	NO	Runs	HS	Avge	S/R	100	50	4s	6s	Ct	St
Tests	12	20	2	544	95	30.22	48.22	0	4	70	2	6	0
ODIs	7	6	1	119	41*	23.80	76.77	0	0	9	3	3	0
T20Is	18	14	4	194	60*	19.40	108.37	0	1	16	5	21	0
First-class	77	127	20	4767	205	44.55	–	8	31	–	–	149	5

Bowling	M	Balls	Runs	Wkts	BB	Avge	RpO	S/R	5i	10m
Tests	12	0	–	–	–	–	–	–	–	–
ODIs	7	0	–	–	–	–	–	–	–	–
T20Is	18	0	–	–	–	–	–	–	–	–
First-class	77	0	–	–	–	–	–	–	–	–

IAN **BELL**

Full name **Ian Ronald Bell**
Born **April 11, 1982, Walsgrave, Coventry**
Teams **Warwickshire**
Style **Right-hand bat, right-arm medium-pace bowler**
Test debut **England v West Indies at The Oval 2004**
ODI debut **England v Zimbabwe at Harare 2004-05**
T20I debut **England v Pakistan at Bristol 2006**

ENGLAND

THE PROFILE Ian Bell was earmarked for greatness long before he was drafted into the England squad in New Zealand in 2001-02, aged 19. Tenacious and technically sound, with a cover-drive to die for, Bell is in the mould of Michael Atherton, who was burdened with similar expectations a generation earlier and was similarly adept at leaving the ball outside off. Bell had played only 13 first-class matches when he got that England call-up, and his form dipped at first. He finally made his Test debut against West Indies in August 2004, making 70 at The Oval, before returning the following summer to lift his average to an obscene 297 against Bangladesh. Such rich pickings soon ceased: Bell mustered just 171 runs in the 2005 Ashes. But he bounced back better for the experience, collecting 313 runs in Pakistan, including a classy century at Faisalabad. And when Pakistan toured in 2006, Bell repeated the dose, with elegant hundreds in each of the first three Tests. He improved his record against the Aussies in 2006-07 without going on to the big score, then in 2008 made 199 against South Africa at Lord's. He missed the start of the 2009 Ashes, returning only when Kevin Pietersen was injured, but has been very productive since: after 140 at Durban, plus two tons against Bangladesh, he hit a cathartic century in the Ashes triumph at Sydney in January 2011, and four hundreds – one a double – against Sri Lanka and India at home. He had a quieter time in Tests in 2012, but stroked three centuries in the following year's Ashes series, and resumed his old role as a 50-overs opener.

THE FACTS After three Tests, and innings of 70, 65* and 162*, Bell's average was 297.00; he raised that to 303.00 before Australia started getting him out – only Lawrence Rowe (336), David Lloyd (308) and "Tip" Foster (306) have ever had better averages in Test history ... Bell has made Test centuries on eight different English grounds (but, oddly, not yet on his home ground of Edgbaston): no-one else has managed more than six ... Bell made 262* for Warwickshire v Sussex at Horsham in May 2004 ...

THE FIGURES to 17.09.13   **ESPNcricinfo.com**

Batting & Fielding	M	Inns	NO	Runs	HS	Avge	S/R	100	50	4s	6s	Ct	St
Tests	93	160	21	6487	235	46.66	49.47	20	37	766	25	74	0
ODIs	135	131	11	4428	126*	36.90	74.87	3	27	428	26	43	0
T20Is	7	7	1	175	60*	29.16	119.86	0	1	21	2	4	0
First-class	228	383	43	15580	262*	45.82	–	44	80	–	–	164	0

Bowling	M	Balls	Runs	Wkts	BB	Avge	RpO	S/R	5i	10m
Tests	93	108	76	1	1–33	76.00	4.22	108.00	0	0
ODIs	135	88	88	6	3–9	14.66	6.00	14.66	0	0
T20Is	7	–	–	–	–	–	–	–	–	–
First-class	228	2827	1598	47	4–4	34.00	3.39	60.14	0	0

TINO **BEST**

Full name **Tino La Bertram Best**
Born **August 26, 1981, Richmond Gap, St Michael, Barbados**
Teams **Barbados**
Style **Right-hand bat, right-arm fast bowler**
Test debut **West Indies v Australia at Bridgetown 2003**
ODI debut **West Indies v Bangladesh at Kingstown 2004**
T20I debut **West Indies v Australia at Brisbane 2012-13**

THE PROFILE If cricket had prizes for enthusiasm and lung-busting effort, Tino Best would win every time. He charges in, confident and energetic, and tries to bowl as fast as possible. In his early days he was likened to a previous Barbadian great, Wes Hall. Best is a bit less fast and a lot less tall, so the comparison is a flattering one – but he was originally capable of nudging the speedo over 90mph, and has tightened his control from his wild and woolly early days: he was banned from bowling in a Test in Sri Lanka in 2005 after delivering three beamers. He came to prominence in 2003, topping the domestic averages with 39 wickets, and played against Australia at home in Barbados that May, without taking a wicket. He impressed in England in 2004, at least with his enthusiasm – his figures, as West Indies slumped to seven defeats out of eight, weren't great, and he was memorably psyched out by Andrew Flintoff while batting at Lord's: jokingly advised to "Mind the windows, Tino," Best tried to blast the next ball into the pavilion, and was immediately stumped. He then injured his back and missed the rest of the tour. He had a spell with Yorkshire, and briefly reappeared in West Indian colours in 2009, when the senior players fell out with the board. That seemed to be that, but he made a surprise return in England in 2012, after injuries to other bowlers, and biffed 95 – the best Test score by a No. 11 – at Edgbaston. Suddenly a first choice at last, he did well at home against New Zealand and Bangladesh – and even cracked the Twenty20 team.

THE FACTS Best made 95, the highest Test score at the time by a No. 11, against England at Edgbaston in June 2012 (Australia's Ashton Agar broke the record in 2013) … Best was banned from bowling after sending down a beamer to Sri Lanka's Rangana Herath at Kandy in July 2005 … Best took 5 for 24, his first Test five-for, against Bangladesh at Mirpur in November 2012 – and added 6 for 40 in the second Test at Khulna … He took 7 for 33 (11 for 66 in the match) for Barbados v Windward Islands in January 2004 …

THE FIGURES *to 17.09.13*   **cricinfo.com**

Batting & Fielding	M	Inns	NO	Runs	HS	Avge	S/R	100	50	4s	6s	Ct	St
Tests	20	28	5	326	95	14.17	58.63	0	1	42	4	5	0
ODIs	25	16	8	76	24	9.50	60.80	0	0	7	0	4	0
T20Is	4	1	1	17	17*	–	188.88	0	0	0	2	0	0
First-class	98	126	23	1312	95	12.73	–	0	2	–	–	33	0

Bowling	M	Balls	Runs	Wkts	BB	Avge	RpO	S/R	5i	10m
Tests	20	3001	1758	47	6–40	37.40	3.51	63.85	2	0
ODIs	25	1246	1087	33	4–35	32.93	5.23	37.75	0	0
T20Is	4	78	77	3	3–18	25.66	5.92	26.00	–	–
First-class	98	12963	7952	290	7–33	27.42	3.68	44.70	12	2

JACKSON **BIRD**

Full name	**Jackson Munro Bird**
Born	**December 11, 1986, Sydney**
Teams	**Tasmania**
Style	**Right-hand bat, right-arm fast-medium bowler**
Test debut	**Australia v Sri Lanka at Melbourne 2012-13**
ODI debut	**No ODIs yet**
T20I debut	**No T20Is yet**

AUSTRALIA

THE PROFILE Jackson Bird is a tall fast bowler who runs up and delivers with a hint of the former Australian paceman Michael Kasprowicz – and like Kasper he doesn't bowl at an express speed. Bird concentrates on attacking the stumps, and generates just enough swing and seam movement to make himself an awkward proposition. He moved from his native New South Wales to Tasmania in search of more opportunities, and it paid off immediately: in his debut Sheffield Shield season in 2011-12 Bird led the tournament wicket-takers with 53 at 16. That included ten in his second match, against Victoria, and 11 for 95 against Western Australia at Hobart in the last game before the final, in which his five wickets weren't quite enough to conjure up victory for Tasmania over Queensland. Bird toured England in 2012 with the A team, dismissing the opposing captain Eoin Morgan for a duck in the first representative game. A good start to the 2012-13 domestic season – including a career-best 6 for 25 against WA – put Bird in the frame for a Test cap as other fast bowlers kept going down injured, and he made his debut on Boxing Day at the MCG. He took two wickets in each innings to help consign Sri Lanka to a heavy defeat, then seven more in another convincing victory at Sydney. In India shortly afterwards he injured his back, but was part of the 2013 Ashes squad, playing in the close encounter at Chester-le-Street. After that, though, the England tour ended in worryingly similar fashion to his Indian one: Bird again flew home early after feeling twinges in his back, joining several other Aussie pacemen on the injured list.

THE FACTS Bird took 5 for 32 and 6 for 63, including a hat-trick, for Tasmania v Western Australia at Hobart in March 2012 ... He claimed 5 for 35 and 5 for 61 in his second first-class match, against Victoria at Melbourne in November 2011 ... Bird's father works in the film industry in Romania, and keeps up with his son's cricket online ... Bird took 6 for 25 for Tasmania v WA at Hobart in November 2012 ...

THE FIGURES to 17.09.13   **ESPN**cricinfo.com

Batting & Fielding	M	Inns	NO	Runs	HS	Avge	S/R	100	50	4s	6s	Ct	St
Tests	3	4	3	7	6*	7.00	13.20	0	0	1	0	1	0
ODIs	0	0	–	–	–	–	–	–	–	–	–	–	–
T20Is	0	0	–	–	–	–	–	–	–	–	–	–	–
First-class	23	22	11	87	26	7.90	28.15	0	0	13	0	10	0

Bowling	M	Balls	Runs	Wkts	BB	Avge	RpO	S/R	5i	10m
Tests	3	633	303	13	4–41	23.30	2.87	48.69	0	0
ODIs	0	0	–	–	–	–	–	–	–	–
T20Is	0	0	–	–	–	–	–	–	–	–
First-class	23	4614	2264	109	6–25	20.77	2.94	42.33	6	2

RAVI **BOPARA**

Full name	**Ravinder Singh Bopara**
Born	**May 4, 1985, Forest Gate, London**
Teams	**Essex**
Style	**Right-hand bat, right-arm medium-pace bowler**
Test debut	**England v Sri Lanka at Kandy 2007-08**
ODI debut	**England v Australia at Sydney 2006-07**
T20I debut	**England v New Zealand at Manchester 2008**

ENGLAND

THE PROFILE Ravi Bopara has had an up-and-down Test career. Uniquely he followed three successive ducks (against Sri Lanka late in 2007, including an embarrassing first-ball run-out) with three successive centuries against West Indies in 2009, despite being dropped after his maiden ton in Barbados. Those hundreds meant he was inked in at No. 3 against Australia for the 2009 Ashes – helping usher Michael Vaughan into retirement – but his wristy technique proved too loose, and he made only 105 runs in seven innings. His usually excellent fielding wavered too, while his energetic medium-pacers proved toothless. He reacted to the chop by making 201 for Essex against Surrey, and was back for the chastening one-day series against Australia. After that, 60 against South Africa in the 2011 World Cup and 96 against India at The Oval in September helped secure a one-day place, but in 2012 he played one Test against South Africa then dropped out for personal reasons, only returning in the end-of-season one-dayers. The following year, unwanted in Tests, he made an ODI hundred against Ireland. Bopara has packed a lot in since he signed for Essex at 17 in 2002. A good county season in 2006 won him a place in the Academy squad which was based in Perth during that winter's Ashes whitewash. When Kevin Pietersen broke a rib in the first match of the one-day tournament, Bopara was summoned: not worried about having such big boots to fill, he made his debut in front of the Sydney Hill, and bowled Australia's "finisher", Michael Hussey, as England began the amazing turnaround that eventually won them that series.

THE FACTS Bopara hit 229 for Essex v Northamptonshire at Chelmsford in June 2007 ... He made 104 (at Bridgetown), 143 (at Lord's) and 108 (at Chester-le-Street) in successive Test innings, all against West Indies, in 2009; his previous three Test innings had all been ducks ... Bopara scored 101* against Ireland at Dublin in September 2013, and shared an ODI-record fifth-wicket stand of 226* with Eoin Morgan ... He made 201* for Essex in the English 50-over competition at Leicester in June 2008 ...

THE FIGURES to 17.09.13   **ESFNcricinfo.com**

Batting & Fielding	M	Inns	NO	Runs	HS	Avge	S/R	100	50	4s	6s	Ct	St
Tests	13	19	1	575	143	31.94	52.89	3	0	71	2	6	0
ODIs	94	86	18	2216	101*	32.58	79.14	1	11	182	30	27	0
T20Is	26	23	4	441	59	23.21	104.75	0	2	35	5	6	0
First-class	137	228	28	8249	229	41.24	53.16	23	31	–	–	79	0

Bowling	M	Balls	Runs	Wkts	BB	Avge	RpO	S/R	5i	10m
Tests	13	434	290	1	1–39	290.00	4.00	434.00	0	0
ODIs	94	1367	1095	30	4–38	36.50	4.80	45.56	0	0
T20Is	26	166	222	9	4–10	24.66	8.02	18.44	0	0
First-class	137	9856	6184	149	5–75	41.50	3.76	66.14	1	0

TRENT **BOULT**

NEW ZEALAND

Full name	Trent Alexander Boult
Born	July 22, 1989, Rotorua
Teams	Northern Districts
Style	Right-hand bat, left-arm fast-medium bowler
Test debut	New Zealand v Australia at Hobart 2011-12
ODI debut	New Zealand v West Indies at Basseterre 2012
T20I debut	New Zealand v England at Auckland 2012-13

THE PROFILE Fast bowler Trent Boult was viewed as an international prospect ever since he was included, as a 17-year-old, in the New Zealand A winter training squad in 2007. One reason the selectors liked the look of him is that he's a left-armer, and New Zealand have always been fond of those, dating back to the likes of Richard Collinge, Graham Troup and Geoff Allott. Boult is also fairly quick, moves the ball away well, and has the potential to be a handy batsman too. He was chosen for the A-team tour of India late in 2008, making his first-class debut in Chennai before he'd played at home (his maiden wicket was Suresh Raina). He came to the fore in 2010-11 with 32 wickets at 25.34, which helped earn him a national contract for the first time. And late in 2011 he got a Test chance when Daniel Vettori was injured – and played his part with four wickets in a rare Kiwi victory over Australia. Boult nailed down a Test place late in 2012, knocking back Sachin Tendulkar's middle stump at Hyderabad in August, then taking seven wickets in Colombo in November. Early in 2013 he demolished England with 6 for 68 at Auckland, then was one of the bright spots for New Zealand in the disappointing return series in May, taking 5 for 57 at Headingley before picking up a side strain that kept him out of the Champions Trophy. Boult's favourite cricketer is Wasim Akram – a pretty good role model for any aspiring left-arm quick.

THE FACTS Boult took 5 for 58 for Northern Districts v Otago in Dunedin in November 2008, in his first first-class match in New Zealand (his third overall) ... He took 6 for 68 against England at Auckland in March 2013 ... In the 2007-08 Under-19 World Cup he took 7 for 20 as Malaysia, the hosts, were shot out for 47 in Johor ... Boult's brother Jonothon has also played for ND ...

THE FIGURES to 17.09.13   **ESPNcricinfo.com**

Batting & Fielding	M	Inns	NO	Runs	HS	Avge	S/R	100	50	4s	6s	Ct	St
Tests	15	24	12	159	33*	13.25	61.62	0	0	13	9	5	0
ODIs	8	4	2	8	5	4.00	57.14	0	0	0	0	1	0
T20Is	3	1	0	4	4	4.00	66.66	0	0	0	0	0	0
First-class	42	57	18	471	46	12.07	47.10	0	0	50	18	17	0

Bowling	M	Balls	Runs	Wkts	BB	Avge	RpO	S/R	5i	10m
Tests	15	2910	1427	49	6-68	29.12	2.94	59.38	2	0
ODIs	8	351	286	6	2-45	47.66	4.88	58.50	0	0
T20Is	3	60	100	2	2-40	50.00	10.00	30.00	0	0
First-class	42	7459	3560	131	6-68	27.17	2.86	56.93	7	0

DOUG **BRACEWELL**

Full name	**Douglas Andrew John Bracewell**
Born	**September 28, 1990, Tauranga, Bay of Plenty**
Teams	**Central Districts**
Style	**Right-hand bat, right-arm fast-medium bowler**
Test debut	**New Zealand v Zimbabwe at Bulawayo 2011-12**
ODI debut	**New Zealand v Zimbabwe at Harare 2011-12**
T20I debut	**New Zealand v Zimbabwe at Harare 2011-12**

THE PROFILE Doug Bracewell is a brawny fast-medium bowler with a fine pedigree: his father Brendon bowled fast for New Zealand, his uncle John played for the national side and later coached them, and two more uncles and a cousin also played first-class cricket. That all meant that Doug had a lot to live up to when he was himself promoted – on promise rather than performance – into the national side late in 2011. But he confirmed that promise by taking nine for 60 in the match as New Zealand pulled off a rare victory at Hobart in December, their first Test win in Australia for 26 years. Bracewell had not expected to be playing Tests so soon: on the preceding trip to Zimbabwe he was initially viewed as more of a one-day player. But he took four wickets in his first two Twenty20 internationals there, and three in his first two ODIs, then injuries to others let him in for the one-off Test at Bulawayo. He took 5 for 85 in the second innings, but 2013 was tougher: he missed the home series against England with a foot injury, and took a solitary wicket in his one appearance in the return series, at Headingley. Bracewell had finished an impressive first year of Test cricket with 40 wickets in 11 matches. Ironically he found it harder going in limited-overs games, although his batting – which once brought him 97 against Wellington – should ensure he remains in the mix. Bracewell is named after the great Australian batsman Doug Walters, one of his father's favourite players – although the son admits "I don't have a favourite Aussie." He was, unsurprisingly, spotted at an early age: he and his cousin Michael played in the Under-19 World Cup in 2010.

THE FACTS Bracewell took 6 for 40 on the final day – including Michael Clarke and Mike Hussey for ducks – at Hobart in December 2012, as New Zealand won a Test in Australia for the first time since 1985-86 ... He scored 97 for Central Districts v Wellington in November 2010, and took 7 for 35 for CD v Canterbury in February 2013 ... Bracewell's father Brendon won six Test caps for New Zealand as a fast bowler, while his uncle John played 41 as an offspinning allrounder, and later coached the national side ...

THE FIGURES to 17.09.13   ESPNcricinfo.com

Batting & Fielding	M	Inns	NO	Runs	HS	Avge	S/R	100	50	4s	6s	Ct	St
Tests	16	30	2	291	43	10.39	42.48	0	0	37	3	5	0
ODIs	7	4	1	14	8*	4.66	48.27	0	0	0	0	2	0
T20Is	13	7	4	70	21*	23.33	129.62	0	0	5	3	5	0
First-class	41	65	8	1161	97	20.36	54.97	0	7	164	13	15	0

Bowling	M	Balls	Runs	Wkts	BB	Avge	RpO	S/R	5i	10m
Tests	16	2836	1599	47	6-40	34.02	3.38	60.34	2	0
ODIs	7	384	336	8	3-55	42.00	5.25	48.00	0	0
T20Is	13	244	391	16	3-25	24.43	9.61	15.25	0	0
First-class	41	7376	4237	125	7-35	33.89	3.44	59.00	4	0

DARREN **BRAVO**

WEST INDIES

Full name	**Darren Michael Bravo**
Born	**February 6, 1989, Santa Cruz, Trinidad**
Teams	**Trinidad & Tobago**
Style	**Left-hand bat, occasional medium-pacer**
Test debut	**West Indies v Sri Lanka at Galle 2010-11**
ODI debut	**West Indies v India at Kingston 2009**
T20I debut	**West Indies v Zimbabwe at Port-of-Spain 2009-10**

THE PROFILE Darren Bravo is the younger half-brother of allrounder Dwayne, but although he can bowl a bit it is his batting – and quicksilver fielding, like Dwayne's – which aroused the interest of the selectors. A left-hander, Bravo junior has a style eerily reminiscent of Brian Lara – not a bad role model. "There are some similarities, like the batting technique, and they look alike a bit," said Chris Gayle, his first international captain. Bravo is actually a distant relative of Lara's, on his mother's side, and, like Lara, was born in Santa Cruz in Trinidad. "I go out there and play my game, the Darren Bravo game," he says, "and if in the eyes of the people it looks like Lara, then that is their judgment. At the end of the day it is just my game." Bravo scored 605 runs at 45 in 2008-09, his first full season for Trinidad & Tobago, including centuries against Barbados and the Windward Islands. This pushed him to the fringes of the West Indian side, and he made his debut alongside Dwayne in the short one-day series against India in June, scoring 19 and 21 in the only two innings the weather allowed him. Later in 2010 he made his Test debut in Sri Lanka, scoring half-centuries in all three matches, and really came of age the following year, extending his maiden Test century in October to 195 against Bangladesh, and following that up with lip-smacking innings of 136 and 166 against sterner foes, India. He had a few problems against the moving ball in England early in 2012, but regained his form against weaker opposition, adding another Test hundred against Bangladesh and a maiden one-day ton at Zimbabwe's expense early in 2013. Given Bravo's flourishing backlift and penchant for the flashing cover-drive, those Lara comparisons are likely to hang around for a while yet.

THE FACTS Darren Bravo made his debut, alongside his half-brother Dwayne, India at home in June 2009 ... He made his first three Test centuries inside six weeks at the end of 2011: 195 against Bangladesh at Mirpur, then 136 and 166 in India in November ... After 12 Tests, Bravo had exactly the same batting record as Brian Lara – 941 runs at an average of 47.05 ...

THE FIGURES to 17.09.13   **ESPNcricinfo.com**

Batting & Fielding	M	Inns	NO	Runs	HS	Avge	S/R	100	50	4s	6s	Ct	St
Tests	23	41	4	1649	195	44.56	46.46	4	8	179	18	17	0
ODIs	65	62	8	1687	100*	31.24	69.39	1	12	143	30	20	0
T20Is	10	9	0	191	42	21.22	109.14	0	0	19	6	0	0
First-class	52	88	7	3238	195	39.97	–	7	17	–	–	45	0

Bowling	M	Balls	Runs	Wkts	BB	Avge	RpO	S/R	5i	10m
Tests	23	0	–	–	–	–	–	–	–	–
ODIs	65	0	–	–	–	–	–	–	–	–
T20Is	10	0	–	–	–	–	–	–	–	–
First-class	52	52	28	1	1–9	28.00	3.23	52.00	0	0

DWAYNE BRAVO

Full name	**Dwayne John Bravo**
Born	**October 7, 1983, Santa Cruz, Trinidad**
Teams	**Trinidad & Tobago, Chennai Super Kings**
Style	**Right-hand bat, right-arm fast-medium bowler**
Test debut	**West Indies v England at Lord's 2004**
ODI debut	**West Indies v England at Georgetown 2003-04**
T20I debut	**West Indies v New Zealand at Auckland 2005-06**

THE PROFILE A genuine allrounder (a rare breed in the Caribbean), Dwayne Bravo was born in Santa Cruz, like Brian Lara, and made his one-day debut in April 2004, on the tenth anniversary of Lara's 375. He won his first Test cap at Lord's three months later, aged 20, took three wickets with his medium-paced swingers, and displayed a cool, straight bat. West Indies lost the series, but at least they knew they had unearthed a special talent. Bravo hit his maiden century against South Africa in April 2005, and played an even better innings the following November, 113 at Hobart against the rampant Australians. He continued to chip in with useful runs, while a selection of slower balls makes him a handful in one-dayers, if less so in Tests. He's also electric in the field. Bravo missed the 2009 home Tests against England with a niggling ankle injury, then was left out for the Tests in England that followed – despite being fit enough to play in the IPL – although he did lift the side visibly in both one-day series. Back in Australia at the end of 2009, he made another century, at Adelaide. Earlier that year Bravo had been one of several players who boycotted the home series against Bangladesh as a contracts dispute festered, and he continues to flit between the international set-up and lucrative 20-over competitions. He hasn't played a Test since December 2010, but remained a one-day regular (although he missed the 2011 World Cup through injury). Early in 2013 – not long after demolishing Zimbabwe with 6 for 43 in Grenada – he replaced Darren Sammy as captain of the 50-overs team.

THE FACTS Dwayne Bravo's second Test century – 113 at Hobart late in 2005 – came during a stand of 182 with his fellow-Trinidadian Denesh Ramdin, the day after Trinidad & Tobago qualified for the football World Cup for the first time ... Bravo averages 30.72 with the ball in Tests against Australia – but 81.66 v Pakistan ... He played 27 Tests before finally finishing on the winning side, against Sri Lanka at Port-of-Spain in April 2008 ... Bravo's half-brother Darren has also played for West Indies ...

THE FIGURES to 17.09.13   cricinfo.com

Batting & Fielding	M	Inns	NO	Runs	HS	Avge	S/R	100	50	4s	6s	Ct	St
Tests	40	71	1	2200	113	31.42	48.59	3	13	269	21	41	0
ODIs	147	124	20	2495	112*	23.99	80.77	1	8	193	48	60	0
T20Is	37	34	9	739	66*	29.56	119.00	0	3	41	32	15	0
First-class	100	180	7	5302	197	30.64	–	8	30	–	–	89	0

Bowling	M	Balls	Runs	Wkts	BB	Avge	RpO	S/R	5i	10m
Tests	40	6466	3426	86	6-55	39.83	3.17	75.18	2	0
ODIs	147	5805	5214	173	6-43	30.13	5.38	33.55	1	0
T20Is	37	498	700	28	4-38	25.00	8.43	17.78	0	0
First-class	100	11025	5918	177	6-11	33.43	3.22	62.28	7	0

TIM **BRESNAN**

Full name **Timothy Thomas Bresnan**
Born **February 28, 1985, Pontefract, Yorkshire**
Teams **Yorkshire**
Style **Right-hand bat, right-arm fast-medium bowler**
Test debut **England v West Indies at Lord's 2009**
ODI debut **England v Sri Lanka at Lord's 2006**
T20I debut **England v Sri Lanka at Southampton 2006**

THE PROFILE The stocky Tim Bresnan was tipped for higher honours in 2001 after becoming Yorkshire's youngest player for 20 years. He quickly progressed to England's youth team, and played in two Under-19 World Cups. The potential took a few years to ripen, but in 2005 he was given more responsibility in a transitional Yorkshire team, and responded with 47 wickets with swinging deliveries which, if a shade short of truly fast, travel at a fair old rate. He can also bat, making three first-class centuries in 2007: he has reached 90 in Tests twice, too. A good start the previous season had resulted in a place in a new-look one-day squad in June 2006, but Bresnan fell victim to the flashing blades of Sanath Jayasuriya and friends, took only two wickets in what became a clean sweep for Sri Lanka, and then suffered a back injury. He responded well with the bat in 2007, although his bowling stats dipped a little (34 wickets at 34), before a return to bowling form the following year led to a one-day recall. He finally made his Test debut in May 2009, but failed to shine at first and had to make way for Andrew Flintoff in the Ashes series. But he returned to Yorkshire, worked on his fitness, and came back a better player ... and a good-luck charm too: England won the first 13 Tests in which Bresnan played, including the victories at Melbourne and Sydney which sealed the 2010-11 Ashes triumph, although the run – and his own superlative form – came to an end in mid-2012. Still, he remained a handy contributor, making useful runs and taking important wickets in the 2013 Ashes before missing the final Test with a stress fracture of the back.

THE FACTS Bresnan made all three of his first-class centuries during 2007, including 126* for England A v India at Chelmsford ... He was on the winning side in his first 13 Tests, an England record: only Adam Gilchrist (15 for Australia) had more ... Bresnan's 80 v Australia at Centurion in October 2009 is the highest score by an England No. 8 in ODIs ... He took 5 for 42 for Yorkshire at Worcester in July 2005 ...

THE FIGURES to 17.09.13   **ESPN**cricinfo.com

Batting & Fielding	M	Inns	NO	Runs	HS	Avge	S/R	100	50	4s	6s	Ct	St
Tests	21	22	4	541	91	30.05	39.57	0	3	62	1	7	0
ODIs	76	56	15	773	80	18.85	90.19	0	1	82	2	20	0
T20Is	25	14	6	80	23*	10.00	100.00	0	0	6	0	6	0
First-class	128	166	29	3731	126*	27.23	47.13	3	17	–	–	50	0

Bowling	M	Balls	Runs	Wkts	BB	Avge	RpO	S/R	5i	10m
Tests	21	4299	2151	67	5–48	32.10	3.00	64.16	1	0
ODIs	76	3780	3418	94	5–48	36.36	5.42	40.21	1	0
T20Is	25	490	610	19	3–10	32.10	7.46	25.78	0	0
First-class	128	22088	11295	363	5–42	31.11	3.06	60.84	6	0

STUART **BROAD**

ENGLAND

Full name	Stuart Christopher John Broad
Born	June 24, 1986, Nottingham
Teams	Nottinghamshire
Style	Left-hand bat, right-arm fast-medium bowler
Test debut	England v Sri Lanka at Colombo 2007-08
ODI debut	England v Pakistan at Cardiff 2006
T20I debut	England v Pakistan at Bristol 2006

THE PROFILE Stuart Broad is a fine allrounder – an aggressive seamer with a good high action, and a free-swinging batsman, especially good driving off the back foot on his day (which, sadly, has come only rarely in the last couple of seasons). But an ability to produce game-changing spells – first apparent as England won the Ashes at The Oval in 2009 – was at its best during the 2013 English summer. First he bounced back from a lacklustre tour of New Zealand by blowing them away in the second Test of the return series: Broad was irresistible at Lord's, claiming 7 for 44 as New Zealand crumbled for 68. Then, with the fourth Ashes Test in the balance (and having taken only six wickets in the first three matches), Broad conjured victory with 6 for 50 after Australia, chasing 299, had seemed likely winners at 147 for 1. He also attracted many column inches for staying put in the first Test after thick-edging a catch but being given not out. Two years previously, in a similarly up-and-down summer, Broad had been disappointing against Sri Lanka before pitching the ball up more as India slipped to a 4-0 whitewash. Broad started as a batsman – as he showed with a stroke-filled 169 against Pakistan at Lord's in 2010 – but a teenage growth spurt encouraged him to try fast bowling: not long after starting with Leicestershire, he was playing for England. A move to more fashionable Nottinghamshire helped his international ambitions, and although injuries have occasionally impinged – he was forced home early from the 2010-11 Ashes tour and the 2011 World Cup – Broad sailed past 200 Test wickets in 2013, and is now England's Twenty20 captain too.

THE FACTS Broad scored 169 – the highest by an England No. 9 in Tests – during a record eighth-wicket partnership of 332 with Jonathan Trott against Pakistan at Lord's in 2010 ... After being part of Peter Siddle's Test hat-trick at Brisbane in November 2010, Broad took one himself against India at Trent Bridge in July 2011 ... Broad took 7 for 44 to demolish New Zealand for 68 at Lord's in 2013 ... His father, Chris, played 25 Tests in the 1980s, scoring 1661 runs with six centuries – he's now a match referee (see page 218) ...

THE FIGURES to 17.09.13   ESPNcricinfo.com

Batting & Fielding	M	Inns	NO	Runs	HS	Avge	S/R	100	50	4s	6s	Ct	St
Tests	62	85	10	1855	169	24.73	62.90	1	10	238	15	18	0
ODIs	102	54	19	430	45*	12.28	74.26	0	0	27	6	21	0
T20Is	48	20	8	75	18*	6.25	98.68	0	0	6	1	20	0
First-class	115	153	25	3033	169	23.69	59.05	1	17	–	–	38	0

Bowling	M	Balls	Runs	Wkts	BB	Avge	RpO	S/R	5i	10m
Tests	62	12925	6637	217	7–44	30.58	3.08	59.56	10	2
ODIs	102	5166	4501	160	5–23	28.13	5.22	32.28	1	0
T20Is	48	1023	1279	57	4–24	22.43	7.50	17.94	0	0
First-class	115	22060	11917	420	8–52	28.37	3.24	52.52	20	3

DEAN **BROWNLIE**

Full name	**Dean Graham Brownlie**
Born	**July 30, 1984, Perth, Western Australia**
Teams	**Canterbury**
Style	**Right-hand bat, occ. right-arm medium-pacer**
Test debut	**New Zealand v Zimbabwe at Bulawayo 2011-12**
ODI debut	**New Zealand v Zimbabwe at Dunedin 2011-12**
T20I debut	**New Zealand v Pakistan at Auckland 2010-11**

THE PROFILE Dean Brownlie is a solid middle-order batsman, good on the cut, who was born in Western Australia, and played for their age-group teams before trying his luck in New Zealand – he qualifies for them through his father, Jim, who was born in Christchurch. "I didn't think I was likely to play for WA," he said. "The players they had there were quality cricketers, and they had good youth coming through." Across the Tasman at 25, Brownlie scored 54 in his first match for Canterbury – a Twenty20 game in January 2010 – and added a century on first-class debut the following month, against Northern Districts at Rangiora. Brownlie was soon back in Australia, playing for New Zealand Emerging Players, and made his national debut in a Twenty20 game on Boxing Day 2010, during a productive domestic season. The following year he stepped up to the Test side in Zimbabwe, making 63 in his first innings, and added two more half-centuries against Australia shortly afterwards, including 56 at Hobart in a rare New Zealand victory over their neighbours. Brownlie had a quiet 2012, with a highest score of 35 in nine international outings, not helped by breaking a finger – but he started the following year with a bang, scoring his first Test century against South Africa at Cape Town in January, saving a modicum of face for his side after their embarrassing collapse to 45 all out in the first innings. He reached three figures in style, moving from 92 to 104 with two sixes off Robin Peterson. Brownlie added a fifty in the second Test, but then played throughout the home-and-away series with England without exceeding 35, although his slip fielding was outstanding.

THE FACTS Brownlie scored half-centuries in each of his first three Tests, a feat achieved for New Zealand previously only by John Reid and Bert Sutcliffe ... Brownlie made 112* on his first-class debut, for Canterbury v Northern Districts at Rangiora in February 2010, and shared a fifth-wicket stand of 236* with Shanan Stewart ... He scored 171 for Canterbury v Auckland at Rangiora in November 2011 ...

THE FIGURES to 17.09.13   ESPNcricinfo.com

Batting & Fielding	M	Inns	NO	Runs	HS	Avge	S/R	100	50	4s	6s	Ct	St
Tests	14	25	1	711	109	29.62	44.80	1	4	96	3	17	0
ODIs	3	3	1	22	19	11.00	51.16	0	0	2	0	1	0
T20Is	4	4	0	6	5	1.50	37.50	0	0	1	0	2	0
First-class	47	84	10	3042	171	41.10	52.48	8	14	387	16	60	0

Bowling	M	Balls	Runs	Wkts	BB	Avge	RpO	S/R	5i	10m
Tests	14	66	52	1	1–13	52.00	4.72	66.00	0	0
ODIs	3	0	–	–	–	–	–	–	–	–
T20Is	4	0	–	–	–	–	–	–	–	–
First-class	47	240	180	1	1–13	180.00	4.50	240.00	0	0

JOS **BUTTLER**

Full name **Joseph Charles Buttler**
Born **September 8, 1990, Taunton, Somerset**
Teams **Lancashire**
Style **Right-hand bat, wicketkeeper**
Test debut **No Tests yet**
ODI debut **England v Pakistan at Dubai 2011-12**
T20I debut **England v India at Manchester 2011**

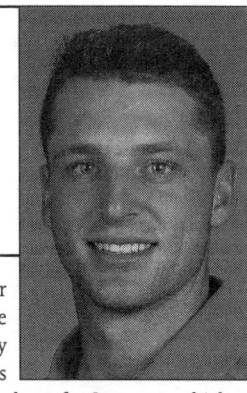

THE PROFILE Broad-beamed Jos Buttler made a name for himself as an uncompromising hitter at an early age, and by the time he was 22 had nailed down the position of England's one-day wicketkeeper, shoving aside the Test incumbent Matt Prior and his Somerset team-mate Craig Kieswetter (who still usually takes the gloves for Somerset, which led to Buttler's move to Lancashire for 2014). Buttler really got noticed with a blistering 32 off ten balls – five of which flew to or over the boundary – against South Africa in a Twenty20 international at Edgbaston in September 2012. Early the following year he added 54 from 30 balls against New Zealand at Hamilton, then started to make his mark in the 50-over format as well: 47 not out from 16 balls against New Zealand at Trent Bridge in June was followed by 75, 65 not out and 42 in successive innings against Australia in September. "Buttler is fearless, unselfish and innovative," wrote Stephen Brenkley in *The Independent*. "The speed of his hands, the weight of his shot and his belief that he can hit the ball a long way from almost any angle make him invariably worth watching." Buttler came to prominence for Somerset as a 19-year-old in 2010, with 440 runs in the CB40 competition. He became a four-day regular too, playing his part as Somerset just missed their first-ever Championship title – they finished level on points with Nottinghamshire, who took the title on the tie-breaker of more matches won. Buttler combined well with the big-hitting West Indian Kieron Pollard as Somerset reached Twenty20 finals day in both 2010 and 2011, and also clouted a valiant 86 from 72 balls in the CB40 final defeat to Surrey in 2011.

THE FACTS Buttler made 144 for Somerset v Hampshire at Southampton in May 2010 ... He made 102* (from 56 balls) and 119 in one-day matches for England Lions v Sri Lanka A in January 2013 ... Buttler scored 227* for King's College Taunton in a school game against King's Bruton in April 2008: he shared an opening stand of 340 with Alex Barrow, who also now plays for Somerset ...

THE FIGURES *to 17.09.13* — espncricinfo.com

Batting & Fielding	M	Inns	NO	Runs	HS	Avge	S/R	100	50	4s	6s	Ct	St
Tests	0	0	–	–	–	–	–	–	–	–	–	–	–
ODIs	19	14	2	298	75	24.83	126.27	0	2	24	11	30	1
T20Is	25	19	7	286	54	23.83	148.95	0	1	22	14	7	0
First-class	47	69	6	2018	144	32.03	60.43	3	9	284	21	79	2

Bowling	M	Balls	Runs	Wkts	BB	Avge	RpO	S/R	5i	10m
Tests	0	0	–	–	–	–	–	–	–	–
ODIs	19	0	–	–	–	–	–	–	–	–
T20Is	25	0	–	–	–	–	–	–	–	–
First-class	47	12	11	0	–	–	5.50	–	0	0

MICHAEL **CARBERRY**

Full name **Michael Alexander Carberry**
Born **September 29, 1980, Croydon, Surrey**
Teams **Hampshire**
Style **Left-hand bat, offspinner**
Test debut **England v Bangladesh at Chittagong 2009-10**
ODI debut **England v Ireland at Dublin 2013**
T20I debut **No T20Is yet**

THE PROFILE Michael Carberry, a talented left-hand batsman and superb fielder, was debating whether to become a Twenty20 specialist before he was recalled by England for the one-day series against Australia at the end of the 2013 season. He had a few problems between the wickets – running Kevin Pietersen out for a duck at the Rose Bowl – but made an important 63, moving across his stumps and trying to work the ball to leg, in the previous match at Cardiff. It had been more than 3½ years since Carberry won his only Test cap – in Bangladesh at the start of 2010 while Andrew Strauss rested – and he had endured an up-and-down time since. He averaged over 50 at home in 2010, but was then laid low by a blood clot on the lung: he made a slow recovery from the emergency operation to remove it. By August 2011, though, he was back to his best, making a wonderful triple-century for Hampshire against Yorkshire in August, when he and Neil McKenzie put on 523, the ninth-biggest partnership in first-class history. But England already had two left-handers at the top of the order, and when Straus retired after the 2012 summer it was Carberry's misfortune to have had a poor season: Nick Compton got the chance to partner Alastair Cook at first, then Joe Root moved up for the Ashes. But Carberry starred for Hampshire in 50- and 20-over matches in 2013, to earn himself another chance. He originally resurrected his career by moving to Hampshire in 2006, following unfulfilling spells with Surrey and Kent. In his first season on the south coast he came close to 1000 runs, and got there in 2007.

THE FACTS Carberry scored 300* for Hampshire v Yorkshire at Southampton in August 2011, sharing a county-record third-wicket stand of 523 with Neil McKenzie ... Four weeks later Carberry made 182 v Somerset at Taunton, and put on 373 for the second wicket with Jimmy Adams ... His maiden first-class century was for Surrey against Cambridge UCCE in 2002: his second was also at Fenner's, but for Kent in 2003 ...

THE FIGURES to 17.09.13 — **cricinfo.com**

Batting & Fielding	M	Inns	NO	Runs	HS	Avge	S/R	100	50	4s	6s	Ct	St
Tests	1	2	0	64	34	32.00	45.71	0	0	9	0	1	0
ODIs	5	5	0	108	63	21.60	62.79	0	1	14	0	2	0
T20Is	0	0	–	–	–	–	–	–	–	–	–	–	–
First-class	145	253	22	10001	300*	43.29	51.82	28	46	–	–	66	0

Bowling	M	Balls	Runs	Wkts	BB	Avge	RpO	S/R	5i	10m
Tests	1	0	–	–	–	–	–	–	–	–
ODIs	5	6	12	0	–	–	12.00	–	0	0
T20Is	0	0	–	–	–	–	–	–	–	–
First-class	145	1429	1010	16	2–85	63.12	4.24	89.31	0	0

REGIS CHAKABVA

Full name **Regis Wiriranai Chakabva**
Born **September 20, 1987, Harare**
Teams **Mashonaland Eagles**
Style **Right-hand bat, wicketkeeper**
Test debut **Zimbabwe v New Zealand at Bulawayo 2011-12**
ODI debut **Zimbabwe v Kenya at Nairobi 2008-09**
T20I debut **Zimbabwe v Pakistan at King City 2008-09**

THE PROFILE Regis Chakabva has long been considered a wicketkeeper of high promise, and a handy batsman too – and Tatenda Taibu's announcement during 2012 that he was retiring to devote himself to the church meant Chakabva got a chance to show his worth. He had already displaced Taibu from behind the stumps in Tests, making his debut late in 2011, and in his second match – in New Zealand early the following year – he showed his class with the bat, despite his small stature, with a plucky 63 as Zimbabwe crumbled to an embarrassing defeat. Diminishing returns, though, meant he lost the gloves to Richmond Mutumbami in 2013. Chakabva had played for the Under-19s back in 2005, but then slipped down the pecking order. One of the others tried was Alester Maregwede, but when he gave up keeping to concentrate on batting, Chakabva was picked for Zimbabwe A in 2007 after only four first-class matches; and when a Zimbabwean XI played in South Africa's one-day competition the following year he reeled off successive scores of 62, 66, 60 and 118. Taibu's return from an earlier retirement meant Chakabva played solely as a batsman for a while, but Taibu's ability to bowl handy medium-pace meant Chakabva was often part of the squad. He made his international debut late in 2008, in a Twenty20 match in far-off Toronto, and a week later played his first ODI, in a triangular tournament in Nairobi. He didn't do much at first, and Taibu regained the gloves for Zimbabwe's Test recall in August 2011 – but Chakabva was still in the mix and, after some consistent displays for Mashonaland Eagles he soon won his first Test cap, and made 37 in a defiant stand of 86 with Malcolm Waller.

THE FACTS Chakabva made 131 for Northerns v Centrals in Harare in April 2009 ... He pulled off three stumpings in a Twenty20 match against a Bangladesh XI in Harare in June 2012 ... Chakabva scored 63 – more than a third of Zimbabwe's runs off the bat in the entire match – against New Zealand at Napier in January 2012 ...

THE FIGURES to 17.09.13 — espncricinfo.com

Batting & Fielding	M	Inns	NO	Runs	HS	Avge	S/R	100	50	4s	6s	Ct	St
Tests	4	8	0	163	63	20.37	35.74	0	1	12	0	5	0
ODIs	17	17	1	250	45	15.62	53.76	0	0	16	1	10	0
T20Is	2	2	0	1	1	0.50	11.11	0	0	0	0	0	0
First-class	61	108	8	3264	131	32.64	52.03	4	19	375	22	134	13

Bowling	M	Balls	Runs	Wkts	BB	Avge	RpO	S/R	5i	10m
Tests	4	0	–	–	–	–	–	–	–	–
ODIs	17	0	–	–	–	–	–	–	–	–
T20Is	2	0	–	–	–	–	–	–	–	–
First-class	61	18	19	0	–	–	6.33	–	0	0

SHIVNARINE **CHANDERPAUL**

Full name **Shivnarine Chanderpaul**
Born **August 16, 1974, Unity Village, Demerara, Guyana**
Teams **Guyana, Derbyshire**
Style **Left-hand bat, occasional legspinner**
Test debut **West Indies v England at Georgetown 1993-94**
ODI debut **West Indies v India at Faridabad 1994-95**
T20I debut **West Indies v New Zealand at Auckland 2005-06**

THE PROFILE Crouched and crabby, Shivnarine Chanderpaul proves there is life beyond the coaching handbook. He never seems to play in the V, or off the front foot, but uses soft hands, canny deflections and a whiplash pull to maintain a Test average of 50-plus. Early on he struggled to convert fifties into hundreds, and also missed several matches through injury. That was rectified in 2000 when a piece of floating bone was removed from his foot: suitably liberated, he set about rectifying his hundreds problem too, and now has 28 (22 against Australia, England, India and South Africa), including 104 as the Windies chased down a record 418 to beat the Aussies in Antigua in May 2003. The following year in England he ended a rare bad trot by narrowly missing twin tons at Lord's. In 2005 he became captain, and celebrated with 203 at home in Guyana. But he stood down after struggling with bat and microphone in Australia, and was back to his limpet best in England in 2007, top-scoring in each of his five innings, and going more than 1000 minutes without being out in Tests for the third time in his career (he did it again in 2008). It's not all defence, though: he can blast with the best when he needs to. Chanderpaul became uncharacteristically vocal after high-level criticism of senior players in 2011. He was omitted from the one-day side, and was somewhat grudgingly restored to the Test team. Now West Indies' most-capped player, he's been around so long that he played with his son, Tagenarine, for Guyana in 2013. He continued to be a stumbling-block for opposition bowlers, scoring 346 runs in three home Tests against Australia in 2012, 203 and 150 (both not out) in Bangladesh later in the year, and another Test hundred against Zimbabwe in 2013.

THE FACTS Chanderpaul scored 303* for Guyana v Jamaica in January 1996 ... At Georgetown in April 2003 he reached his century against Australia in only 69 balls ... Chanderpaul became West Indies' most-capped player against India in July 2011 (and celebrated with a century) ... He once shot a policeman in the hand in his native Guyana, mistaking him for a mugger ...

THE FIGURES to 17.09.13   **ESPNcricinfo.com**

Batting & Fielding	M	Inns	NO	Runs	HS	Avge	S/R	100	50	4s	6s	Ct	St
Tests	148	251	42	10830	203*	51.81	42.94	28	61	1177	34	63	0
ODIs	268	251	40	8778	150	41.60	70.74	11	59	722	85	73	0
T20Is	22	22	5	343	41	20.17	98.84	0	0	34	5	7	0
First-class	305	495	92	22527	303*	55.89	–	67	112	–	–	171	0

Bowling	M	Balls	Runs	Wkts	BB	Avge	RpO	S/R	5i	10m
Tests	148	1740	883	9	1–2	98.11	3.04	193.33	0	0
ODIs	268	740	636	14	3–18	45.42	5.15	52.85	0	0
T20Is	22	0	–	–	–	–	–	–	–	–
First-class	305	4700	2492	57	4–48	43.71	3.18	82.45	0	0

DINESH CHANDIMAL

Full name	**Lokuge Dinesh Chandimal**
Born	**November 18, 1989, Balapitiya**
Teams	**Nondescripts, Uthura**
Style	**Right-hand bat, wicketkeeper**
Test debut	**Sri Lanka v South Africa at Durban 2011-12**
ODI debut	**Sri Lanka v Zimbabwe at Bulawayo 2010**
T20I debut	**Sri Lanka v New Zealand at Providence 2009-10**

THE PROFILE Dinesh Chandimal is a batsman who can keep wicket, like one of his heroes Romesh Kaluwitharana. He's taller than the diminutive "Kalu", though, at 5ft 9ins (175cm), and collected a full national contract after a seamless run through Sri Lanka's age-group sides. First-class cricket also seemed to pose few terrors: he scored a century in his second match, against the New Zealand tourists in August 2009, and added two more in his next five games. He finished his first full home season with 895 runs at 52.64, and did well enough in limited-overs cricket to earn selection for the World Twenty20 in the West Indies early in 2010. He was also called up to keep wicket for the 50-overs team in a tri-series in Zimbabwe in June while Kumar Sangakkara took a rest. Still only 20, Chandimal did a passable impersonation of Sangakkara behind the stumps – and in front of them, too, spanking a superb 111 in only his second ODI, against India at Harare. Another cool century at Lord's followed not long afterwards. An injury to Prasanna Jayawardene gave Chandimal a Test chance in December 2011, which he grabbed with innings of 58 and 54. By 2013 he was entrenched as the No. 1 keeper, showing that the dual role didn't affect him too much by following a chancy maiden Test century, against Bangladesh, with another in the next game. Soon he had even more responsibility, being named as captain of the national Twenty20 team. With Angelo Mathews struggling for form, Chandimal might be in line for the Test leadership sooner rather than later. And he's still only 24.

THE FACTS Chandimal scored 111 in an ODI against India at Harare in June 2010, and 105 not out against England at Lord's in July 2011 ... He was only the second wicketkeeper, after Dilawar Hussain of India in 1933-34, to score two half-centuries on his Test debut ... Chandimal scored 116* v Bangladesh at Galle in March 2013, and 102 in the next Test in Colombo ... He made 244 for Sri Lanka A v South Africa A in Colombo in August 2010 ...

THE FIGURES to 17.09.13   espncricinfo.com

Batting & Fielding	M	Inns	NO	Runs	HS	Avge	S/R	100	50	4s	6s	Ct	St
Tests	7	12	2	583	116*	58.30	58.30	2	4	70	4	10	4
ODIs	66	59	10	1525	111	31.12	73.17	2	9	116	19	24	1
T20Is	18	16	0	211	56	13.18	91.73	0	1	17	2	2	0
First-class	46	74	10	3698	244	57.78	71.51	11	21	415	68	78	16

Bowling	M	Balls	Runs	Wkts	BB	Avge	RpO	S/R	5i	10m
Tests	7	0	–	–	–	–	–	–	–	–
ODIs	66	0	–	–	–	–	–	–	–	–
T20Is	18	0	–	–	–	–	–	–	–	–
First-class	46	36	18	1	1–13	18.00	3.00	36.00	0	0

JOHNSON **CHARLES**

WEST INDIES

Full name	Johnson Charles
Born	January 14, 1989, St Lucia
Teams	Windward Islands
Style	Right-hand bat, occasional wicketkeeper
Test debut	No Tests yet
ODI debut	West Indies v Australia at Kingstown 2011-12
T20I debut	West Indies v England at The Oval 2011

THE PROFILE Johnson Charles, a right-hander from St Lucia who usually opens, elbowed his way into the West Indian one-day reckoning with a string of forthright displays for the Windward Islands, starting with 55 (from 40 balls) against Guyana in only his third Twenty20 game, in July 2010. The following year he was one of several unfamiliar names in the team which took on England in two late-season Twenty20 internationals: he let no-one down with 36 and 21. Early in 2012 he stepped up to the 50-overs team when Australia toured. Strongly built, with the power to muscle the ball down the ground and also swat it forcefully square of the wicket, Charles made his presence felt, the highlight 45 in a tie in St Vincent. Against England in the World Twenty20 in Sri Lanka later in 2012 he biffed 84 from 56 balls – remarkably, his highest score in any form of senior cricket. He improved that with a round 100 in a one-day international against Australia at Melbourne in February 2013: his inexperience of such landmarks possibly showed when he was out the ball after reaching three figures. Less than a fortnight later, though, he made no such mistake against Zimbabwe in Grenada, powering to 130 from just 111 deliveries. In June he hit 60 against India in the Champions Trophy at The Oval, despite having to keep wicket as Denesh Ramdin was banned, and a month later added 97 when the Indians came to Jamaica. Charles still hasn't made a first-class hundred, although that may soon change, as he has vowed to tone down his attacking batting and focus on building an innings as he bids to become Chris Gayle's full-time opening partner.

THE FACTS Charles made 100 against Australia in an ODI at Melbourne in February 2013: it was his maiden century in all forms of senior cricket (his highest first-class score at the time was 66, for Windward Islands v Trinidad & Tobago at Kingstown in February 2011) ... He added 130 against Zimbabwe in an ODI in Grenada two weeks later ... Charles hit 84 from 56 balls against England during the World Twenty20 in Colombo in September 2012 ...

THE FIGURES to 17.09.13   ESPNcricinfo.com

Batting & Fielding	M	Inns	NO	Runs	HS	Avge	S/R	100	50	4s	6s	Ct	St
Tests	0	0	–	–	–	–	–	–	–	–	–	–	–
ODIs	23	23	0	764	130	33.21	81.44	2	2	80	20	13	1
T20Is	18	17	0	402	84	23.64	115.18	0	2	54	9	4	2
First-class	21	41	3	677	66	17.81	–	0	3	–	–	30	0

Bowling	M	Balls	Runs	Wkts	BB	Avge	RpO	S/R	5i	10m
Tests	0	0	–	–	–	–	–	–	–	–
ODIs	23	0	–	–	–	–	–	–	–	–
T20Is	18	0	–	–	–	–	–	–	–	–
First-class	21	84	80	1	1–27	80.00	5.71	84.00	0	0

TENDAI **CHATARA**

Full name	**Tendai Larry Chatara**
Born	**February 28, 1991, Chimanimani**
Teams	**Mountaineers**
Style	**Right-hand bat, right-arm fast-medium bowler**
Test debut	**Zimbabwe v West Indies at Bridgetown 2012-13**
ODI debut	**Zimbabwe v West Indies at St George's 2012-13**
T20I debut	**Zimbabwe v India at Harare 2010**

THE PROFILE Tall and wiry, Tendai Chatara sends the ball down at a lively pace from a front-on action, which doesn't stop him moving the ball away from the right-handers, as he showed while inspiring Zimbabwe to a rare Test victory in September 2013. After making some useful runs in the first innings, Chatara led the charge at the end with 5 for 61 as Pakistan – needing 264 to win – stuttered to 239 all out at Harare. He started by dismissing Mohammad Hafeez and Azhar Ali (for 0) then, on a tense final day, returned to trap Adnan Akmal and Saeed Ajmal in front before Junaid Khan was caught in the gully in the first over with the second new ball. A run-out shortly afterwards completed Zimbabwe's triumph, their first Test victory over a team other than Bangladesh for 12 years. A former athlete – he represented Manicaland at 200 and 400 metres while still at school – Chatara rose quickly after making his first-class debut for Mountaineers in October 2009, when he was 18: within a year he had played his first Twenty20 international, taking the wicket of India's Yusuf Pathan at Harare. That was it for a while, but after consistent domestic performances – he took 56 first-class wickets at 19 in 2010-11, including 11 for 49 in one Logan Cup game – he was recalled early in 2013. He made his Test debut in the West Indies, and claimed a distinguished maiden scalp in Chris Gayle. When Pakistan toured later in 2013 Chatara made early inroads in both innings of the first Test, finishing with five wickets in the match – which turned out to be just a warm-up for his heroics in the second Test.

THE FACTS Chatara took 5 for 61 as Zimbabwe pulled off a rare Test victory – by just 24 runs – over Pakistan at Harare in September 2013 ... He took 6 for 33 and 5 for 16 for Mountaineers v Southern Rocks at Masvingo in March 2011 ... After taking no wickets in his first two first-class matches, Chatara took 5 for 42 against Mid West Rhinos in the third ...

THE FIGURES to 17.09.13 — espncricinfo.com

Batting & Fielding	M	Inns	NO	Runs	HS	Avge	S/R	100	50	4s	6s	Ct	St
Tests	4	8	0	41	21	5.12	34.74	0	0	6	0	0	0
ODIs	11	6	3	27	23	9.00	46.55	0	0	2	1	1	0
T20Is	4	0	–	–	–	–	–	–	–	–	–	1	0
First-class	35	45	12	298	35*	9.03	52.65	0	0	41	5	8	0

Bowling	M	Balls	Runs	Wkts	BB	Avge	RpO	S/R	5i	10m
Tests	4	889	405	15	5–61	27.00	2.73	59.26	1	0
ODIs	11	591	475	14	3–48	33.92	4.82	42.21	0	0
T20Is	4	90	133	4	2–30	33.25	8.86	22.50	0	0
First-class	35	6155	2907	134	6–33	21.69	2.83	45.93	8	1

ELTON **CHIGUMBURA**

ZIMBABWE

Full name	**Elton Chigumbura**
Born	**March 14, 1986, Kwekwe**
Teams	**Mashonaland Eagles**
Style	**Right-hand bat, right-arm fast-medium bowler**
Test debut	**Zimbabwe v Sri Lanka at Harare 2004**
ODI debut	**Zimbabwe v Sri Lanka at Bulawayo 2004**
T20I debut	**Zimbabwe v Bangladesh at Khulna 2006-07**

THE PROFILE Elton Chigumbura, who was fast-tracked into the national side not long after his 18th birthday when several leading players fell out with the board, made his first-class debut in the Logan Cup when only 15. A genuine allrounder, he is a big hitter fond of the lofted drive, bowls at a sharp pace, and is an athletic fielder. He looked out of his depth in his first Test, in May 2004, but was more at home by the time of the Champions Trophy in England that September. Three years later he played a vital role in the shock victory over Australia at the inaugural World Twenty20, removing both openers and rotating the strike well as Zimbabwe squeaked home. Then, after a poor run, he pounded the Kenyans in Nairobi in 2009, smashing 79, 68, 43 and 36 in successive innings at a strike-rate well above 100, and picking up seven wickets for good measure. Early in 2010 Chigumbura took over as captain when Prosper Utseya stood down, but after a promising start – and a county stint with Northamptonshire – the responsibility seemed to affect him and his form fell away: in 20 matches in charge he failed to reach 50 and took only two wickets. He was replaced in 2011 by Brendan Taylor, but kept his place in the side, and chipped in with three important wickets in the historic Test-comeback victory over Bangladesh at Harare in August. But soon after that he injured his knee, and missed the Test against Pakistan that followed. He remains a dangerous hitter and handy bowling option, and in September 2013 showed his maturity with a responsible three-hour 69 as Zimbabwe took a rare first-innings lead in a Test against Pakistan at Harare.

THE FACTS Chigumbura scored 186 for Northerns v Westerns at Harare in April 2008 ... In May 2009 he hit 103* from 56 balls in a Twenty20 match for Northerns v Centrals at Bulawayo ... Chigumbura has the highest strike-rate of anyone who has scored 1000 runs in ODIs for Zimbabwe ... He took 6 for 24 against Sri Lanka A in a one-day match at Harare in July 2012 ...

THE FIGURES to 17.09.13   **ESPNcricinfo.com**

Batting & Fielding	M	Inns	NO	Runs	HS	Avge	S/R	100	50	4s	6s	Ct	St
Tests	11	21	0	434	86	20.66	47.74	0	3	55	4	3	0
ODIs	153	141	16	2998	79	23.98	82.45	0	15	243	84	46	0
T20Is	24	23	3	389	48	19.45	149.61	0	0	32	20	10	0
First-class	85	149	9	4649	186	33.20	–	5	31	–	–	36	0

Bowling	M	Balls	Runs	Wkts	BB	Avge	RpO	S/R	5i	10m
Tests	11	1353	779	16	5-54	48.68	3.45	84.56	1	0
ODIs	153	3955	3879	95	4-28	40.83	5.88	41.63	0	0
T20Is	24	270	411	16	4-31	25.68	9.13	16.87	0	0
First-class	85	10256	5641	194	5-33	29.07	3.30	52.86	4	0

MICHAEL CLARKE

Full name **Michael John Clarke**
Born **April 2, 1981, Liverpool, New South Wales**
Teams **New South Wales**
Style **Right-hand bat, left-arm orthodox spinner**
Test debut **Australia v India at Bangalore 2003-04**
ODI debut **Australia v England at Adelaide 2002-03**
T20I debut **Australia v New Zealand at Auckland 2004-05**

THE PROFILE Michael Clarke was being touted as an Australian captain before he'd even played a Test. And when he marked his debut with 151 against India in October 2004, his future looked even brighter than the yellow motorbike he received as Man of the Match. Another thrilling century followed on his home debut, and his first Test season ended with the Allan Border Medal. Then came the fall. Barely a year later he was dropped after 15 centuryless Tests, and told to tighten his technique, especially early on against swing. He had to wait until the low-key Bangladesh series early in 2006 to reclaim that Test spot, cemented his place with two tons in the 2006-07 Ashes whitewash, and has been a fixture ever since. In England in 2009 Clarke was the classiest batsman on show, finishing with two centuries: soon afterwards he was entrusted with the Twenty20 captaincy, and took over as Test skipper too after the 2010-11 Ashes debacle. He showed himself to be a shrewd tactician, and the responsibility didn't seem to affect him: he creamed 329 not out against India at the SCG in January 2012, and two matches later added 210 at Adelaide. The run-fest continued, threatened only by back problems – and, to an extent, by England's tall quick bowlers during a third successive Ashes defeat for Clarke in 2013. He started as a ravishing shotmaker who did not so much take guard as take off: he radiated a pointy-elbowed elegance reminiscent of the young Greg Chappell or Mark Waugh. His bouncy fielding adds to his value, while his slow left-armers once shocked six Indians in a Test. A cricket nut since he was in nappies, the young "Pup" honed his technique against the bowling machine at his dad's indoor centre.

THE FACTS Clarke scored 151 v India at Bangalore on his Test debut in 2004-05, and the following month added 141 v New Zealand at Brisbane in his first home Test ... Clarke averages 60.55 in ODIs v Sri Lanka, but only 17.50 v Scotland (and 0.00 v Ireland) ... He took 6 for 9 against India at Mumbai in November 2004 ... He made 329* against India at Sydney in January 2012, and 259* and 230 in successive innings v South Africa in November 2012 ...

THE FIGURES to 17.09.13   **espncricinfo.com**

Batting & Fielding	M	Inns	NO	Runs	HS	Avge	S/R	100	50	4s	6s	Ct	St
Tests	97	164	17	7656	329*	52.08	55.91	24	27	865	35	111	0
ODIs	232	211	43	7581	130	45.12	78.65	8	55	625	50	97	0
T20Is	34	28	5	488	67	21.21	103.17	0	1	29	10	13	0
First-class	164	283	27	12446	329*	48.61	–	41	45	–	–	176	0

Bowling	M	Balls	Runs	Wkts	BB	Avge	RpO	S/R	5i	10m
Tests	97	2310	1129	30	6-9	37.63	2.93	77.00	2	0
ODIs	232	2525	2113	56	5-35	37.73	5.02	45.08	1	0
T20Is	34	156	225	6	1-2	37.50	8.65	26.00	0	0
First-class	164	3502	1831	41	6-9	44.65	3.13	85.41	2	0

ALASTAIR **COOK**

Full name	Alastair Nathan Cook
Born	December 25, 1984, Gloucester
Teams	Essex
Style	Left-hand bat, occasional offspinner
Test debut	England v India at Nagpur 2005-06
ODI debut	England v Sri Lanka at Manchester 2006
T20I debut	England v West Indies at The Oval 2007

THE PROFILE Wise judges were saying that the tall, dark and handsome Alastair Cook was destined for great things very early on. A left-hander strong on the pull, Cook was thrown in at the deep end by Essex the year after leaving Bedford School with a fistful of batting records, and has barely looked back since. He makes his runs with a languid ease reminiscent of David Gower, if slightly more stiff-legged. His early England career was full of successes, although a barren spell in 2010 – he looked vulnerable around off stump, with a tendency to play around the front pad – briefly threatened his place. But then he piled up 766 runs in the 2010-11 Ashes triumph, and added a colossal 294 against India at Edgbaston. Cook was in the Caribbean with the A team when the original England SOS came early in 2006, after a crop of injuries: he flew to India and, unfazed, stroked 60 and an unbeaten 104 in a memorable debut at Nagpur. He lost his one-day place for a while, not helped by some occasionally ponderous fielding, and missed the 2011 World Cup, but returned afterwards, and showed that he could up the tempo if required, hitting three one-day hundreds in 2012. Appointed captain after Andrew Strauss retired, Cook started with centuries in three successive Tests in India, to orchestrate a fine come-from-behind series victory. The third ton made him England's most prolific century-maker. Two more followed against New Zealand in 2013 before a quiet time in the Ashes series at home.

THE FACTS Cook was the 16th England batsman to make a century on Test debut ... He made 766 runs against Australia in 2010-11, a number exceeded in an Ashes series only by Don Bradman (twice), Wally Hammond and Mark Taylor ... Cook's stand of 127 with Marcus Trescothick v Sri Lanka at Lord's in 2006 was the second-highest in Tests by unrelated players who share a birthday (they were both born on Christmas Day), behind 163 by Vic Stollmeyer and Kenneth Weekes (Jan 24) for West Indies at The Oval in 1939 ...

THE FIGURES to 17.09.13   cricinfo.com

Batting & Fielding	M	Inns	NO	Runs	HS	Avge	S/R	100	50	4s	6s	Ct	St
Tests	97	173	10	7801	294	47.85	47.03	25	32	896	10	89	0
ODIs	72	72	3	2681	137	38.85	78.39	5	18	306	8	24	0
T20Is	4	4	0	61	26	15.25	112.96	0	0	10	0	1	0
First-class	191	340	26	14899	294	47.44	51.49	44	71	–	–	179	0

Bowling	M	Balls	Runs	Wkts	BB	Avge	RpO	S/R	5i	10m
Tests	97	6	1	0	–	–	1.00	–	0	0
ODIs	72	0	–	–	–	–	–	–	–	–
T20Is	4	0	–	–	–	–	–	–	–	–
First-class	191	270	205	6	3-13	34.16	4.55	45.00	0	0

ED COWAN

AUSTRALIA

Full name	**Edward James McKenzie Cowan**
Born	**June 16, 1982, Paddington, Sydney**
Teams	**Tasmania, Gloucestershire**
Style	**Left-hand bat**
Test debut	**Australia v India at Melbourne 2011-12**
ODI debut	**No ODIs yet**
T20I debut	**No T20Is yet**

THE PROFILE Ed Cowan, a patient and correct left-hander – something of a throwback to an earlier type of opening batsman – looked to be drifting out of first-class cricket after playing only three times for New South Wales in 2008-09. But a move to Tasmania was just what he needed: in his first season there he made 957 runs at 53, the second-highest aggregate in that summer's Sheffield Shield, including a career-best 225 against South Australia. He followed that with a hundred for Australia A, then hit a purple patch – four centuries in four matches – at the start of the 2011-12 home season. That got him into the Boxing Day Test against India, and he made a watchful start, batting almost five hours for 68. In the third Test at Perth he dropped anchor while David Warner exploded at the other end – they eventually put on 214, of which Cowan's share was 74. He remained in the side, and batted for more than six hours for 136 – his maiden Test century – against South Africa at Brisbane in November 2012. But after one indifferent Test in the 2013 Ashes he was rather harshly dropped – he was ill and also batting out of position at No. 3 – but the success of the similarly adhesive Chris Rogers threatened Cowan's long-term place. Cowan is one of the most thoughtful characters in Australian cricket – and one of the game's best users of Twitter. He has already written a book (a diary of a season), has a degree, and worked as an analyst for an investment bank. He played a few matches for Oxford University in 2003, and scored 137 not out for the British Universities against the touring Zimbabweans.

THE FACTS Cowan scored 225 for Tasmania v South Australia at Hobart in November 2009 … He scored 137*, his maiden first-class hundred, for British Universities against Zimbabwe at Edgbaston in 2003 … Cowan fielded for Australia as a substitute before he had played for NSW: called from the Members' Bar, he was on the SCG for about five minutes against Pakistan in 2004-05 …

THE FIGURES to 17.09.13

espncricinfo.com

Batting & Fielding	M	Inns	NO	Runs	HS	Avge	S/R	100	50	4s	6s	Ct	St
Tests	18	32	0	1001	136	31.28	41.27	1	6	123	2	24	0
ODIs	0	0	–	–	–	–	–	–	–	–	–	–	–
T20Is	0	0	–	–	–	–	–	–	–	–	–	–	–
First-class	100	180	12	6712	225	39.95	47.06	16	30	–	–	77	0

Bowling	M	Balls	Runs	Wkts	BB	Avge	RpO	S/R	5i	10m
Tests	18	0	–	–	–	–	–	–	–	–
ODIs	0	0	–	–	–	–	–	–	–	–
T20Is	0	0	–	–	–	–	–	–	–	–
First-class	100	24	36	0	–	–	9.00	–	0	0

PAT **CUMMINS**

AUSTRALIA

Full name	**Patrick James Cummins**
Born	**May 8, 1993, Westmead, Sydney**
Teams	**New South Wales**
Style	**Right-hand bat, right-arm fast bowler**
Test debut	**Australia v South Africa at Johannesburg 2011-12**
ODI debut	**Australia v South Africa at Centurion 2011-12**
T20I debut	**Australia v South Africa at Cape Town 2011-12**

THE PROFILE Few have had as meteoric a rise as pacy Pat Cummins. He made his initial mark in the Twenty20 Big Bash in 2010-11, taking 3 for 29 against Tasmania in his first match: he finished with 11 wickets and a fine economy-rate. There was a first-class debut too: his third game was the Sheffield Shield final in which, still only 17, he bowled 48 overs in eventual winners Tasmania's first innings, taking 3 for 118. Cummins then became the youngest player to be given a central contract for Australia, and toured South Africa after doing well for New South Wales in the Champions League T20. He was an instant success at international level, too, taking 3 for 25 in his first Twenty20 game, and 3 for 28 in his maiden ODI. Cummins missed the first Test in South Africa in November 2011 – when Australia were skittled for 47 – but in the second became, at 18, their second-youngest debutant. He claimed 6 for 79 in the second innings, a spell which included an impressive working-over of Jacques Kallis. Then Cummins strode in with his side still 18 short of the victory that would square the series ... and nervelessly biffed 13 of them, including the winning boundary. Then, though, the bandwagon stopped as injuries struck with worrying regularity. He picked up a heel niggle, and missed the 2011-12 home season. Back for the limited-overs series in England in July 2012, he injured his side, before returning against Pakistan in the UAE in September. The following year, frustratingly, he reported back pain and again returned home early from the Australia A tour of South Africa. Still, Cummins has been deemed so important to the national side's future that a three-year plan has been drawn up for his management and development.

THE FACTS Cummins was 18 years 185 days old when he made his Test debut – the only younger man to play for Australia was 17-year-old Ian Craig in 1952-53 – in only his fourth first-class match ... Cummins took 6 for 79 in his first Test, the best debut figures by an Australian fast bowler since Tony Dodemaide's 6 for 58 in 1987-88 ...

THE FIGURES to 17.09.13   **ESPNcricinfo.com**

Batting & Fielding	M	Inns	NO	Runs	HS	Avge	S/R	100	50	4s	6s	Ct	St
Tests	1	2	1	15	13*	15.00	68.18	0	0	2	0	1	0
ODIs	5	3	2	21	11*	21.00	95.45	0	0	3	0	0	0
T20Is	11	5	1	22	13	5.50	91.66	0	0	1	1	1	0
First-class	6	10	5	39	13*	7.80	39.39	0	0	4	0	2	0

Bowling	M	Balls	Runs	Wkts	BB	Avge	RpO	S/R	5i	10m
Tests	1	264	117	7	6-79	16.71	2.65	37.71	1	0
ODIs	5	216	214	7	3-28	30.57	5.94	30.85	0	0
T20Is	11	258	315	16	3-15	19.68	7.32	16.12	0	0
First-class	6	1350	656	22	6-79	29.81	2.91	61.36	1	0

NARSINGH **DEONARINE**

Full name	**Narsingh Deonarine**
Born	**August 16, 1983, Albion, Berbice, Guyana**
Teams	**Guyana**
Style	**Left-hand bat, offspinner**
Test debut	**West Indies v South Africa at Georgetown 2004-05**
ODI debut	**West Indies v India at Dambulla 2005**
T20I debut	**West Indies v Australia at Hobart 2009-10**

THE PROFILE In many respects Narsingh Deonarine is a carbon copy of his distinguished Guyana team-mate Shivnarine Chanderpaul. Both are small, wiry left-handers, although Deonarine is rather chunkier and not quite so open and unorthodox at the crease. He also affects the anti-glare patches under the eyes that Chanderpaul borrowed from baseball. Deonarine started as a handy offspinner, with an easy delivery not unlike Carl Hooper's. His bowling helped him into the regional team in 2005, and he toured Sri Lanka later that year after several senior players dropped out following a contracts dispute. When they returned, however, there was no place for Deonarine – and for four years it looked as if that was his solitary flirtation with the international game. But in 2008-09 he topped 1000 runs for Guyana, finishing as the leading scorer in the regional tournament, and was recalled for the tours of England and Australia, where he scored 82 at Perth. Some handy innings followed against South Africa in mid-2010, to suggest that Guyana might be providing much of the West Indian middle-order fibre for a while yet, but Deonarine's career stalled later that year when he was cut from the board's contracts list, a no-nonsense press release stating that his fitness was "regrettably unacceptable for an international cricketer". He worked on that, started bowling more, and was back for the England tour in 2012: he played in the final Test, and kept his place for the New Zealand series that followed at home, making 79 as the first Test was won then taking six wickets in another victory in the second. After that, though, he did little in Australia or at home to Zimbabwe early in 2013, and lost his place.

THE FACTS Deonarine scored 198 for Guyana v Combined Campuses & Colleges at Georgetown in March 2009: that season he was the leading runscorer in the West Indian domestic tournament with 1068 ... Deonarine's maiden first-class century was 100 for West Indies B v India A at Bridgetown in March 2003 ... He took 7 for 26 as Guyana bowled Barbados out for 58 at Bridgetown in March 2012 ...

THE FIGURES *to 17.09.13*   **cricinfo.com**

Batting & Fielding	M	Inns	NO	Runs	HS	Avge	S/R	100	50	4s	6s	Ct	St
Tests	14	22	2	588	82	29.40	40.52	0	4	66	6	12	0
ODIs	25	23	3	587	65*	29.35	70.29	0	4	46	8	8	0
T20Is	8	7	2	55	36*	11.00	103.77	0	0	5	0	2	0
First-class	105	179	19	5846	198	36.53	–	9	38	–	–	69	0

Bowling	M	Balls	Runs	Wkts	BB	Avge	RpO	S/R	5i	10m
Tests	14	1169	531	19	4-37	27.94	2.72	61.52	0	0
ODIs	25	447	413	6	2-18	68.83	5.54	74.50	0	0
T20Is	8	54	87	0	–	–	9.66	–	0	0
First-class	105	8360	3889	124	7-26	31.36	2.79	67.41	3	0

AB de VILLIERS

SOUTH AFRICA

Full name	Abraham Benjamin de Villiers
Born	February 17, 1984, Pretoria
Teams	Titans, Royal Challengers Bangalore
Style	Right-hand bat, wicketkeeper, occ. medium-pacer
Test debut	South Africa v England at Port Elizabeth 2004-05
ODI debut	South Africa v England at Bloemfontein 2004-05
T20I debut	South Africa v Australia at Johannesburg 2005-06

THE PROFILE A batsman of breathtaking chutzpah and enterprise. A superb fielder, also perfectly at ease donning pads and gloves. A fine rugby, golf and tennis player. All AB de Villiers needs to show off his abundant gifts is a ball ... just about any ball. Few drive as sweetly and as regularly, and – in South Africa, at any rate – even fewer possess the silkily snappy footwork required to put spinners in their place. He adjusts seamlessly to all formats, averaging around 50 in both Tests and ODIs. His potential was recognised years before he made the leap to senior international level as an opening batsman against England in 2004-05. After a slump, de Villiers returned to the straight and narrow early in 2008 with a blistering 103 not out against West Indies at Durban. Later that year came an undefeated 217 at Ahmedabad, South Africa's first double-century against India: he bettered that, statistically anyway, with 278 not out (a national record at the time) against Pakistan in November 2010. South Africans do not take easily to the precociously talented, but it helps if they do not come across all precocious. Such is the case with de Villiers, whose lazy smile under a thatch of blond hair has helped convince the nation that he's worth feeding despite all that talent. He obviously convinced the selectors, anyway, because he was appointed limited-overs captain in 2011. His workload was increased the following year when Mark Boucher's eye injury meant de Villiers had to keep wicket in Tests, too. He enjoyed it so much – equalling the Test record with 11 catches against Pakistan at Jo'burg in February 2013 – that he asked that the temporary solution become permanent ... but the dual burden might be unsustainable in the long term.

THE FACTS de Villiers scored 278* against Pakistan at Abu Dhabi in November 2010 ... He made 217* at Ahmedabad in April 2008, after India had been bowled out for 76 ... He averages 81.42 in Tests against Sri Lanka, but 17.25 in four matches against Bangladesh ... de Villiers went a Test-record 78 innings before falling for a duck, against Bangladesh in November 2008 ... His record includes five ODIs for the Africa XI ...

THE FIGURES to 17.09.13   espncricinfo.com

Batting & Fielding	M	Inns	NO	Runs	HS	Avge	S/R	100	50	4s	6s	Ct	St
Tests	85	142	16	6364	278*	50.50	54.66	16	32	734	45	142	2
ODIs	148	142	23	5817	146	48.88	92.98	14	34	534	95	125	3
T20Is	48	46	8	849	79*	22.34	121.11	0	4	64	26	46	6
First-class	111	187	21	8251	278*	49.70	56.67	19	46	–	–	193	3

Bowling	M	Balls	Runs	Wkts	BB	Avge	RpO	S/R	5i	10m
Tests	85	198	99	2	2–49	49.50	3.00	99.00	0	0
ODIs	148	12	22	0	–	–	11.00	–	0	0
T20Is	48	0	–	–	–	–	–	–	–	–
First-class	111	228	133	2	2–49	66.50	3.50	114.00	0	0

SHIKHAR **DHAWAN**

INDIA

Full name	**Shikhar Dhawan**
Born	**December 5, 1985, Delhi**
Teams	**Delhi, Sunrisers Hyderabad**
Style	**Left-hand bat, occasional offspinner**
Test debut	**India v Australia at Mohali 2012-13**
ODI debut	**India v Australia at Visakhapatnam 2010-11**
T20I debut	**India v West Indies v India at Port-of-Spain 2011**

THE PROFILE By late 2012 it looked as if Shikhar Dhawan's Test hopes had been terminally stymied by the long-time presence of his Delhi team-mates Virender Sehwag and Gautam Gambhir atop the Indian order. Dhawan had been the star of the 2003-04 Under-19 World Cup – man of the tournament after piling up 505 runs – but almost a decade later had hardly had a sniff at international level, beyond a handful of nondescript one-dayers: his domestic form, while consistent, hardly demanded inclusion. And then everything changed. Sehwag could hardly buy a run, Gambhir was dropped after a lean spell, and Dhawan was finally called up. At the advanced age for an Indian of 27, he played in the third match against Australia at Mohali early in 2013, and smashed the fastest century by any Test debutant, marauding to 187 to set up victory even though the first day had been lost to rain. After that stellar start, he could hardly be left out of the one-day side, and shook up the Champions Trophy in England with centuries in the first two matches: again, he picked up another player of the tournament award after India's victory in the final. After those two tons he reached double figures in his next dozen innings, including another century in Zimbabwe. Dhawan is a showman, from his dazzling left-handed strokeplay to the jaunty moustache which currently sits underneath an ever-changing hairstyle. He stands upright in the stance, is a bit stiff with his hands when he pushes forward, and is partial to the cover-drive. The whole of India held its breath for his second Test appearance – he missed the whitewash-clincher against Australia after picking up a hand injury.

THE FACTS Dhawan's hundred against Australia at Mohali in March 2013 came up in just 85 balls, the fastest by any Test debutant (beating Dwayne Smith's 93 balls for West Indies v South Africa at Cape Town in January 2004) ... Dhawan's 187 was the highest of 13 Test-debut centuries for India (previously Gundappa Viswanath's 137 in 1969-70, also against Australia) ... Dhawan hit 248 for India A in a 50-over match against South Africa A in Pretoria in August 2013 ... He made 224 for Delhi v Baroda at Vadodara in November 2009 ...

THE FIGURES *to 17.09.13*   **ESPNcricinfo.com**

Batting & Fielding	M	Inns	NO	Runs	HS	Avge	S/R	100	50	4s	6s	Ct	St
Tests	1	1	0	187	187	187.00	107.47	1	0	33	2	0	0
ODIs	19	19	1	776	116	43.11	88.28	3	3	81	10	7	0
T20Is	1	1	0	5	5	5.00	45.45	0	0	0	0	0	0
First-class	82	134	9	5866	224	46.92	–	17	24	–	–	83	0

Bowling	M	Balls	Runs	Wkts	BB	Avge	RpO	S/R	5i	10m
Tests	1	0	–	–	–	–	–	–	–	–
ODIs	19	0	–	–	–	–	–	–	–	–
T20Is	1	0	–	–	–	–	–	–	–	–
First-class	82	244	124	3	2–30	41.33	3.04	81.33	0	0

MAHENDRA SINGH **DHONI**

Full name	**Mahendra Singh Dhoni**
Born	**July 7, 1981, Ranchi, Bihar**
Teams	**Jharkhand, Chennai Super Kings**
Style	**Right-hand bat, wicketkeeper**
Test debut	**India v Sri Lanka at Chennai 2005-06**
ODI debut	**India v Bangladesh at Chittagong 2004-05**
T20I debut	**India v South Africa at Johannesburg 2006-07**

THE PROFILE The odds against a Virender Sehwag clone emerging from the backwaters of Jharkhand were highly remote – until MS Dhoni arrived (a one-time railway ticket collector, his first love was football). His batting is swashbuckling, and his wicketkeeping usually secure. A rapid hundred as East Zone clinched the Deodhar Trophy, an audacious 60 in the Duleep Trophy final, and two tons against Pakistan A established him as a clinical destroyer of bowling attacks, and in just his fifth ODI – against Pakistan in April 2005 – Dhoni cracked a dazzling 148. He followed that with 183 against Sri Lanka in November, beating Adam Gilchrist's highest ODI score by a wicketkeeper. He made an instant impact in Tests, too, pounding 148 at Faisalabad in his fifth match, when India were struggling to avoid the follow-on. He stepped up to captain India to the inaugural World Twenty20 title in September 2007, and was then the most expensive signing ($1.5m) for the inaugural IPL in 2008. He took over as full-time Test captain when Anil Kumble retired that November, rubber-stamping victory over Australia then defeating England and New Zealand. He won eight of his first 11 Tests – an unprecedented start for an Indian skipper – then turned his attention to 50-over cricket, leading from the front with the bat to make sure the 2011 World Cup was won, and then the Champions Trophy in England in 2013. He was criticised as India slumped to 4-0 Test whitewashes in England and Australia – but he remained calm, and continued to lead with panache (in one-day games at least), then, after England upset India at home late in 2012, spanked 224 against Australia in what became a 4-0 Test whitewash.

THE FACTS Dhoni's 183* against Sri Lanka at Jaipur in November 2005 is the highest score in ODIs by a wicketkeeper, while only Andy Flower among Test keepers has exceeded Dhoni's 224 v Australia at Chennai in February 2013 ... Of players with 4000 runs in ODIs, only Michael Bevan (53.88) has a higher average than Dhoni's 51.45 ... Dhoni's record includes three ODIs for the Asia XI ...

THE FIGURES to 17.09.13   cricinfo.com

Batting & Fielding	M	Inns	NO	Runs	HS	Avge	S/R	100	50	4s	6s	Ct	St
Tests	77	121	15	4209	224	39.70	60.04	6	28	452	75	212	36
ODIs	226	200	57	7358	183*	51.45	88.17	8	48	565	154	212	75
T20Is	42	39	15	748	48*	31.16	114.90	0	0	51	20	21	8
First-class	118	187	18	6371	224	37.69	–	9	42	–	–	320	55

Bowling	M	Balls	Runs	Wkts	BB	Avge	RpO	S/R	5i	10m
Tests	77	78	58	0	–	–	4.46	–	0	0
ODIs	226	36	31	1	1-14	31.00	5.16	31.00	0	0
T20Is	42	0	–	–	–	–	–	–	–	–
First-class	118	108	78	0	–	–	4.33	–	0	0

TILLEKERATNE **DILSHAN**

SRI LANKA

Full name	**Tillekeratne Mudiyanselage Dilshan**
Born	**October 14, 1976, Kalutara**
Teams	**Tamil Union, Ruhuna, Royal Challengers Bangalore**
Style	**Right-hand bat, offspinner**
Test debut	**Sri Lanka v Zimbabwe at Bulawayo 1999-2000**
ODI debut	**Sri Lanka v Zimbabwe at Bulawayo 1999-2000**
T20I debut	**Sri Lanka v England at Southampton 2006**

THE PROFILE Tillekeratne Dilshan, who started life as Tuwan Mohamad Dilshan before converting to Buddhism, is a light-footed right-hander and an electric fielder who made an unbeaten 163 against Zimbabwe in only his second Test in November 1999. Technically sound, comfortable against pace, with quick feet and strong wrists, Dilshan has talent in abundance. But that bright start was followed by a frustrating time when he was shovelled up and down the order. After a lean series against England in 2001 he didn't play another Test until late 2003. He returned determined to play his own aggressive game, and was immediately successful. He continued to do well, and was one of four centurions in an innings victory over India in July 2008 then the following January against Bangladesh at Chittagong hit 162 and 143 then wrapped up the match with four wickets. Later that year Dilshan lit up the World Twenty20 in England with some spectacular batting, including his own trademark cheeky scoop over the shoulder. He made ten international centuries in 2009, then on the march to the 2011 World Cup final was in fine form, scoring two centuries. He inherited the captaincy shortly afterwards when Kumar Sangakkara stepped down, and led from the front in England, making a superb 193 in the Lord's Test, but a run of defeats cost him the job early the following year. He remained an important member of the side, though, hitting two Test centuries against Pakistan in mid-2012, and a sparkling 164 against Australia at Hobart at the end of the year. Then, after feasting on Bangladesh's bowlers at the start of 2013, he caned South Africa's for 115 not out and 99 in successive ODIs in July.

THE FACTS Dilshan's 193 in 2011 was Sri Lanka's highest score in a Test at Lord's ... He hit 168 against Bangladesh in Colombo in September 2005, putting on 280 with Thilan Samaraweera, a Sri Lankan fifth-wicket record in Tests ... Dilshan made his first ODI century in the record total of 443 for 9 against the Netherlands at Amstelveen in July 2006 ... He made 200* while captaining North Central Province v Central in Colombo in February 2005 ...

THE FIGURES to 17.09.13   **ESPNcricinfo.com**

Batting & Fielding	M	Inns	NO	Runs	HS	Avge	S/R	100	50	4s	6s	Ct	St
Tests	87	145	11	5492	193	40.58	65.54	16	23	677	24	88	0
ODIs	267	242	38	7643	160*	37.46	86.15	17	30	790	46	101	1
T20Is	50	49	8	1203	104*	29.34	121.14	1	7	138	24	25	2
First-class	226	371	22	13701	200*	39.25	–	38	57	–	–	352	23

Bowling	M	Balls	Runs	Wkts	BB	Avge	RpO	S/R	5i	10m
Tests	87	3385	1711	39	4-10	43.87	3.03	86.79	0	0
ODIs	267	4411	3453	76	4-4	45.43	4.69	58.03	0	0
T20Is	50	192	231	5	2-4	46.20	7.21	38.40	0	0
First-class	226	6255	3117	87	5-49	35.82	2.98	71.89	1	0

J-P DUMINY

SOUTH AFRICA

Full name	Jean-Paul Duminy
Born	April 14, 1984, Strandfontein, Cape Town
Teams	Cape Cobras
Style	Left-hand bat, occasional offspinner
Test debut	South Africa v Australia at Perth 2008-09
ODI debut	South Africa v Sri Lanka at Colombo 2004-05
T20I debut	South Africa v Bangladesh at Cape Town 2007-08

THE PROFILE Slightly built but stylish, left-hander Jean-Paul Duminy had trouble finding a place in South Africa's strong middle order – but when an injury to Ashwell Prince finally let him into the Test side in Australia late in 2008, more than four years after his one-day debut, he certainly made it count. First Duminy stroked a nerveless 50 not out as his side made light of a target of 414 to start with victory at Perth, then he set up a series-winning triumph at Melbourne with a superb 166, most of it coming during an eye-popping ninth-wicket stand of 180 with Dale Steyn. A four-hour 73 followed in the return series in a defeat at Durban. Duminy had first featured in a one-day series in Sri Lanka in 2004. He struggled there, scoring only 29 runs in five attempts, and dropped off the national radar for a couple of years. But he continued to score heavily at home, and was given an extended one-day run after the 2007 World Cup, showing signs of developing into a late-innings "finisher": he batted into the final over in three successive victories against West Indies. A horror run in Tests in 2009-10 – only one score above 11 in nine innings – cost him his place, but Duminy remained a one-day fixture, missing a century against Ireland during the 2011 World Cup by just one run. He returned to the Test side after more than two years with 103 against New Zealand at Wellington in March 2012, then batted tidily in England later in the year. But he ruptured his Achilles tendon during the Brisbane Test in November 2012, and was out for six months, marking his return by hammering the Dutch bowlers for 150 in an ODI in May 2013. He is also a superb fielder, while his part-time offbreaks occasionally come in handy.

THE FACTS Duminy scored 169 as Cape Cobras followed on against the Eagles at Stellenbosch in February 2007 ... He scored 200* – with nine sixes – for the Cobras against the Dolphins at Paarl in December 2010 ... Duminy scored 150* v Holland in an ODI in May 2013 ... Against Ireland in 2011 he became only the second man (after Adam Gilchrist) to be out for 99 in a World Cup match ...

THE FIGURES to 17.09.13   espncricinfo.com

Batting & Fielding	M	Inns	NO	Runs	HS	Avge	S/R	100	50	4s	6s	Ct	St
Tests	17	26	5	789	166	37.57	43.32	2	4	92	6	14	0
ODIs	104	95	21	2959	150*	39.98	83.84	3	16	187	40	44	0
T20Is	45	42	11	1084	96*	34.96	122.20	0	6	85	32	19	0
First-class	75	120	21	5029	200*	50.79	49.85	15	25	–	–	55	0

Bowling	M	Balls	Runs	Wkts	BB	Avge	RpO	S/R	5i	10m
Tests	17	875	510	12	3–89	42.50	3.49	72.91	0	0
ODIs	104	1632	1341	33	3–31	40.63	4.93	49.45	0	0
T20Is	45	168	198	10	3–18	19.80	7.07	16.80	0	0
First-class	75	3222	1839	43	5–108	42.76	3.42	74.93	1	0

FAF **DU PLESSIS**

SOUTH AFRICA

Full name	**Francois du Plessis**
Born	**July 13, 1984, Pretoria**
Teams	**Titans, Chennai Super Kings**
Style	**Right-hand bat, legspinner**
Test debut	**South Africa v Australia at Adelaide 2012-13**
ODI debut	**South Africa v India at Cape Town 2010-11**
T20I debut	**South Africa v England at Chester-le-Street 2012**

THE PROFILE Francois "Faf" du Plessis made one of the most remarkable Test debuts of all late in 2012. After J-P Duminy was injured during the first Test in Australia, one columnist lamented that South Africa had "no specialist batsman in reserve", even though du Plessis was there and had played 26 one-day internationals. Dean Elgar flew in, but du Plessis was preferred for the second Test at Adelaide even though his first-class average was around 40 to Elgar's 50. It proved to be an inspired decision: after warming up with 78 in the first innings, du Plessis dropped anchor for almost eight hours in the second, making 110 not out and preventing certain defeat. At tea on the final day, the flagging du Plessis was revived by AB de Villiers, who said: "Keep fighting, because you don't understand how much this means for the people back home. If you get through this, your career will be changed." It certainly was: within a year du Plessis was captaining the one-day teams. Before that he had added 78 not out and 27 in the next Test, at Perth, as South Africa pinched the series, then made 137 against New Zealand at Port Elizabeth, reaching three figures with six off Jeetan Patel. But du Plessis could easily have been lost to South African cricket: in 2008 he signed as a Kolpak player for Lancashire, where he made a big impression, especially with his electric fielding. He returned home after two seasons, and produced a stunning display in the MTN40 competition in 2010-11 – the leading run-scorer with 567 in ten matches, including three centuries – and made his ODI debut just before the 2011 World Cup.

THE FACTS du Plessis was only the fourth batsman to score a century on Test debut for South Africa, following Andrew Hudson (1991-92), Jacques Rudolph (2002-03) and Alviro Petersen (2009-10) ... Just before being dismissed for the second time, du Plessis had a Test average of 293.00 ... He scored 176 for Titans v Lions at Centurion in November 2008 ... du Plessis made 144, sharing a stand of 292 with Dean Elgar, while captaining South Africa A v Sri Lanka A at Durban in July 2012 ...

THE FIGURES to 17.09.13   espncricinfo.com

Batting & Fielding	M	Inns	NO	Runs	HS	Avge	S/R	100	50	4s	6s	Ct	St
Tests	7	10	2	558	137	69.75	44.35	2	2	73	3	4	0
ODIs	42	40	5	967	72	27.62	88.79	0	6	83	13	23	0
T20Is	11	11	1	303	85	30.30	127.84	0	3	32	7	3	0
First-class	85	137	14	4963	176	40.34	–	10	31	–	–	79	0

Bowling	M	Balls	Runs	Wkts	BB	Avge	RpO	S/R	5i	10m
Tests	7	60	60	0	–	–	6.00	–	0	0
ODIs	42	150	142	2	1–8	71.00	5.59	75.00	0	0
T20Is	11	8	3	0	–	–	2.25	–	0	0
First-class	85	2540	1468	41	4–39	35.80	3.46	61.95	0	0

DEAN **ELGAR**

SOUTH AFRICA

Full name	**Dean Elgar**
Born	**June 11, 1987, Welkom, Orange Free State**
Teams	**Knights, Somerset**
Style	**Left-hand bat, slow left-arm orthodox spinner**
Test debut	**South Africa v Australia at Perth 2012-13**
ODI debut	**South Africa v England at Cardiff 2012**
T20I debut	**No T20Is yet**

THE PROFILE A compact left-hander, Dean Elgar was a consistent scorer at domestic level after playing in the Under-19 World Cup in 2006. Two years later he was selected for South Africa A, and made 86 not out against Sri Lanka in his first match – but a senior spot proved frustratingly elusive. He strung together several good domestic scores, and remained an A-team regular, hitting 169 not out against Bangladesh A in April 2011, to round off a season in which he made 1193 first-class runs at 62. Elgar followed that with 74, 105, 174 and 78 in two A-team Tests in Sri Lanka in August, and continued to score heavily at home, ending 2011-12 with 816 runs. Finally he got a chance in the senior side, when a couple of senior batsmen skipped the one-day series in England in 2012. He made 42 at The Oval and 35 at Lord's, without quite stamping his authority or dispelling the notion that he was more suited to the longer formats. He got his five-day chance later in the year, being summoned to Australia after J-P Duminy was injured during the first Test at Brisbane. But Elgar had to watch his less-trumpeted Knights team-mate Faf du Plessis make an astonishing Test debut with the bat in Adelaide, then, when called up for his own first cap in the third Test at Perth in November, Elgar bagged a pair. Things were rather easier when New Zealand toured South Africa shortly afterwards, and he made a solid maiden century at Port Elizabeth. But three Tests against Pakistan brought a highest score of 27, threatening his place – although a career-best 268 against Australia A in July 2013 did his cause no harm.

THE FACTS Elgar scored 268 – his fifth century for South Africa A – against Australia A at Pretoria in July 2013 ... He made 225 for Eagles v Titans at Bloemfontein in February 2007, when he was 19 ... Elgar was the 10th man to bag a pair on Test debut for South Africa, but the first of them to go on to make a Test century later ...

THE FIGURES to 17.09.13   espncricinfo.com

Batting & Fielding	M	Inns	NO	Runs	HS	Avge	S/R	100	50	4s	6s	Ct	St
Tests	6	8	2	192	103*	32.00	50.39	1	0	23	2	6	0
ODIs	5	4	0	93	42	23.25	58.86	0	0	4	0	3	0
T20Is	0	0	–	–	–	–	–	–	–	–	–	–	–
First-class	87	150	14	6101	268	44.86	50.22	18	23	782	25	63	0

Bowling	M	Balls	Runs	Wkts	BB	Avge	RpO	S/R	5i	10m
Tests	6	18	18	0	–	–	6.00	–	0	0
ODIs	5	96	67	2	1–11	33.50	4.18	48.00	0	0
T20Is	0	0	–	–	–	–	–	–	–	–
First-class	87	2383	1563	30	4–25	52.10	3.93	79.43	0	0

ELIAS SUNNY

Full name	**Mohammad Elias Sunny**
Born	**August 2, 1986, Dhaka**
Teams	**Dhaka**
Style	**Left-hand bat, slow left-arm orthodox spinner**
Test debut	**Bangladesh v West Indies at Chittagong 2011-12**
ODI debut	**Bangladesh v Pakistan at Mirpur 2011-12**
T20I debut	**Bangladesh v Ireland at Belfast 2012**

THE PROFILE He may be one of Bangladesh's production line of slow left-armers, but Elias Sunny has more than one string to his bow. He's a livewire in the field, and is also a better batsman than most of his rivals: his three first-class centuries include 176, back in 2005, although he has not yet had much chance with the bat at international level. In the 2010-11 Bangladesh domestic season Sunny finished in the top ten of both sets of averages, with 498 runs at 45 and 24 wickets at 26. He made his first-class debut at 17, but with so many other spinners around it took him almost a decade to break into the national set-up. When he did, towards the end of 2011, he made it count: despite having two early catches dropped, he ran through the West Indian batting at Chittagong, and finished with 6 for 94. *Wisden* observed that he "flighted the ball craftily", despite a slightly round-arm action, and he became only the third Bangladeshi (after Javed Omar and Mohammad Ashraful in 2001) to lift the match award on debut. An untimely stomach upset kept him out of the next Test, but he was back when Pakistan visited, and persisted manfully to take three of the five wickets that fell as they ran up nearly 600. In 2012, Sunny took a cheap five-for in a Twenty20 game against Ireland, but his only Test of 2013 was a chastening experience – 0 for 165 against Sri Lanka at Galle. He started playing cricket with a taped-up tennis ball in the Hajaribagh district of Dhaka – and remains much in demand on the popular tape-ball circuit.

THE FACTS Elias took 6 for 94 in his first Test in October 2011: only two left-arm spinners (Alf Valentine of West Indies and England's James Langridge) have had better figures on debut ... Sunny took 5 for 13, Bangladesh's best figures in Twenty20 internationals, against Ireland at Belfast in July 2012 ... His best first-class figures are 7 for 79 (13 for 107 in the match) for Dhaka v Sylhet in October 2008 ... Sunny hit 176 for Chittagong v Barisal in February 2005, sharing a fourth-wicket stand of 365 with Ehsanul Haque ...

THE FIGURES to 17.09.13   **cricinfo.com**

Batting & Fielding	M	Inns	NO	Runs	HS	Avge	S/R	100	50	4s	6s	Ct	St
Tests	4	6	1	38	20*	7.60	26.57	0	0	4	1	1	0
ODIs	4	4	2	2	1*	1.00	18.18	0	0	0	0	0	0
T20Is	7	4	2	9	5	4.50	100.00	0	0	1	0	4	0
First-class	70	108	15	2115	176	22.74	40.76	3	8	–	–	38	0

Bowling	M	Balls	Runs	Wkts	BB	Avge	RpO	S/R	5i	10m
Tests	4	863	518	12	6–94	43.16	3.60	71.91	1	0
ODIs	4	204	161	5	2–21	32.20	4.73	40.80	0	0
T20Is	7	138	146	9	5–13	16.22	6.34	15.33	1	0
First-class	70	13889	6759	250	7–79	27.03	2.91	55.55	11	1

ENAMUL HAQUE

Full name	Mohammad Enamul Haque
Born	December 5, 1986, Sylhet
Teams	Sylhet
Style	Right-hand bat, slow left-arm orthodox spinner
Test debut	Bangladesh v England at Dhaka 2003-04
ODI debut	Bangladesh v Zimbabwe at Chittagong 2004-05
T20I debut	No T20Is yet

THE PROFILE Enamul Haque was born in the hill country of Sylhet, on Bangladesh's eastern border, and there was some confusion about his age when he played for the Board President's XI in the opening match of England's 2003-04 tour: he was supposedly 16, most people had him pegged as two years older than that, and he bowled like a veteran – at one point four wickets went down for no runs, three of them to Enamul. It propelled him straight into the following week's Test, where he bowled with skill and impressive composure to embarrass England's batsmen again. He gives the ball a big rip from a high, economical action, and took 6 for 45 – including the historic final wicket – to send the country wild with an inaugural Test victory over Zimbabwe in January 2005. He added 12 more wickets in the drawn second Test. Kept out of the firing line in England later that year, he bounced back as Bangladesh nearly embarrassed Australia in the first Test of their 2006 tour. His form dipped after that, and other spinners were tried. Enamul played for Maharashtra in India's Ranji Trophy late in 2008, and was briefly recalled to the national side while Abdur Razzak's bowling action was investigated: in the second Test in the Caribbean in July 2009, Enamul took three wickets in each innings as Bangladesh completed a 2-0 clean sweep over a depleted West Indies side. But a quiet time followed, before he roared back with 59 wickets in the domestic first-class competition in 2011-12: still officially only 26, Enamul played his first Test for almost four years in Zimbabwe in April 2013, and took three rather expensive wickets.

THE FACTS Enamul took 7 for 95 – and 12 for 200 in the match, a Bangladesh record – against Zimbabwe at Dhaka in 2004-05 ... He took 7 for 47 in an A-team Test against Zimbabwe at Bulawayo in February 2005 ... The "junior" is added to Enamul's name to distinguish him from an earlier Bangladesh left-arm spinner of the same name (born February 27, 1966, Enamul Haque senior played ten Tests, and is now an international umpire) ...

THE FIGURES to 17.09.13   espncricinfo.com

Batting & Fielding	M	Inns	NO	Runs	HS	Avge	S/R	100	50	4s	6s	Ct	St
Tests	15	26	16	59	13	5.90	21.77	0	0	7	0	3	0
ODIs	10	5	1	12	5	3.00	63.15	0	0	0	0	8	0
T20Is	0	0	–	–	–	–	–	–	–	–	–	–	–
First-class	88	137	47	1190	60	13.22	–	0	2	–	–	38	0

Bowling	M	Balls	Runs	Wkts	BB	Avge	RpO	S/R	5i	10m
Tests	15	3549	1787	44	7-95	40.61	3.02	80.65	3	1
ODIs	10	576	422	14	3-16	30.14	4.39	41.14	0	0
T20Is	0	0	–	–	–	–	–	–	–	–
First-class	88	21477	10189	355	7-47	28.70	2.84	60.49	27	5

SHAMINDA **ERANGA**

Full name	**Ranaweera Mudiyanselage Shaminda Eranga**
Born	**June 23, 1986, Chilaw**
Teams	**Tamil Union, Uthura**
Style	**Right-hand bat, right-arm fast-medium bowler**
Test debut	**Sri Lanka v Australia at Colombo 2011**
ODI debut	**Sri Lanka v Australia at Hambantota 2011**
T20I debut	**Sri Lanka v India at Pallekele 2012**

SRI LANKA

THE PROFILE A brisk fast-medium bowler who can nudge 90mph on the speed-gun, Shaminda Eranga made a spectacular start in international cricket, dismissing Brad Haddin with his second ball in ODIs (and adding Ricky Ponting a few overs later). A month later he went one better, taking a wicket with his first ball in Tests, a widish delivery which Shane Watson obligingly sliced to backward point. Eranga added Michael Clarke, Mike Hussey and Haddin (again) to a distinguished bag to finish with 4 for 65. He was spotted in 2006 at an all-island pace-bowling competition by the former Test fast bowler Champaka Ramanayake. Eranga, who is also a handy tailend batsman with a first-class century to his name, joined the Chilaw Marians, and did enough to earn a place in the national development squad. He made his debut for Sri Lanka A in 2010, and was in the squad that faced West Indies late that year. "This young lad is fit and looks a willing horse," observed Aravinda de Silva, Sri Lanka's chief selector. In 2011, after some good displays for the A team on tour in England – he took seven wickets in the match against Durham – Eranga was flown back to Sri Lanka to join up with the main squad for the Australian series. Back and shoulder injuries kept him out for almost a year, but he roared back at the end of 2012, completing his set by taking a wicket (Gautam Gambhir) with his first ball in Twenty20 internationals, and nudging 90mph during the Tests in Australia. He did well in the Champions Trophy in England in 2013, then set up a one-day-win over West Indies with three important wickets in Trinidad.

THE FACTS Eranga was the second Sri Lankan (after Chamila Gamage) to take a wicket with his first ball in a Test match, dismissing Shane Watson in Colombo in September 2011 ... The previous month Eranga had struck with his second ball in ODIs, and next year took a wicket with his fourth ball in a Twenty20 international ... Eranga scored 100* for Chilaw Marians v Sinhalese Sports Club in February 2012 ...

THE FIGURES to 17.09.13   **cricinfo.com**

Batting & Fielding	M	Inns	NO	Runs	HS	Avge	S/R	100	50	4s	6s	Ct	St
Tests	7	9	3	49	15	8.16	37.40	0	0	8	0	3	0
ODIs	13	8	5	17	7*	5.66	38.63	0	0	0	0	5	0
T20Is	3	1	0	6	6	6.00	85.71	0	0	1	0	1	0
First-class	50	66	24	916	100*	21.80	60.50	1	4	84	34	26	0

Bowling	M	Balls	Runs	Wkts	BB	Avge	RpO	S/R	5i	10m
Tests	7	1344	781	21	4–65	37.19	3.48	64.00	0	0
ODIs	13	482	447	16	3–46	27.93	5.56	30.12	0	0
T20Is	3	66	90	3	2–30	30.00	8.18	22.00	0	0
First-class	50	5580	3495	112	6–21	31.20	3.75	49.82	2	0

FAISAL IQBAL

PAKISTAN

Full name	**Faisal Iqbal**
Born	**December 30, 1981, Karachi, Sind**
Teams	**Karachi Blues, Pakistan International Airlines**
Style	**Right-hand bat, occasional right-arm medium-pacer**
Test debut	**Pakistan v New Zealand at Auckland 2000-01**
ODI debut	**Pakistan v Sri Lanka at Lahore 1999-2000**
T20I debut	**No T20Is yet**

THE PROFILE A gutsy middle-order batsman with a sound defence and attitude to boot, Faisal Iqbal was a prolific junior performer, but his elevation to the national squad was criticised as nepotism – he's the nephew of the great Javed Miandad, the coach when Faisal made his Test debut in 2000-01. But he silenced the critics with three pleasing knocks then, and a counter-attacking 83 off 85 balls against Australia in Colombo in October 2002. He was particularly impressive against Shane Warne, using his feet superbly to seize the momentum, and did it all with a swagger reminiscent of his uncle. However, he couldn't do it again in that series, or in South Africa shortly afterwards, and lost his place. Recalled against India at Karachi in January 2006 when Inzamam-ul-Haq was injured, Faisal made an attractive maiden Test hundred, with some assured back-foot play and composed defence, to help Pakistan to a comfortable series-clinching win. Another good season in 2008-09, which included his second double-century, ensured he stayed in the mix, but after the Sydney Test of January 2010 – which Pakistan somehow lost after taking a first-innings lead of 206 – Faisal was one of those jettisoned. That seemed to be that, but he remained a consistent runscorer at home, and when he made 1013 runs at 53 in 2011-12 – with five hundreds – he was recalled for the Sri Lankan tour in June 2012, but did not actually play. After another fine domestic season he was chosen to go to Zimbabwe late in 2013 – and again did not get a game. But he remained upbeat: "I am always optimistic and ready to grab the chance."

THE FACTS Faisal Iqbal's maiden Test century, 139 at Karachi in January 2006, helped Pakistan defeat India by 341 runs, even though they were 0 for 3 after the first over of the match ... He scored 200* for PIA v Sui Southern Gas in January 2009 ... Faisal made 100* v Zimbabwe at Harare in November 2002, but in 17 other ODIs his highest score is 32 ... His uncle Javed Miandad is Pakistan's leading scorer, with 8832 runs from 124 Tests ...

THE FIGURES to 17.09.13 ESPNcricinfo.com

Batting & Fielding	M	Inns	NO	Runs	HS	Avge	S/R	100	50	4s	6s	Ct	St
Tests	26	44	2	1124	139	26.76	44.16	1	8	136	5	22	0
ODIs	18	16	2	314	100*	22.42	60.50	1	0	24	4	3	0
T20Is	0	0	–	–	–	–	–	–	–	–	–	–	–
First-class	183	286	28	10432	200*	40.59	–	24	55	–	–	152	0

Bowling	M	Balls	Runs	Wkts	BB	Avge	RpO	S/R	5i	10m
Tests	26	6	7	0	–	–	7.00	–	0	0
ODIs	18	18	33	0	–	–	11.00	–	0	0
T20Is	0	0	–	–	–	–	–	–	–	–
First-class	183	216	155	1	1–6	155.00	4.30	216.00	0	0

JAMES **FAULKNER**

Full name **James Peter Faulkner**
Born **April 29, 1990, Launceston, Tasmania**
Teams **Tasmania, Rajasthan Royals**
Style **Right-hand bat, left-arm fast-medium bowler**
Test debut **Australia v England at The Oval 2013**
ODI debut **Australia v West Indies at Perth 2012-13**
T20I debut **Australia v India at Sydney 2011-12**

THE PROFILE James Faulkner, a busy bowling allrounder, has had great success for Tasmania in recent seasons, and has also been much in demand in Twenty20 cricket: he's played for three IPL teams – he was snapped up for $400,000 by the Rajasthan Royals in 2013 – and Shane Warne's Melbourne Stars in the Australian Big Bash. Faulkner has been voted Tasmania's best player in each of the last three domestic seasons, the best of which (2012-13) brought him 444 runs and 39 wickets. He is a forthright batsman, who made 46 and 89 in the 2013 Shield final (that, and four wickets, earned him the match award as Tasmania came out on top against Queensland at Hobart), and a bustling long-legged left-arm bowler. He was initially pigeonholed as a short-form specialist, and it was a surprise when he was called up for his debut in the final Test of the 2013 Ashes – but he biffed some quick runs and took six wickets, including Alastair Cook and Jonathan Trott as England tried to press for victory in their second innings, to show he could hack the longer game too. Faulkner also proved he was no shrinking violet, cheekily suggesting in a press conference that England's earlier batting had been boring. Earlier in the year he was fined after giving Chris Gayle an over-enthusiastic sendoff after bowling him in one of his early one-day international appearances. Faulkner's father, Peter, was also a handy allrounder for Tasmania in the 1980s, and was later their chairman of selectors. Junior says his dad was the biggest influence on his career – although at 16 he brazenly told him to step aside and let others take up the mantle.

THE FACTS Faulkner took 5 for 5 as Tasmania bowled South Australia out for 55 at Hobart in November 2010: two years later he took 5 for 23 against SA at Hobart ... He took two five-fors for Rajasthan Royals against Sunrisers Hyderabad in the 2013 IPL ... Faulkner's father, Peter, also played for Tasmania ...

THE FIGURES to 17.09.13   **cricinfo.com**

Batting & Fielding	M	Inns	NO	Runs	HS	Avge	S/R	100	50	4s	6s	Ct	St
Tests	1	2	0	45	23	22.50	104.65	0	0	4	1	0	0
ODIs	13	9	2	178	54*	25.42	90.81	0	1	15	2	3	0
T20Is	5	3	1	17	7	8.50	121.42	0	0	1	0	1	0
First-class	38	56	10	1379	89	29.97	51.60	0	8	130	10	18	0

Bowling	M	Balls	Runs	Wkts	BB	Avge	RpO	S/R	5i	10m
Tests	1	166	98	6	4–51	16.33	3.54	27.66	0	0
ODIs	13	577	481	18	4–48	26.72	5.00	32.05	0	0
T20Is	5	108	146	7	3–28	20.85	8.11	15.42	0	0
First-class	38	6221	3118	138	5–5	22.59	3.00	45.07	4	0

FAWAD AHMED

Full name	Fawad Ahmed
Born	February 5, 1982, Merguz, Pakistan
Teams	Victoria
Style	Right-hand bat, legspinner
Test debut	No Tests yet
ODI debut	Australia v Scotland at Edinburgh 2013
T20I debut	Australia v England at Southampton 2013

THE PROFILE It was one of the romantic stories of 2013: the asylum-seeking legspinner fast-tracked to Australian citizenship and into the national squad. Fawad Ahmed had played ten first-class matches in his native Pakistan before fleeing to Australia in 2010. He had apparently inflamed extremists by coaching women as part of his work in the northern frontier province of Khyber-Pakhtunkwa. Newly settled in Melbourne, Fawad joined the University club, and worked in a warehouse while his asylum claim was considered. Initially it was rejected, but after Cricket Australia spoke up for him Fawad was granted permanent residency late in 2012. Early the following year he was selected for Victoria, taking 5 for 83 in his first match, and was soon being hailed as a potential international: Damien Martyn faced him in the nets and said he was the best spinner in Australia since Shane Warne. There was talk of unleashing Fawad on the Ashes in England, but even though his citizenship was rushed through (causing sniggers in an English media accustomed to fielding jibes from Aussies about their dependence on overseas imports) it was eventually decided, sensibly, not to pile extra pressure on him. Instead Fawad toured with Australia A, then made a low-key international debut against Scotland before playing some of the end-of season games in England. He showed himself to be a tight bowler, with a Warne-ish stroll up the stumps. He can turn it a lot, although a soggy September in England wasn't conducive to that. Fawad may now be blooded in the 2013-14 Ashes series Down Under. There's one final mystery: some sources suggest he is three years older than the 32 he admits to in his passport.

THE FACTS Fawad Ahmed took 6 for 109 for Pakistan Customs v Karachi Whites in January 2009 ... He took 5 for 83 on his first-class debut in Australia for Victoria v Queensland at Melbourne in February 2013 ... A devout Muslim, Fawad has been allowed to remove alcohol advertising from his Australian cricket kit ...

THE FIGURES to 17.09.13   espncricinfo.com

Batting & Fielding	M	Inns	NO	Runs	HS	Avge	S/R	100	50	4s	6s	Ct	St
Tests	0	0	–	–	–	–	–	–	–	–	–	–	–
ODIs	3	1	1	4	4*	–	200.00	0	0	0	0	0	0
T20Is	2	1	1	3	3*	–	60.00	0	0	0	0	0	0
First-class	18	27	10	170	23	10.00	–	0	0	–	–	9	0

Bowling	M	Balls	Runs	Wkts	BB	Avge	RpO	S/R	5i	10m
Tests	0	0	–	–	–	–	–	–	–	–
ODIs	3	144	145	3	1–39	48.33	6.04	48.00	0	0
T20Is	2	48	68	3	3–25	22.66	8.50	16.00	0	0
First-class	18	2878	1761	56	6–109	31.44	3.67	51.39	2	0

AARON **FINCH**

Full name **Aaron James Finch**
Born **November 17, 1986, Colac, Victoria**
Teams **Victoria, Pune Warriors**
Style **Right-hand bat, left-arm medium-pace bowler**
Test debut **No Tests yet**
ODI debut **Australia v Sri Lanka at Melbourne 2012-13**
T20I debut **Australia v England at Adelaide 2010-11**

THE PROFILE Stocky Aaron Finch propelled his name into the record books late in 2013, hammering 156 in a Twenty20 international against England at Southampton in September 2013. His muscular onslaught included 11 fours and no fewer than 14 sixes from just 63 balls, and was easily the highest score in T20 internationals, beating Brendon McCullum's 123. As an encore, a few days later Finch blitzed 148 in an ODI against Scotland, dominating a national-record opening stand of 246 with Shaun Marsh, who went on to 151 himself. Finch's returns against England were less spectacular, but nonetheless he had finally arrived in international cricket after a long apprenticeship: in 13 previous games, dating back to January 2013, he had managed only one fifty. Finch hails from the country town of Colac in south-west Victoria, and has been a consistent performer for Victoria in first-class cricket, quite apart from his Twenty20 success, which has led to stints in New Zealand and Sri Lanka as well as the IPL. He is also the poster-boy for the Melbourne Renegades in Australia's Big Bash. Finch made his first-class debut against the touring Indians in December 2007, but didn't get to bat in a rain-affected game, and had to wait more than two years for another chance. He made 50 in his second match, and 102 in his sixth – but was already more of a star in the limited-overs formats. When Victoria won the Twenty20 Big Bash in 2009-10 Finch led the runscoring lists (alongside Kieron Pollard) with 190, which earned him his first IPL contract, with Shane Warne's Rajasthan Royals. He played only once for them, but has since been a regular for Delhi and Pune.

THE FACTS Finch hit 156, the highest score in Twenty20 internationals, for Australia v England at Southampton in August 2013 (the previous-best was 123): his 14 sixes in that innings was also a record ... Finch made 148 against Scotland at Edinburgh in September 2013, putting on 246 with Shaun Marsh, the best for Australia's first wicket in ODIs ... Finch made 154 in a Ryobi Cup one-day game for Victoria v Queensland in October 2012 ...

THE FIGURES to 17.09.13   espncricinfo.com

Batting & Fielding	M	Inns	NO	Runs	HS	Avge	S/R	100	50	4s	6s	Ct	St
Tests	0	0	–	–	–	–	–	–	–	–	–	–	–
ODIs	12	11	0	324	148	29.45	95.57	1	0	39	8	9	0
T20Is	8	8	2	277	156	46.16	181.04	1	1	24	16	1	0
First-class	33	58	1	1685	122	29.56	52.47	2	11	199	18	31	0

Bowling	M	Balls	Runs	Wkts	BB	Avge	RpO	S/R	5i	10m
Tests	0	0	–	–	–	–	–	–	–	–
ODIs	12	6	2	0	–	–	2.00	–	0	0
T20Is	8	6	9	0	–	–	9.00	–	0	0
First-class	33	158	132	1	1-9	132.00	5.01	158.00	0	0

STEVEN **FINN**

Full name	Steven Thomas Finn
Born	April 4, 1989, Watford, Hertfordshire
Teams	Middlesex
Style	Right-hand bat, right-arm fast-medium bowler
Test debut	England v Bangladesh at Chittagong 2009-10
ODI debut	England v Australia at Brisbane 2010-11
T20I debut	England v West Indies at The Oval 2011

ENGLAND

THE PROFILE In 2010 Steven Finn, who measures up at 6ft 7ins (201cm), became the latest beanpole fast bowler to carry England's hopes, and his impressive arrival sounded the death knell for the international career of the previous one, Steve Harmison. Finn pings the ball down from the clouds with a heady blend of pace and bounce, and can rattle the best. After 53 Championship wickets in 2009, Finn went with the England Lions to the UAE, and when injuries struck at the start of the Bangladesh tour early in 2010, he was parachuted in as cover. He did well in the warm-up game against Bangladesh A, and three days later made his Test debut, displaying good pace and bounce on a docile Chittagong track. Back in England Finn took 14 wickets in a match for Middlesex, then claimed five-fors in both early-season Tests against Bangladesh. He started the 2010-11 Ashes tour strongly – 6 for 125 at Brisbane – but was supplanted by Chris Tremlett and Tim Bresnan. Their successes meant that after taking 46 Test wickets in 2010 Finn played only once in 2011 – he took four wickets against Sri Lanka at Lord's to become the youngest Englishman to reach 50 – but he was back the following year, and used his local knowledge of the Lord's slope to take eight wickets in a close-fought Test against South Africa. He started to make headlines with his habit of demolishing the non-striker's stumps with his knee: the Law was eventually changed to make this a no-ball. Trying to modify his approach, Finn took 18 wickets in the five home-and-away Tests against New Zealand in 2013, but was dropped after one match in the Ashes series that followed.

THE FACTS Finn took 9 for 37 (after 5 for 69 in the first innings) for Middlesex at Worcester in April 2010: his next two five-fors were in Tests against Bangladesh ... In 2011 Finn became the youngest bowler to reach 50 Test wickets for England, a record previously held by Ian Botham ... At 16 in 2005 Finn was the youngest player to appear in a first-class match for Middlesex, beating the record set by Fred Titmus in 1949 ...

THE FIGURES to 17.09.13   ESPNcricinfo.com

Batting & Fielding	M	Inns	NO	Runs	HS	Avge	S/R	100	50	4s	6s	Ct	St
Tests	23	29	14	169	56	11.26	28.98	0	1	22	0	6	0
ODIs	39	13	6	96	35	13.71	85.71	0	0	10	3	8	0
T20Is	18	3	3	14	8*	–	73.68	0	0	1	0	4	0
First-class	91	110	34	552	56	7.26	30.73	0	1	69	1	29	0

Bowling	M	Balls	Runs	Wkts	BB	Avge	RpO	S/R	5i	10m
Tests	23	4348	2646	90	6–125	29.40	3.65	48.31	4	0
ODIs	39	2084	1637	59	4–34	27.74	4.71	35.32	0	0
T20Is	18	408	487	25	3–16	19.48	7.16	16.32	0	0
First-class	91	16035	9168	326	9–37	28.12	3.43	49.18	8	1

JAMES **FRANKLIN**

NEW ZEALAND

Full name	**James Edward Charles Franklin**
Born	**November 7, 1980, Wellington**
Teams	**Wellington**
Style	**Left-hand bat, left-arm fast-medium bowler**
Test debut	**New Zealand v Pakistan at Auckland 2000-01**
ODI debut	**New Zealand v Zimbabwe at Taupo 2000-01**
T20I debut	**New Zealand v West Indies at Auckland 2005-06**

THE PROFILE James Franklin first represented New Zealand in 2000-01, when barely out of his teens, but made little impact at first. Back then he was a left-arm medium-pacer who swung the ball around, but he has worked on his batting and now has a double-century to his name. He was playing club cricket in Lancashire in 2004 when he was summoned for the third Test at Trent Bridge after Shane Bond was injured. Although New Zealand lost, Franklin took six wickets, five of them Test century-makers. In the one-dayers that followed he took 5 for 42 at Chester-le-Street as England were skittled for 101: not long afterwards he grabbed a Test hat-trick at Dhaka. In April 2006 he did his allrounder claims no harm with 122 – and a stand of 256 with Stephen Fleming – against South Africa at Cape Town. A stubborn knee injury, which eventually required surgery, kept him out for most of 2007-08 and the England tour that followed, but he was back for the Tests against India early in 2009, doing more with bat than ball (1 for 290 in 89 overs). Rather surprisingly, since he hadn't been in the one-day side since the 2007 World Cup, he did play in the World Twenty20 in England in 2009, during a successful stint with Gloucestershire – but after that he fell out of favour and lost his central contract. After two injury-restricted seasons Franklin averaged 53 at home in 2011-12, and was slotted back into the national side – usually batting at No. 6 and bowling a bit although he had lost a bit of nip, and Test appearances were rare. He made 47 and 53 – both not out – against South Africa in January 2013, but had a poor run with the bat over the next few months.

THE FACTS Franklin was the fourth of seven men to take a hat-trick and score a century in Tests ... The only other New Zealander to take a Test hat-trick was Peter Petherick in 1976-77 ... Franklin made 219 for Wellington at Auckland in November 2008: in the next match (v Northern Districts) he scored 160 ... He took 7 for 14 as Derbyshire were bowled out for 44 on the first morning at Bristol in August 2010 – but Gloucestershire still lost the match ...

THE FIGURES *to 17.09.13*   **cricinfo.com**

Batting & Fielding	M	Inns	NO	Runs	HS	Avge	S/R	100	50	4s	6s	Ct	St
Tests	31	46	7	808	122*	20.71	37.35	1	2	82	5	12	0
ODIs	110	80	27	1270	98*	23.96	76.92	0	4	97	17	26	0
T20Is	38	31	8	463	60	20.13	118.41	0	2	28	23	13	0
First-class	148	228	32	6831	219	34.85	–	14	29	–	–	56	0

Bowling	M	Balls	Runs	Wkts	BB	Avge	RpO	S/R	5i	10m
Tests	31	4767	2786	82	6–119	33.97	3.50	58.13	3	0
ODIs	110	3848	3554	81	5–42	41.40	5.22	47.50	1	0
T20Is	38	327	417	20	4–15	20.85	7.65	16.35	0	0
First-class	148	22068	11604	437	7–14	26.55	3.15	50.49	14	1

PETER **FULTON**

NEW ZEALAND

Full name	**Peter Gordon Fulton**
Born	**February 1, 1979, Christchurch**
Teams	**Canterbury**
Style	**Right-hand bat, occ. right-arm medium-pacer**
Test debut	**New Zealand v West Indies at Auckland 2005-06**
ODI debut	**New Zealand v Bangladesh at Chittagong 2004-05**
T20I debut	**New Zealand v West Indies at Auckland 2005-06**

THE PROFILE The international career of Peter Fulton, an imposingly tall batsman nicknamed "Two-Metre Peter", seemed be over late in 2009 after a disappointing run, culminating in ducks in successive home Tests against Pakistan. But three seasons later, Fulton hit twin centuries for Canterbury against Otago, and added 79 and 104 in the next game, against Wellington. By now opening, after starting in the middle order, Fulton was thus in pole position when the injured Martin Guptill missed the home series with England – and Fulton capitalised with 55 in his first match back, then, at 34, compiled twin centuries as New Zealand dominated the drawn third Test at Auckland in March 2013. This kept him in the side, ahead of Guptill, in England, where he looked ponderous against the early-season swing. Fulton is a product of Canterbury Country, an area rich in cricket history but which had never previously produced an international player, and initially hit the headlines by extending his maiden century to a triple in March 2003, in only his second full season. The following summer he made 728 runs at 42.82, including two more centuries, and was called up to the senior one-day squad for the Bangladesh tour in November 2004. He played one match there, but it was another 12 months before he featured again. This time he made the most of his chance, making a one-day hundred against Sri Lanka which led to a Test baptism: he made 75 in his second match, as New Zealand took an unbeatable lead over West Indies. He did well in the 2007 World Cup, but then struggled against England early in 2008, not reaching double figures in five international innings.

THE FACTS Fulton's 301*, for Canterbury v Auckland at Christchurch in March 2003, was the fifth-highest maiden century in all first-class cricket: the highest is 337* by Pervez Akhtar for Pakistan Railways in 1964-65 ... Fulton scored 136 and 110 against England at Auckland in March 2013 ... He averages 52 in ODIs against Sri Lanka, but 13.83 v England (and 4.00 v Scotland) ... His uncle, Roddy Fulton, played for Canterbury and Northern Districts in the 1970s ...

THE FIGURES to 17.09.13   espncricinfo.com

Batting & Fielding	M	Inns	NO	Runs	HS	Avge	S/R	100	50	4s	6s	Ct	St
Tests	15	25	1	697	136	29.04	42.39	2	2	90	15	15	0
ODIs	49	46	5	1334	112	32.53	72.77	1	8	111	20	18	0
T20Is	12	12	1	127	25	11.54	90.71	0	0	7	6	4	0
First-class	119	208	16	8079	301*	42.07	–	14	48	–	–	90	0

Bowling	M	Balls	Runs	Wkts	BB	Avge	RpO	S/R	5i	10m
Tests	15	0	–	–	–	–	–	–	–	–
ODIs	49	0	–	–	–	–	–	–	–	–
T20Is	12	0	–	–	–	–	–	–	–	–
First-class	119	727	445	11	4-49	40.45	3.67	66.09	0	0

SHANNON **GABRIEL**

Full name	**Shannon Terry Gabriel**
Born	**April 28, 1988, Trinidad**
Teams	**Trinidad & Tobago**
Style	**Right-hand bat, right-arm fast bowler**
Test debut	**West Indies v England at Lord's 2012**
ODI debut	**No ODIs yet**
T20I debut	**West Indies v Zimbabwe at North Sound 2012-13**

THE PROFILE The Trinidad fast bowler Shannon Gabriel has been compared to the young Ian Bishop, his fellow countryman who ended up with 161 Test wickets. Gabriel was one of the first 15 youngsters picked for the Sagicor High Performance Centre when the West Indian board set it up in 2010, and credits the coaches there for improving his fitness and technique. He made his debut for Trinidad & Tobago early in 2010, and although he was not a big wicket-taker to start with he did well enough to be named in T&T's squad for the Champions League Twenty20 in India in 2011 – something of a surprise as he had rarely featured in domestic limited-overs games – although he didn't actually play. First-class wickets started to come in greater numbers, and in March 2012 he took a timely career-best 5 for 78 against Barbados: all his victims were out in single figures, and four of them were Test players. This earned Gabriel a spot on the early-season tour of England which followed. He wasn't really expected to play in the Tests, but won his first cap at Lord's after his T&T team-mate Ravi Rampaul was injured. Gabriel looked good, bowling with genuine pace and removing Ian Bell, Matt Prior and Graeme Swann in the first innings, then adding Kevin Pietersen, who bottom-edged an attempted pull in the second. Sadly, though, Gabriel was then struck with injury himself: a back problem sent him home, and Tino Best stepped in to claim a place for a while. Still, Gabriel was back to face Zimbabwe early in 2013, defying two spin-friendly surfaces to take four wickets in the first Test and two more in the second.

THE FACTS Gabriel took 5 for 78 for Trinidad & Tobago v Barbados at Port-of-Spain in March 2012: the next time he bowled in a first-class match was his Test debut … He was only the seventh West Indian since the Second World War to make his Test debut at Lord's … Gabriel was Man of the Match in the Caribbean Twenty20 final in St Lucia in January 2013, after taking 2 for 16 in his four overs against Guyana …

THE FIGURES to 17.09.13   **cricinfo.com**

Batting & Fielding	M	Inns	NO	Runs	HS	Avge	S/R	100	50	4s	6s	Ct	St
Tests	3	3	1	13	13	6.50	39.39	0	0	2	0	1	0
ODIs	0	0	–	–	–	–	–	–	–	–	–	–	–
T20Is	2	0	–	–	–	–	–	–	–	–	–	1	0
First-class	34	44	16	126	14	4.50	–	0	0	–	–	7	0

Bowling	M	Balls	Runs	Wkts	BB	Avge	RpO	S/R	5i	10m
Tests	3	355	170	10	3–10	17.00	2.87	35.50	0	0
ODIs	0	0	–	–	–	–	–	–	–	–
T20Is	2	42	56	3	3–44	18.66	8.00	14.00	0	0
First-class	34	4625	2612	88	5–78	29.68	3.38	52.55	1	0

GAUTAM **GAMBHIR**

INDIA

Full name	Gautam Gambhir
Born	October 14, 1981, Delhi
Teams	Delhi, Essex, Kolkata Knight Riders
Style	Left-hand bat, occasional legspinner
Test debut	India v Australia at Mumbai 2004-05
ODI debut	India v Bangladesh at Dhaka 2002-03
T20I debut	India v Scotland at Durban 2006-07

THE PROFILE Gautam Gambhir has set tongues wagging ever since he was a schoolboy. Compact footwork and high bat-speed meant defence was often replaced by the aerial route over point. He pasted successive double-centuries in 2002, and joined the one-day squad when several seniors took a rest after the World Cup. He finally made the Test side late the following year, hitting 96 against South Africa in his second match and 139 against Bangladesh in his fifth. Leaner times followed, punctuated by cheap runs in Zimbabwe, and although he celebrated his one-day return after 30 months on the sidelines with 103 against Sri Lanka in April 2005, he struggled for big scores and soon found himself out again. After the disasters of the 2007 World Cup Gambhir was given another chance, and this time immediately looked the part. He made two one-day centuries in Australia early in 2008, and carried his good form into the inaugural IPL. He crashed 67, 104 and a superb 206 as Australia were beaten in October 2008, then helped ensure a series victory over England with 179 and 97 in the second Test. In ODIs he crashed 150 against Sri Lanka in Colombo in February 2009. Gambhir kept up this astonishing run of form with centuries in five successive Tests in 2009-10, and was a star at the 2011 World Cup, never failing to reach double figures and taking India close to glory with 97 in the final. However, he had gone off the boil in Tests, and was finally dropped early in 2013 after 26 matches – and three years – without a century. Shikhar Dhawan's turbocharged arrival displaced Gambhir from the one-day side, too, and he faced a battle to regain his place.

THE FACTS Gambhir made 206 against Australia at Delhi in October 2008: VVS Laxman also scored a double-century, the first time Australia had ever conceded two in the same innings ... Gambhir scored centuries in five successive Test matches in 2009 and 2010: only Don Bradman (six) has ever done better ... He made 214 (for Delhi v Railways) and 218 (for the Board President's XI v Zimbabwe) in successive innings early in 2002 ...

THE FIGURES to 17.09.13   ESPNcricinfo.com

Batting & Fielding	M	Inns	NO	Runs	HS	Avge	S/R	100	50	4s	6s	Ct	St
Tests	54	96	5	4021	206	44.18	51.55	9	21	502	8	38	0
ODIs	147	143	11	5238	150*	39.68	85.25	11	34	561	17	36	0
T20Is	37	36	2	932	75	27.41	119.02	0	7	109	10	11	0
First-class	141	240	21	11274	233*	51.47	–	33	50	–	–	87	0

Bowling	M	Balls	Runs	Wkts	BB	Avge	RpO	S/R	5i	10m
Tests	54	12	4	0	–	–	2.00	–	0	0
ODIs	147	6	13	0	–	–	13.00	–	0	0
T20Is	37	0	–	–	–	–	–	–	–	–
First-class	141	397	281	7	3-12	40.14	4.24	56.71	0	0

CHRIS **GAYLE**

Full name **Christopher Henry Gayle**
Born **September 21, 1979, Kingston, Jamaica**
Teams **Jamaica, Royal Challengers Bangalore**
Style **Left-hand bat, offspinner**
Test debut **West Indies v Zimbabwe at Port-of-Spain 1999-2000**
ODI debut **West Indies v India at Toronto 1999-2000**
T20I debut **West Indies v New Zealand at Auckland 2005-06**

THE PROFILE An attacking left-hander, Chris Gayle earned himself a black mark on his first tour when the new boys were felt to be insufficiently respectful of their elders. But a lack of respect, for opposition bowlers at least, has served him well since then. Tall and imposing, he loves to carve through the covers off either foot (without moving either of them much), and can take any bowling apart on his day. His lack of positive footwork was exposed in England in 2004 – but men with little footwork often baffle experts, and in May 2005 he punched 317 against South Africa in Antigua. Gayle also bowls brisk non-turning offspin, which makes him a genuine one-day allrounder. He took over the captaincy in 2007, and immediately showed unexpected flair for the job. But it ended in tears: after several acrimonious disputes with the board, Gayle declined a central contract, preferring to keep his options open for lucrative Twenty20 offers. He was stripped of the captaincy, responded by scoring 333 against Sri Lanka in his next Test in December 2010, then – after battling injury in the World Cup – was dropped altogether after another public row with the board. Gayle stomped off to the IPL, and was the leading runscorer ... but was left out of the West Indian side for 15 months. The standoff was finally resolved in mid-2012 – and Gayle roared back with a magnificent 150 against New Zealand in Antigua. A fallow period followed – 17 international innings with a fifty – but ended that with a Test century against Zimbabwe, and soon added another one-day ton against India. Earlier in 2013, though, he had thrashed 175 not out in an IPL game, leaving the Pune bowlers "scared", according to their coach Allan Donald.

THE FACTS Gayle's 333 against South Africa in Antigua in May 2005 has been exceeded for West Indies only by Brian Lara (twice) and Garry Sobers ... The only others to have scored two Test triple-centuries are Lara, Don Bradman and Virender Sehwag ... Gayle hit the first century in Twenty20 internationals, 117 v South Africa at Johannesburg in September 2007 ... His record includes three ODIs for the World XI ...

THE FIGURES *to 17.09.13* espncricinfo.com

Batting & Fielding	M	Inns	NO	Runs	HS	Avge	S/R	100	50	4s	6s	Ct	St
Tests	97	170	9	6836	333	42.45	59.77	15	34	992	89	89	0
ODIs	254	249	17	8743	153*	37.68	84.24	21	45	1009	204	108	0
T20Is	34	33	3	999	117	33.30	143.32	1	10	88	60	9	0
First-class	173	307	24	12772	333	45.13	–	32	60	–	–	151	0

Bowling	M	Balls	Runs	Wkts	BB	Avge	RpO	S/R	5i	10m
Tests	97	6899	3024	72	5–34	42.00	2.62	95.81	2	0
ODIs	254	7032	5556	157	5–46	35.38	4.74	44.78	1	0
T20Is	34	295	351	15	2–15	23.40	7.13	19.66	0	0
First-class	173	12289	5095	131	5–34	38.89	2.48	93.80	2	0

MARTIN **GUPTILL**

Full name **Martin James Guptill**
Born **September 30, 1986, Auckland**
Teams **Auckland**
Style **Right-hand bat, occasional offspinner**
Test debut **New Zealand v India at Hamilton 2008-09**
ODI debut **New Zealand v West Indies at Auckland 2008-09**
ODI debut **New Zealand v Australia at Sydney 2008-09**

NEW ZEALAND

THE PROFILE A tall right-hander, Martin Guptill made a bittersweet entry into first-class cricket in March 2006, not long after playing in the Under-19 World Cup, collecting a duck in his first innings then making 99 in the second before tickling a catch behind. By 2007-08 Guptill was tickling the selectors, too: he topped the State Shield runlists that season as Auckland reached the final. His rise continued with an A-team tour of India and, after a maiden first-class century at home, he was called up for the one-day series against the touring West Indians early in 2009. He lit up his debut in familiar surroundings in Auckland, reaching three figures with a huge six off Chris Gayle and finishing with a superb unbeaten 122 – the second-highest score by anyone in their first ODI. He was dropped three times before he reached 30, but his running (not one of New Zealand's strengths) was notable. Indeed, Guptill's turn of speed – between wickets or in the outfield, from a high-stepping run – is particularly remarkable as he has only two toes on his left foot after a forklift accident when he was 13. He consolidated his place in 2009-10, although his stats were boosted by 91 in a one-dayer against Bangladesh, and a massive 189 against them in the Hamilton Test. Now a regular in all three formats, he had a reasonable World Cup in 2011 before widening his experience with a county stint for Derbyshire, where he turned heads, not least with his sumptuous straight and cover-drives. A thumb injury kept him out early in 2013, but he returned in June for the one-day series in England, where he spanked 103 and 189 (a New Zealand record) in successive games.

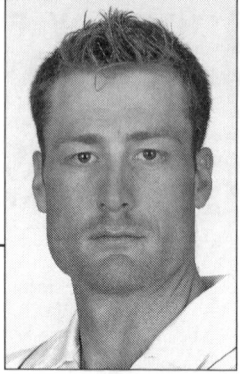

THE FACTS Guptill was the fifth batsman to score a century in his first one-day international ... He hit 189*, a New Zealand record in ODIs, against England at Southampton in June 2013 ... Guptill made 189 v Bangladesh at Hamilton in February 2010, sharing a sixth-wicket partnership of 339 with Brendon McCullum ... On his first-class debut, against Wellington in Auckland in March 2006, Guptill made 0 and 99 ...

THE FIGURES *to 17.09.13*   **ESPNcricinfo.com**

Batting & Fielding	M	Inns	NO	Runs	HS	Avge	S/R	100	50	4s	6s	Ct	St
Tests	31	59	1	1718	189	29.62	43.40	2	12	210	16	33	0
ODIs	75	73	9	2555	189*	39.92	82.79	4	17	254	50	31	0
T20Is	41	39	6	1168	101*	35.39	124.38	1	5	101	48	19	0
First-class	75	137	8	4300	195*	33.33	48.38	7	24	583	40	73	0

Bowling	M	Balls	Runs	Wkts	BB	Avge	RpO	S/R	5i	10m
Tests	31	332	258	5	3-37	51.60	4.66	66.40	0	0
ODIs	75	67	55	2	2-7	27.50	4.92	33.50	0	0
T20Is	41	6	11	0	–	–	11.00	–	0	0
First-class	75	530	387	6	3-37	64.50	4.38	88.33	0	0

BRAD **HADDIN**

AUSTRALIA

Full name	Bradley James Haddin
Born	October 23, 1977, Cowra, New South Wales
Teams	New South Wales, Kolkata Knight Riders
Style	Right-hand bat, wicketkeeper
Test debut	Australia v West Indies at Kingston 2007-08
ODI debut	Australia v Zimbabwe at Hobart 2000-01
T20I debut	Australia v South Africa at Brisbane 2005-06

THE PROFILE For years Brad Haddin held the most nerve-fraying position in Australian cricket – wicketkeeper-in-waiting, warming the seat whenever Adam Gilchrist needed a rest. Finally he became Australia's 400th Test cricketer in the West Indies early in 2008, and played through the series despite breaking a finger early on, which affected his batting. But he cemented his place with a blazing – almost Gilchristian – 169 against New Zealand at Adelaide in November, pulling and cutting strongly, and added another century in the first Ashes Test in 2009, before a valiant 80 in defeat at Lord's. After that, though, his fortunes waned: he broke another finger and had to surrender the gloves to Tim Paine for the one-dayers that followed. Then an elbow-tendon problem forced him out of the internationals in England in 2010: Paine again showed himself to be a capable deputy. Haddin returned with some feisty displays in the 2010-11 Ashes defeat, including another century at Brisbane, but he was forced home from the West Indian tour in April 2012 by the illness of his young daughter – which allowed another rival, Matthew Wade, to stake an impressive claim. But Haddin was preferred for the 2013 Ashes – as much for his leadership qualities as his glovework – and set a new record with 29 catches in the series. Haddin has long been a consistent scorer at domestic level, making 916 runs at 57.25 in 2004-05, leading NSW to a one-wicket Shield final victory over Queensland. He began his senior domestic career in 1997-98 with the Australian Capital Territory in their debut season in Australia's one-day competition.

THE FACTS Haddin took up a novel batting position behind the stumps for a free hit after a Shoaib Akhtar no-ball early in 2005: he reasoned that he had more time to sight the ball, and if it hit the stumps it would confuse the fielders (it did hit the stumps, and he managed a bye) ... Haddin's 29 catches in the 2013 Ashes were a record for any Test series, beating Rod Marsh's 28 in 1982-83 ... Haddin scored 169 against New Zealand at Adelaide in November 2008 ...

THE FIGURES to 17.09.13   **espn**cricinfo.com

Batting & Fielding	M	Inns	NO	Runs	HS	Avge	S/R	100	50	4s	6s	Ct	St
Tests	49	83	9	2514	169	33.97	56.60	3	12	281	38	193	5
ODIs	96	90	8	2614	110	31.87	81.84	2	16	244	57	133	9
T20Is	26	24	4	364	47	18.20	113.39	0	0	27	12	12	4
First-class	162	265	33	9033	169	38.93	–	16	49	–	–	528	37

Bowling	M	Balls	Runs	Wkts	BB	Avge	RpO	S/R	5i	10m
Tests	49	0	–	–	–	–	–	–	–	–
ODIs	96	0	–	–	–	–	–	–	–	–
T20Is	26	0	–	–	–	–	–	–	–	–
First-class	162	0	–	–	–	–	–	–	–	–

ALEX HALES

Full name **Alexander David Hales**
Born **January 3, 1989, Hillingdon, Middlesex**
Teams **Nottinghamshire**
Style **Right-hand bat, right-arm medium-pace bowler**
Test debut **No Tests yet**
ODI debut **No ODIs yet**
T20I debut **England v India at Manchester 2011**

THE PROFILE Alex Hales is an aggressive top-order batsman whose performances in limited-overs cricket – he once pounded 150 not out in a 40-over game for Nottinghamshire – earned him a call-up to England's Twenty20 side at the end of the 2011 season, and he has been a short-from regular ever since. Hales is 6ft 5ins (196cm) tall, and likes to give the ball a hearty thump. But he's not just a one-day basher: he has overcome the tough batting conditions at Trent Bridge, comfortably passing 1000 first-class runs in 2011 – despite missing a chunk of the season with a broken jaw – and falling just short in 2012 before a dip the following summer, during which he was dropped. When he joined Nottinghamshire from the Lord's groundstaff in 2008, MCC's head coach Clive Radley said he was "a natural timer of a ball", and Hales showed that was true almost from the start, hitting 62 and 78 against Durham in one of his early games and completing his maiden first-class century – 136 against Hampshire – in his first match of 2010. In Twenty20 cricket for Notts in 2011 he biffed 544 runs at a strike-rate of 146, which led to that international call-up later in the season. He started with a debut duck against India, but clouted 62 in his second game, against West Indies. And when the West Indians returned the following year, Hales made 99 from 68 deliveries in front of his home crowd at Trent Bridge: he reached the nineties again with 94 against Australia in August 2013. Sporting talent runs in Hales's genes: his grandfather Dennis once took tennis great Rod Laver to five sets in a Wimbledon qualifying match.

THE FACTS Hales was the first man to be dismissed for 99 in a Twenty20 international, against West Indies at Trent Bridge in June 2012: no-one has yet made a higher T20 score for England ... He hit 150* – with eight sixes and 13 fours – in a 40-over match for Nottinghamshire v Worcestershire at Trent Bridge in August 2009 ... Hales made 184 for Notts v Somerset at Trent Bridge in July 2011 ...

THE FIGURES to 17.09.13   **cricinfo.com**

Batting & Fielding	M	Inns	NO	Runs	HS	Avge	S/R	100	50	4s	6s	Ct	St
Tests	0	0	–	–	–	–	–	–	–	–	–	–	–
ODIs	0	0	–	–	–	–	–	–	–	–	–	–	–
T20Is	21	21	4	665	99	39.11	135.99	0	6	69	19	9	0
First-class	61	104	5	3367	184	34.01	56.37	6	22	489	13	57	0

Bowling	M	Balls	Runs	Wkts	BB	Avge	RpO	S/R	5i	10m
Tests	0	0	–	–	–	–	–	–	–	–
ODIs	0	0	–	–	–	–	–	–	–	–
T20Is	21	0	–	–	–	–	–	–	–	–
First-class	61	281	167	3	2–63	55.66	3.56	93.66	0	0

HARBHAJAN SINGH

Full name	Harbhajan Singh Plaha
Born	July 3, 1980, Jullundur, Punjab
Teams	Punjab, Mumbai Indians
Style	Right-hand bat, offspinner
Test debut	India v Australia at Bangalore 1997-98
ODI debut	India v New Zealand at Sharjah 1997-98
T20I debut	India v South Africa at Johannesburg 2006-07

THE PROFILE Harbhajan Singh represents the spirit of the new Indian cricketer: arrogance and cockiness translate into self-belief and passion on the field. An offspinner with a windmilling, whiplash delivery, remodelled after questions about his action, he exercises great command over the ball, has the ability to vary his length and pace, and bowls a deadly doosra too – although his main wicket-taking ball is the one that climbs wickedly from a length. In March 2001 it proved too much for the previously all-conquering Australians, as "Bhajji" collected 32 wickets in three Tests while none of his team-mates managed more than three. Harbhajan's rivalry with the Aussies – against whom he has taken 95 wickets in 18 Tests – boiled over in Sydney in January 2008 when he was charged with racially abusing Andrew Symonds. He was initially given a three-Test ban before the charge was reduced on appeal. Then in April Harbhajan slapped his Indian team-mate Sreesanth after an IPL game, which cost him an 11-match ban. He took 16 wickets in three Tests in New Zealand early in 2009, but although he took his 400th Test wicket in the West Indies in mid-2011, he looked jaded on the England tour that followed. Ravichandran Ashwin took his place and grabbed his chance – and although Harbhajan played three Tests in 2012-13 (including his 100th) he made little impression. Muttiah Muralitharan once suggested that Harbhajan might be the man to threaten his stratospheric wicket-tally of 800 – but that's looking increasingly unlikely.

THE FACTS Harbhajan's match figures of 15 for 217 against Australia at Chennai in 2000-01 have been bettered for India only by Narendra Hirwani (16 for 136 in 1987-88, also at Chennai) ... Harbhajan took 32 wickets at 17.03 in that three-match series: his haul at Kolkata included India's first Test hat-trick ... He has taken 56 wickets at 22.60 in Tests against West Indies, but 25 at 52.04 v Pakistan ... His record includes two ODIs for the Asia XI ...

THE FIGURES to 17.09.13   ESPNcricinfo.com

Batting & Fielding	M	Inns	NO	Runs	HS	Avge	S/R	100	50	4s	6s	Ct	St
Tests	101	142	22	2202	115	18.35	65.03	2	9	274	42	42	0
ODIs	229	123	33	1190	49	13.22	80.51	0	0	89	34	69	0
T20Is	25	11	4	100	21	14.28	120.48	0	0	10	4	6	0
First-class	179	239	42	3865	115	19.61	–	2	13	–	–	91	0

Bowling	M	Balls	Runs	Wkts	BB	Avge	RpO	S/R	5i	10m
Tests	101	28293	13372	413	8–84	32.37	2.83	68.50	25	5
ODIs	229	12059	8651	259	5–31	33.40	4.30	46.55	3	0
T20Is	25	540	573	22	4–12	26.04	6.36	24.54	0	0
First-class	179	45198	21146	726	8–84	29.12	2.80	62.25	39	7

RYAN **HARRIS**

AUSTRALIA

Full name **Ryan James Harris**
Born **October 11, 1979, Sydney**
Teams **Queensland, Kings XI Punjab**
Style **Right-hand bat, right-arm fast bowler**
Test debut **Australia v New Zealand at Wellington 2009-10**
ODI debut **Australia v South Africa at Hobart 2008-09**
T20I debut **Australia v West Indies at Sydney 2009-10**

THE PROFILE Ryan Harris leapt onto the international stage in 2009-10, a season he initially feared would be a write-off after knee surgery. He remains susceptible to injury, and is generally mothballed for Tests – hence his new nickname "TMO" (Test Matches Only – a label originally coined for Terry Alderman). A stocky, skiddy bowler who is faster than he looks, Harris quickly became too good to ignore. He made a dream start to his international career: in only his second ODI, against Pakistan in January 2010, he collected five wickets, and did the same in the next game. All this led to a Test debut in New Zealand, and he did well during both matches there, taking nine wickets in terribly windy conditions at Wellington. Then he took 6 for 47 as Australia bounced back to win the second Ashes Test of 2010-11 at Perth, and there was widespread disappointment when he limped out of the series during the next Test with an ankle injury. He was back in Sri Lanka later in 2011, taking 11 wickets in the first two Tests before a hamstring niggle kept him out of the third. In 2012 his five wickets contributed to a win in Bridgetown, but he was rested for the next Test on fitness grounds. In England in 2013 the body held together for four consecutive Tests for the first time – and Harris looked the pick of the Australian attack while scalping 24 victims. He is also a handy attacking batsman – an early limited-overs highlight was lofting a six over long-on when South Australia needed five to win against Queensland at Adelaide in December 2006. However, until his international debut at 29, he almost qualified as a journeyman. He was South Australia's top wicket-taker in 2007-08, and they might have tried harder to stop him moving to Queensland. He also played briefly for Sussex and Surrey.

THE FACTS Harris took five-fors in his second and third ODIs, a unique feat at the time (since bettered by Brian Vitori of Zimbabwe) ... Harris took 7 for 117 v England at Chester-le-Street in August 2013 ... Harris scored 94 for Surrey at Northampton in June 2009 ... He took 7 for 60 for Queensland v Tasmania at Brisbane in October 2011 ...

THE FIGURES to 17.09.13 ESPNcricinfo.com

Batting & Fielding	M	Inns	NO	Runs	HS	Avge	S/R	100	50	4s	6s	Ct	St
Tests	16	25	8	311	68*	18.29	56.85	0	1	31	3	6	0
ODIs	21	13	7	48	21	8.00	100.00	0	0	3	1	6	0
T20Is	3	1	1	2	2*	–	200.00	0	0	0	0	0	0
First-class	66	103	17	1638	94	19.04	60.91	0	8	–	–	32	0

Bowling	M	Balls	Runs	Wkts	BB	Avge	RpO	S/R	5i	10m
Tests	16	3285	1581	71	7–117	22.26	2.88	46.26	4	0
ODIs	21	1031	832	44	5–19	18.90	4.84	23.43	3	0
T20Is	3	70	95	4	2–27	23.75	8.14	17.50	0	0
First-class	66	13079	6489	245	7–60	26.48	2.97	53.38	9	0

RANGANA **HERATH**

SRI LANKA

Full name	Herath Mudiyanselage Rangana Keerthi Bandara Herath
Born	March 19, 1978, Kurunegala
Teams	Tamil Union, Basnahira
Style	Left-hand bat, left-arm orthodox spinner
Test debut	Sri Lanka v Australia at Galle 1999-2000
ODI debut	Sri Lanka v Zimbabwe at Harare 2003-04
T20I debut	Sri Lanka v Australia at Pallekele 2011

THE PROFILE Slow left-armer Rangana Herath first came to prominence late in 1999, when his so-called mystery ball – *Wisden* called it "a wonderful delivery, bowled out of the front of his hand, which turned back into right-handers" – befuddled the touring Australians. He took four wickets on Test debut at Galle, including Steve Waugh and Ricky Ponting, but was soon unceremoniously dumped as other spinners were tried as foils for Muttiah Muralitharan. But he has blossomed since Murali's retirement, taking 129 wickets in 25 Tests, including ten-fors to inspire victories over England, New Zealand and Bangladesh. He sprinted to 200 wickets in March 2013, as Sri Lankans realised there could indeed be some success in the post-Muralitharan era. Originally, Herath's unprepossessing body shape – he's rather short with a hint of excess padding around the midriff – may have counted against him, but he has long been a regular wicket-taker in domestic cricket. He took 17 wickets in four Tests in 2004, including seven in a rare Murali-less Sri Lankan victory over Pakistan at Faisalabad, flighting the ball well and making it grip and turn. However, he was soon left out again, seemingly for good. But the domestic wickets still kept coming and he was eventually recalled in 2008, although he might have returned to anonymity but for an injury which forced Murali out of the home series against Pakistan in July 2009. Herath took five wickets in each of the three Tests, then 11 in three in India that winter, but lost his place after an underwhelming bowling performance in Murali's final Test in July 2010, although he did manage a career-best with the bat.

THE FACTS Herath took 8 for 43 (11 for 72 in the match) for Moors v Police in Colombo in 2002-03 ... In January 2002 he took 8 for 47 (and caught one of the others) for Moors v Galle ... Of his 200 Test wickets, 169 have come in Asia, and 31 in 11 Tests elsewhere, at an average of 38.77 ... Herath took 72 wickets at 13.59 in Sri Lanka in 2000-01 ... He made 80* against India in Colombo in July 2010 ...

THE FIGURES to 17.09.13   espncricinfo.com

Batting & Fielding	M	Inns	NO	Runs	HS	Avge	S/R	100	50	4s	6s	Ct	St
Tests	47	66	15	707	80*	13.86	49.54	0	1	76	5	11	0
ODIs	52	22	10	106	17*	8.83	61.62	0	0	4	2	8	0
T20Is	6	2	2	1	1*	–	100.00	0	0	0	0	0	0
First-class	215	305	71	3823	80*	16.33	–	0	12	–	–	93	0

Bowling	M	Balls	Runs	Wkts	BB	Avge	RpO	S/R	5i	10m
Tests	47	12780	5904	200	7–89	29.52	2.77	63.90	16	3
ODIs	52	2395	1673	51	4–20	32.80	4.19	46.96	0	0
T20Is	6	108	121	6	3–25	20.16	6.72	18.00	0	0
First-class	215	45012	20256	818	8–43	24.81	2.70	55.02	51	8

PHILLIP **HUGHES**

AUSTRALIA

Full name	Phillip Joel Hughes
Born	November 30, 1988, Macksville, New South Wales
Teams	New South Wales, Worcestershire
Style	Left-hand bat
Test debut	Australia v South Africa at Johannesburg 2008-09
ODI debut	Australia v South Africa at Melbourne 2012-13
T20I debut	No T20Is yet

THE PROFILE Phillip Hughes made an unconvincing start in Tests – a four-ball duck at the Wanderers after becoming Australia's youngest player for 25 years – but he scored 75 in the second innings. But in the next Test he became the youngest to make two centuries in the same match, bringing up the first with two sixes. His 415 runs in the series were followed by centuries in each of three Championship matches for Middlesex, irritating England supporters angry he had been given the chance to fine-tune before the 2009 Ashes. It didn't do him much good, as he did little in the first two Tests and was replaced by Shane Watson, a change made public by Hughes on Twitter before the official announcement, which provoked reactions ranging from rage to raucous laughter. His country-baked technique includes compulsive slicing through point and slashing to cover, as well as stepping away to provide room for tennis-style drives down the ground. He did make 86 not out at Wellington in March 2010 when Watson was injured – but then a dislocated shoulder, suffered while boxing, knocked Hughes himself out. After that he continued to score heavily in domestic cricket ... and continued to struggle in Tests. He was jettisoned after making only 97 runs in the first three Tests of the 2010-11 Ashes debacle, but restated his case in Sri Lanka, with an important century in Colombo. Twin 80s against Sri Lanka at home late in 2012 earned him another Ashes tour – and a long-delayed ODI chance, scoring 112 on debut against Sri Lanka. But after scoring 81 not out in the first Test in England he was left out again after two failures in the second one.

THE FACTS Hughes made 115 and 160 in only his second Test, against South Africa at Durban in March 2009: at 20 years 98 days he was the youngest to hit twin centuries in a Test, beating George Headley (20 years 271 days for West Indies v England in 1929-30) ... Hughes hit 198 for NSW v South Australia at Adelaide in November 2008 ... He shared a Test-record tenth-wicket stand of 163 with Ashton Agar at Trent Bridge in July 2013 ...

THE FIGURES to 17.09.13 **ESPNcricinfo.com**

Batting & Fielding	M	Inns	NO	Runs	HS	Avge	S/R	100	50	4s	6s	Ct	St
Tests	26	49	2	1535	160	32.65	53.55	3	7	199	11	15	0
ODIs	14	13	1	461	138*	38.41	74.71	2	1	51	3	3	0
T20Is	0	0	–	–	–	–	–	–	–	–	–	–	–
First-class	101	187	12	7832	198	44.75	57.95	21	43	1072	42	63	0

Bowling	M	Balls	Runs	Wkts	BB	Avge	RpO	S/R	5i	10m
Tests	26	0	–	–	–	–	–	–	–	–
ODIs	14	0	–	–	–	–	–	–	–	–
T20Is	0	0	–	–	–	–	–	–	–	–
First-class	101	24	14	0	–	–	3.50	–	0	0

IMRAN TAHIR

Full name	**Mohammad Imran Tahir**
Born	**March 27, 1979, Lahore, Pakistan**
Teams	**Lions**
Style	**Right-hand bat, legspinner**
Test debut	**South Africa v Australia at Cape Town 2011-12**
ODI debut	**South Africa v West Indies at Delhi 2010-11**
T20I debut	**South Africa v Sri Lanka at Colombo 2013**

THE PROFILE Legspinner Imran Tahir is the ultimate journeyman cricketer. Since starting his first-class career in his native Pakistan in 1996-97 he has played for almost 20 first-class teams, ranging from Sui Gas to Yorkshire. He has helped out four English counties, but he finally settled in South Africa, after marrying a local girl. He has a fine record, with nearly 700 first-class wickets at a good average. Early on he played for Pakistan Under-19s, but after his marriage threw in his lot with South Africa. Match-winning spinners have always been scarce there, and the bouncy Tahir – who has all the variations, including a well-disguised googly – was soon being mentioned as a Test candidate. In fact he was selected for the Test squad – against England in January 2010 – before he was even eligible, which caused red faces all round. The situation was formalised after that, and he became a naturalised South African early in 2011. He had been picking up plenty of wickets on the domestic circuit, and was immediately chosen in the squad for the one-dayers against India. But the selectors kept him under wraps, and finally blooded him in the World Cup. He made up for lost time, taking four West Indian wickets in his first game, three in his second (against the Netherlands) and four more against England. He was hindered after that by a cracked thumb, but finished with 14 wickets at 10.71, a fine start. Tahir finally made his Test debut at 32 late in 2011, and performed respectably enough – at least until the Australians caned him (23-0-180-0) at Adelaide in November 2012. He hasn't played a Test since, but was recalled for the one-dayers in Sri Lanka in August 2013.

THE FACTS Imran Tahir took 8 for 76 for Redco Pakistan v Lahore Blues at Lahore in December 1999 ... He took 8 for 114 for Warwickshire (his fourth English county) against Durham at Edgbaston in May 2010 ... Tahir's first ODI was during the 2011 World Cup: he took 4 for 41 against West Indies ...

THE FIGURES to 17.09.13

espncricinfo.com

Batting & Fielding	M	Inns	NO	Runs	HS	Avge	S/R	100	50	4s	6s	Ct	St
Tests	11	12	5	88	29*	12.57	66.66	0	0	10	1	4	0
ODIs	5	2	2	1	1*	–	50.00	0	0	0	0	2	0
T20Is	3	0	–	–	–	–	–	–	–	–	–	1	0
First-class	164	204	48	2220	77*	14.23	–	0	4	–	–	69	0

Bowling	M	Balls	Runs	Wkts	BB	Avge	RpO	S/R	5i	10m
Tests	11	2151	1305	26	3–55	50.19	3.64	82.73	0	0
ODIs	5	237	150	14	4–38	10.71	3.79	16.92	0	0
T20Is	3	72	63	3	1–20	21.00	5.25	24.00	0	0
First-class	164	32481	17674	673	8–76	26.26	3.26	48.26	47	10

COLIN **INGRAM**

Full name **Colin Alexander Ingram**
Born **July 3, 1985, Port Elizabeth**
Teams **Warriors**
Style **Left-hand batsman, occasional legspinner**
Test debut **No Tests yet**
ODI debut **South Africa v Zimbabwe at Bloemfontein 2010-11**
T20I debut **South Africa v Zimbabwe at Bloemfontein 2010-11**

THE PROFILE A blond, bruising left-hander who answers to the nickname "Bozie", Colin Ingram is among the brightest talents produced by the Eastern Cape in recent years. Happily for a region of South Africa that has often seen its budding stars bloom fully elsewhere, Ingram has remained true to his roots and stayed with the Warriors. He brings a bracing brand of aggression to the batting, and made an immediate impact to being elevated to the senior one-day side after a successful stint in the A team. In his first ODI, against Zimbabwe at Bloemfontein in October 2010, Ingram hit 124 from 126 balls, and a fortnight later he repeated the dose, this time against Pakistan in Abu Dhabi, making a round 100. Things calmed down a little after that, and for a while he lost his place to David Miller, but it was Ingram who made the 2011 World Cup squad (he played only once, scoring 46 against Ireland), and Ingram who was preferred for a national contract afterwards. He lost his place early in 2012, but remained in the frame with consistent runs for the A team, and cracked another ODI hundred against Pakistan at Bloemfontein in March 2013. Some put his fluctuations in form down to being shuffled around the order: he usually opens for the Warriors, and scored his first two one-day hundreds at No. 3. But Jacques Kallis is the immovable object there in the national side, and when Ingram moved down to No. 6 he looked less assured. Ingram, however, says: "I pride myself on being adaptable and flexible as a cricketer. When you are batting lower down the order, the situation dictates what you have to do, rather than when you are at No. 3 and you can just decide for yourself."

THE FACTS Ingram was the first South African – and only the sixth from any country – to score a century in his first one-day international, with 124 against Zimbabwe in October 2010 ... He scored 190 for Eastern Province v KwaZulu-Natal in Port Elizabeth in January 2009 ... Ingram made 78 from 50 balls in a Twenty20 international against India at Johannesburg in March 2012 ...

THE FIGURES *to 17.09.13*   **cricinfo.com**

Batting & Fielding	M	Inns	NO	Runs	HS	Avge	S/R	100	50	4s	6s	Ct	St
Tests	0	0	–	–	–	–	–	–	–	–	–	–	–
ODIs	29	27	3	839	124	34.95	82.41	3	3	81	10	11	0
T20Is	9	9	1	210	78	26.25	129.62	0	1	23	7	2	0
First-class	58	103	5	3377	190	34.45	–	6	16	–	–	38	0

Bowling	M	Balls	Runs	Wkts	BB	Avge	RpO	S/R	5i	10m
Tests	0	0	–	–	–	–	–	–	–	–
ODIs	29	6	17	0	–	–	17.00	–	0	0
T20Is	9	0	–	–	–	–	–	–	–	–
First-class	58	2042	1207	33	4-16	36.57	3.54	61.87	0	0

RAVINDRA **JADEJA**

Full name	**Ravindrasinh Anirudsinh Jadeja**
Born	**December 6, 1988, Navagam-Khed, Saurashtra**
Teams	**Saurashtra, Chennai Super Kings**
Style	**Left-hand bat, slow left-arm orthodox spinner**
Test debut	**India v England at Nagpur 2012-13**
ODI debut	**India v Sri Lanka at Colombo 2008-09**
T20I debut	**India v Sri Lanka at Colombo 2008-09**

THE PROFILE Left-handed allrounder Ravindra Jadeja elbowed his way into national contention with a superb 2008-09 season, which followed a good showing in the inaugural IPL, during which Shane Warne labelled him "a superstar in the making". He extended his maiden first-class hundred for Saurashtra in November 2008 to 232 not out, although even that was overshadowed by his batting partner Cheteshwar Pujara's triple-century. They put on 520, a fifth-wicket record for all first-class cricket, erasing the Waugh twins' 464 for New South Wales in 1990-91. Jadeja collected his best bowling figures, and another century, the following month, finishing the Ranji Trophy season with 739 runs and 42 wickets. He leapfrogged Pujara into the national side, making his limited-overs debuts in Sri Lanka early in 2009 ... but then the fairytale went sour for a while. He was criticised during the World Twenty20 for using up 35 balls over 25 in the defeat by England (in truth the blame lay with whoever put him in at No. 4, ahead of hitters like Yuvraj Singh and MS Dhoni). Then he was banned from the third IPL for allegedly trying to negotiate terms with another team. Jadeja remained in the one-day mix, to the bemusement of those who thought his bowling was unthreatening, but he made them eat their words with some spectacular returns in 2012-13. Finally chosen for the Test side, he claimed 24 wickets as Australia were whitewashed 4-0, and by September was the top-ranked bowler in the one-day rankings. And, although his batting has not yet hit the same heights at international level, the only Indian to score three first-class triple-centuries obviously has the potential to make it big there too.

THE FACTS Jadeja scored 232* for Saurashtra v Orissa at Rajkot in November 2008: he shared a world-record fifth-wicket stand of 520* with Cheteshwar Pujara ... Jadeja is the only Indian to make three first-class triple-centuries, all for Saurashtra: 314 v Orissa in November 2011, 303* v Gujarat in November 2012, and 331 v Railways the following month ... He took 7 for 31 (10 for 88 in the match) for Saurashtra v Hyderabad at Rajkot in December 2008 ...

THE FIGURES to 17.09.13   ESPNcricinfo.com

Batting & Fielding	M	Inns	NO	Runs	HS	Avge	S/R	100	50	4s	6s	Ct	St
Tests	5	6	1	97	43	19.40	63.81	0	0	15	1	1	0
ODIs	80	54	16	1242	78	32.68	80.23	0	6	95	21	28	0
T20Is	14	10	3	74	25	10.57	84.09	0	0	3	1	6	0
First-class	48	70	6	3263	331	50.98	59.66	7	12	365	48	41	0

Bowling	M	Balls	Runs	Wkts	BB	Avge	RpO	S/R	5i	10m
Tests	5	1580	536	27	5–58	19.85	2.03	58.51	1	0
ODIs	80	3773	2907	95	5–36	30.60	4.62	39.71	1	0
T20Is	14	274	331	7	2–26	47.28	7.24	39.14	0	0
First-class	48	11025	4400	171	7–31	25.73	2.39	64.47	11	2

JAHURUL ISLAM

BANGLADESH

Full name	**Mohammad Jahurul Islam**
Born	**December 12, 1986, Rajshahi**
Teams	**Rajshahi**
Style	**Right-hand bat, occ. wicketkeeper and offspinner**
Test debut	**Bangladesh v England at Mirpur 2009-10**
ODI debut	**Bangladesh v Pakistan at Dambulla 2010**
T20I debut	**Bangladesh v Australia at Bridgetown 2010**

THE PROFILE A superb domestic season in 2009-10, during which he was the only man to pass 1000 runs, with four centuries, propelled the tall, aggressive Jahurul Islam into national contention, and when Raqibul Hasan fell out with the selectors and announced a short-lived retirement just before the home Test series against England in March 2010, "Aumi" got the call. He made a duck in his first Test innings, courtesy of Graeme Swann, but took his revenge in the second, getting off the mark with a six off Swann over long-on, and adding another shortly afterwards to become only the second player (after his team-mate Shafiul Islam) to open his Test account with two sixes. Jahurul had long been earmarked for high honours: a product of the national academy, he made 78 on first-class debut in 2002-03, although he was into his fifth season before he finally cracked the three-figure barrier. In England in 2010 he hit 158 against Surrey, and did reasonably well in the first Test at Lord's (20 and 46) before two low scores in the second. He is also a handy stopgap wicketkeeper, and deputised in some of the one-dayers in Britain later in 2010 after Mushfiqur Rahim was injured. It didn't seem to affect his batting: at Bristol Jahurul made 40 during an important stand of 83 with Imrul Kayes, in a match Bangladesh ended up winning by five runs, their first-ever victory over England. After a spell on the sidelines he made 53 in a rare ODI victory over India at Mirpur during the Asia Cup in March 2012, but he played in all four of Bangladesh's Tests early in 2013 without nailing a big score – or even a half-century.

THE FACTS Jahurul Islam's first two scoring shots in Test cricket were both sixes (against England in March 2010), equalling the feat of his team-mate Shafiul Islam earlier in the year ... Jahurul's 53 helped Bangladesh overhaul India's 289 in the Asia Cup in March 2012 ... He scored 167 for Rajshahi against Dhaka at Sylhet in December 2011, sharing a stand of 345 with Junaid Siddique ...

THE FIGURES to 17.09.13   espncricinfo.com

Batting & Fielding	M	Inns	NO	Runs	HS	Avge	S/R	100	50	4s	6s	Ct	St
Tests	7	14	1	347	48	26.69	38.47	0	0	37	4	7	0
ODIs	14	13	1	270	53	22.50	72.77	0	1	25	2	7	0
T20Is	3	3	0	31	18	10.33	134.78	0	0	3	1	3	0
First-class	90	165	15	5452	167	36.34	–	10	31	–	–	96	5

Bowling	M	Balls	Runs	Wkts	BB	Avge	RpO	S/R	5i	10m
Tests	7	0	–	–	–	–	–	–	–	–
ODIs	14	0	–	–	–	–	–	–	–	–
T20Is	3	0	–	–	–	–	–	–	–	–
First-class	90	18	10	1	1–0	10.00	3.33	18.00	0	0

MAHELA **JAYAWARDENE**

SRI LANKA

Full name	**Denagamage Proboth Mahela de Silva Jayawardene**
Born	**May 27, 1977, Colombo**
Teams	**Sinhalese Sports Club, Uthura, Delhi Daredevils**
Style	**Right-hand bat, right-arm medium-pacer**
Test debut	**Sri Lanka v India at Colombo 1997-98**
ODI debut	**Sri Lanka v Zimbabwe at Colombo 1997-98**
T20I debut	**Sri Lanka v England at Southampton 2006**

THE PROFILE A fine technician with an excellent temperament, Mahela Jayawardene's arrival heralded a new era for Sri Lanka's middle order. Perhaps mindful of his first Test, when he went in at 790 for 4, he soon developed an appetite for big scores. His 66 then, in the world-record 952 for 6 against India, was followed by a masterful 167 on a Galle minefield against New Zealand in only his fourth Test, and a marathon 242 against India in his seventh. However he lost form, hardly scored a run in the 2003 World Cup, and was briefly dropped. Jayawardene benefited from a settled spot at No. 4 after Aravinda de Silva retired: a good series against England was followed by more runs in 2004. He took over as captain in England in 2006, producing a stunning double of 61 and 119 to lead the rearguard that saved the Lord's Test. Later he put South Africa to the sword in Colombo, compiling a colossal 374 in a world-record stand of 624 with Kumar Sangakkara. In 2007 he inspired his side to the World Cup final with 548 runs at 60, including a century in the semi-final, then became Sri Lanka's leading Test runscorer during 2007-08, a period that included three successive centuries, one of them a double against England. He stepped down as captain early in 2009 to concentrate on his batting – not that leadership seemed to affect it much. He made a classy century in the 2011 World Cup final – in vain – and early the following year got the captaincy back, after Tillekeratne Dilshan was dumped. Jayawardene made a brilliant 180 against England in his first match back in charge, but gladly handed over to Angelo Mathews in 2013. He's now passed 10,000 runs in both Tests and ODIs.

THE FACTS Jayawardene made 374 against South Africa in July 2006, the highest by a right-hander in Tests … He took 77 Test catches off Muttiah Muralitharan, a record for a fielder-bowler combination … Jayawardene has scored 2698 runs and ten centuries in Tests at the SSC in Colombo, a record for a single ground: he's also made 2284 at Galle … His record includes five ODIs for the Asia XI …

THE FIGURES to 17.09.13   cricinfo.com

Batting & Fielding	M	Inns	NO	Runs	HS	Avge	S/R	100	50	4s	6s	Ct	St
Tests	138	232	14	10806	374	49.56	51.51	31	45	1281	53	194	0
ODIs	404	378	38	11354	144	33.39	78.36	16	70	982	67	201	0
T20Is	48	48	7	1322	100	32.48	134.40	1	8	153	30	14	0
First-class	223	359	23	16648	374	49.54	–	48	73	–	–	292	0

Bowling	M	Balls	Runs	Wkts	BB	Avge	RpO	S/R	5i	10m
Tests	138	553	297	6	2–32	49.50	3.22	92.16	0	0
ODIs	404	582	558	7	2–56	79.71	5.75	83.14	0	0
T20Is	48	6	8	0	–	–	8.00	–	0	0
First-class	223	2965	1616	52	5–72	31.07	3.27	57.01	1	0

MITCHELL **JOHNSON**

Full name **Mitchell Guy Johnson**
Born **November 2, 1981, Townsville, Queensland**
Teams **Western Australia, Mumbai Indians**
Style **Left-hand bat, left-hand fast-medium bowler**
Test debut **Australia v Sri Lanka at Brisbane 2007-08**
ODI debut **Australia v New Zealand at Christchurch 2005-06**
T20I debut **Australia v Zimbabwe at Cape Town 2007-08**

AUSTRALIA

THE PROFILE He's quick, he's tall, he's talented ... but most of all, Mitchell Johnson is a left-armer, and only two others before him (Alan Davidson and Bruce Reid) took 100 Test wickets for Australia. Dennis Lillee spotted him at 17, and called him a "once-in-a-generation bowler". In December 2005 Johnson was supersubbed into the final one-dayer in New Zealand. Johnson, who runs up as if carrying a crate of milk bottles in his left hand, started by reducing India to 35 for 5 in a one-dayer in Kuala Lumpur, but narrowly missed out to the steadier Stuart Clark for the 2006-07 Ashes, then sat out the World Cup. Test rewards finally came in 2007-08, with 16 wickets against India and ten in the West Indies. Next season Johnson was superb against South Africa both home and away, adding a wicked in-ducker to his repertoire and claiming 33 wickets in six Tests (and also hammering a maiden century), but then he struggled in England, spraying the ball around from an arm seemingly lower than usual. The start of 2010 was similarly up-and-down – ten wickets against New Zealand at Hamilton, but only 11 in five other matches, and it was the same story at the end of the year in the Ashes: dropped for the second Test, matchwinner in the third with nine wickets and a handy 62, then down to earth again. Injuries then kept him out for a while in 2012, but he said they probably stopped him from retiring. He did well when recalled to the Test side in 2012-13, and was then a hit in the IPL – before a disastrous Indian Test tour when he was one of the players disciplined for failing to complete a "homework" task. He missed the 2013 Ashes, but looked lively in the one-day series that followed.

THE FACTS Johnson took 8 for 61 – the best bowling figures in Tests by any left-arm fast bowler – against South Africa at Perth in 2008-09 ... He was the world's leading Test wicket-taker in 2009, with 63 ... Johnson took 6 for 51 (and 10 for 106 in the match) for Queensland v Victoria in the Pura Cup final at Brisbane in March 2006 ... He reached his maiden Test (and first-class) century against South Africa at Cape Town in March 2009 with a six ...

THE FIGURES *to 17.09.13* ESPNcricinfo.com

Batting & Fielding	M	Inns	NO	Runs	HS	Avge	S/R	100	50	4s	6s	Ct	St
Tests	51	76	12	1406	123*	21.96	58.58	1	7	166	23	17	0
ODIs	129	74	26	788	73*	16.41	93.36	0	2	63	18	27	0
T20Is	30	17	7	109	28*	10.90	114.73	0	0	8	3	5	0
First-class	92	132	25	2416	123*	22.57	–	2	11	–	–	26	0

Bowling	M	Balls	Runs	Wkts	BB	Avge	RpO	S/R	5i	10m
Tests	51	11338	6341	205	8–61	30.93	3.35	55.30	7	2
ODIs	129	6280	5019	200	6–31	25.09	4.79	31.40	3	0
T20Is	30	656	797	38	3–15	20.97	7.28	17.26	0	0
First-class	92	18456	10455	342	8–61	30.57	3.39	53.96	12	3

JUNAID KHAN

Full name **Mohammad Junaid Khan**
Born **December 24, 1989, Matra, NW Frontier Province**
Teams **Abbottabad, WAPDA**
Style **Right-hand bat, left-arm fast-medium bowler**
Test debut **Pakistan v Zimbabwe at Bulawayo 2011**
ODI debut **Pakistan v West Indies at Gros Islet 2010-11**
T20I debut **Pakistan v West Indies at Gros Islet 2010-11**

THE PROFILE Junaid Khan had an unenviable task as the left-arm fast bowler called up in 2011 to replace the banned Mohammad Aamer. Junaid bowls at a good pace – the upper 80s mph according to the man himself – and moves the ball around when conditions are right. He was called up for Pakistan's 2011 World Cup squad as a late replacement, but didn't actually get a game. His debut had to wait until the West Indian tour that followed, and he made a slow start – only three wickets in six internationals, one of them a Twenty20 game. Junaid did grab six cheap scalps in two subsequent matches in Ireland, which was enough to keep him in the squad for the Zimbabwe tour that followed (in between he had a promising stint in limited-overs cricket for Lancashire). He made his Test debut at Bulawayo in September 2011, but although he kept things quiet in the first innings he took only one wicket. Things improved after that, though, with 5 for 38 against Sri Lanka in Abu Dhabi, and when Pakistan toured Sri Lanka in mid-2012 he added further five-fors in Colombo and Pallekele. The following year he looked more the part of pack leader, especially against Zimbabwe's undercooked batsmen in August and September. Junaid is from the Khyber-Pakhtunkhwa (formerly North West Frontier) province, and plays at home for Abbottabad, who are among the weaker sides on Pakistan's domestic circuit. But he still managed to catch the selectors' eye, taking 75 wickets at a fraction under 24 apiece in first-class cricket in 2009-10.

THE FACTS Junaid Khan took 7 for 46 (13 for 77 in the match) for Abbottabad at Peshawar in November 2007 ... He had figures of 4-0-4-5 as Khan Research Laboratories bowled Customs out for 79 – the last nine wickets went down for 13 – in a first-class match in February 2009 ... Junaid's first three Test five-fors all came against Sri Lanka ... He played for Lancashire in 2011 ...

THE FIGURES to 17.09.13

Batting & Fielding	M	Inns	NO	Runs	HS	Avge	S/R	100	50	4s	6s	Ct	St
Tests	11	14	4	65	17	6.50	36.31	0	0	10	0	1	0
ODIs	33	12	5	42	25	6.00	52.50	0	0	3	1	4	0
T20Is	5	2	2	3	3*	–	75.00	0	0	0	0	0	0
First-class	56	79	23	643	71	11.48	–	0	2	–	–	8	0

Bowling	M	Balls	Runs	Wkts	BB	Avge	RpO	S/R	5i	10m
Tests	11	2205	1012	38	5–38	26.63	2.75	58.02	3	0
ODIs	33	1524	1239	52	4–12	23.82	4.87	29.30	0	0
T20Is	5	90	136	3	2–23	45.33	9.06	30.00	0	0
First-class	56	11143	5573	255	7–46	21.85	3.00	43.69	18	3

JUNAID SIDDIQUE

Full name **Mohammad Junaid Siddique**
Born **October 30, 1987, Rajshahi**
Teams **Rajshahi**
Style **Left-hand bat, occasional offspinner**
Test debut **Bangladesh v New Zealand at Dunedin 2007-08**
ODI debut **Bangladesh v New Zealand at Auckland 2007-08**
T20I debut **Bangladesh v Pakistan at Cape Town 2007-08**

THE PROFILE Left-hander Junaid Siddique made a sensational start in Test cricket, when he and fellow debutant Tamim Iqbal flayed New Zealand's bowlers in an opening stand of 161 to light up the inaugural Test at Dunedin's University Oval at the start of 2008. *Wisden* said they began "with an entrancing display of classical strokes, their timing perfect as the ball was distributed around the short boundaries". Sadly, this fine start came to nothing: the other batsmen made only 83 between them, and Bangladesh lost yet again. "Imrose" also made a stylish 74 against South Africa at Mirpur – no-one else made more than 24 – and added 71 on his Twenty20 international debut. However, the faster bowlers noticed a compulsion to get onto the front foot – bred on slow, low pitches in Bangladesh – and Junaid began to cop a lot of short stuff. But he persevered, making 78 in victory over a depleted West Indian side in St Vincent in July 2009, while his ODI performances improved: after an anaemic start (62 runs in eight innings), he hit 85 against New Zealand in November 2008, then scored consistently against admittedly modest attacks in the West Indies and Zimbabwe. He made his first Test century against England at Chittagong in March 2010, before adding a maiden one-day international hundred against Ireland a few months later. Typically, though, Bangladesh lost both matches. After an up-and-down 2011, during which he struggled at the World Cup, Junaid was dropped for a while – but kept his name on the selectors' radar with a career-best 181 for Rajshahi against Barisal in November 2012, which led to a Test recall against West Indies.

THE FACTS Junaid Siddique scored 74 on his Test debut at Dunedin in January 2008, putting on 161 for the first wicket with Tamim Iqbal, who was also winning his first cap: it was the highest opening stand between debutants in Tests since Billy Ibadulla and Abdul Kadir put on 249 for Pakistan v Australia at Karachi in 1964-65 ... Junaid hit 71 off 49 balls in his first Twenty20 international, against Pakistan at Cape Town in September 2007 ...

THE FIGURES to 17.09.13   espncricinfo.com

Batting & Fielding	M	Inns	NO	Runs	HS	Avge	S/R	100	50	4s	6s	Ct	St
Tests	19	37	0	969	106	26.18	41.39	1	7	123	1	11	0
ODIs	54	53	1	1196	100	23.00	68.22	1	6	118	7	23	0
T20Is	7	7	0	159	71	22.71	147.22	0	1	16	7	1	0
First-class	61	109	1	3003	181	27.80	–	4	16	–	–	47	0

Bowling	M	Balls	Runs	Wkts	BB	Avge	RpO	S/R	5i	10m
Tests	19	18	11	0	–	–	3.66	–	0	0
ODIs	54	12	13	0	–	–	6.50	–	0	0
T20Is	7	0	–	–	–	–	–	–	–	–
First-class	61	209	130	1	1–30	127.00	3.73	209.00	0	0

JACQUES **KALLIS**

Full name	Jacques Henry Kallis
Born	October 16, 1975, Pinelands, Cape Town
Teams	Cape Cobras, Kolkata Knight Riders
Style	Right-hand bat, right-arm fast-medium bowler
Test debut	South Africa v England at Durban 1995-96
ODI debut	South Africa v England at Cape Town 1995-96
T20I debut	South Africa v New Zealand at Johannesburg 2005-06

SOUTH AFRICA

THE PROFILE In an era of fast scoring and high-octane entertainment, Jacques Kallis is a throwback – an astonishingly effective one – to a more sedate age, when your wicket was to be guarded with your life. He blossomed after a quiet start into arguably the world's leading batsman, with the adhesive qualities of a Cape Point limpet. In 2005, he was the ICC's first Test Player of the Year, but his batting is not for the romantic: a Kallis century (of which there have now been 61 in international cricket) tends to see ruthless efficiency taking precedence over derring-do, and he has never quite dispelled the notion that he is a selfish batsman, something the Aussies played on during the 2007 World Cup. His team-mates, though, agree that he bats the way he does precisely *because* he puts his team first and his personal ambitions some way behind. He had a purple patch at the turn of 2010-11, scoring five Test centuries – including a long-awaited maiden 200 – inside two months. In 2012 he made another double-century – 224 against Sri Lanka at Cape Town – and almost bagged another (182 not out) against England at The Oval in July. Kallis has sailed to the top of South Africa's batting charts, and is a fine bowler too, capable of swinging the ball sharply at a surprising pace. Strong, with powerful shoulders and a deep chest, Kallis has the capacity to play a wide array of attacking strokes, and has a good Twenty20 record, although he picks and chooses his one-day games these days. He has a Test batting average in the mid-fifties to go with nearly 600 international wickets all told. He's also a fine slip fielder.

THE FACTS Kallis and Shaun Pollock were the first South Africans to play 100 Tests, reaching the mark, appropriately enough, at Centurion in April 2006 ... Kallis averages 169.75 in Tests against Zimbabwe, and scored 388 runs against them in two Tests in 2001-02 without being dismissed ... Including his next innings he batted for a record 1241 minutes in Tests without getting out ... Kallis's record includes one Test and three ODIs for the World XI, and two ODIs for the Africa XI ...

THE FIGURES to 17.09.13   **ESPNcricinfo.com**

Batting & Fielding	M	Inns	NO	Runs	HS	Avge	S/R	100	50	4s	6s	Ct	St
Tests	162	274	40	13128	224	56.10	46.08	44	58	1469	97	194	0
ODIs	321	307	53	11498	139	45.26	72.97	17	85	903	136	125	0
T20Is	25	23	4	666	73	35.05	119.35	0	5	56	20	7	0
First-class	253	415	57	19534	224	54.56	–	61	97	–	–	258	0

Bowling	M	Balls	Runs	Wkts	BB	Avge	RpO	S/R	5i	10m
Tests	162	19842	9341	288	6-54	32.43	2.82	68.89	5	0
ODIs	321	10636	8558	270	5-30	31.69	4.82	39.39	2	0
T20Is	25	276	333	12	4-15	27.75	7.23	23.00	0	0
First-class	253	28643	13338	423	6-54	31.53	2.79	67.71	8	0

KAMRAN AKMAL

Full name	**Kamran Akmal**
Born	**January 13, 1982, Lahore, Punjab**
Teams	**Lahore, National Bank**
Style	**Right-hand bat, wicketkeeper**
Test debut	**Pakistan v Zimbabwe at Harare 2002-03**
ODI debut	**Pakistan v Zimbabwe at Bulawayo 2002-03**
T20I debut	**Pakistan v England at Bristol 2006**

THE PROFILE Kamran Akmal made his first-class debut at 15 as a useful wicketkeeper and a hard-hitting batsman. He has had good times since – and bad ones, as his keeping fell away, leading to several costly errors, none more so than in an iron-gloved performance that cost Pakistan victory at Sydney in January 2010: Akmal dropped four catches, most of them sitters, failed with the bat too, and later had to fend off accusations of match-fixing. After that he was briefly dropped, and replaced again after the 2011 World Cup by his brother Adnan (another brother, Umar, has also kept wicket for Pakistan). But Kamran is a survivor, and returned after 18 months for the limited-overs matches against Australia in the UAE late in 2012. Since then he has been inked in as the limited overs keeper, with Adnan doing the job in Tests. Kamran plugged on throughout 2013, and although runs were scarce he did make an important 81 in Dublin in May to stave off embarrassment by Ireland. It all started so promisingly: by October 2004 Kamran was Pakistan's first-choice keeper, and the following year hit five international centuries. Three of them came while opening in one-dayers, and two in Tests, one to save the match against India at Mohali, and a blistering 154 in the emphatic series-sealing win over England at Lahore. However, a nightmare series in England in 2006 set him back again. Since then he has rarely regained his best touch with bat or gloves: he did make an important 119 against India in the Kolkata Test in November 2007, and started 2009 with an unbeaten 158 in a Test against Sri Lanka and a century against Australia. He also played his part in winning the World Twenty20 in England in June 2010.

THE FACTS Kamran Akmal scored five international hundreds in December 2005 and January 2006, including 154 in the Lahore Test against England, when he shared a sixth-wicket stand of 269 with Mohammad Yousuf ... Akmal has scored more Test hundreds than any other Pakistan wicketkeeper: Moin Khan made four and Imtiaz Ahmed three ... His brothers Umar and Adnan Akmal have both also played – and kept wicket – for Pakistan ...

THE FIGURES to 17.09.13   **ESPNcricinfo.com**

Batting & Fielding	M	Inns	NO	Runs	HS	Avge	S/R	100	50	4s	6s	Ct	St
Tests	53	92	6	2648	158*	30.79	63.10	6	12	372	14	184	22
ODIs	154	135	14	3168	124	26.18	83.83	5	10	371	34	156	31
T20Is	50	45	6	849	73	21.76	123.22	0	5	82	27	24	30
First-class	183	286	29	8591	268	33.42	–	17	42	–	–	622	52

Bowling	M	Balls	Runs	Wkts	BB	Avge	RpO	S/R	5i	10m
Tests	53	0	–	–	–	–	–	–	–	–
ODIs	154	0	–	–	–	–	–	–	–	–
T20Is	50	0	–	–	–	–	–	–	–	–
First-class	183	0	–	–	–	–	–	–	–	–

DINESH **KARTHIK**

Full name	**Krishnakumar Dinesh Karthik**
Born	**June 1, 1985, Madras (now Chennai)**
Teams	**Tamil Nadu, Mumbai Indians**
Style	**Right-hand bat, wicketkeeper**
Test debut	**India v Australia at Mumbai 2004-05**
ODI debut	**India v England at Lord's 2004**
T20I debut	**India v South Africa at Johannesburg 2006-07**

THE PROFILE For a while it seemed as if Dinesh Karthik owed his place in the Indian squad to the back trouble which sometimes afflicts MS Dhoni, meaning a spare wicketkeeper was a necessity. Karthik originally had a run in the side after making his debut in September 2004, when he pulled off a superb stumping to dispose of Michael Vaughan on debut at Lord's. Shortly after that he won his first Test cap but, after just one fifty in ten matches, was replaced by Dhoni, whose instant success meant Karthik had to rethink. He reinvented himself as a specialist batsman, with some success. After India's forgettable 2007 World Cup, he made a maiden Test century in Bangladesh, and forged a successful opening partnership with Wasim Jaffer which continued in England, where Karthik was India's leading scorer in the Tests. In 2008-09 he passed 1000 runs in the domestic first-class season, hitting five centuries (one of them a double), and also did well in the IPL. But leaner times followed at international level – he was left out, seemingly for good, after six single-figure scores in ten innings: Parthiv Patel had a spell as the spare keeper, and Karthik was marooned on 1000 Test runs from exactly 2000 deliveries. He was ignored for almost three years, but some eye-catching performances as Mumbai Indians won the IPL in 2013 – particularly 86 from 48 balls against Delhi Daredevils, after Ricky Ponting and Sachin Tendulkar had departed for one run between them – earned him a recall for the Champions Trophy in England in June, which India won, and Karthik did enough to retain his place for the successful visits to Zimbabwe and the West Indies that followed.

THE FACTS Karthik hit 213 for Tamil Nadu v Uttar Pradesh at Ghaziabad in November 2008 ... He made 153 and 103 for South Zone v Central Zone in the Duleep Trophy at Bangalore in January 2009 ... Karthik averages 49.33 in Tests against South Africa, but only 1.00 in two Tests against Zimbabwe ... For a while he asked that his surname should be spelt with two As ("Kaarthik") as it was more astrologically propitious ...

THE FIGURES to 17.09.13   **espncricinfo.com**

Batting & Fielding	M	Inns	NO	Runs	HS	Avge	S/R	100	50	4s	6s	Ct	St
Tests	23	37	1	1000	129	27.77	50.00	1	7	132	4	51	5
ODIs	67	56	11	1263	79	28.06	73.64	0	7	133	12	46	6
T20Is	9	8	2	100	31*	16.66	113.63	0	0	14	1	5	2
First-class	108	164	11	6227	213	40.69	58.65	18	28	–	–	270	26

Bowling	M	Balls	Runs	Wkts	BB	Avge	RpO	S/R	5i	10m
Tests	23	0	–	–	–	–	–	–	–	–
ODIs	67	0	–	–	–	–	–	–	–	–
T20Is	9	0	–	–	–	–	–	–	–	–
First-class	108	114	125	0	–	–	6.57	–	0	0

DIMUTH **KARUNARATNE**

Full name	Frank Dimuth Madushankar Karunaratne
Born	April 21, 1988, Colombo
Teams	Sinhalese Sports Club, Basnahira
Style	Left-hand bat, occ. right-arm medium pace bowler
Test debut	Sri Lanka v New Zealand at Galle 2012-13
ODI debut	Sri Lanka v England at Manchester 2011
T20I debut	No T20Is yet

THE PROFILE Dimuth Karunaratne is a solid opening batsman, who was at St Joseph's College with Angelo Mathews and Thisara Perera. He's quite tall, at 6ft, plays well off his legs, and is not afraid to loft the ball on the leg side. He made his first-class debut for Sinhalese Sports Club in 2008-09, starting brightly with 63 and 55 in his first two matches. He tailed off a little after that, and averaged less than 20. It was a different story next season, though, as he amassed 1186 runs at 56. That included his maiden century, 147 against Colts, and 185 in the inter-provincial tournament, when he and Kaushal Silva added 306. In August 2010 he made a superb 184 against South Africa A at the SSC, when he and Dinesh Chandimal (244) put on 369 against an attack that included Vernon Philander. A leanish spell followed, but Karunaratne got a one-day chance in Britain in 2011, making 60 against Scotland. He then toured South Africa without making the Test side, but he was back there the following July, captaining the A team, and hit 83 and 150 not out in the second representative game at Durban. This put him in line for a Test debut, which came when Tillekeratne Dilshan was injured shortly before the series against New Zealand in November 2012: Karunaratne filled the problem opening position at Galle, and made 60 not out after a third-ball duck in the first innings. That got him on the plane to Australia, where he did reasonably well in a dispiriting tour, making a sprightly 85 at Sydney. Later in 2013 he added twin centuries against West Indies A in St Kitts.

THE FACTS Karunaratne scored 210* for Sinhalese Sports Club v Ragama in Colombo in February 2012 ... He scored 184 for Sri Lanka A v South Africa A in Colombo in August 2010, and 150* against them at Durban in July 2012 ... Karunaratne made 100 and 100* for Sri Lanka A v West Indies A at Basseterre in June 2013 ...

THE FIGURES to 17.09.13

Batting & Fielding	M	Inns	NO	Runs	HS	Avge	S/R	100	50	4s	6s	Ct	St
Tests	6	12	1	277	85	25.18	61.01	0	2	31	2	5	0
ODIs	2	2	0	64	60	32.00	71.91	0	1	4	0	0	0
T20Is	0	0	–	–	–	–	–	–	–	–	–	–	–
First-class	63	99	8	4212	210*	46.28	63.60	14	19	508	17	73	1

Bowling	M	Balls	Runs	Wkts	BB	Avge	RpO	S/R	5i	10m
Tests	6	0	–	–	–	–	–	–	–	–
ODIs	2	0	–	–	–	–	–	–	–	–
T20Is	0	0	–	–	–	–	–	–	–	–
First-class	63	79	58	0	–	–	4.40	–	0	0

ZAHEER **KHAN**

Full name **Zaheer Khan**
Born **October 7, 1978, Shrirampur, Maharashtra**
Teams **Mumbai, Royal Challengers Bangalore**
Style **Right-hand bat, left-arm fast-medium bowler**
Test debut **India v Bangladesh at Dhaka 2000-01**
ODI debut **India v Kenya at Nairobi 2000-01**
T20I debut **India v South Africa at Johannesburg 2006-07**

THE PROFILE Like Waqar Younis before him, Zaheer Khan yorked his way into the cricket world's consciousness: his performances at the Champions Trophy in September 2000 announced the arrival of an all-too-rare star in the Indian fast-bowling firmament. Zaheer can move the ball both ways off the pitch and swing the old ball at a decent pace. After initial struggles, he came of age in the West Indies in 2002, when he led the attack with great heart. His subsequent displays in England and New Zealand – and some eye-catching moments at the 2003 World Cup – established him at the forefront of the new pace generation, but a hamstring injury relegated him to bit-part performer as India enjoyed some of their finest moments away in Australia and Pakistan. In a bid to jump the queue of left-arm hopefuls, Zaheer put in the hard yards for Worcestershire in 2006. It worked: Zaheer reclaimed his Test place, survived the fallout from the World Cup, and led the way in England in 2007, where his nine wickets at Trent Bridge clinched the match and the series: he was one of *Wisden*'s Cricketers of the Year. After an ankle injury he led the attack in the 2011 World Cup success – but his early exit from the England tour that followed, after a hamstring problem in the first Test, visibly deflated India, who subsided to a 4-0 whitewash. He returned for the Australian tour that followed, and made it to the World Twenty20 in Sri Lanka in September 2012 – but then a calf injury disrupted 2013, and threatened his future just as he was poised to reach 300 wickets in both Tests and ODIs.

THE FACTS Zaheer Khan's 75 against Bangladesh at Dhaka in December 2004 was the highest Test score by a No. 11 at the time: he dominated a last-wicket stand of 133 with Sachin Tendulkar ... He took 9 for 138 (including a spell of 9 for 28) for Worcestershire v Essex at Chelmsford in June 2006, but a last-wicket stand of 97 cost him the chance of taking all ten wickets ... Zaheer averages 17.46 with the ball in ODIs against Zimbabwe, but 46.39 v Australia, and 40.85 v Pakistan ... His record includes six ODIs for the Asia XI ...

THE FIGURES to 17.09.13   espncricinfo.com

Batting & Fielding	M	Inns	NO	Runs	HS	Avge	S/R	100	50	4s	6s	Ct	St
Tests	88	120	23	1146	75	11.81	51.18	0	3	130	25	19	0
ODIs	200	101	35	792	34*	12.20	73.46	0	0	69	24	43	0
T20Is	17	4	2	13	9	6.50	130.00	0	0	0	1	2	0
First-class	158	207	39	2250	75	13.39	–	0	4	–	–	45	0

Bowling	M	Balls	Runs	Wkts	BB	Avge	RpO	S/R	5i	10m
Tests	88	17612	9545	295	7–87	32.35	3.25	59.70	10	1
ODIs	200	10097	8301	282	5–42	29.43	4.93	35.80	1	0
T20Is	17	352	448	17	4–19	26.35	7.63	20.70	0	0
First-class	158	31939	17505	630	9–138	27.78	3.28	50.69	33	8

USMAN **KHAWAJA**

Full name **Usman Tariq Khawaja**
Born **December 18, 1986, Islamabad, Pakistan**
Teams **New South Wales, Derbyshire**
Style **Left-hand bat, occ. right-arm medium-pacer**
Test debut **Australia v England at Sydney 2010-11**
ODI debut **Australia v Sri Lanka at Melbourne 2012-13**
T20I debut **No T20Is yet**

THE PROFILE Born in Pakistan, Usman Khawaja was taken to Australia when young, and achieved his dream of becoming the first Muslim to play for them in the final Test of the 2010-11 Ashes. Khawaja replaced the injured Ricky Ponting, and marked his arrival in style, pulling his second ball to the midwicket boundary, almost emulating the watching David Gower, another languid left-hander, who did the same first ball back in 1978. Khawaja made only 37 and 21, but his poise and temperament seemed to mark him out as a future star. However, he failed to nail a big score, and was left out later in 2011. He didn't return until the start of 2013: again the returns were modest, with 54 in the Ashes Test at Lord's his only international score above 24 in nine attempts, and he was dropped before the end of the series in England. Before that there were whispers about his attitude, notably as one of four players disciplined for failing to complete a task set by the team management in India. Khawaja originally came to the fore with 554 runs for NSW in 2008-09, then 698 – with three Sheffield Shield centuries – the following season. That earned him a trip to England for the "neutral" Tests against his native Pakistan, although there was no great conflict of loyalty: "I will never forget where I come from, and no-one should," he said, "but Australia has been my home every since I can remember." Khawaja didn't feature there, but laid the groundwork for his Ashes call-up with 214 in a Shield match at Adelaide in October 2010. While cricket is his first love, Khawaja is also a qualified pilot.

THE FACTS Khawaja scored 214 for New South Wales against South Australia at Adelaide in October 2010 ... He made 210* and 228 in successive matches for NSW's 2nd XI in October 2008 ... Khawaja was the first Muslim (and the first man born in Pakistan) to play Test cricket for Australia ... He played for Derbyshire in 2012 ...

THE FIGURES to 17.09.13

Batting & Fielding	M	Inns	NO	Runs	HS	Avge	S/R	100	50	4s	6s	Ct	St
Tests	9	17	2	377	65	25.13	40.14	0	2	37	3	5	0
ODIs	3	3	1	14	8*	7.00	35.00	0	0	1	0	0	0
T20Is	0	0	–	–	–	–	–	–	–	–	–	–	–
First-class	69	120	11	4425	214	40.59	50.60	11	23	568	27	46	0

Bowling	M	Balls	Runs	Wkts	BB	Avge	RpO	S/R	5i	10m
Tests	9	0	–	–	–	–	–	–	–	–
ODIs	3	0	–	–	–	–	–	–	–	–
T20Is	0	0	–	–	–	–	–	–	–	–
First-class	69	102	69	1	1–21	69.00	4.05	102.00	0	0

KHURRAM MANZOOR

Full name **Khurram Manzoor**
Born **June 10, 1986, Karachi, Sind**
Teams **Karachi Blues, Port Qasim Authority**
Style **Right-hand bat, occasional offspinner**
Test debut **Pakistan v Sri Lanka at Karachi 2008-09**
ODI debut **Pakistan v Zimbabwe at Sheikhupura 2007-08**
T20I debut **No T20Is yet**

THE PROFILE Khurram Manzoor is a solid but aggressive opener with a distinctive stance not unlike the former Pakistan batsman Ijaz Ahmed – backside jutting out and legs planted wide apart. It served him well on his first-class debut, at the tender age of 16, when he made 73 for Karachi Blues – but he did little for a couple of seasons before hitting two centuries, and nearly 500 runs, in 2004-05. Three years later he made 1283 first-class runs with four centuries (one of them a double), and made his one-day international debut early in 2008, marking it with an impressive half-century: he added another in his next match, against West Indies in Abu Dhabi the following November. Pakistan's seemingly perennial struggle to find a settled Test opening pair led to Manzoor being given a run in 2009, and he responded with 59 at Lahore in his second Test (he was one of the not-out batsmen when the match was abandoned after the terrorist attack on the Sri Lankans), and adding a confident 93 in Colombo later in the year. In that innings Manzoor played well off the back foot, and showed good judgment of which deliveries to play, until nerves got the better of him in the nineties. Not long afterwards he buckled down for a five-hour 77 in a Test against Australia at Hobart – and was promptly dropped for more than three years. After captaining Karachi Blues to the Quaid-e-Azam Trophy in 2012-13, in a season that brought him 1065 runs, Manzoor was finally recalled for the Zimbabwe tour late in 2013. In the second Test at Harare he played two attractive innings of 51 and 54 – but couldn't prevent an embarrassing defeat.

THE FACTS Khurram Manzoor made 241 for PIA v Khan Research Laboratories at Karachi in October 2009 ... He scored 201* (in 708 minutes) for Sind v Punjab at Lahore in November 2008, and 200 for Karachi Urban v Mumbai in the Mohammad Nissar Trophy match in September 2007 ... Manzoor made 50 (v Zimbabwe) and 63 (v West Indies) in his first two ODIs in 2007-08 ...

THE FIGURES to 17.09.13   espncricinfo.com

Batting & Fielding	M	Inns	NO	Runs	HS	Avge	S/R	100	50	4s	6s	Ct	St
Tests	9	16	1	447	93	29.80	41.69	0	5	60	0	4	0
ODIs	7	7	0	236	83	33.71	62.93	0	3	21	0	3	0
T20Is	0	0	–	–	–	–	–	–	–	–	–	–	–
First-class	107	185	14	6801	241	39.77	–	20	28	–	–	83	0

Bowling	M	Balls	Runs	Wkts	BB	Avge	RpO	S/R	5i	10m
Tests	9	0	–	–	–	–	–	–	–	–
ODIs	7	0	–	–	–	–	–	–	–	–
T20Is	0	0	–	–	–	–	–	–	–	–
First-class	107	468	206	3	1-14	68.66	2.64	156.00	0	0

RORY **KLEINVELDT**

Full name	**Rory Keith Kleinveldt**
Born	**March 15, 1983, Cape Town**
Teams	**Cape Cobras**
Style	**Right-hand bat, right-arm fast-medium bowler**
Test debut	**South Africa v Australia at Brisbane 2012-13**
ODI debut	**South Africa v New Zealand at Paarl 2012-13**
T20I debut	**South Africa v Bangladesh at Johannesburg 2008-09**

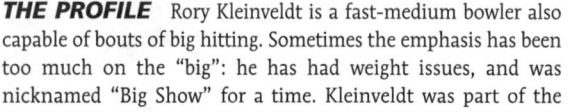

THE PROFILE Rory Kleinveldt is a fast-medium bowler also capable of bouts of big hitting. Sometimes the emphasis has been too much on the "big": he has had weight issues, and was nicknamed "Big Show" for a time. Kleinveldt was part of the South African team which reached the Under-19 World Cup final in 2002, and made his first-class bow for Western Province shortly afterwards. He was consigned to the B team for a while, before some consistent performances – including a spell he counts among his best, 6 for 22 against Border at Newlands – resulted in a regular first-team spot. He was consistent without being devastating over the next few seasons for Cape Cobras, and was occasionally mentioned in despatches: he took part in the Hong Kong Sixes a couple of times, and made the odd appearance for South Africa A before, in November 2008, a disastrous Twenty20 international debut against Bangladesh at the Wanderers, when his only over disappeared for 20. In his next international, in the World Twenty20 in the West Indies 18 months later, India carted his four overs for 48. That might have been that, but the success of Vernon Philander – a similar type of bowler – meant the selectors remained interested, and after Kleinveldt took 32 wickets at a shade under 18 apiece in 2011-12 he made his Test debut at Brisbane in November 2012. Again, it was a chastening experience – no wicket for 97 – but he bounced back with four wickets in the next match, at Adelaide, and four more against New Zealand at Port Elizabeth early in 2013. Kleinveldt is a handy fast-bowling reserve – but Kyle Abbott's remarkable debut may have pushed him even further down the queue.

THE FACTS Kleinveldt took 8 for 47 (10 for 80 in the match) for Cape Cobras v Warriors at Stellenbosch in March 2006 ... He took 7 for 43 from 25 overs for Cape Cobras v Eagles at Cape Town in February 2009 ... Kleinveldt scored 115* for Western Province against KwaZulu-Natal at Chatsworth in October 2005 ...

THE FIGURES to 17.09.13   ESPNcricinfo.com

Batting & Fielding	M	Inns	NO	Runs	HS	Avge	S/R	100	50	4s	6s	Ct	St
Tests	4	5	2	27	17*	9.00	44.26	0	0	1	2	2	0
ODIs	10	7	0	105	43	15.00	84.67	0	0	9	5	4	0
T20Is	6	3	2	25	22	25.00	250.00	0	0	1	3	1	0
First-class	83	112	14	1816	115*	18.53	65.84	1	8	-	-	35	0

Bowling	M	Balls	Runs	Wkts	BB	Avge	RpO	S/R	5i	10m
Tests	4	667	422	10	3–65	42.20	3.79	66.70	0	0
ODIs	10	513	448	12	4–22	37.33	5.23	42.75	0	0
T20Is	6	122	173	9	3–18	19.22	8.50	13.55	0	0
First-class	83	13916	6673	232	8–47	28.76	2.87	59.98	9	1

VIRAT **KOHLI**

Full name **Virat Kohli**
Born **November 5, 1988, Delhi**
Teams **Delhi, Royal Challengers Bangalore**
Style **Right-hand bat, occasional medium-pacer**
Test debut **India v West Indies at Kingston 2011**
ODI debut **India v Sri Lanka at Dambulla 2008**
T20I debut **India v Zimbabwe at Harare 2010**

THE PROFILE An attacking player with a cool head and the hint of a swagger, Virat Kohli has been making big scores from a young age. By the time he captained India to victory in the Under-19 World Cup in 2008, he had already made his Ranji Trophy debut, making 90 (after Delhi had been 14 for 4) against Karnataka in his fourth match. The upward curve continued with a maiden century against Rajasthan, and a superb 169 against Karnataka. He was called up for India's one-day series in Sri Lanka in August 2008. He wasn't expected to play, but injuries gave him a chance: he reached double figures in all five innings, with 54 in the fourth game. Another good domestic season followed – 613 runs at 55, with a career-best 197 against Pakistan's national champions – then he improved his IPL form after a disappointing first campaign. Kohli enjoyed a dream run in ODIs in 2009-10: successive innings against Sri Lanka and Bangladesh produced 54, 107, 9, 91, 71 not out and 102 not out. He couldn't quite keep that up, but he kicked off the 2011 World Cup with a hundred against Bangladesh, and later made 35 as the final was won. After a slow start in Tests Kohli blossomed in 2012, making hundreds against Australia and New Zealand – but it was in the 50-overs game that he really caught the eye, turning into a prolific scorer, and an accomplished "finisher". One purple patch included five centuries in eight innings, including a rollicking 183 against Pakistan in the Asia Cup in Dhaka. The following year, with Sachin Tendulkar's star on the wane, Kohli became the poster boy of Indian cricket, adding Test tons against England and Australia before, late in 2013, skippering India to a one-day whitewash in Zimbabwe.

THE FACTS Kohli scored 197 for Delhi against Pakistan's champions Sui Northern Gas in the Mohammad Nissar Trophy match at Delhi in September 2008 ... He made 183 against Pakistan at Dhaka in the Asia Cup in March 2012, during a run of four centuries in five ODI innings (and 66 in the other one) ... Kohli took a wicket with his first delivery in Twenty20 internationals (Kevin Pietersen stumped off a wide) at Old Trafford in August 2011 ...

THE FIGURES to 17.09.13   espncricinfo.com

Batting & Fielding	M	Inns	NO	Runs	HS	Avge	S/R	100	50	4s	6s	Ct	St
Tests	18	31	3	1175	116	41.96	46.94	4	6	139	6	23	0
ODIs	113	108	16	4575	183	49.72	86.64	15	24	436	30	55	0
T20Is	20	18	2	558	78*	34.87	130.37	0	4	70	8	8	0
First-class	49	77	10	3363	197	50.19	53.63	11	14	446	19	51	0

Bowling	M	Balls	Runs	Wkts	BB	Avge	RpO	S/R	5i	10m
Tests	18	66	35	0	–	–	3.18	–	0	0
ODIs	113	387	376	2	1-20	188.00	5.82	193.50	0	0
T20Is	20	124	159	3	1-13	53.00	7.69	41.33	0	0
First-class	49	534	289	3	1-19	96.33	3.24	178.00	0	0

NUWAN **KULASEKARA**

Full name	Kulasekara Mudiyanselage Dinesh Nuwan Kulasekara
Born	July 22, 1982, Nittambuwa
Teams	Colts, Kandurata
Style	Right-hand bat, right-arm fast-medium bowler
Test debut	Sri Lanka v New Zealand at Napier 2004-05
ODI debut	Sri Lanka v England at Dambulla 2003-04
T20I debut	Sri Lanka v Pakistan at King City 2008-09

THE PROFILE Nuwan Kulasekara has a bustling run-up and a whippy open-chested action, and moves the ball off the seam at around 80mph. He maintains a tight line and length, and, after adding a yard or two of pace, suddenly emerged as a formidable bowler, especially in one-day internationals. He did so well in 2008 (33 wickets at 20.87) that by March 2009 he was proudly sitting on top of the ICC's world one-day rankings for bowlers. He maintained that form in 2009, and also began to look the part in Tests, too: he grabbed four wickets in each innings as Pakistan lost in Colombo in August, and ending that series with 17 victims. After that, though, the old worries about his supposed lack of pace returned, and he has been in and out of the side ever since, although he did play six matches in the 2011 World Cup, including the final. After that, nine ODIs against England and Australia produced only three wickets, but he was back in favour by 2012 – and in June took five wickets against Pakistan in his first Test for 19 months. A maiden one-day five-for followed in Australia early in 2013, although he went wicketless in his only Test there. Kulasekara's initial mark on Test cricket was with the bat: at Lord's in May 2006 he hung on for more than three hours for 64, helping Chaminda Vaas ensure that Sri Lanka drew after following on 359 behind. Kulasekara also made an instant impression in his first one-dayer, taking 2 for 19 in nine overs as England subsided for 88 at Dambulla in November 2003. That came soon after a fine first season, in which he took 61 wickets at 21.06 for Colts. He started as a softball enthusiast before turning to cricket, first with Negegoda CC and then with Galle.

THE FACTS Playing for North Central Province at Dambulla in March 2005, Kulasekara dismissed all of Central Province's top six, finishing with 6 for 71 ... He took 7 for 27 for Colts v Bloomfield in January 2008 ... In March 2009 Kulasekara was top of the ICC world rankings for ODI bowlers ... He took 5 for 22 in an ODI against Australia at Brisbane in January 2013 ... Kulasekara made 95 for Galle v Nondescripts in Colombo in October 2003 ...

THE FIGURES to 17.09.13   ESPNcricinfo.com

Batting & Fielding	M	Inns	NO	Runs	HS	Avge	S/R	100	50	4s	6s	Ct	St
Tests	20	26	1	381	64	15.24	42.52	0	1	45	8	8	0
ODIs	140	89	29	1004	73	16.73	81.69	0	3	71	26	33	0
T20Is	29	15	4	99	26	9.00	112.50	0	0	5	4	8	0
First-class	83	109	21	1571	95	17.85	–	0	4	–	–	32	0

Bowling	M	Balls	Runs	Wkts	BB	Avge	RpO	S/R	5i	10m
Tests	20	3345	1646	46	4–21	35.78	2.95	72.71	0	0
ODIs	140	6545	5061	154	5–22	32.86	4.63	42.50	1	0
T20Is	29	611	735	30	3–4	24.50	7.21	20.36	0	0
First-class	83	12011	6321	264	7–27	23.94	3.15	45.49	9	1

BHUVNESHWAR **KUMAR**

Full name **Bhuvneshwar Kumar Singh**
Born **February 5, 1990, Meerut, Uttar Pradesh**
Teams **Uttar Pradesh, Pune Warriors**
Style **Right-hand bat, right-arm fast-medium bowler**
Test debut **India v Australia at Chennai 2012-13**
ODI debut **India v Pakistan at Chennai 2012-13**
T20I debut **India v Pakistan at Bangalore 2012-13**

THE PROFILE Bhuvneshwar Kumar hails from Meerut, like his near-namesake Praveen Kumar, another wily swing bowler who preceded him into the Indian side. Meerut is mainly known for the production of sporting goods – including the Indian ball of choice, the SG. Perhaps it's therefore not too surprising that Bhuvneshwar can hoop the SG ball around. He's not the fastest, rarely nudging the speedo above the low 80s mph, but his ability to swing it – and make the occasional one hold its line – makes him a genuine threat. He's also a handy batsman, with a first-class century under his belt. Bhuvneshwar made a remarkable start in international cricket. His Twenty20 debut came on Christmas Day 2012, and he gave himself a present by bowling Pakistan's Nasir Jamshed with his sixth delivery. Five days later he marked his ODI debut by bowling Mohammad Hafeez with the first ball of the match. Bhuvneshwar couldn't quite complete the hat-trick during his Test debut soon afterwards – he went wicketless in the first innings at Chennai – but he played his part as India whitewashed Australia 4-0, twice knocking over the openers cheaply during the second and third Tests. After that he bustled in during the successful Champions Trophy campaign in England, failing to strike only in the rain-shortened final, and shortly afterwards singlehandedly reduced Sri Lanka to 31 for 4 in a one-dayer in the Caribbean. Bhuvneshwar first hit the headlines early in 2009, when he was still only 18, by dismissing Sachin Tendulkar in the Ranji Trophy final for his first duck in a domestic first-class match in India.

THE FACTS Bhuvneshwar Kumar took a wicket with his sixth ball in international cricket, bowling Pakistan's Nasir Jamshed in a T20I at Bangalore in December 2012 … Five days later, at Chennai, he added a wicket with his first ball in ODIs, bowling Mohammad Hafeez … Kumar took 6 for 77 for Uttar Pradesh v Haryana at Mohan Nagar in December 2010 … He made 128 for Central Zone v South Zone in the Duleep Trophy semi-final at Hyderabad in October 2012 …

THE FIGURES to 17.09.13   espncricinfo.com

Batting & Fielding	M	Inns	NO	Runs	HS	Avge	S/R	100	50	4s	6s	Ct	St
Tests	4	4	1	80	38	26.66	41.02	0	0	10	0	2	0
ODIs	17	8	4	65	31	16.25	82.27	0	0	8	1	6	0
T20Is	2	1	1	6	6*	–	100.00	0	0	0	0	1	0
First-class	50	72	8	1928	128	30.12	42.27	1	11	245	7	11	0

Bowling	M	Balls	Runs	Wkts	BB	Avge	RpO	S/R	5i	10m
Tests	4	384	239	6	3–31	39.83	3.73	64.00	0	0
ODIs	17	828	549	25	4–8	21.96	3.97	33.12	0	0
T20Is	2	48	55	4	3–9	13.75	6.87	12.00	0	0
First-class	50	8817	4116	155	6–77	26.55	2.80	56.88	8	0

SURANGA LAKMAL

Full name **Ranasinghe Arachchige Suranga Lakmal**
Born **March 10, 1987, Matara**
Teams **Tamil Union, Basnahira**
Style **Right-hand bat, right-arm fast-medium bowler**
Test debut **Sri Lanka v West Indies at Colombo 2010-11**
ODI debut **Sri Lanka v India at Nagpur 2009-10**
T20I debut **Sri Lanka v England at Bristol 2011**

THE PROFILE A fast-medium bowler who generates fair pace from a slingy action, Suranga Lakmal was spotted by the Sri Lankan board's fast-bowling coaches while still a schoolboy. They liked his height, and consequent ability to get bounce and swing. But early on he lacked the stamina to bowl long spells, and when he did manage one he often fell ill. This stemmed from a lack of nutrition, apparently quite a common problem in fast bowlers from outside Colombo (Lakmal hails from the southern city of Matara, Sanath Jayasuriya's home town), and as soon as he joined the academy the coaches started work on his stamina. It paid off: after some good A-team showings he broke into the senior one-day side towards the end of 2009. He got a bit of tap in his first match, before removing Virender Sehwag and Sachin Tendulkar early in his second. Lakmal's first Tests came late the following year, in the soggy home series against West Indies. He dismissed Chris Gayle with the first ball of the third Test, and impressed his coach, Trevor Bayliss: "He is the least experienced in the team but he's been one of our better bowlers." Lakmal toiled away equally enthusiastically in England in 2011, taking three wickets in the first innings at Lord's, although he leaked runs at more than five an over. Soon after that his four scalps in the first Test against Australia at Galle included Ricky Ponting. Injuries – including an ankle problem that needed an operation – affected him for a while, but he bounced in at Sydney in January 2013 after being summoned as a replacement, and continued on the fringes of the team throughout the year.

THE FACTS Lakmal took 6 for 68 for Tamil Union v Nondescripts in Colombo in March 2013 ... The previous month he took 5 for 63 against Colombo CC and 5 for 21 v Galle ... Lakmal took a wicket (England's Michael Lumb) with his third ball in Twenty20 internationals, at Bristol in June 2011 ... He scored 58* for Tamil Union v Navy at Welisara in March 2013 ...

THE FIGURES to 17.09.13   ESPNcricinfo.com

Batting & Fielding	M	Inns	NO	Runs	HS	Avge	S/R	100	50	4s	6s	Ct	St
Tests	14	19	7	77	18	6.41	36.32	0	0	13	0	3	0
ODIs	17	9	5	2	1*	0.50	8.00	0	0	0	0	5	0
T20Is	3	0	–	–	–	–	–	–	–	–	–	0	0
First-class	62	66	15	502	58*	9.84	54.98	0	1	56	10	21	0

Bowling	M	Balls	Runs	Wkts	BB	Avge	RpO	S/R	5i	10m
Tests	14	2165	1315	20	3–55	65.75	3.64	108.25	0	0
ODIs	17	731	725	21	3–22	34.52	5.95	34.80	0	0
T20Is	3	66	78	4	2–26	19.50	7.09	16.50	0	0
First-class	62	8222	5270	153	6–68	34.44	3.84	53.73	4	0

NATHAN **LYON**

Full name	**Nathan Michael Lyon**
Born	**November 20, 1987, Young, New South Wales**
Teams	**South Australia**
Style	**Right-hand bat, offspinner**
Test debut	**Australia v Sri Lanka at Galle 2011**
ODI debut	**Australia v Sri Lanka at Adelaide 2011-12**
T20I debut	**No T20Is yet**

THE PROFILE As rags-to-riches stories go, it's right up there: Nathan Lyon is a groundsman at Adelaide Oval, bowls a bit in the nets when he can, gets noticed by the coach, plays for the state and does reasonably well, then, in a time of an Australia-wide drought of quality spin, is called up for the tour of Sri Lanka in 2011. If that doesn't sound implausible enough, Lyon then goes even further – a first-ball wicket, and figures of 5 for 34. The dream debut of the lanky Lyon started when he replaced his fellow newcomer, Trent Copeland, who had earlier taken a wicket with his second ball. Lyon went one better, sending down a venomous offbreak which Kumar Sangakkara – a veteran of almost 100 Tests and more than 8000 runs – could only edge low to slip. Unlike some, Lyon built on that early success, polishing off the tail to finish with five wickets. Things got harder after that, but Lyon was level-headed enough to know that he was, as Australia's wicketkeeper Brad Haddin put it, still "work in progress" as a bowler, although his repertoire has been increased, with a sneaky legbreak from time to time. That first Test was, after all, just the sixth match of a first-class career which had begun only seven months earlier. Lyon did well in the Caribbean early in 2012, following an important 40 not out from No. 11 in victory at Bridgetown with 5 for 68 at Port-of-Spain. In 2013, after a second respectable home Test summer, he took 15 wickets in three Tests in India, than performed capably in England after being left out of the first two Tests. Lyon's early cricket was for the Australian Capital Territory in Canberra, where he worked as a groundsman before he got the job in Adelaide.

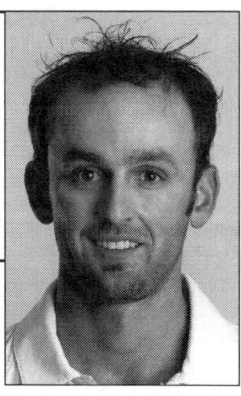

THE FACTS Lyon was the third Australian (after Tom Horan in 1882-83 and Arthur Coningham in 1894-95) to take a wicket with his first ball in a Test, dismissing Kumar Sangakkara of Sri Lanka at Galle in September 2011 ... Lyon took 7 for 94 v India at Delhi in March 2013 ... All three of his first-class five-fors have come in Tests ...

THE FIGURES to 17.09.13

espncricinfo.com

Batting & Fielding	M	Inns	NO	Runs	HS	Avge	S/R	100	50	4s	6s	Ct	St
Tests	25	32	14	244	40*	13.55	37.13	0	0	32	0	7	0
ODIs	2	2	1	4	4*	4.00	66.66	0	0	0	0	1	0
T20Is	0	0	–	–	–	–	–	–	–	–	–	–	–
First-class	46	60	19	450	40*	10.97	38.20	0	0	56	0	10	0

Bowling	M	Balls	Runs	Wkts	BB	Avge	RpO	S/R	5i	10m
Tests	25	5549	2825	85	7–94	33.23	3.05	65.28	3	0
ODIs	2	96	77	1	1–4	77.00	4.81	96.00	0	0
T20Is	0	0	–	–	–	–	–	–	–	–
First-class	46	9718	5214	136	7–94	38.33	3.21	71.45	3	0

MITCHELL **McCLENAGHAN**

NEW ZEALAND

Full name	**Mitchell John McClenaghan**
Born	**June 11, 1986, Hastings, Hawke's Bay**
Teams	**Auckland, Lancashire**
Style	**Left-hand bat, left-arm fast-medium bowler**
Test debut	**No Tests yet**
ODI debut	**New Zealand v South Africa at Paarl 2012-13**
T20I debut	**New Zealand v South Africa at Durban 2012-13**

THE PROFILE Mitchell McClenaghan is a tall left-arm fast bowler with an open-chested action. He can dig the ball in or push it across the right-handers, and proved a handful when first called up to New Zealand's one-day side: he took 29 wickets in his first ten matches, more than anyone else has ever managed. McClenaghan started with Central Districts, but made little impression until he moved to Auckland in 2011-12, his progress not helped by a genetic hip condition: doctors eventually had to fracture the hip sockets and screw the cartilages back into place, a process McClenaghan laconically described as "painful". He took 5 for 30 in his first one-day match for Auckland, and followed that with 6 for 41 in the next game. He finished that season with 16 one-day wickets, and also claimed 35 in first-class matches. He was rewarded with a place on the tour of South Africa later in 2012, and took 4 for 20 in his maiden one-day international, only the second man to take four on ODI debut for New Zealand after Dayle Hadlee. McClenaghan made surprising new opponents something of a speciality: he also took four wickets in his first one-dayers against England, Sri Lanka and Australia (and, by September 2013, hadn't played against anyone else). After taking ten wickets in three matches in the Champions Trophy in England in June 2013, he was signed up by Lancashire for their Twenty20 campaign, and took 5 for 29 against Nottinghamshire at Old Trafford. New Zealand have no shortage of left-arm pacemen, but McClenaghan's one-day successes will have the likes of Trent Boult and Neil Wagner looking over their shoulders as the new season gets under way.

THE FACTS McClenaghan took a record 29 wickets in his first ten ODIs ... He took 8 for 23 as Auckland bowled Otago out for 63 in March 2012 ... McClenaghan took 4 for 20 – the best figures on ODI debut for New Zealand – against South Africa in January 2013 ... He took 5 for 36 for NZ's Emerging Players v England Lions in February 2009 ...

THE FIGURES to 17.09.13   **ESPNcricinfo.com**

Batting & Fielding	M	Inns	NO	Runs	HS	Avge	S/R	100	50	4s	6s	Ct	St
Tests	0	0	–	–	–	–	–	–	–	–	–	–	–
ODIs	10	4	3	7	4	7.00	29.16	0	0	0	0	3	0
T20Is	8	3	2	7	6*	7.00	63.63	0	0	1	0	2	0
First-class	26	31	12	175	34	9.21	26.04	0	0	13	0	6	0

Bowling	M	Balls	Runs	Wkts	BB	Avge	RpO	S/R	5i	10m
Tests	0	0	–	–	–	–	–	–	–	–
ODIs	10	550	479	29	4–20	16.51	5.22	18.96	0	0
T20Is	8	158	206	9	2–24	22.88	7.82	17.55	0	0
First-class	26	4986	2967	76	8–23	39.03	3.57	65.60	2	0

BRENDON McCULLUM

NEW ZEALAND

Full name	**Brendon Barrie McCullum**
Born	**September 27, 1981, Dunedin, Otago**
Teams	**Otago, Kolkata Knight Riders**
Style	**Right-hand bat, wicketkeeper**
Test debut	**New Zealand v South Africa at Hamilton 2003-04**
ODI debut	**New Zealand v Australia at Sydney 2001-02**
T20I debut	**New Zealand v Australia at Auckland 2004-05**

THE PROFILE Short but power-packed, Brendon McCullum stepped up to the national side as a wicketkeeper-batsman after an outstanding career in youth cricket, where he often dominated opposition attacks. Not surprisingly he found it hard to replicate that at the highest level at first, although there were occasional fireworks in domestic cricket. But he finally made his mark in England in 2004, with an entertaining 96 at Lord's. He collected his maiden century in Bangladesh that October, and hammered 86 as New Zealand overhauled Australia's 346 at Hamilton in February 2007 with one wicket to spare. But he really made his mark in April 2008, on the opening night of the inaugural IPL, by smacking 158 not out from 73 balls for Kolkata Knight Riders. There were signs he was having trouble tempering his natural attacking instincts in the longer game, but in the summer of 2008 he lit up Lord's again with 97, before walloping ten sixes in 166 in a one-day mismatch against Ireland. McCullum showed he could still hack it in Tests with 84 and 115 against India in March 2009 and 185 against Bangladesh a year later. After regular back niggles, he announced that he would no longer keep wicket in Tests, and in only his second match unencumbered by the gloves applied himself for 543 minutes to score 225 against India at Hyderabad in November 2010. The runs continued to flow, although similar big scores proved elusive: in the next three years he made only three limited-overs hundreds, against Canada, Bangladesh and Zimbabwe. Early in 2013 he took over as captain, doing well at home against England but powerless to prevent heavy defeats at Lord's and Headingley in the return series.

THE FACTS McCullum made 185, the highest score by a New Zealand wicketkeeper in Tests, against Bangladesh at Hamilton in February 2010 ... He was the first man to score 1000 runs in Twenty20 internationals ... McCullum hit 166, and shared an opening stand of 274 with James Marshall, in an ODI against Ireland at Aberdeen in July 2008 ... His brother Nathan has also played for New Zealand ...

THE FIGURES to 17.09.13   ESPncricinfo.com

Batting & Fielding	M	Inns	NO	Runs	HS	Avge	S/R	100	50	4s	6s	Ct	St
Tests	77	134	8	4459	225	35.38	60.41	6	28	539	55	182	11
ODIs	218	188	27	4952	166	30.75	89.98	4	25	443	147	240	15
T20Is	62	61	8	1882	123	35.50	135.49	2	11	183	75	34	8
First-class	124	217	12	7169	225	34.97	–	11	43	–	–	290	19

Bowling	M	Balls	Runs	Wkts	BB	Avge	RpO	S/R	5i	10m
Tests	77	36	18	0	–	–	3.00	–	0	0
ODIs	218	0	–	–	–	–	–	–	–	–
T20Is	62	0	–	–	–	–	–	–	–	–
First-class	124	36	18	0	–	–	3.00	–	0	0

NATHAN **McCULLUM**

NEW ZEALAND

Full name	Nathan Leslie McCullum
Born	September 1, 1980, Dunedin, Otago
Teams	Otago, Glamorgan, Sunrisers Hyderabad
Style	Right-hand bat, offspinner
Test debut	No Tests yet
ODI debut	New Zealand v Sri Lanka at Colombo 2009
T20I debut	New Zealand v South Africa at Durban 2007-08

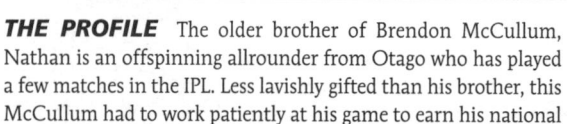

THE PROFILE The older brother of Brendon McCullum, Nathan is an offspinning allrounder from Otago who has played a few matches in the IPL. Less lavishly gifted than his brother, this McCullum had to work patiently at his game to earn his national colours. He was in the 30-man preliminary squad for the Champions Trophy in 2006 but didn't make the cut, and had to wait until the inaugural World Twenty20 in South Africa in September 2007 for the chance to appear alongside Brendon in New Zealand colours. He scored a single in his only match and didn't bowl – and promptly returned to domestic cricket for nearly 18 months. He was back for the next World Twenty20, in England in 2009, and this time added more to the cause, particularly with some tight bowling and taut fielding. Three 50-overs outings produced fewer runs and even fewer wickets, but McCullum was back for the third edition of the World Twenty20 in the West Indies in 2010, where he turned the match against Sri Lanka with a four and a six in the last over, after earlier taking a wicket and three catches: for once he overshadowed his brother, who failed to score. He then took 3 for 16 in his four overs against Zimbabwe to ensure New Zealand reached the second phase. McCullum took eight wickets on helpful pitches at the 2011 World Cup, and made a half-century against Australia. The following year he made 50, then took 2 for 40, as West Indies were demolished in St Kitts. Limited-overs cricket is his forte: he has only one century and three five-fors (one for Glamorgan in 2013) in a first-class career spanning more than a decade. In his younger days, he was also a useful footballer.

THE FACTS McCullum took 6 for 90 for New Zealand A v India A at Chennai in September 2008 ... He scored 106 not out for Otago v Northern Districts at Hamilton in March 2008 ... He has played Twenty20 matches in India (for two IPL teams), England (Lancashire) and Australia (Sydney Sixers) ... McCullum's brother Brendon has also played for New Zealand, while their father Stu represented Otago ...

THE FIGURES to 17.09.13 espncricinfo.com

Batting & Fielding	M	Inns	NO	Runs	HS	Avge	S/R	100	50	4s	6s	Ct	St
Tests	0	0	–	–	–	–	–	–	–	–	–	–	–
ODIs	52	43	4	769	65	19.71	85.16	0	4	51	20	23	0
T20Is	47	29	10	238	36*	12.52	101.27	0	0	13	7	17	0
First-class	58	90	8	2114	106*	25.78	–	1	13	–	–	66	0

Bowling	M	Balls	Runs	Wkts	BB	Avge	RpO	S/R	5i	10m
Tests	0	0	–	–	–	–	–	–	–	–
ODIs	52	2150	1725	38	3–24	45.39	4.81	56.57	0	0
T20Is	47	788	902	42	4–16	21.47	6.86	18.76	0	0
First-class	58	10532	5018	122	6–90	41.13	2.85	86.32	3	0

RYAN McLAREN

Full name	**Ryan McLaren**
Born	**February 9, 1983, Kimberley**
Teams	**Knights, Kolkata Knight Riders**
Style	**Left-hand bat, right-arm fast-medium bowler**
Test debut	**South Africa v England at Johannesburg 2009-10**
ODI debut	**South Africa v Zimbabwe at Benoni 2009-10**
T20I debut	**South Africa v England at Johannesburg 2009-10**

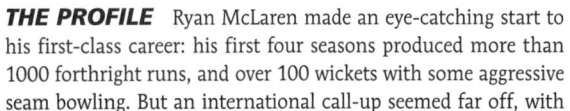

THE PROFILE Ryan McLaren made an eye-catching start to his first-class career: his first four seasons produced more than 1000 forthright runs, and over 100 wickets with some aggressive seam bowling. But an international call-up seemed far off, with Shaun Pollock and Jacques Kallis entrenched. Like several of his compatriots McLaren opted for county cricket as a Kolpak player, and soon became a key performer for Kent, taking a hat-trick as they won the Twenty20 Cup final in 2007. After signing a three-year contract before another impressive county season in 2008 McLaren was named in South Africa's one-day squad that October – but Kent refused to release him, and he was forced to return to Canterbury. At the end of 2009, though, they did let him go – and South Africa lost no time in blooding him. McLaren kept things tight against Zimbabwe and England, then injuries to others led to a first Test cap on a bowler-friendly pitch at Johannesburg, where the England series was emphatically squared: his contribution was some handy runs and the wicket of England's first-innings top-scorer Paul Collingwood. McLaren is accurate and bowls at a nagging pace, factors which helped him pick up 5 for 19 in a Twenty20 international in the West Indies in May 2010. He missed the 2011 World Cup, but remains marketable in the Twenty20 game. An English type of bowler, he was recalled for the one-day leg of South Africa's triumphant 2012 tour, and was back in England the following year for the Champions Trophy, claiming eight wickets in his four games, and coming close to upsetting the eventual winners, India, with an unbeaten 71 in a big chase at Cardiff.

THE FACTS McLaren took a hat-trick for Kent v Gloucestershire in the English Twenty20 Cup final at Edgbaston in August 2007 ... He made 140 for Eagles v Warriors at Bloemfontein in March 2006 ... McLaren took 5 for 19 in a T20 international against West Indies in May 2010 ... He took 8 for 38 for Eagles v Cape Cobras at Stellenbosch in February 2007 ... His father, uncle and cousin all played for Griqualand West ...

THE FIGURES to 17.09.13   **cricinfo.com**

Batting & Fielding	M	Inns	NO	Runs	HS	Avge	S/R	100	50	4s	6s	Ct	St
Tests	1	1	1	33	33*	–	58.92	0	0	5	0	0	0
ODIs	30	23	8	270	71*	18.00	70.31	0	1	22	3	9	0
T20Is	8	3	3	8	6*	–	88.88	0	0	0	0	1	0
First-class	102	151	27	3811	140	30.73	–	3	20	–	–	49	0

Bowling	M	Balls	Runs	Wkts	BB	Avge	RpO	S/R	5i	10m
Tests	1	78	43	1	1–30	43.00	3.30	78.00	0	0
ODIs	30	1369	1167	39	4–19	29.92	5.11	35.10	0	0
T20Is	8	191	222	14	5–19	15.85	6.97	13.64	1	0
First-class	102	16400	8252	326	8–38	25.31	3.01	50.30	12	1

MAHMUDULLAH

Full name	Mohammad Mahmudullah
Born	February 4, 1986, Mymensingh
Teams	Dhaka
Style	Right-hand bat, offspinner
Test debut	Bangladesh v West Indies at Kingstown 2009
ODI debut	Bangladesh v Sri Lanka at Colombo 2007
T20I debut	Bangladesh v Kenya at Nairobi 2007-08

THE PROFILE An offspinning allrounder who is also an assured close-in fielder, Mahmudullah was something of a surprise selection for Bangladesh's chastening tour of Sri Lanka in mid-2007 (all three Tests were lost by an innings, and all three ODIs ended in defeat too). He made his international debut in the second one-dayer, scoring 36 and picking up two wickets in his five overs. As a bowler he does turn the ball, and can also keep the runs down. Mahmudullah spent the summer of 2005 on the groundstaff at Lord's: MCC's head coach, Clive Radley, remembered him delivering "from quite wide of the crease – he spun it a lot and bowled a good doosra". Bangladesh have a lot of slow left-armers, but not many offspinners made a mark before "Riyad" – although so far he has been needed more for his batting, which improved as he got to grips with international cricket. He was stranded on 96 not out against India at Mirpur early in 2010, but made sure of his maiden century in the next Test, with 115 against New Zealand, before making assured fifties in both home Tests against England, and two more in a tight home series against West Indies late in 2012. Mahmudullah's bowling, after a good start against a depleted West Indian side in July 2009 – 12 wickets in his first two Tests – has proved less incisive, but he looks set to remain a fixture in the team for some time. He came to prominence after a superb domestic season in 2008-09, when 710 runs at 54.61 earned him a place on that West Indian tour. He anchored Bangladesh's upset victory over England in the 2011 World Cup, and has quietly matured into a fine player.

THE FACTS Mahmudullah took 5 for 51 (and 8 for 110 in the match) on his Test debut, against West Indies in St Vincent in July 2009 ... His first four first-class centuries all came within a month at the end of 2008, including 152 for Dhaka at Khulna ... After being stranded on 96 against India at Mirpur in January 2010, Mahmudullah completed his maiden Test century in his next match, against New Zealand at Hamilton ...

THE FIGURES to 17.09.13   **cricinfo.com**

Batting & Fielding	M	Inns	NO	Runs	HS	Avge	S/R	100	50	4s	6s	Ct	St
Tests	17	33	2	865	115	27.90	57.24	1	6	114	6	15	0
ODIs	91	77	25	1763	75*	33.90	71.78	0	9	129	16	22	0
T20Is	24	23	1	279	64*	12.68	96.87	0	1	18	10	8	0
First-class	64	115	12	3422	152	33.22	–	5	19	–	–	60	0

Bowling	M	Balls	Runs	Wkts	BB	Avge	RpO	S/R	5i	10m
Tests	17	2198	1262	28	5–51	45.07	3.44	78.50	1	0
ODIs	91	2761	2327	54	3–4	43.09	5.05	51.12	0	0
T20Is	24	277	350	9	2–28	38.88	7.58	30.77	0	0
First-class	64	5798	3152	88	5–51	35.81	3.26	65.88	1	0

LASITH **MALINGA**

Full name **Separamadu Lasith Malinga Swarnajith**
Born **August 28, 1983, Galle**
Teams **Nondescripts, Ruhuna, Mumbai Indians**
Style **Right-hand bat, right-arm fast bowler**
Test debut **Sri Lanka v Australia at Darwin 2004**
ODI debut **Sri Lanka v United Arab Emirates at Dambulla 2004**
T20I debut **Sri Lanka v England at Southampton 2006**

THE PROFILE A rare Sri Lankan cricketer from the south, Lasith Malinga - whose exotic hairstyles make him stand out on and off the park - played hardly any proper cricket until he was 17, preferring the softball version in the coconut groves of Rathgama, a village near Galle. But once he was unearthed, he took eight wickets in his first-class debut, and hardly looked back. He bowls with a distinctive explosive round-arm action, and generates genuine pace, often disconcerting batsmen who struggle to pick up the ball's trajectory. "Slinga" Malinga was a surprise selection for the 2004 tour of Australia, and started with 6 for 90 in a warm-up game. That led to a first Test cap, and he grabbed six wickets in his first match and four in the second: he added nine at Napier in April 2005, when the New Zealanders complained his action meant the ball often got lost in the umpires' clothing. He was originally thought too erratic for one-dayers, but buried that reputation with 13 wickets in the 5-0 whitewash of England in 2006. The following year he scalped 18 during the World Cup, including four in four balls against South Africa. After that he became a fixture in limited-overs matches, where his toe-crushing yorkers proved hard to get away. He officially retired from the five-day game in 2011 when only 27, ostensibly to spare his body wear and tear, although the lure of lucrative Twenty20 contracts might have helped make up his mind. Malinga remained a stunning limited-overs sledgehammer, picking up two more ODI hat-tricks, including another in the 2011 World Cup. He reached 200 wickets late in 2012, and struck twice in the first over - blowing away Mike Hussey and Suresh Raina - as Mumbai Indians won the IPL for the first time in 2013.

THE FACTS Malinga is the only bowler to take four wickets in four balls in international cricket, against South Africa during the 2007 World Cup ... He has taken two further ODI hat-tricks, against Kenya in the 2011 World Cup and Australia in August 2011 ... Malinga took 6 for 17 as Galle bowled out the Police for 51 in Colombo in November 2003 ...

THE FIGURES to 17.09.13   ESPNcricinfo.com

Batting & Fielding	M	Inns	NO	Runs	HS	Avge	S/R	100	50	4s	6s	Ct	St
Tests	30	37	13	275	64	11.45	44.42	0	1	36	6	7	0
ODIs	152	74	24	405	56	8.10	80.51	0	1	31	17	20	0
T20Is	45	16	7	69	27	7.66	84.14	0	0	3	3	13	0
First-class	83	100	41	584	64	9.89	40.58	0	1	–	–	23	0

Bowling	M	Balls	Runs	Wkts	BB	Avge	RpO	S/R	5i	10m
Tests	30	5209	3349	101	5–50	33.15	3.85	51.57	3	0
ODIs	152	7350	6235	235	6–38	26.53	5.08	31.27	5	0
T20Is	45	936	1154	51	3–12	22.62	7.39	18.35	0	0
First-class	83	11867	7751	255	6–17	30.39	3.91	46.53	7	0

SHAUN MARSH

Full name	**Shaun Edward Marsh**
Born	**July 9, 1983, Narrogin, Western Australia**
Teams	**Western Australia, Kings XI Punjab**
Style	**Left-hand bat, occasional left-arm spinner**
Test debut	**Australia v Sri Lanka at Galle 2011**
ODI debut	**Australia v West Indies at Kingstown 2007-08**
T20I debut	**Australia v West Indies at Bridgetown 2008**

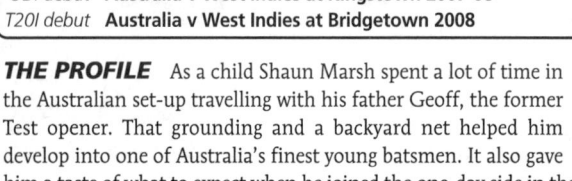

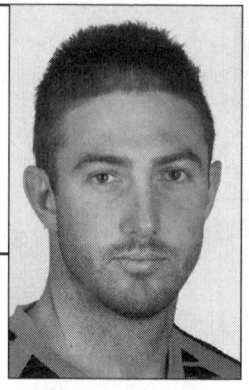

AUSTRALIA

THE PROFILE As a child Shaun Marsh spent a lot of time in the Australian set-up travelling with his father Geoff, the former Test opener. That grounding and a backyard net helped him develop into one of Australia's finest young batsmen. It also gave him a taste of what to expect when he joined the one-day side in the Caribbean in 2008. That came after a fine domestic season: he was also the surprise hit of the inaugural IPL. More gifted than his father – "He's got a few more shots than me," Geoff once admitted – Shaun is a left-hander who reached his maiden first-class hundred in 2003 with successive sixes over midwicket off Mark Waugh. The second century had to wait until 2004-05 as Marsh struggled with concentration, the finest trait of his father's batting. In 2008-09 he made 79 and 78 against South Africa, but then tore a hamstring while fielding against New Zealand, and later hurt his leg again, which kept him out of the World Twenty20 in England in June 2009. He returned with a century in India then, after a back injury, made a classy 59 as Australia ended the one-day series against England in July 2010 with a victory at Lord's. He finally got a Test chance in Sri Lanka in 2011, with Ricky Ponting on paternity leave. Watched by his dad, Marsh grabbed the opportunity greedily, making a superb 141 and adding 81 in the next Test. When Ponting returned, Marsh stayed at No. 3 … but not for long. He endured a horror run against India at home at the start of 2012 – 17 runs in six innings, with three ducks – and was sent back to Shield cricket, although he remained in the one-day frame, and hammered 151 against Scotland in September 2013.

THE FACTS Marsh was the 19th Australian to score a century on Test debut, five years after he hit 81 in his first ODI … Marsh made 166* for Western Australia v Queensland at Perth in November 2007 … His father Geoff won 50 Test caps (they were only the second father-son combination to play Tests for Australia), and his younger brother Mitchell played his first limited-overs internationals in October 2011 …

THE FIGURES to 17.09.13

espncricinfo.com

Batting & Fielding	M	Inns	NO	Runs	HS	Avge	S/R	100	50	4s	6s	Ct	St
Tests	7	11	0	301	141	27.36	41.00	1	1	36	0	4	0
ODIs	41	40	1	1490	151	38.20	76.92	3	8	142	18	8	0
T20Is	13	13	1	223	47*	18.58	104.69	0	0	12	10	3	0
First-class	79	144	16	4489	166*	35.07	45.87	7	25	–	–	70	0

Bowling	M	Balls	Runs	Wkts	BB	Avge	RpO	S/R	5i	10m
Tests	7	0	–	–	–	–	–	–	–	–
ODIs	41	0	–	–	–	–	–	–	–	–
T20Is	13	0	–	–	–	–	–	–	–	–
First-class	79	174	131	2	2–20	65.50	4.51	87.00	0	0

HAMILTON **MASAKADZA**

ZIMBABWE

Full name	**Hamilton Masakadza**
Born	**August 9, 1983, Harare**
Teams	**Mountaineers**
Style	**Right-hand bat, right-arm medium-pacer**
Test debut	**Zimbabwe v West Indies at Harare 2001**
ODI debut	**Zimbabwe v South Africa at Bulawayo 2001-02**
T20I debut	**Zimbabwe v Bangladesh at Khulna 2006-07**

THE PROFILE Hamilton Masakadza was still a schoolboy when he set the record – since beaten by Bangladesh's Mohammad Ashraful – as the youngest man to score a century on Test debut. Against West Indies in July 2001, he made a composed 119 from No. 3 – driving well, and showing few signs of nerves in the nineties. A year later, though, he put his cricket career on hold while at university in South Africa. Masakadza's return to the team brought mixed results at first, but he was their best batsman, technically, in South Africa early in 2005, showing an application lacking in his team-mates. Masakadza's form in one-day cricket – admittedly largely against lesser teams like Bangladesh and Kenya – has steadily improved: 2009 was a bumper year, bringing him more than 1000 runs in ODIs at an average of 43.48 and a strike-rate of 88. It included two towering scores of more than 150, both against Kenya in October. Late the following year, though, he went through a lean patch, and was rather surprisingly left out of the 2011 World Cup. But Masakadza was soon back, and helped set up Zimbabwe's victory in their comeback Test, against Bangladesh at Harare in August, with a five-hour 104, a second Test century more than ten years after his first. He remained in the runs during an otherwise disappointing tour of New Zealand early in 2012, making 53 and 62 in the two Twenty20 internationals. The following year he made up for a poor tour of the West Indies with another Test hundred, against Bangladesh, and added a responsible 75 in the victory over Pakistan at Harare in September 2013.

THE FACTS Masakadza was only the second Zimbabwean, after Dave Houghton in 1992-93, to make a century on Test debut: he made 119 against West Indies in July 2001, when 11 days short of his 18th birthday … His second Test hundred came more than ten years later, against Bangladesh in August 2011 … Masakadza is the only man ever to make two scores above 150 in the same ODI series – 156 and 178* v Kenya in October 2009 … His brother Shingirai, a fast bowler, made his Test debut in 2012 …

THE FIGURES to 17.09.13   ESPNcricinfo.com

Batting & Fielding	M	Inns	NO	Runs	HS	Avge	S/R	100	50	4s	6s	Ct	St
Tests	25	50	2	1292	119	26.91	41.12	3	4	159	12	12	0
ODIs	129	129	4	3429	178*	27.43	73.33	3	20	341	46	52	0
T20Is	28	28	1	767	79	28.40	115.16	0	7	68	23	7	0
First-class	110	194	11	7379	208*	40.32	–	18	34	–	–	84	0

Bowling	M	Balls	Runs	Wkts	BB	Avge	RpO	S/R	5i	10m
Tests	25	762	270	10	3–24	27.00	2.12	76.20	0	0
ODIs	129	1425	1258	33	3–39	38.12	5.29	43.18	0	0
T20Is	28	54	82	2	1–4	41.00	9.11	27.00	0	0
First-class	110	3560	1553	53	4–11	29.30	2.61	67.16	0	0

SHINGI **MASAKADZA**

ZIMBABWE

Full name	**Shingirai Winston Masakadza**
Born	**September 4, 1986, Harare**
Teams	**Mountaineers**
Style	**Right-hand bat, right-arm fast-medium bowler**
Test debut	**Zimbabwe v New Zealand at Napier 2011-12**
ODI debut	**Zimbabwe v West Indies at Providence 2009-10**
T20I debut	**Zimbabwe v West Indies at Port-of-Spain 2009-10**

THE PROFILE Shingi Masakadza, an honest fast-medium seamer who opens the bowling for the Mountaineers franchise, has a lot to live up to – his older brother Hamilton was the first black African to hit a Test century (and, for a short time, the youngest to do so on debut). Born in Harare's Highfield township, Shingi first learned the game at Mbizi Primary School, and eventually joined the prominent Takashinga club. He made his first-class debut in 2007-08, and caused a stir with 21 wickets in four Logan Cup matches at the remarkable average of 11.95. He remained a consistent wicket-taker in first-class cricket, picking up 24 in 2008-09 and 40 the following season, which earned him a call-up to the national side for the West Indies tour early in 2010. His first over in international cricket was despatched for 14, but he bounced back well, grabbing three quick wickets late on to seal a tense two-run victory in the first one-day international in Guyana. He was out of the side for a while, but was on the fringe when Zimbabwe returned to Test cricket late in 2011: he duly made his Test debut in New Zealand early the following year, but had a rough baptism, collecting the wicket of Martin Guptill but going for 102 in his 23 overs. He did better against Bangladesh at home in April 2013, taking five wickets in both Tests, but may have to add a yard or two of pace to prosper at the top level. Masakadza is a handy lower-order batsman, and has a first-class century to his name. He was a promising footballer before opting for cricket.

THE FACTS Shingi Masakadza took 6 for 54 for Mountaineers v Mid West Rhinos at Kwekwe in January 2010 (his brother Hamilton, who also played for Zimbabwe, scored 155 in the same game) ... Shingi equalled his best figures with 6 for 54 (9 for 75 in the match) against Mashonaland Eagles at Harare in January 2012 ... He hit 100*, from 79 balls, against Southern Rocks at Mutare in January 2010 ...

THE FIGURES to 17.09.13 — espncricinfo.com

Batting & Fielding	M	Inns	NO	Runs	HS	Avge	S/R	100	50	4s	6s	Ct	St
Tests	4	7	1	88	24	14.66	38.59	0	0	9	0	2	0
ODIs	12	8	2	148	45*	24.66	100.00	0	0	15	7	6	0
T20Is	7	5	1	18	9	4.50	75.00	0	0	1	0	2	0
First-class	50	73	14	991	100*	16.79	49.72	1	2	116	15	23	0

Bowling	M	Balls	Runs	Wkts	BB	Avge	RpO	S/R	5i	10m
Tests	4	865	410	14	4–32	29.28	2.84	61.78	0	0
ODIs	12	595	704	22	4–46	32.00	7.09	27.04	0	0
T20Is	7	117	211	4	2–39	52.75	10.82	29.25	0	0
First-class	50	8959	4564	206	6–54	22.15	3.05	43.49	7	0

MASHRAFE MORTAZA

BANGLADESH

Full name **Mashrafe bin Mortaza**
Born **October 5, 1983, Norail, Jessore, Khulna**
Teams **Khulna**
Style **Right-hand bat, right-arm fast-medium bowler**
Test debut **Bangladesh v Zimbabwe at Dhaka 2001-02**
ODI debut **Bangladesh v Zimbabwe at Chittagong 2001-02**
T20I debut **Bangladesh v Zimbabwe at Khulna 2006-07**

THE PROFILE Mashrafe Mortaza has long been the standard-bearer for Bangladesh's pacemen, although injuries have bedevilled him: he hurt his right knee after only 6.3 overs in the first Test in West Indies in July 2009, and had to undergo an operation (on both knees, in fact). This was doubly disappointing as it was his first match as captain, and it ended in only Bangladesh's second Test victory – their first overseas. He returned in Britain in 2010, leading Bangladesh to their first win over England, but injured the knee again at the end of the year. He was not thought ready for the 2011 World Cup, and although he played two ODIs against Australia shortly afterwards – and took five wickets – his long-suffering right knee then went under the knife again. However, he was back among the wickets when Bangladesh toured Europe in mid-2012, before being sidelined by another injury (heel this time). But, slimmer and trimmer, he targeted an international return at the end of 2013. "Koushik" has proved adept at reining in his attacking instincts to concentrate on line and length. He won his first Test cap in 2001-02, in what was also his first-class debut, and did well in the second Test against England in 2003-04, taking 4 for 60 to keep Bangladesh in touch, but then twisted his knee, which kept him out of Tests for over a year. Mashrafe's 4 for 38 in the 2007 World Cup set up a famous defeat of India, and he remains the only fast bowler to take 100 ODI wickets for Bangladesh. He is not a complete mug with the bat: he has a first-class century to his name, and over 20% of his ODI runs have come in sixes.

THE FACTS Mashrafe Mortaza was the first Bangladeshi to make his first-class debut in a Test match: only three others have done this since 1899 ... Mashrafe started the famous ODI victory over Australia at Cardiff in 2005 by dismissing Adam Gilchrist for 0 ... His 6 for 26 v Kenya in Nairobi in August 2006 remain Bangladesh's best bowling figures in ODIs ... Only Mike Hendrick of England has claimed more Test wickets (87) without ever taking a five-for ... Mashrafe's record includes two ODIs for the Asia XI ...

THE FIGURES to 17.09.13   **ESFT cricinfo.com**

Batting & Fielding	M	Inns	NO	Runs	HS	Avge	S/R	100	50	4s	6s	Ct	St
Tests	36	67	5	797	79	12.85	67.20	0	3	95	22	9	0
ODIs	128	97	17	1220	51*	15.25	86.52	0	1	98	42	39	0
T20Is	20	16	4	196	36	16.33	134.24	0	0	7	14	3	0
First-class	52	93	7	1413	132*	16.43	–	1	6	–	–	23	0

Bowling	M	Balls	Runs	Wkts	BB	Avge	RpO	S/R	5i	10m
Tests	36	5990	3239	78	4–60	41.52	3.24	76.79	0	0
ODIs	128	6411	4990	162	6–26	30.80	4.67	39.57	1	0
T20Is	20	447	612	19	4–19	32.21	8.21	23.52	0	0
First-class	52	8487	4407	124	4–27	35.54	3.11	68.44	0	0

ANGELO **MATHEWS**

Full name	**Angelo Davis Mathews**
Born	**June 2, 1987, Colombo**
Teams	**Colts, Basnahira, Pune Warriors**
Style	**Right-hand bat, right-arm fast-medium bowler**
Test debut	**Sri Lanka v Pakistan at Galle 2009**
ODI debut	**Sri Lanka v Zimbabwe at Harare 2008-09**
T20I debut	**Sri Lanka v Australia at Nottingham 2009**

THE PROFILE Angelo Mathews was long seen as a potential Sri Lankan captain, and it was no great shock when he finally took over the Test leadership in February 2013. What was a surprise, though, was that his form then declined: after a Champions Trophy fifty was followed by another in the West Indies, he went ten innings without exceeding 30. Still, it was too soon to panic: Mathews had looked good ever since his international debut late in 2008. Early on he bowled at a lively medium-pace, but the odd injury has reduced his effectiveness and, as always seemed likely, he is now basically an attacking batsman who bowls a bit. After two A-team hundreds in South Africa in August 2008, he really made his presence felt the following year, following 52 not out in his third ODI, in Bangladesh in January, with 270 in a domestic match. Later that year he helped Sri Lanka to the World Twenty20 final in England, notably with three West Indian wickets to effectively settle the semi in the first over, then in December he made 99 – and cried when he was narrowly run out – in a Test against India in Mumbai. After a consistent time the following year more heartache followed in 2011: a late six in the semi helped ensure Sri Lanka reached the World Cup final, but Mathews already knew he wouldn't be playing in that, as he had injured his leg. He missed the IPL and the England tour, but was back for the home series against Australia, reaching that elusive century in the third Test, after another near-miss (trying for a six when 95) in the first one at Galle.

THE FACTS Mathews was run out for 99 against India in Mumbai in December 2009 ... He made 270 for Basnahira North v Kandurata in Colombo in February 2009 ... Mathews took 6 for 20 in an ODI against India in Colombo in September 2009 ... In the World Twenty20 in England in 2009 his shirt had "Mathew" on the back before he added the final "s" with a marker pen ...

THE FIGURES to 17.09.13   cricinfo.com

Batting & Fielding	M	Inns	NO	Runs	HS	Avge	S/R	100	50	4s	6s	Ct	St
Tests	33	54	10	1762	105*	40.04	47.90	1	11	207	16	19	0
ODIs	105	84	23	2048	80*	33.57	82.18	0	15	143	26	26	0
T20Is	42	32	12	498	58	24.90	114.22	0	1	33	12	11	0
First-class	67	106	17	4401	270	49.44	51.18	10	22	474	53	43	0

Bowling	M	Balls	Runs	Wkts	BB	Avge	RpO	S/R	5i	10m
Tests	33	1584	808	11	2–60	73.45	3.06	144.00	0	0
ODIs	105	3058	2304	67	6–20	34.38	4.52	45.64	1	0
T20Is	42	577	644	24	3–16	26.83	6.69	24.04	0	0
First-class	67	4097	1958	41	5–47	47.75	2.86	99.92	1	0

TINO **MAWOYO**

ZIMBABWE

Full name	**Tinotenda Mbiri Kanayi Mawoyo**
Born	**January 8, 1986, Umtali (now Mutare)**
Teams	**Mountaineers**
Style	**Right-hand bat, occasional medium-pacer**
Test debut	**Zimbabwe v Bangladesh at Harare 2011**
ODI debut	**Zimbabwe v Bangladesh at Dhaka 2006-07**
T20I debut	**No T20Is yet**

THE PROFILE A top-order batsman, Tino Mawoyo had already played first-class cricket when he captained Zimbabwe at the Under-19 World Cup in 2004. To start with his appearances were limited by educational commitments, but he played for the A team against Bangladesh in 2006. He made his full ODI debut later that year, also in Bangladesh. Mawoyo appeared to be set for a more permanent place when he was appointed captain of Zimbabwe A, but was subsequently reduced to the ranks after some supposedly inappropriate behaviour while the team was in a training camp. Nevertheless, he remained one of Zimbabwe's most talented young batsmen, and when Easterns completed the domestic double in 2006-07, Mawoyo was their leading runscorer in the first-class Logan Cup. By 2009-10 he was heading the run-charts in the national one-day competition too, but then experienced wildly varied emotions as the 2011 World Cup approached. Initially left out, he was called up when Sean Ervine withdrew – then had to pull out himself shortly before the tournament after injuring a stomach muscle. The disappointment forced a rethink: Mawoyo lost weight, and elbowed his way into the side for Zimbabwe's comeback Tests later in the year. He shared opening stands of 102 and 69 with Vusi Sibanda in the first Test, against Bangladesh at Harare, and carried his bat for 163 in the second, resisting Pakistan's bowlers for well over ten hours. He than made 52 in a narrow loss to New Zealand, but fared less well as Zimbabwe were walloped in the return Test at Napier. The following year he made 50 at Bridgetown – his side's only half-century in two horror Tests in the West Indies – but struggled when Pakistan visited Harare in September 2013.

THE FACTS Mawoyo carried his bat for 163* in only his second Test, against Pakistan at Bulawayo in September 2011: he was only the third opener to do this for Zimbabwe, after Mark Dekker and Grant Flower, also against Pakistan ... Mawoyo scored 208* for Mountaineers against New Zealand A in a non-first-class game in October 2010 ...

THE FIGURES to 17.09.13   **ESPNcricinfo.com**

Batting & Fielding	M	Inns	NO	Runs	HS	Avge	S/R	100	50	4s	6s	Ct	St
Tests	8	16	1	454	163*	30.26	37.09	1	3	58	0	6	0
ODIs	4	4	0	42	14	10.50	42.00	0	0	3	0	1	0
T20Is	0	0	–	–	–	–	–	–	–	–	–	–	–
First-class	88	156	9	4113	163*	27.97	43.34	4	23	–	–	63	0

Bowling	M	Balls	Runs	Wkts	BB	Avge	RpO	S/R	5i	10m
Tests	8	0	–	–	–	–	–	–	–	–
ODIs	4	0	–	–	–	–	–	–	–	–
T20Is	0	0	–	–	–	–	–	–	–	–
First-class	88	72	44	2	1–0	22.00	3.66	36.00	0	0

AJANTHA MENDIS

Full name	Balapuwaduge Ajantha Winslo Mendis
Born	March 11, 1985, Moratuwa
Teams	Army, Wayamba
Style	Right-hand bat, right-arm off- and legspinner
Test debut	Sri Lanka v India at Colombo 2008
ODI debut	Sri Lanka v West Indies at Port-of-Spain 2007-08
T20I debut	Sri Lanka v Zimbabwe at King City 2008-09

THE PROFILE Those batsmen who thought one Sri Lankan mystery spinner was enough found more on their plate during 2008, when Ajantha Mendis stepped up to join Muttiah Muralitharan in the national side. Mendis sends down a mixture of offbreaks, legbreaks, top-spinners, googlies and flippers, plus his very own "carrom ball" – one flicked out using a finger under the ball, in the style of the old Australians Jack Iverson and John Gleeson. Mendis was a prolific wicket-taker in 2007-08 for the Army (he received not one but two promotions following his meteoric rise) and was called up for the West Indian tour early in 2008 after taking 46 wickets in six matches. After doing well there he ran rings round the Indians – the supposed masters of spin – in the Asia Cup, rather ruining the final with 6 for 13. In his first Test series he took 26 Indian wickets at 18.38 in three home games, and even achieved the rare feat of outperforming Murali (21 wickets at 22.23). Soon, though, batsmen began to work out Mendis's variations. Some tight spells were instrumental in Sri Lanka reaching the World Twenty20 final in England in 2009, but shortly after that he lost his place in the Test side. He remained effective in one-dayers, and it was a surprise when, after keeping things tight in the 2011 World Cup, he was left out for the final. Test success continued to be elusive, but it was a different story in the shorter stuff: he took 6 for 16 in a Twenty20 game against Australia in August 2011, improved that with 6 for 8 v Zimbabwe the following year, and showed there was still petrol in the tank with ten South African wickets in three ODIs in July 2013.

THE FACTS Mendis claimed 26 wickets in his first Test series, against India in 2008, the most by anyone in a debut series of three Tests, beating Alec Bedser's 24 for England v India in 1946 ... Mendis took 6 for 8, the best figures in Twenty20 internationals, against Zimbabwe at Hambantota in September 2012 ... He took 6 for 13 in the Asia Cup final against India at Karachi in July 2008, and 7 for 37 for Army v Lankan CC at Panagoda in February 2008 ...

THE FIGURES to 17.09.13   espncricinfo.com

Batting & Fielding	M	Inns	NO	Runs	HS	Avge	S/R	100	50	4s	6s	Ct	St
Tests	17	17	6	164	78	14.90	43.50	0	1	19	1	2	0
ODIs	65	30	13	111	15*	6.52	61.32	0	0	8	0	9	0
T20Is	32	8	5	8	4*	2.66	47.05	0	0	1	0	3	0
First-class	54	71	6	1045	101	16.07	69.75	1	3	102	30	18	0

Bowling	M	Balls	Runs	Wkts	BB	Avge	RpO	S/R	5i	10m
Tests	17	4251	2189	64	6–117	34.20	3.08	66.42	3	1
ODIs	65	3095	2270	109	6–13	20.82	4.40	28.39	3	0
T20Is	32	732	745	58	6–8	12.84	6.10	12.62	1	0
First-class	54	11018	5713	264	7–37	21.64	3.11	41.73	16	3

JEEVAN MENDIS

Full name	Balapuwaduge Manukulasuriya Amith Jeevan Mendis
Born	January 15, 1983, Colombo
Teams	Tamil Union, Uthura, Delhi Daredevils
Style	Left-hand bat, legspinner
Test debut	No Tests yet
ODI debut	Sri Lanka v Zimbabwe at Bulawayo 2010
T20I debut	Sri Lanka v England at Bristol 2011

THE PROFILE Jeevan Mendis was a young achiever, winning the national schoolboy cricketer of the year award in 2001, and the player of the tournament prize early the following year in the Under-19 World Cup, where his feats included 7 for 19 against Zimbabwe. But it took him a long time to translate that into form good enough to interest the national selectors: he wasn't helped that, for most of his six years with Sinhalese Sports Club, his legspin hardly got an airing. But he moved to Tamil Union in 2008-09, and immediately began to bowl more, an important extra string to his bow to go with forceful left-hand batting and superb fielding. He says batsmen find it difficult to pick his googly because of the way he grips the ball. In his first season for Tamil Union he took 22 wickets to go with 570 runs, then 35 and 846 in 2009-10. He also lit up the domestic one-day tournament, and soon the selectors remembered his name. Mendis made his one-day debut in Zimbabwe in June 2010, and has been a regular member of the 50- and 20-overs squads since, although he did miss out on the 2011 World Cup. His best return with the bat so far was 72 against India at Pallekele in August 2012, and three months later at Hambantota he took 3 for 15 against New Zealand – although his legbreaks have so far proved fairly unthreatening in internationals. Mendis hasn't quite cracked the Test side yet, although two first-class double-centuries suggest he could do a job there too. He has played for Delhi Daredevils in the IPL, and for Sydney Sixers in the Australian Big Bash.

THE FACTS Mendis scored 206* (and 44*) for Tamil Union v Colombo CC in February 2013: it was his first first-class hundred since 205 (and 5 for 80) against Ragama in Colombo in May 2011 ... He took 6 for 37 for Tamil Union v Saracens in August 2011 ... Mendis took 5 for 32 against Pakistan A in September 2010, after 5 for 74 v South Africa A the previous month ...

THE FIGURES to 17.09.13

Batting & Fielding	M	Inns	NO	Runs	HS	Avge	S/R	100	50	4s	6s	Ct	St
Tests	0	0	–	–	–	–	–	–	–	–	–	–	–
ODIs	39	29	6	468	72	20.34	80.96	0	1	38	6	8	0
T20Is	16	12	3	197	43*	21.88	124.68	0	0	18	5	4	0
First-class	111	176	25	5317	206*	35.21	–	11	27	–	–	97	0

Bowling	M	Balls	Runs	Wkts	BB	Avge	RpO	S/R	5i	10m
Tests	0	0	–	–	–	–	–	–	–	–
ODIs	39	947	781	23	3–15	33.95	4.94	41.17	0	0
T20Is	16	108	116	6	3–24	19.33	6.44	18.00	0	0
First-class	111	7410	4217	160	6–37	26.35	3.41	46.31	9	0

DAVID MILLER

Full name **David Andrew Miller**
Born **June 10, 1989, Pietermaritzburg**
Teams **Dolphins, Kings XI Punjab**
Style **Left-hand bat, occasional offspinner**
Test debut **No Tests yet**
ODI debut **South Africa v West Indies at North Sound 2010**
T20I debut **South Africa v West Indies at North Sound 2010**

SOUTH AFRICA

THE PROFILE An explosive left-hander, David Miller was called up to the South African limited-overs sides at 20 in the wake of the disappointing performance at the World Twenty20 in the Caribbean in 2010. His first assignment was back in the West Indies – and he did as well as could have been expected, smashing his sixth ball in international cricket (from Sulieman Benn) into the stands on the way to 33 in the first Twenty20 match. He made a similarly brisk start in one-day internationals, calmly swinging the pacy Ravi Rampaul over square leg for six more during another cameo. Miller joined the South African Academy in mid-2009, and then caught the eye during a successful domestic season, in which he was the Dolphins' leading scorer in both 50- and 20-overs cricket. A rapid unbeaten 90 from 52 balls against the Lions in a Pro20 match at Potchefstroom in February 2010 ensured his selection for a triangular A-team tournament in Bangladesh, and it was while he was there that Miller received the call from the national selectors. But his form fell away in 2010-11, with four successive single-figure scores in ODIs against Pakistan and India: others moved ahead in the queue and Miller missed the 2011 World Cup. He was back for the one-dayers against Australia later in the year, making 59 at Port Elizabeth, but was then overtaken again. He played for Yorkshire in 2012, after a Twenty20 stint with Durham the previous year, and returned to the one-day side after 15 months in January 2013. He did well in the Champions Trophy in England in June, making 56 not out against the hosts, then added an unbeaten 85, from 72 balls with five sixes, against Sri Lanka at Pallekele the following month.

THE FACTS Miller hit four sixes en route to his maiden first-class century, 108* for Dolphins v Eagles at Kimberley in December 2009 ... He raised his highest score to 149 against the Lions at Durban in April 2011 ... Miller also made a century in 55 balls in a 50-over match for South Africa A v Bangladesh A at Mirpur in April 2010 ...

THE FIGURES to 17.09.13   ESPNcricinfo.com

Batting & Fielding	M	Inns	NO	Runs	HS	Avge	S/R	100	50	4s	6s	Ct	St
Tests	0	0	–	–	–	–	–	–	–	–	–	–	–
ODIs	29	26	8	618	85*	34.33	100.32	0	5	41	20	7	0
T20Is	15	13	3	284	36*	28.40	130.87	0	0	20	10	8	0
First-class	40	65	6	1745	149	29.57	54.29	2	8	239	28	37	0

Bowling	M	Balls	Runs	Wkts	BB	Avge	RpO	S/R	5i	10m
Tests	0	0	–	–	–	–	–	–	–	–
ODIs	29	0	–	–	–	–	–	–	–	–
T20Is	15	0	–	–	–	–	–	–	–	–
First-class	40	26	23	0	–	–	5.30	–	0	0

KYLE **MILLS**

Full name **Kyle David Mills**
Born **March 15, 1979, Auckland**
Teams **Auckland, Middlesex**
Style **Right-hand bat, right-arm fast-medium bowler**
Test debut **New Zealand v England at Nottingham 2004**
ODI debut **New Zealand v Pakistan at Sharjah 2000-01**
T20I debut **New Zealand v Australia at Auckland 2004-05**

NEW ZEALAND

THE PROFILE Injuries at inopportune times have hampered Kyle Mills. They delayed his arrival as an international player, and impinged again in 2009-10, when knee and shoulder problems shortened his season and kept him out of the IPL: he did, however, make it to the World Twenty20 in the West Indies, although he proved expensive in his two matches there. A genuine swing bowler of lively pace, Mills yo-yoed in and out of the team after the 2003 World Cup, but he did enough to tour England in 2004, and made his Test debut in the third match at Trent Bridge. But he suffered a side strain there, and missed the one-day series. That was a shame, as one-day cricket is really his forte: he played throughout 2005-06, chipping in with wickets in almost every game, even if his once-promising batting had diminished to the point that he managed double figures only once in 16 matches. A feisty temper remains, though: he was fined after an on-field incident in the 2011 World Cup ... and he was only the 12th man at the time. Then, early in 2012, he slammed the small boundaries on many New Zealand grounds, although he did admit: "I'm a bowler so I'm going to be a little bit biased." Ankle surgery, then knee trouble – which necessitated another op – sidelined him early in 2007, but after missing that year's World Cup, Mills bounced back, following up 5 for 25 in a one-dayer in South Africa with a Test-best 4 for 16 against England at Hamilton in March 2008. He lost his Test spot after some anaemic performances the following season, but has remained a one-day force, taking 4 for 30 against England at Cardiff in June 2013, more than four years after his last Test.

THE FACTS Mills's only first-class hundred came from No. 9 at Wellington in 2000-01, helping Auckland recover from 109 for 7 ... His 5 for 25 at Durban in November 2007 remain NZ's best one-day figures v South Africa ... Mills is the leading wicket-taker in the ICC Champions Trophy, with 28 ... Only Daniel Vettori (276) has taken more ODI wickets for New Zealand ...

THE FIGURES to 17.09.13   **cricinfo.com**

Batting & Fielding	M	Inns	NO	Runs	HS	Avge	S/R	100	50	4s	6s	Ct	St
Tests	19	30	5	289	57	11.56	38.58	0	1	37	3	4	0
ODIs	153	94	32	958	54	15.45	80.23	0	2	70	34	38	0
T20Is	35	17	6	127	33*	11.54	114.41	0	0	9	5	7	0
First-class	75	108	25	2166	117*	26.09	–	1	14	–	–	26	0

Bowling	M	Balls	Runs	Wkts	BB	Avge	RpO	S/R	5i	10m
Tests	19	2902	1453	44	4–16	33.02	3.00	65.95	0	0
ODIs	153	7455	5837	222	5–25	26.29	4.69	33.58	1	0
T20Is	35	742	1029	35	3–33	29.40	8.32	21.20	0	0
First-class	75	12176	5981	203	5–33	29.46	2.94	59.98	5	2

MISBAH-UL-HAQ

Full name	Misbah-ul-Haq Khan Niazi
Born	May 28, 1974, Mianwali, Punjab
Teams	Faisalabad, Sui Northern Gas
Style	Right-hand bat, occasional legspinner
Test debut	Pakistan v New Zealand at Auckland 2000-01
ODI debut	Pakistan v New Zealand at Lahore 2001-02
T20I debut	Pakistan v Bangladesh at Nairobi 2007-08

THE PROFILE An orthodox right-hander with a tight technique, Misbah-ul-Haq caught the eye in a one-day tournament in Nairobi in 2002, making 50 in the final against Australia. But then his form slumped: his highest score in three Tests against Australia was 17. Misbah remained a consistent domestic performer, making 951 runs at 50 in 2004-05, 882 the following season, and capping that with 1108 at 61 in 2006-07, but it was nonetheless a shock when he was called up for the inaugural World Twenty20 in South Africa late in 2007. But he was a surprise hit there, and added 464 runs in three Tests against India, including two important centuries. Suddenly, in his mid-thirties but with a first-class average which remains close to 50, he was an automatic choice. He played his part in winning the World Twenty20 in 2009, but then had a poor time in Australia, and wasn't required for the tour of England in 2010. That ended in turmoil, with three players banned for spot-fixing ... and from the ruins strode Misbah, suddenly the Test captain. He celebrated with six successive fifties then, after a decent World Cup, made a hundred in the West Indies in May 2011. Hardly a long-term solution – he's 40 in 2014 – Misbah turned out to be an inspired choice as a stopgap. Series victories came against Zimbabwe, Sri Lanka and Bangladesh, before a satisfying 3-0 clean sweep against top-ranked England in the UAE early in 2012. The following year was a prolific one for Misbah, especially in one-day internationals where he repeatedly baled his side out. He did well in Tests, too, although he couldn't prevent defeat in South Africa at the start of the year and embarrassment in Zimbabwe in September 2013.

THE FACTS Misbah-ul-Haq has made six first-class double-centuries, the highest 284 for Sui Northern Gas v Lahore Shalimar in October 2009 ... He also made 208* (in a total of 723 for 4) for Punjab v Baluchistan at Sialkot in March 2008 ... He scored 161* and 133* in successive Tests against India in 2007-08 ...

THE FIGURES to 17.09.13   ESPNcricinfo.com

Batting & Fielding	M	Inns	NO	Runs	HS	Avge	S/R	100	50	4s	6s	Ct	St
Tests	41	71	12	2636	161*	44.67	40.62	3	21	292	27	36	0
ODIs	128	117	29	3972	96*	45.13	73.59	0	31	268	58	57	0
T20Is	39	34	13	788	87*	37.52	110.20	0	3	45	26	14	0
First-class	186	304	36	13374	284	49.90	–	35	72	–	–	178	0

Bowling	M	Balls	Runs	Wkts	BB	Avge	RpO	S/R	5i	10m
Tests	41	0	–	–	–	–	–	–	–	–
ODIs	128	24	30	0	–	–	7.50	–	0	0
T20Is	39	0	–	–	–	–	–	–	–	–
First-class	186	318	242	3	1-2	80.66	4.56	106.00	0	0

AMIT MISHRA

Full name	**Amit Mishra**
Born	**November 24, 1982, Delhi**
Teams	**Haryana, Sunrisers Hyderabad**
Style	**Right-hand bat, legspinner**
Test debut	**India v Australia at Mohali 2008-09**
ODI debut	**India v South Africa at Dhaka 2002-03**
T20I debut	**India v Zimbabwe at Harare 2010**

THE PROFILE Amit Mishra is a confident cricketer, but even he might have thought his international chance had gone when five years went by after a flirtation with the one-day team early in 2003. The diminutive Mishra, who bowls big loopy legbreaks and has a fizzing googly, took only two wickets in three matches after several players were rested following the World Cup: he was seen as too slow through the air, and went back to the domestic grind. But Mishra remained a consistent force for Haryana, and also did well in the inaugural IPL, taking a hat-trick against Adam Gilchrist's team. Early the following season Mishra took 6 for 81 (and nine in the match) against New Zealand A, which earned him a Test call-up against Australia a fortnight later at Mohali after Anil Kumble injured his shoulder. Mishra grabbed his big chance, becoming the first Indian to take a debut five-for since Narendra Hirwani, one of the selectors who finally chose him. The googly accounted for three of his wickets, but the pick was arguably the legbreak which pinned top-scorer Shane Watson in front. Mishra took 14 wickets in three Tests, then six more against England later in 2008. He wasn't required for the 2011 World Cup, then made little impression when replacing the injured Harbhajan Singh in England, although he did collect 84 as a nightwatchman at The Oval. The success of Ravichandran Ashwin and Pragyan Ojha – with Ravindra Jadeja also in the mix – meant that Mishra sat on the sidelines for almost two years until, recalled in mid-2013 while Ashwin and Ojha took a breather, he bamboozled the Zimbabweans with 18 wickets, a record for a five-match one-day series.

THE FACTS Mishra took 5 for 71 against Australia at Mohali in October 2008: he was only the sixth Indian to take a five-for on Test debut ... He took 6 for 66 for Haryana v Jharkhand in March 2005 ... Mishra came in as nightwatchman in the 2011 Oval Test, and made 84 ... He scored 202* for Haryana v Karnataka at Hubli in December 2012 ... Mishra took 18 wickets against Zimbabwe in 2013, a record for a five-match bilateral one-day series ...

THE FIGURES to 17.09.13   **cricinfo.com**

Batting & Fielding	M	Inns	NO	Runs	HS	Avge	S/R	100	50	4s	6s	Ct	St
Tests	13	19	2	392	84	23.05	58.24	0	2	50	2	6	0
ODIs	20	4	1	14	9	4.66	56.00	0	0	1	0	3	0
T20Is	1	–	–	–	–	–	–	–	–	–	–	0	0
First-class	123	174	25	3313	202*	22.23	–	1	13	–	–	63	0

Bowling	M	Balls	Runs	Wkts	BB	Avge	RpO	S/R	5i	10m
Tests	13	3497	1862	43	5–71	43.30	3.19	81.32	1	0
ODIs	20	1048	784	37	6–48	21.18	4.48	28.32	1	0
T20Is	1	24	21	1	1–21	21.00	5.25	24.00	0	0
First-class	123	26014	12970	448	6–66	28.95	2.99	58.06	20	1

MOHAMMAD HAFEEZ

PAKISTAN

Full name	**Mohammad Hafeez**
Born	**October 17, 1980, Sargodha, Punjab**
Teams	**Faisalabad, Sui Northern Gas**
Style	**Right-hand bat, offspinner**
Test debut	**Pakistan v Bangladesh at Karachi 2003**
ODI debut	**Pakistan v Zimbabwe at Sharjah 2002-03**
T20I debut	**Pakistan v England at Bristol 2006**

THE PROFILE For years Mohammad Hafeez – stylish opener, handy offspinner, brilliant fielder – was in and out of the Pakistan side. But finally he put together the sort of run that ensured he couldn't be dropped, and in 2012 took over as Twenty20 captain, suitable perhaps for someone with the nickname "Professor". His first chance followed the 2003 World Cup, after Pakistan's poor showing led to a clearout. Hafeez made 50 on debut and 102 in his second Test, against Bangladesh, but then struggled against South Africa – just 33 runs in five one-day innings – and was briefly dropped, then lost his place again early in 2005. He was not originally chosen for the 2006 England tour, but 180 against Australia A in Darwin in July, while Pakistan struggled to find an opening combination worth the name in England, led to a surprise call-up for the final Test at The Oval, and he made a tidy 95 before the ball-tampering row overshadowed everything. Another century followed against West Indies, but then he was left out for more than two years before a surprise recall for the World Twenty20 in the Caribbean and the one-day portion of the England tour later in 2010; a maiden ODI hundred followed in New Zealand early in 2011. After a consistent World Cup he was a star in the Caribbean – another one-day hundred and a surprise bowling hit, dismissing Devon Smith in six successive innings, often taking the new ball so he could get at the opener quickly. Hafeez confirmed his arrival with his first Test century for five years, against Zimbabwe in September 2011, and the following July added a seven-hour 196 against Sri Lanka in Colombo. In 2013 he boosted his ODI average with not-out centuries against Ireland and Zimbabwe, although he had less success in Tests.

THE FACTS Mohammad Hafeez scored 50 in his first Test, against Bangladesh in August 2003, and added 102* in his second, a week later ... He is the only man to open the batting and bowling in the same Test, ODI and T20I ... Hafeez scored 196 against Sri Lanka in Colombo in June 2012 ... He took 8 for 57 for Faisalabad v Quetta in December 2004 ...

THE FIGURES to 17.09.13 espncricinfo.com

Batting & Fielding	M	Inns	NO	Runs	HS	Avge	S/R	100	50	4s	6s	Ct	St
Tests	34	66	5	2061	196	33.78	53.71	5	8	261	12	24	0
ODIs	129	129	7	3527	139*	28.90	71.28	6	18	380	42	41	0
T20Is	47	45	1	1093	86	24.84	118.16	0	6	121	27	15	0
First-class	167	287	11	9560	196	34.63	–	20	46	–	–	143	0

Bowling	M	Balls	Runs	Wkts	BB	Avge	RpO	S/R	5i	10m
Tests	34	2693	1134	34	4-16	33.35	2.52	79.20	0	0
ODIs	129	5376	3589	104	3-17	34.50	4.00	51.69	0	0
T20Is	47	758	830	42	4-10	19.76	6.56	18.04	0	0
First-class	167	12785	5710	211	8-57	27.06	2.67	60.59	6	2

MOHAMMAD IRFAN

PAKISTAN

Full name **Mohammad Irfan**
Born **June 6, 1982, Gaggu Mandi, Punjab**
Teams **Baluchistan, Khan Research Laboratories**
Style **Right-hand bat, left-arm fast-medium bowler**
Test debut **Pakistan v South Africa at Cape Town 2012-13**
ODI debut **Pakistan v England at Chester-le-Street 2010**
T20I debut **Pakistan v India at Bangalore 2012-13**

THE PROFILE Few fast bowlers have generated as much advance publicity as Mohammad Irfan, selected at the relatively advanced age of 28 for the one-day portion of the 2010 England tour, after the first-choice new-ball bowlers Mohammad Aamer and Mohammad Asif were suspended during the spot-fixing affair. But the interest in Irfan was entirely unrelated to that sorry business: it concerned his height, which was variously reported as between 6ft 8ins and 7ft 4ins. Most people seem to have settled on 7ft 1in (216cm), which still makes him comfortably the tallest man ever to play international cricket. His early appearances failed to inspire: he looked nervous and cumbersome when he bowled, and also upset his captain with some amateurish fielding, dropping the century-bound Andrew Strauss early on at Headingley: "Cricket is not all about just batting and bowling, nowadays fielding is very important," said Shahid Afridi. It seemed that Irfan was a novelty act – but he went back to domestic cricket, worked on increasing his pace and fitness, and looked a different prospect when he was recalled in 2012, for a limited-overs series in India. He troubled everyone with his pace and bounce, and did likewise in South Africa in 2012-13. Irfan is from a rural town, and at one stage retired from cricket to work in a pipe factory to support his family. He was hooked out of club cricket to join the national academy, and was soon turning heads on the domestic scene, taking nine wickets in his second first-class match and 11 in his third: he ended 2009-10, his first season, with 43 wickets and a place in the preliminary squad for the World Twenty20 in the West Indies.

THE FACTS Mohammad Irfan is thought to be the tallest international player of all, surpassing Joel Garner and Bruce Reid (both 6ft 8ins/203cm) ... Irfan took 7 for 113 for Khan Research Laboratories v Habib Bank at Karachi in only his second first-class match, in October 2009, and added 5 for 27 and 6 for 96 for KRL v Karachi Whites a week later ...

THE FIGURES to 17.09.13 — ESPNcricinfo.com

Batting & Fielding	M	Inns	NO	Runs	HS	Avge	S/R	100	50	4s	6s	Ct	St
Tests	2	4	1	14	6*	4.66	26.41	0	0	1	0	0	0
ODIs	22	10	7	13	4*	4.33	38.23	0	0	2	0	5	0
T20Is	5	0	–	–	–	–	–	–	–	–	–	0	0
First-class	38	46	16	201	31	6.70	38.43	0	0	20	6	9	0

Bowling	M	Balls	Runs	Wkts	BB	Avge	RpO	S/R	5i	10m
Tests	2	317	201	3	3–86	67.00	3.80	105.66	0	0
ODIs	22	1073	821	30	4–33	27.36	4.59	35.76	0	0
T20Is	5	102	129	3	1–25	43.00	7.58	34.00	0	0
First-class	38	6211	3638	134	7–113	27.14	3.51	46.35	8	1

EOIN MORGAN

Full name **Eoin Joseph Gerard Morgan**
Born **September 10, 1986, Dublin, Ireland**
Teams **Middlesex, Kolkata Knight Riders**
Style **Left-hand bat, occasional right-arm medium-pacer**
Test debut **England v Bangladesh at Lord's 2010**
ODI debut **Ireland v Scotland at Ayr 2006**
T20I debut **England v Netherlands at Lord's 2009**

THE PROFILE Eoin Morgan is an impish batsman capable of inventive and audacious strokeplay, and he's a natural "finisher", a role England struggled to fill for a decade. A compact left-hander, he gained initial recognition with Ireland, playing 23 one-day internationals for them, although he was disappointing at the 2007 World Cup. He had joined his fellow Dubliner, Ed Joyce, at Middlesex in 2006, and two years later helped them win the Twenty20 Cup. In 2009 he was called up by England. After a quiet start in which his fielding was probably more impressive than his batting, Morgan did well as England won the World Twenty20 in the West Indies early in 2010 then, although not widely viewed as a five-day player, he was a surprise inclusion for the first Test of the home summer, against Bangladesh: he confidently collected his first boundary with a reverse-sweep. He added a gutsy 130 to set up victory over Pakistan in the first Test at Trent Bridge, and finished the season with a fine century to seal a 3-2 victory in a fractious one-day series. With a middle-order spot up for grabs in 2011, Morgan claimed it with 193 for the Lions against Sri Lanka, and cemented it with three gritty seventies before making 104 against India at Edgbaston ... all this despite adding a curious low squat in the stance. Morgan lost his Test place after struggling against Pakistan's spinners in the UAE early in 2012 – only 82 runs in six innings – but remained a one-day fixture, adding a century *against* his native country late in a 2013 season disrupted by a broken finger.

THE FACTS Morgan is the only player to be out (run out, too!) for 99 in his first ODI, v Scotland in August 2006 ... His first 23 ODIs were for Ireland: he made 744 runs at 35.42 for them ... Morgan hit 124* – and shared an ODI-record fifth-wicket stand of 226* with Ravi Bopara – for England v Ireland at Dublin in September 2013 ... He scored 209* for Ireland v UAE in Abu Dhabi in February 2007 ... Morgan was the third Irish-born player to score a Test century, after Fred Fane for England in 1905-06 and Australia's Tom Horan (1881-82) ...

THE FIGURES to 17.09.13   espncricinfo.com

Batting & Fielding	M	Inns	NO	Runs	HS	Avge	S/R	100	50	4s	6s	Ct	St
Tests	16	24	1	700	130	30.43	54.72	2	3	77	6	11	0
ODIs	107	101	21	3165	124*	39.56	86.07	5	19	269	65	45	0
T20Is	38	37	10	898	85*	33.25	131.47	0	4	80	32	20	0
First-class	78	127	15	3859	209*	34.45	51.13	9	18	–	–	63	1

Bowling	M	Balls	Runs	Wkts	BB	Avge	RpO	S/R	5i	10m
Tests	16	0	–	–	–	–	–	–	–	–
ODIs	107	0	–	–	–	–	–	–	–	–
T20Is	38	0	–	–	–	–	–	–	–	–
First-class	78	97	83	2	2–24	41.50	5.13	48.50	0	0

MORNE **MORKEL**

Full name	**Morne Morkel**
Born	**October 6, 1984, Vereeniging, Transvaal**
Teams	**Titans, Delhi Daredevils**
Style	**Left-hand bat, right-arm fast bowler**
Test debut	**South Africa v India at Durban 2006-07**
ODI debut	**Africa XI v Asia XI at Bangalore 2007**
T20I debut	**South Africa v West Indies at Johannesburg 2007-08**

THE PROFILE Morne Morkel, the taller, faster brother of Easterns allrounder Albie, has been a hot property ever since his first-class debut in 2003-04, when he and Albie put on 141 against the West Indians at Benoni. Morne excelled with 20 wickets at 18.20 apiece in 2004-05, and impressed Allan Donald: "He gets serious bounce, and he's got really great pace – genuine pace." Morkel used that to shake up the Indians for the Rest of South Africa in December 2006, bowling Sehwag with his first ball and adding Laxman, Tendulkar and Dhoni as the tourists lurched to 69 for 5. That earned him a call-up for the second Test when Dale Steyn was injured, although three wickets and some handy runs in a crushing victory weren't enough to keep him in when Steyn was fit again. A stress fracture temporarily halted the rise, but he returned in England in 2008, without ever quite being at his best as South Africa won the Test series. Early the following year Morne had the unusual experience of being replaced in the Test side by his brother, but later cemented his place with seven wickets in a crushing victory over England at Johannesburg, and six more in another comfortable win over West Indies at Port-of-Spain later in 2010. After that he took 15 in three matches against India at the turn of 2010-11, but was less effective on subcontinental pitches at the World Cup. Back on juicier tracks, though, he consistently proved a handful, taking 6 for 23 against New Zealand at Wellington in March 2012, then 11 wickets as South Africa won again in England to claim top spot in the Test rankings. The fast-bowling pair of Steyn and Morkel was the most-feared in the world, too.

THE FACTS Morkel took 6 for 43 and 6 for 48 for Titans v Eagles at Bloemfontein in March 2009, a week after being dropped from the Test side ... He took 6 for 23 v New Zealand at Wellington in March 2012 ... Morkel's first three ODIs were for the Africa XI: in one he opened the bowling with his brother Albie, the first instance of siblings sharing the new ball in an ODI since Kenya's Martin and Tony Suji during the 1999 World Cup ...

THE FIGURES to 17.09.13   espncricinfo.com

Batting & Fielding	M	Inns	NO	Runs	HS	Avge	S/R	100	50	4s	6s	Ct	St
Tests	49	57	9	657	40	13.68	50.07	0	0	102	2	12	0
ODIs	66	26	8	151	25	8.38	76.26	0	0	14	4	17	0
T20Is	34	3	1	8	6	4.00	100.00	0	0	0	1	4	0
First-class	85	103	15	1365	82*	15.51	49.81	0	4	–	–	32	0

Bowling	M	Balls	Runs	Wkts	BB	Avge	RpO	S/R	5i	10m
Tests	49	9646	5246	175	6–23	29.97	3.26	55.12	6	0
ODIs	66	3288	2677	111	5–38	24.11	4.88	29.62	1	0
T20Is	34	736	857	43	4–17	19.93	6.98	17.11	0	0
First-class	85	15631	8522	309	6–23	27.57	3.27	50.58	13	2

MUSHFIQUR RAHIM

BANGLADESH

Full name	Mohammad Mushfiqur Rahim
Born	September 1, 1988, Bogra
Teams	Rajshahi
Style	Right-hand bat, wicketkeeper
Test debut	Bangladesh v England at Lord's 2005
ODI debut	Bangladesh v Zimbabwe at Harare 2006
T20I debut	Bangladesh v Zimbabwe at Khulna 2006-07

THE PROFILE A wild-card inclusion for Bangladesh's maiden tour of England in 2005, the diminutive Mushfiqur Rahim was just 16 when he was selected for that daunting trip. He was principally chosen as understudy to long-serving wicketkeeper Khaled Mashud, but he had also shown signs of promise with the bat (a century in an A-team Test in Zimbabwe, and 88 against England Under-19s). He showed more evidence of grit with the full team, with a hundred at Northampton, which earned him a call-up – as a batsman – to become the youngest player to appear in a Test at Lord's: Mushfiqur was one of only three players to reach double figures in a disappointing first innings. Two years later he supplanted Mashud for the 2007 World Cup, anchoring the win over India with 56 not out, and soon established himself as the first-choice keeper. He is now one of Bangladesh's most consistent batsmen, and their captain too: he just missed a one-day hundred against Zimbabwe in August 2009, but made sure in Tests with 101 against India at Chittagong in January 2010, Bangladesh's fastest hundred in Tests at the time. After a modest 2011 World Cup with the bat, Mushfiqur bounced back with 126 runs for once out in three one-dayers against Australia, then made a 99-ball hundred in an ODI in Zimbabwe – although it was not enough to prevent another defeat on that embarrassing tour, after which he replaced Shakib Al Hasan as captain. The results remained disappointing, but Mushfiqur's batting kept getting better, and in Sri Lanka in March 2013 he compiled Bangladesh's first Test double-century shortly afterwards, though, he resigned the captaincy after a disappointing series in Zimbabwe – but was persuaded to carry on.

THE FACTS Mushfiqur Rahim's 200 against Sri Lanka at Galle in March 2013 was Bangladesh's first double-century in Tests … His hundred against Northants in 2005 made him the youngest century-maker in English first-class cricket: at 16 years 261 days old, he was 211 days younger than Sachin Tendulkar in 1990 … He had played two Tests before he appeared in a first-class match at home …

THE FIGURES to 17.09.13   espncricinfo.com

Batting & Fielding	M	Inns	NO	Runs	HS	Avge	S/R	100	50	4s	6s	Ct	St
Tests	34	66	4	1993	200	32.14	45.90	2	11	250	13	57	9
ODIs	119	109	19	2326	101	25.84	67.14	1	11	179	26	84	34
T20Is	29	26	6	335	41*	16.75	112.04	0	0	16	13	12	16
First-class	65	116	12	3458	200	33.25	–	4	21	–	–	111	16

Bowling	M	Balls	Runs	Wkts	BB	Avge	RpO	S/R	5i	10m
Tests	34	0	–	–	–	–	–	–	–	–
ODIs	119	0	–	–	–	–	–	–	–	–
T20Is	29	0	–	–	–	–	–	–	–	–
First-class	65	60	23	1	1–23	23.00	2.30	60.00	0	0

RICHMOND **MUTUMBAMI**

Full name	**Richmond Mutumbami**
Born	**June 11, 1989, Masvingo**
Teams	**Southern Rocks**
Style	**Right-hand bat, wicketkeeper**
Test debut	**Zimbabwe v Bangladesh at Harare 2012-13**
ODI debut	**No ODIs yet**
T20I debut	**No T20Is yet**

THE PROFILE A slightly built wicketkeeper, Richmond Mutumbami is also an aggressive middle-order batsman. He played a one-day game for Masvingo at 16, and made his first-class debut for Southerns (now Southern Rocks) in April 2007, when he was still not quite 18. He started with a duck, but had better luck with his keeping, taking four catches in each innings. It took him a while to make a mark with the bat, but he made a maiden century in March 2010 – a round 100 against Matabeleland Tuskers. He went in at No. 8, and put on 125 with Craig Ervine. Soon Mutumbami was creeping up the order, and in 2012-13 he blossomed, finishing as the leading scorer in the Zimbabwean domestic season, with 686 at 49. He started with 141 against Mashonaland Eagles at Harare, and later added a patient 150 against Mountaineers at Mutare in February 2013. Rather surprisingly, he was overlooked for Zimbabwe's tour of the West Indies shortly after that, but he was called up for the Tests against Bangladesh in April when Regis Chakabva was injured (Chakabva's batting had, in any case, been underwhelming). Mutumbami did little with the bat at first, collecting a golden duck in the second innings, but an attacking 42 in the second Test meant he kept his place for the Pakistan series later in the year. Again runs proved elusive, but his keeping was tidy: he took three catches in each innings of the first Test at Harare. Zimbabwe have been casting around for a keeper who can bat ever since Tatenda Taibu's surprise decision to quit cricket for the church, and Mutumbami has a chance to cement the position.

THE FACTS Mutumbami scored 150 for Southern Rocks against Mountaineers at Mutare in February 2013: earlier the same season he made 141 v Mashonaland Eagles at Harare ... Mutumbami took eight catches on his first-class debut, for Southerns v Easterns at Mutare in April 2007: he claimed eight more dismissals in his fourth game ... His brother, Ashby, has also played for Southern Rocks ...

THE FIGURES to 17.09.13

Batting & Fielding	M	Inns	NO	Runs	HS	Avge	S/R	100	50	4s	6s	Ct	St
Tests	4	8	1	131	42	18.71	49.74	0	0	18	1	12	2
ODIs	0	0	–	–	–	–	–	–	–	–	–	–	–
T20Is	0	0	–	–	–	–	–	–	–	–	–	–	–
First-class	47	81	4	2076	150	26.96	45.63	3	11	279	10	105	9

Bowling	M	Balls	Runs	Wkts	BB	Avge	RpO	S/R	5i	10m
Tests	4	0	–	–	–	–	–	–	–	–
ODIs	0	0	–	–	–	–	–	–	–	–
T20Is	0	0	–	–	–	–	–	–	–	–
First-class	47	81	163	3	2–121	54.33	12.07	27.00	0	0

SUNIL **NARINE**

Full name	**Sunil Philip Narine**
Born	**May 26, 1988, Trinidad**
Teams	**Trinidad & Tobago, Kolkata Knight Riders**
Style	**Left-hand bat, right-arm offspinner**
Test debut	**West Indies v England at Birmingham 2012**
ODI debut	**West Indies v India at Ahmedabad 2011-12**
T20I debut	**West Indies v Australia at Gros Islet 2011-12**

THE PROFILE Few cricketers have had as meteoric a rise as Sunil Narine, an unorthodox offspinner from Trinidad. Virtually unknown outside his native island, he bamboozled several distinguished batsmen during the Champions League T20 in India in October 2011, taking ten wickets with his mixture of offbreaks and hard-to-fathom "knuckle" balls, and was snapped up by Kolkata at the IPL auction the following spring for $700,000. He went on to be the player of the tournament as his side won their first IPL title. Narine took 24 wickets (more than anyone else except Morne Morkel) at an unmatched average of 13.50 and – arguably more importantly – went for less than five and a half runs per over. Just before this he had befuddled the Australians in the limited-overs portion of their tour of the Caribbean – they were highly relieved when Narine, without a West Indian contract at the time, toddled off to the IPL and missed the Tests. He was hurried back for the end of the 2012 England tour, and although rain ruined his Test debut there, he soon proved his worth with 32 wickets in the nine internationals of New Zealand's visit, including eight in a thumping Test victory on Antigua's usually batsman-friendly pitch in July. His Test returns since have been modest, but he continues to bewitch in the shorter formats. Narine originally came to notice by taking all ten wickets in a trial game, which led to his inclusion in the T&T squad early in 2009. Doubts were raised about his action a couple of years later, but remedial work with biomechanical experts in Australia, who made him go more side-on, seemed to do the trick.

THE FACTS Narine took only three wickets in his first three first-class matches for Trinidad, but then in February 2012 collected 5 for 22 and 8 for 17 against Combined Campuses & Colleges, 5 for 78 and 3 for 54 v Barbados, and 5 for 49 and 5 for 78 v Windward Islands ... His next match (his seventh) was his Test debut ... In the home ODIs against Australia early in 2012 Narine bowled 20 balls to Matthew Wade, and dismissed him three times ...

THE FIGURES to 17.09.13   **espncricinfo.com**

Batting & Fielding	M	Inns	NO	Runs	HS	Avge	S/R	100	50	4s	6s	Ct	St
Tests	5	5	1	38	22*	9.50	54.28	0	0	4	1	2	0
ODIs	39	27	5	258	36	11.72	79.14	0	0	24	8	8	0
T20Is	18	6	2	38	28	9.50	146.15	0	0	4	1	0	0
First-class	12	16	5	211	40*	19.18	–	0	0	–	–	10	0

Bowling	M	Balls	Runs	Wkts	BB	Avge	RpO	S/R	5i	10m
Tests	5	1299	721	15	5–132	48.06	3.33	86.60	1	0
ODIs	39	2123	1464	60	5–27	24.40	4.13	35.38	1	0
T20Is	18	406	402	24	4–12	16.75	5.94	16.91	0	0
First-class	12	2672	1268	59	8–17	21.49	2.84	45.28	7	3

NASIR HOSSAIN

BANGLADESH

Full name	**Mohammad Nasir Hossain**
Born	**November 30, 1991, Rangpur**
Teams	**Rangpur**
Style	**Right-hand bat, offspinner**
Test debut	**Bangladesh v West Indies at Chittagong 2011-12**
ODI debut	**Bangladesh v Zimbabwe at Harare 2011**
T20I debut	**Bangladesh v West Indies at Mirpur 2011-12**

THE PROFILE Nasir Hossain is a true allrounder: a batsman who can change gear according to the match situation, an offspinner with control and accuracy and – perhaps most excitingly – a fine fielder. So far it has been Nasir's batting which has been of most value to the national side: usually going in around No. 7 in a notoriously brittle batting order, he has added solidity. His first ten Tests brought him six half-centuries and, after nineties in his previous two Tests, a round 100 against Sri Lanka at Galle in March 2013. Nasir has also biffed a century in a one-day international – exactly 100 again – this time with Pakistan on the receiving end. He started well, with 63 in his first ODI, against Zimbabwe in October 2011, which led to a Test debut a couple of months later, when he was still a few weeks shy of his 20th birthday. Nasir had long been tipped for stardom: in 2004, when he was only 13, he joined BKSP, Bangladesh's only sports institute, quickly became an important member of their league team, and played in the Under-19 World Cup in 2008 at the age of 16. A move to Abahani, one of Dhaka's biggest clubs, was a risk – but he held his nerve in several tight games, including one where he had to open the bowling against Sanath Jayasuriya, who was playing for Mohammedans. Nasir started slowly in first-class cricket with Khulna, then moved to Rajshahi, for whom he recorded his maiden first-class hundred, against Khulna in February 2010. But he has looked more at home with his native Rangpur, after they were added to the domestic competition in 2011-12.

THE FACTS Nasir Hossain scored 100 in a Test against Sri Lanka at Galle in March 2013 – and 100 in an ODI against Pakistan at Mirpur in December 2011 ... He made 213 runs between dismissals in ODIs in 2012-13 – 39* v West Indies, 73* and 33* v Sri Lanka and 68 v Zimbabwe ... Nasir made 134, putting on 259 with Mominul Haque, in an A-team Test against West Indies in Antigua in November 2011 ...

THE FIGURES to 17.09.13   espncricinfo.com

Batting & Fielding	M	Inns	NO	Runs	HS	Avge	S/R	100	50	4s	6s	Ct	St
Tests	10	18	1	794	100	46.70	57.36	1	6	84	9	5	0
ODIs	25	22	5	771	100	45.35	80.56	1	6	68	9	12	0
T20Is	14	12	3	228	50*	25.33	120.63	0	2	21	4	6	0
First-class	41	70	4	2606	134	39.48	–	4	15	–	–	30	0

Bowling	M	Balls	Runs	Wkts	BB	Avge	RpO	S/R	5i	10m
Tests	10	600	267	3	3-52	89.00	2.67	200.00	0	0
ODIs	25	184	163	3	2-3	54.33	5.31	61.33	0	0
T20Is	14	12	14	1	1-14	14.00	7.00	12.00	0	0
First-class	41	2824	1299	38	3-22	34.18	2.75	74.31	0	0

NASIR JAMSHED

PAKISTAN

Full name	**Nasir Jamshed**
Born	**December 6, 1989, Lahore**
Teams	**Lahore, National Bank**
Style	**Left-hand bat**
Test debut	**Pakistan v South Africa at Johannesburg 2012-13**
ODI debut	**Pakistan v Zimbabwe at Karachi 2007-08**
T20I debut	**Pakistan v Australia at Dubai 2012-13**

THE PROFILE A hard-hitting left-hand opener prone to ugly hoicks but also capable of some lovely drives and pulls, Nasir Jamshed leapt to prominence early in 2008, called up for the one-day series against the touring Zimbabweans after flaying them for 182 from 240 balls in a warm-up game. He kick-started his international career with an awardwinning 61 (from 48 balls) in the first game, and 74 (from 64 balls with 14 fours) in the second. Leaner pickings followed, almost inevitably, until he peeled off successive unbeaten scores of 53 and 52 against India and Bangladesh in the Asia Cup in July. It looked as if he had nailed down a spot: but a poor run later in the year in Sri Lanka cost him his place, not helped by murmurs about his weight and attitude to training. It was 30 months before Jamshed was recalled, for the Asia Cup in Bangladesh in March 2012, but he made 54 in his first match before hitting 112 against India. Then, at the turn of 2012-13, he clouted two centuries in successive matches, with India on the receiving end again. That finally earned him a Test chance, in South Africa – but 46 in the second innings of his debut in Johannesburg, after Pakistan had been humbled for 49 in the first, was his only decent score, and he was confined to one-day duty again in Zimbabwe later in 2013. Jamshed made his first-class debut shortly after turning 15, and made 74. Three seasons later, in 2007-08, he topped the domestic first-class run-lists with 1353 – 800 of them in the Quaid-e-Azam Trophy – including six centuries, which earned him that initial run in the national team.

THE FACTS Nasir Jamshed made 74 on his first-class debut for National Bank v Defence Housing Authority in February 2005, two months after his 15th birthday ... The following month he made 204 for Pakistan Under-19s in the first Test against Sri Lanka in Karachi ... Jamshed scored 61 and 74 in his first two ODIs, against Zimbabwe in January 2008 ...

THE FIGURES to 17.09.13   espncricinfo.com

Batting & Fielding	M	Inns	NO	Runs	HS	Avge	S/R	100	50	4s	6s	Ct	St
Tests	2	4	0	51	46	12.75	47.66	0	0	8	0	1	0
ODIs	39	39	3	1356	112	37.66	78.06	3	8	147	18	12	0
T20Is	15	15	1	307	56	21.92	119.92	0	2	25	12	4	0
First-class	75	131	8	5117	182	41.60	–	15	23	–	–	64	0

Bowling	M	Balls	Runs	Wkts	BB	Avge	RpO	S/R	5i	10m
Tests	2	0	–	–	–	–	–	–	–	–
ODIs	39	0	–	–	–	–	–	–	–	–
T20Is	15	0	–	–	–	–	–	–	–	–
First-class	75	12	8	0	–	–	4.00	–	0	0

PRAGYAN OJHA

Full name	Pragyan Prayash Ojha
Born	September 5, 1986, Bhubaneshwar
Teams	Hyderabad, Mumbai Indians
Style	Left-hand bat, left-arm orthodox spinner
Test debut	India v Sri Lanka at Kanpur 2009-10
ODI debut	India v Bangladesh at Karachi 2008
T20I debut	India v Bangladesh at Nottingham 2009

THE PROFILE A left-arm spinner of teasing flight and pleasing loop, Pragyan Ojha made a stunning start in first-class cricket: in the Ranji Trophy semi-final in March 2005, he took the first five wickets to fall in eventual champions Railways' first innings, starting with the Test allrounder Sanjay Bangar. Ojha showed his control in the inaugural IPL in 2008: with 11 wickets, then took 21 – four more than anyone else – in 2010. He also made an immediate impact in his first ODI, in the Asia Cup in June 2008, with three outfield catches and an absolute ripper which foxed Bangladesh's Raqibul Hasan. Ojha started the 2009 World Twenty20 in England well, taking a wicket with his first ball on the way to 4 for 21 against Bangladesh, but was omitted later in the tournament, then missed out as legspinner Amit Mishra was tried as Harbhajan Singh's partner. But Ojha did win his first Test cap late in 2009, taking a catch off his first ball in the field, and collected 21 wickets in his first six matches, with seven – including danger men Sangakkara and Jayawardene in both innings – as India squared the series in Sri Lanka in August 2010. By 2012 he was forming a potent spin partnership with Ravichandran Ashwin – they claimed 103 wickets between them in their first eight Tests together – with Ojha taking six-fors against West Indies at Delhi and Mumbai, and adding 5 for 99 as New Zealand went down fighting in Bangalore in September 2012. He added 20 wickets in the series defeat by England, and although omitted in favour of Harbhajan for the start of the Australian series early in 2013, he was back to take seven wickets as the whitewash was completed at Mohali and Delhi.

THE FACTS Ojha took a wicket (Bangladesh's Shakib Al Hasan) with his first ball in Twenty20 internationals, at Trent Bridge in June 2009, and finished with 4 for 21 ... On his first-class debut, against Railways at Delhi in March 2005, Ojha took the first five wickets to fall, finishing with 5 for 55 ... Ojha took 7 for 114 for Hyderabad v Rajasthan in December 2006: the previous week he took 6 for 84 against Maharashtra ...

THE FIGURES to 17.09.13   espncricinfo.com

Batting & Fielding	M	Inns	NO	Runs	HS	Avge	S/R	100	50	4s	6s	Ct	St
Tests	22	25	16	87	18*	9.66	17.93	0	0	6	0	8	0
ODIs	18	10	8	46	16*	23.00	41.07	0	0	3	0	7	0
T20Is	6	1	1	10	10*	–	166.66	0	0	0	1	1	0
First-class	71	90	36	509	35	9.42	28.67	0	0	51	1	25	0

Bowling	M	Balls	Runs	Wkts	BB	Avge	RpO	S/R	5i	10m
Tests	22	7235	3242	102	6–47	31.78	2.68	70.93	5	0
ODIs	18	876	652	21	4–38	31.04	4.46	41.71	0	0
T20Is	6	126	132	10	4–21	13.20	6.28	12.60	0	0
First-class	71	18376	8676	309	7–114	28.07	2.83	59.46	18	1

GRAHAM **ONIONS**

Full name	Graham Onions
Born	September 9, 1982, Gateshead
Teams	Durham
Style	Right-hand bat, right-arm fast-medium bowler
Test debut	England v West Indies at Lord's 2009
ODI debut	England v Australia at Chester-le-Street 2009
T20I debut	No T20Is yet

THE PROFILE A brisk seam bowler, with a name that is a headline-writer's dream (especially when Durham's keeper Phil Mustard does the catching), Graham Onions first took the eye in 2006, with 54 wickets. He maintained an impressive workload for Durham, and didn't just take wickets on helpful surfaces at Chester-le-Street. The following two seasons were more of a struggle, but Onions began 2009 in rare form, and made the early-season Tests against West Indies. He started in fairytale fashion at Lord's, mopping up the tail with four wickets in seven balls to finish with 5 for 38, bowling at a lively pace and swinging the ball away. He played in three of the Ashes Tests without quite recapturing this form. Although he was left out for the final Test he was at The Oval as the urn was regained, then returned to Durham as they retained the Championship. After that he picked up 11 wickets in three Tests in South Africa – although he will be better remembered for his obstinate batting, twice surviving the last over to stave off defeats. But he also picked up a stress fracture in the back, which wiped out the whole of 2010. Onions returned to form and fitness the following year, taking 53 first-class wickets, and he played one Test in 2012, although more noteworthy was what happened when he was left out of the final XI for the Lord's Test against South Africa in August. Onions drove to Nottingham, missed his lunch, and went out and took 9 for 67 for Durham. And he ran the tenth one out, for good measure. Another fine season followed in 2013, as Durham won the Championship again, although he could not quite regain his Test place.

THE FACTS Onions took 9 for 67 for Durham v Nottinghamshire at Trent Bridge in 2012: he ran the other man out with a direct hit ... At Edgbaston in July 2009 Onions took wickets with the first two balls of the second day's play against Australia: this is believed to have happened only once before in Test history, when Australia's "Chuck" Fleetwood-Smith did it against England at Melbourne in 1936-37 ...

THE FIGURES to 17.09.13

Batting & Fielding	M	Inns	NO	Runs	HS	Avge	S/R	100	50	4s	6s	Ct	St
Tests	9	10	7	30	17*	10.00	30.92	0	0	4	0	0	0
ODIs	4	1	0	1	1	1.00	50.00	0	0	0	0	1	0
T20Is	0	0	–	–	–	–	–	–	–	–	–	–	–
First-class	112	146	51	1237	41	13.02	52.17	0	0	–	–	25	0

Bowling	M	Balls	Runs	Wkts	BB	Avge	RpO	S/R	5i	10m
Tests	9	1606	957	32	5–38	29.90	3.57	50.18	1	0
ODIs	4	204	185	4	2–58	46.25	5.44	51.00	0	0
T20Is	0	0	–	–	–	–	–	–	–	–
First-class	112	19327	11043	424	9–67	26.04	3.42	45.58	21	3

MONTY **PANESAR**

ENGLAND

Full name **Mudhsuden Singh Panesar**
Born **April 25, 1982, Luton, Bedfordshire**
Teams **Sussex, Essex**
Style **Left-hand bat, slow left-arm orthodox spinner**
Test debut **England v India at Nagpur 2005-06**
ODI debut **England v Australia at Melbourne 2006-07**
T20I debut **England v Australia at Sydney 2006-07**

THE PROFILE Monty Panesar made himself a cult hero to English crowds enchanted by his enthusiastic celebrations and endearingly erratic fielding. That, and equally amateurish batting, had threatened to hold him back, but when Ashley Giles was ruled out of the 2005-06 Indian tour Panesar received a late summons. He's a throwback to an earlier slow left-armer, Bishan Bedi, who also twirled away for Northants in a patka, teasing and tempting with flight and guile, although Panesar gives it more of a rip. In 2005 he took 46 Championship wickets at 21.54, and made his Test debut at Nagpur that winter, picking up Sachin Tendulkar as his first wicket. At home in 2006 he delivered the ball of the season to bowl Younis Khan and set up victory at Leeds; next summer he claimed 31 wickets in seven home Tests, and remained the crowd's favourite as Montymania showed no sign of abating. But he struggled in Sri Lanka at the end of 2007, while his antics and frequent appealing rubbed some up the wrong way. By the start of 2009 he had lost his place as England's No. 1 spinner to Graeme Swann (ironically, since Panesar's arrival had hastened Swann's departure from Northants), and his only contribution to the Ashes series was an unlikely match-saving display with the bat in the first Test. A move to Sussex paid off: Panesar passed 50 wickets in both 2010 and 2011. Early the next year he took Test five-fors against Pakistan in Abu Dhabi and Dubai, then late in the year claimed 11 wickets at Mumbai then five in the next Test as England rallied to win from behind. He was less impressive in New Zealand, where he played as the sole spinner as Swann was injured, and did not feature at home in 2013. His love affair with Sussex came to a soggy end with a drunken incident outside a Brighton nightspot, and Panesar decamped to Essex.

THE FACTS Panesar took 7 for 60 (13 for 137 in the match) for Sussex v Somerset at Taunton in August 2012 ... He was the first Sikh to play Test cricket for anyone other than India ... Panesar took 6 for 37 for England v New Zealand at Old Trafford in 2008 ... He averages 25.00 in Tests against West Indies – but 44.90 v Australia ...

THE FIGURES *to 17.09.13*   **espncricinfo.com**

Batting & Fielding	M	Inns	NO	Runs	HS	Avge	S/R	100	50	4s	6s	Ct	St
Tests	48	64	23	216	26	5.26	31.53	0	0	23	1	10	0
ODIs	26	8	3	26	13	5.20	28.57	0	0	2	0	3	0
T20Is	1	1	0	1	1	1.00	50.00	0	0	0	0	0	0
First-class	193	237	80	1347	46*	8.57	34.43	0	0	–	–	38	0

Bowling	M	Balls	Runs	Wkts	BB	Avge	RpO	S/R	5i	10m
Tests	48	12050	5540	164	6–37	33.78	2.75	73.47	12	2
ODIs	26	1308	980	24	3–25	40.83	4.49	54.50	0	0
T20Is	1	24	40	2	2–40	20.00	10.00	12.00	0	0
First-class	193	43629	19743	637	7–60	30.99	2.71	68.49	34	5

IRFAN **PATHAN**

Full name **Irfan Khan Pathan**
Born **October 27, 1984, Baroda, Gujarat**
Teams **Baroda, Delhi Daredevils**
Style **Left-hand bat, left-arm fast-medium bowler**
Test debut **India v Australia at Adelaide 2003-04**
ODI debut **India v Australia at Melbourne 2003-04**
T20I debut **India v South Africa at Johannesburg 2006-07**

INDIA

THE PROFILE Irfan Pathan was initially rated the most talented swing and seam bowler to emerge from India since Kapil Dev, and was soon being thought of as a possible successor for Kapil in the allround department too. He was strikingly composed in his Test debut at 19. A potent left-armer's outswinger helped him to a hat-trick in the first over of the Karachi Test in January 2006, and he could reverse it too, although his pace has reduced in recent years. When batting, he was regularly pushed up the order, sometimes even opening in one-dayers. At No. 3 he produced a spectacular 83 against Sri Lanka, and he often bailed India out in Tests as well, with 93 and 82 against Sri Lanka late in 2005. After that he struggled with shoulder trouble, but returned to the one-day side in 2007, then celebrated his first Test for 19 months – against Pakistan in December – by clubbing his first century, reaching it with his fourth six. Early in 2008 he played two important innings and took five wickets as Australia were beaten at Perth, but after that other left-arm pacemen shoved him down the queue. After the World Twenty20 in England in 2009 Pathan disappeared from the national scene, seemingly for good – but he popped up in the one-day team again in 2012, taking 4 for 32 against Sri Lanka in the Asia Cup in March, and 5 for 61 against them at Pallekele later in the year. In 2013 he was part of the Champions Trophy-winning squad, before missing the tri-series in the West Indies with a hamstring strain. A Test return looks unlikely, but since he's still only 29 there's time for that too.

THE FACTS Pathan was the first bowler to take a hat-trick in the first over of a Test match, when he dismissed Salman Butt, Younis Khan and Mohammad Yousuf at Karachi in January 2006: from 0 for 3, Pakistan recovered to win by 341 runs ... Pathan took 12 for 126 in the match against Zimbabwe at Harare in September 2005 ... He is one of only seven players to have scored a century and taken a hat-trick in Tests ... His half-brother Yusuf Pathan has also played for India ...

THE FIGURES to 17.09.13   **cricinfo.com**

Batting & Fielding	M	Inns	NO	Runs	HS	Avge	S/R	100	50	4s	6s	Ct	St
Tests	29	40	5	1105	102	31.57	53.22	1	6	131	18	8	0
ODIs	120	87	21	1544	83	23.39	79.54	0	5	142	37	21	0
T20Is	24	14	7	172	33*	24.57	119.44	0	0	9	7	2	0
First-class	94	129	24	3303	121	31.45	–	3	18	–	–	27	0

Bowling	M	Balls	Runs	Wkts	BB	Avge	RpO	S/R	5i	10m
Tests	29	5884	3226	100	7–59	32.26	3.28	58.84	7	2
ODIs	120	5855	5143	173	5–27	29.72	5.27	33.84	2	0
T20Is	24	462	618	28	3–16	22.07	8.02	16.50	0	0
First-class	94	17495	9251	324	7–35	28.55	3.17	53.99	17	3

JAMES **PATTINSON**

Full name	**James Lee Pattinson**
Born	**May 3, 1990, Melbourne**
Teams	**Victoria**
Style	**Left-hand bat, right-arm fast-medium bowler**
Test debut	**Australia v New Zealand at Brisbane 2011-12**
ODI debut	**Australia v Bangladesh at Mirpur 2010-11**
T20I debut	**Australia v South Africa at Cape Town 2011-12**

THE PROFILE A strong fast bowler who hits the bat hard, James Pattinson will be one of Australia's players to watch over the next few years – or so the selectors thought when they surprised him with a national contract in 2011. He made a dream start in Test cricket, demolishing New Zealand at Brisbane in December with 5 for 27, and adding 5 for 51 in the next Test at Hobart. After four Tests he had 25 wickets, but a back injury led to an early return home from the West Indies in mid-2012. He caught the eye again at home in 2012-13, with five wickets against South Africa, then toiled hard in the heat of Chennai to take 5 for 96. He started the 2013 Ashes with five wickets at Trent Bridge, but joined the long casualty list of Australian bowlers after the Lord's Test, returning home with a stress fracture of the back. Pattinson had first made his mark in one-day cricket: in December 2009 he swung the ball impressively against New South Wales at the SCG, finishing with 6 for 48, the best figures by a Victorian in a domestic one-day game, breaking Graeme Watson's 40-year-old record. He is the younger brother of the former Nottinghamshire seamer Darren Pattinson – with whom he competes for a spot in the Victoria side – who played one Test for England in 2008. Unlike Darren, who was born in Grimsby, James popped out in Melbourne after the family emigrated, so his only passport is an Australian one. James honed his skills against his brother, who is ten years older, in the back yard of their Melbourne home: both of them played for the Dandenong club in the eastern suburbs.

THE FACTS Pattinson took 6 for 32 for Victoria v Queensland at Brisbane in October 2012 ... He took 5 for 27 (singlehandedly reducing New Zealand to 28 for 5) on his Test debut at Brisbane in December 2011 ... His brother Darren played one match for England in 2008: they were the first brothers to play Test cricket for different countries since the 19th century ...

THE FIGURES to 17.09.13   **ESPNcricinfo.com**

Batting & Fielding	M	Inns	NO	Runs	HS	Avge	S/R	100	50	4s	6s	Ct	St
Tests	12	18	7	331	42	30.09	40.07	0	0	38	3	1	0
ODIs	11	6	3	36	13	12.00	57.14	0	0	2	0	2	0
T20Is	4	2	2	5	5*	–	166.66	0	0	1	0	3	0
First-class	29	38	9	620	66	21.37	38.50	0	1	66	3	7	0

Bowling	M	Balls	Runs	Wkts	BB	Avge	RpO	S/R	5i	10m
Tests	12	2275	1242	47	5–27	26.42	3.27	48.40	3	0
ODIs	11	553	468	15	4–51	31.20	5.07	36.86	0	0
T20Is	4	78	104	3	2–17	34.66	8.00	26.00	0	0
First-class	29	5400	2861	120	6–32	23.84	3.17	45.00	4	0

THISARA **PERERA**

Full name **Narangoda Liyanaarachchilage Thisara Chirantha Perera**
Born **April 3, 1989, Colombo**
Teams **Colts, Uthura, Sunrisers Hyderabad**
Style **Left-hand bat, right-arm fast-medium bowler**
Test debut **Sri Lanka v England at Cardiff 2011**
ODI debut **Sri Lanka v India at Kolkata 2009-10**
T20I debut **Sri Lanka v Zimbabwe at Providence 2009-10**

THE PROFILE A big-hitting left-hander who also bowls at a lively pace, Thisara Perera was originally primarily seen as a bowler, taking the new ball for the national under-19 side. He played in the Under-19 World Cup in 2008, and received his first senior call late the following year, replacing the injured Angelo Mathews on tour in India. Perera made his ODI debut there, hammering 31 from just 14 balls at the death. He proved less successful with the ball – none for 66 from nine overs as Gautam Gambhir and Virat Kohli gambolled to centuries. Two matches later he was at it again, slamming 36 from 15 balls to set up another victory, one which improved his bank balance as it led to an IPL contract. Then his bowling kicked in: 5 for 28 as India were skittled for 103 at Dambulla in August 2010, and not long afterwards he bounced in combatively at Melbourne for another five-for, his victims including Michael Clarke and Brad Haddin. After being a fringe performer at the 2011 World Cup – he played only four matches, but that did include the final, in which he slammed 22 from nine balls and took one expensive wicket – Perera made his Test debut at Cardiff in 2011. He made 25 in the first innings and 20 in the second ... but that was the top score as Sri Lanka crashed to 82 all out and a defeat that had looked impossible when the last day began. He hasn't done much in Tests yet, beyond 75 against Pakistan at Pallekele in July 2012 (in his last Test to date, as it happens), but has started to make his mark in the shorter formats, maintaining a phenomenal strike-rate with the bat, and taking wickets consistently with the ball.

THE FACTS Perera took 5 for 28 as India were bowled out for 103 at Dambulla in August 2010, and 5 for 46 v Australia at Melbourne six weeks later ... He took 6 for 44 in an ODI against Pakistan at Pallekele in June 2012 ... Perera scored 113*, with eight sixes, for Colts v Moors in December 2009, then took a career-best 5 for 69 when Moors batted ...

THE FIGURES to 17.09.13   ESPNcricinfo.com

Batting & Fielding	M	Inns	NO	Runs	HS	Avge	S/R	100	50	4s	6s	Ct	St
Tests	6	10	0	203	75	20.30	73.02	0	1	21	4	1	0
ODIs	63	45	9	630	69*	17.50	109.56	0	2	52	21	24	0
T20Is	27	23	12	291	35*	26.45	154.78	0	0	20	17	9	0
First-class	28	45	6	1225	113*	31.41	87.31	1	7	111	49	19	0

Bowling	M	Balls	Runs	Wkts	BB	Avge	RpO	S/R	5i	10m
Tests	6	954	653	11	4-63	59.36	4.10	86.72	0	0
ODIs	63	2375	2161	82	6-44	26.35	5.45	28.96	3	0
T20Is	27	322	430	16	2-19	26.87	8.01	20.12	0	0
First-class	28	3101	1960	47	5-69	41.70	3.79	65.97	1	0

ALVIRO **PETERSEN**

Full name	**Alviro Nathan Petersen**
Born	**November 25, 1980, Port Elizabeth**
Teams	**Lions, Somerset**
Style	**Right-hand bat, occasional medium-pacer**
Test debut	**South Africa v India at Kolkata 2009-10**
ODI debut	**South Africa v Zimbabwe at East London 2006-07**
T20I debut	**South Africa v West Indies at North Sound 2009-10**

THE PROFILE Alviro Petersen grew up in the suburbs of Cape Town, honing his skills at the Gelvandale club, which also produced Ashwell Prince. A century in only his second first-class match kick-started his career in 2001-02, and he was soon playing for South Africa A: but the next step eluded him until 2006, when he hit 80 against Zimbabwe in his second one-day international. However, opportunities at the top of the order were few, and by mid-2008 Petersen had played only three more one-dayers. But it all changed in 2008-09, when he hit a record 1376 first-class runs, including six centuries. With Gibbs out of favour, Petersen was given another one-day chance, and capitalised with half-centuries in each of his three innings against England. That got him on the plane to India, and he finally made his Test debut at 29 in February 2010. He opened, with his old pal Prince sliding down the order, and made a round 100, pulling and hooking well. It was a particularly sweet moment for Petersen's father, Isaac, who had driven journalists around Cape Town for years and rarely missed an opportunity to remind them of his son's abilities. However, eight further Tests produced only three fifties, and Petersen agreed a return to Glamorgan (who he captained in 2011) as a Kolpak player. But a surprise Test recall in January 2012 resulted in a century against Sri Lanka – and a change of mind (and county: he appeared as an overseas player for Essex in 2012 and Somerset in 2013). He added 156 against New Zealand then, after a duck in the run-fest at The Oval, Petersen made 182 in nearly nine hours against England at Headingley in August.

THE FACTS At Kolkata in February 2010 Petersen became only the third South African to score a century on Test debut, after Andrew Hudson (in 1991-92) and Jacques Rudolph (2002-03) ... Petersen's 210 for Glamorgan v Surrey in May 2011, contained every scoring shot from one to seven ... He scored 129 and 105* for Lions v Titans in April 2009, and finished the season with 1376 runs, a South African record ...

THE FIGURES to 17.09.13   espncricinfo.com

Batting & Fielding	M	Inns	NO	Runs	HS	Avge	S/R	100	50	4s	6s	Ct	St
Tests	24	43	2	1589	182	38.75	50.86	5	5	192	9	19	0
ODIs	21	19	1	504	80	28.00	82.62	0	4	54	3	5	0
T20Is	2	2	0	14	8	7.00	73.68	0	0	1	0	1	0
First-class	163	289	14	10915	210	39.69	–	33	43	–	–	126	0

Bowling	M	Balls	Runs	Wkts	BB	Avge	RpO	S/R	5i	10m
Tests	24	114	62	1	1–2	62.00	3.26	114.00	0	0
ODIs	21	6	7	0	–	–	7.00	–	0	0
T20Is	2	0	–	–	–	–	–	–	–	–
First-class	163	1244	660	12	2–7	55.00	3.18	103.66	0	0

ROBIN **PETERSON**

Full name	**Robin John Peterson**
Born	**August 4, 1979, Port Elizabeth**
Teams	**Cape Cobras**
Style	**Left-hand bat, slow left-arm orthodox spinner**
Test debut	**South Africa v Bangladesh at Dhaka 2003**
ODI debut	**South Africa v India at Colombo 2002**
T20I debut	**South Africa v Australia at Johannesburg 2006**

THE PROFILE For almost a decade it seemed as if Robin Peterson was going to be a nearly man in Test cricket: he was a handy batsman and a superb fielder, but his left-arm spin looked just too plain for the five-day game, although he does have a doosra, which slants in to the right-handers. He was a regular in South Africa's one-day squads, but by November 2012 had played only six Tests since 2003, the last of them four years previously, and 11 of his 14 wickets had come against Bangladesh. And then a funny thing happened. After Imran Tahir was mercilessly mauled by the Aussies at Adelaide, Peterson played in the third Test, on the traditional spinners' graveyard at Perth – and claimed six wickets, including Ricky Ponting in his final innings. Finally given a run as the No. 1 spinner, Peterson did reasonably well against New Zealand and Pakistan – and suddenly looked at home in Test cricket. The highlight of his "first" career was 5 for 33 against Bangladesh early in 2008, the lowlight being pummelled for a Test-record 28 runs in an over by Brian Lara at the end of 2003. The amiable Peterson has taken part in three World Cups, although he made only three appearances in 2003 and 2007 before a more central role on subcontinental tracks in 2011, when his 15 wickets included reducing England to 15 for 3 after being handed the new ball at Chennai. Still, he is probably best-remembered for a batting feat: his thick-edged four completed a last-gasp victory over Sri Lanka in Guyana in 2007 after Lasith Malinga's four wickets in four balls had derailed what had seemed a routine run-chase.

THE FACTS Peterson's unlucky 13th over against West Indies at Johannesburg in December 2003 was the most expensive in Test history: Brian Lara hit it for 28 (466444) ... Peterson made 130 for Eastern Province v Gauteng at Johannesburg in October 2002 ... He also made 108 for South Africa A v India A at Bloemfontein in April 2002 ... Peterson took 6 for 67 for Eastern Province v Border at East London in December 1999, and 6 for 16 in a one-day game for EP v Namibia in November 2002 ...

THE FIGURES to 17.09.13

Batting & Fielding	M	Inns	NO	Runs	HS	Avge	S/R	100	50	4s	6s	Ct	St
Tests	12	15	2	320	84	24.61	68.23	0	2	43	1	8	0
ODIs	76	39	14	543	68	21.72	80.56	0	1	51	4	27	0
T20Is	20	11	3	120	34	15.00	110.09	0	0	13	2	9	0
First-class	130	197	24	4384	130	25.34	–	6	17	–	–	63	0

Bowling	M	Balls	Runs	Wkts	BB	Avge	RpO	S/R	5i	10m
Tests	12	1862	1006	31	5–33	32.45	3.24	60.06	1	0
ODIs	76	3163	2575	70	4–12	36.78	4.88	45.18	0	0
T20Is	20	335	423	21	3–30	20.14	7.57	15.95	0	0
First-class	130	23364	11730	368	6–67	31.87	3.01	63.48	15	1

VERNON **PHILANDER**

Full name **Vernon Darryl Philander**
Born **June 24, 1985, Bellville**
Teams **Cape Cobras, Kent**
Style **Right-hand bat, right-arm fast-medium bowler**
Test debut **South Africa v Australia at Cape Town 2011-12**
ODI debut **South Africa v Ireland at Belfast 2007**
T20I debut **South Africa v West Indies at Johannesburg 2007-08**

THE PROFILE The possessor of one of international cricket's more remarkable surnames (Brian Johnston would have loved it, and his initials), the muscular Vernon Philander is a powerful allrounder – mainly a bowler who swings the ball at a decent pace, but also a handy batsman whose two forthright innings did much to tilt the 2012 Lord's Test South Africa's way. After a good domestic season, Philander received his first international call-up in 2007 for a low-key tour of Ireland, and in his first match – on his 22nd birthday – he took 4 for 12 to make sure the Irish did not approach South Africa's modest total in a rain-hit game. Philander played a few Twenty20 internationals before apparently fading out of the picture. It seemed that his face didn't fit ... but he was still a force in domestic cricket, following 56 wickets at less than 13 apiece in 2009-10 with 35 at 16 next season, and eventually the selectors brought him back, to face Australia in the criminally short two-Test series late in 2011. Philander made hay, and hasn't stopped harvesting since. He marked his debut with 5 for 15 as Australia were rolled for 47 at Cape Town, collected another five-for in the next Test, then ten in victory over Sri Lanka at Centurion. Philander sprinted to 50 wickets in just seven Tests: only one man has ever done it quicker. And the success continued in England, where he took 5 for 30 at Lord's as South Africa cemented their rise to the No. 1 Test ranking. He finally went wicketless at Brisbane in November 2012 (0 for 103), but it proved only a temporary blip: there were seven wickets against New Zealand at Cape Town, then 15 in three matches against Pakistan – including nine in a tight encounter at Cape Town in February 2013.

THE FACTS Philander reached 50 wickets in only his seventh Test: only Charles Turner, the 19th-century Australian, got there quicker (six) ... Philander's strike-rate of 36.84 balls per wicket is the best by any current bowler ... He scored 168 for Western Province v Griqualand West at Kimberley in November 2004, in only his fourth first-class match ... He took 7 for 61 for Cape Cobras v Knights at Cape Town in February 2012 ...

THE FIGURES *to 17.09.13*   **cricinfo.com**

Batting & Fielding	M	Inns	NO	Runs	HS	Avge	S/R	100	50	4s	6s	Ct	St
Tests	16	19	3	364	74	22.75	49.65	0	2	41	3	5	0
ODIs	8	6	3	75	23	25.00	85.22	0	0	7	0	2	0
T20Is	7	4	0	14	6	3.50	50.00	0	0	0	0	1	0
First-class	99	128	19	2765	168	25.36	47.73	2	8	–	–	26	0

Bowling	M	Balls	Runs	Wkts	BB	Avge	RpO	S/R	5i	10m
Tests	16	3279	1525	89	6–44	17.13	2.79	36.84	9	2
ODIs	8	311	248	7	4–12	35.42	4.78	44.42	0	0
T20Is	7	83	114	4	2–23	28.50	8.24	20.75	0	0
First-class	99	17615	7723	382	7–61	20.21	2.63	46.11	20	2

KEVIN **PIETERSEN**

ENGLAND

Full name	Kevin Peter Pietersen
Born	June 27, 1980, Pietermaritzburg, Natal, South Africa
Teams	Surrey
Style	Right-hand bat, offspinner
Test debut	England v Australia at Lord's 2005
ODI debut	England v Zimbabwe at Harare 2004-05
T20I debut	England v Australia at Southampton 2005

THE PROFILE Expansive with bat and explosive with bombast, Kevin Pietersen is not one for the quiet life. Bold-minded and big-hitting, he first ruffled feathers by quitting South Africa – he was disenchanted with the race-quota system – in favour of England, his eligibility coming courtesy of an English mother. As soon as he was eligible, he was chosen for a one-day series in Zimbabwe, where he averaged 104. Then, in South Africa, he hammered a robust century in the second match, undeterred by hostile crowds. Test cricket was next. In 2005 he replaced Graham Thorpe, against Australia, at Lord's ... and coolly blasted a brace of fifties. Then, with the Ashes at stake, he hit 158 on the final day at The Oval: "KP" had arrived. The runs kept coming: 158 at Adelaide and 226 against West Indies at Headingley sandwiched two tons in the 2007 World Cup. Late the following year he succeeded Michael Vaughan as captain, starting with a hundred as South Africa were beaten in the Oval Test. But his captaincy ended in tears after a fallout with the coach, then his form dipped as he battled an Achilles problem. But just as people were beginning to wonder, Pietersen hammered 227 at Adelaide in December 2010 then hit another double-century against India at Lord's and 175 at The Oval to emphasise that he wasn't going anywhere just yet. Things went pear-shaped, though, in 2012: Pietersen was dropped – despite just having stroked a superb 149 – from the final Test of the summer, after it emerged that he had been texting the South Africans with derogatory remarks about Andrew Strauss. He was soon "reintegrated", and celebrated with a superb 186 at Mumbai. A dicky knee restricted him a little in 2013, although he played his part in the retention of the Ashes, with 113 at Old Trafford.

THE FACTS Pietersen reached 100 against South Africa at East London in February 2005 in 69 balls, the fastest for England in ODIs ... He averages 64.60 in ODIs v South Africa – but 14.80 v Bangladesh ... Pietersen was out for 158 three times in Tests before going on to 226 against West Indies in May 2007 ... His record includes two ODIs for the World XI ...

THE FIGURES to 17.09.13   ESPNcricinfo.com

Batting & Fielding	M	Inns	NO	Runs	HS	Avge	S/R	100	50	4s	6s	Ct	St
Tests	99	171	8	7887	227	48.38	62.27	23	33	960	76	59	0
ODIs	136	125	16	4440	130	40.73	86.58	9	25	427	77	40	0
T20Is	37	36	5	1176	79	37.93	141.51	0	7	119	32	14	0
First-class	206	339	23	15688	254*	49.64	–	49	67	–	–	147	0

Bowling	M	Balls	Runs	Wkts	BB	Avge	RpO	S/R	5i	10m
Tests	99	1287	869	10	3–52	86.90	4.05	128.70	0	0
ODIs	136	400	370	7	2–22	52.85	5.55	57.14	0	0
T20Is	37	30	53	1	1–27	53.00	10.60	30.00	0	0
First-class	206	6407	3735	73	4–31	51.16	3.49	87.77	0	0

KIERON **POLLARD**

Full name **Kieron Adrian Pollard**
Born **May 12, 1987, Cacariqua, Trinidad**
Teams **Trinidad & Tobago, Mumbai Indians**
Style **Right-hand bat, right-arm medium-pacer**
Test debut **No Tests yet**
ODI debut **West Indies v South Africa at St George's 2006-07**
T20I debut **West Indies v Australia at Bridgetown 2008**

THE PROFILE Kieron Pollard shot to prominence in 2006-07 when still only 19, his muscular batting doing much to take Trinidad to the final of the inaugural Stanford 20/20 competition: in the semi-final, against Nevis, he clobbered 83 in only 38 balls, and then grabbed a couple of wickets with his medium-pacers. That won him a first-class start against Barbados: he got off the mark with a six, and added six more on his way to 126. Another hundred, with six more sixes, followed in his third match, and in between he hit 87 off 58 balls – seven sixes this time – in a one-dayer against Guyana. That was followed by inclusion in West Indies' squad for the 2007 World Cup. The cometary rise almost inevitably tailed off a little: he finished his first Carib Beer season with 420 runs at 42, and played only once in the World Cup itself. Pollard spent some time on the sidelines after that, but his big-hitting potential earned him megabucks contracts in the IPL, and in England and Australia (he thumped 52 off 22 balls against Victoria early in 2010). But while his bank balance rocketed, international success proved elusive: Pollard's first 50 limited-overs internationals featured only one half-century, and although he added three more in the first half of 2011, two of them came against Netherlands and Ireland in the World Cup. He finally made a century – with ten sixes – against India at Chennai in December 2011. He added a second (only eight sixes this time) against Australia in St Vincent in March 2012, and another at Sydney the following year – but there was still no sign of a Test cap.

THE FACTS Pollard made 126 on his first-class debut, for Trinidad v Barbados in January 2007: he hit 11 fours and seven sixes, one of which got him off the mark ... In his next match he hit 69 (31 balls, six sixes), and in his third 117 from 87 balls with 11 fours and six more sixes ... In a Twenty20 match for Somerset in 2010 Pollard failed by inches to become only the second person ever to hit a ball over the Lord's pavilion ...

THE FIGURES to 17.09.13

Batting & Fielding	M	Inns	NO	Runs	HS	Avge	S/R	100	50	4s	6s	Ct	St
Tests	0	0	–	–	–	–	–	–	–	–	–	–	–
ODIs	85	79	4	1869	119	24.92	93.54	3	6	123	87	45	0
T20Is	37	32	7	569	63*	22.76	149.73	0	2	44	33	19	0
First-class	24	39	2	1421	174	38.40	–	3	7	–	–	39	0

Bowling	M	Balls	Runs	Wkts	BB	Avge	RpO	S/R	5i	10m
Tests	0	0	–	–	–	–	–	–	–	–
ODIs	85	1788	1655	44	3-27	37.61	5.55	40.63	0	0
T20Is	37	342	475	17	3-30	27.94	8.33	20.11	0	0
First-class	24	691	376	7	2-29	53.71	3.26	98.71	0	0

KIERAN **POWELL**

Full name	**Kieran Omar Akeem Powell**
Born	**March 6, 1990, Nevis**
Teams	**Leeward Islands**
Style	**Left-hand bat**
Test debut	**West Indies v India at Roseau 2011**
ODI debut	**West Indies v Bangladesh at Basseterre 2009**
T20I debut	**No T20Is yet**

THE PROFILE A powerful opener, Kieran Powell started playing cricket when he was eight – initially alongside his brother Alan, who followed him into Nevis's youth teams. But Kieran trained on, and made the West Indian Under-19 squad. His first taste of big cricket came in the Stanford 20/20 competition in 2006, and two years later he scored at a healthy clip in the Under-19 World Cup. Powell was drafted into the makeshift squad that took on Bangladesh – and lost – in mid-2009, when the senior players withdrew in a contracts dispute. Powell made his one-day debut near home in St Kitts … and was lbw to the first ball of the match. Not long afterwards the dispute was finally settled, and the seniors returned – but Powell kept his name in the frame with a century against England Lions early in 2011, and made his Test debut against India that July … but failed again with 3 and 4. But then he came up against Bangladesh, hit 72 in a Test at Mirpur, and added 81 against India shortly afterwards. Powell, like several of his team-mates, struggled in England in the first part of the 2012 summer, but looked a different prospect back home, especially once Chris Gayle was restored to the top of the order. Powell made his maiden century in the first Test against New Zealand in July, helping Gayle add 254 for the first wicket, then really cashed in against Bangladesh, striking twin hundreds in the first Test at Mirpur later in 2012. That earned him a sustained run in the one-day side, too, and he made 83 against Australia at Perth early in 2013, then did well against Zimbabwe at home.

THE FACTS Powell was only the sixth Test cricketer from Nevis, following Elquemedo Willett, Derick Parry, Keith Arthurton, Stuart Williams and the late Runako Morton … Powell scored 117 and 110 against Bangladesh at Mirpur in November 2012 … He made 131 for Leeward Islands v England Lions at Basseterre in February 2011 … Powell and Chris Gayle put on 254 against New Zealand in Antigua in July 2012, West Indies' fourth-highest opening stand in Tests …

THE FIGURES to 17.09.13   espncricinfo.com

Batting & Fielding	M	Inns	NO	Runs	HS	Avge	S/R	100	50	4s	6s	Ct	St
Tests	15	28	1	819	134	30.33	50.12	3	2	114	3	16	0
ODIs	19	19	0	486	83	25.57	76.77	0	3	54	8	6	0
T20Is	0	0	–	–	–	–	–	–	–	–	–	–	–
First-class	49	86	5	2893	139	35.71	–	6	14	–	–	33	0

Bowling	M	Balls	Runs	Wkts	BB	Avge	RpO	S/R	5i	10m
Tests	15	0	–	–	–	–	–	–	–	–
ODIs	19	0	–	–	–	–	–	–	–	–
T20Is	0	0	–	–	–	–	–	–	–	–
First-class	49	43	34	0	–	–	4.74	–	0	0

NUWAN PRADEEP

Full name	Aththachchi Nuwan Pradeep Roshan Fernando
Born	October 19, 1986, Negombo
Teams	Bloomfield, Wayamba
Style	Right-hand bat, right-arm fast-medium bowler
Test debut	Sri Lanka v Pakistan at Abu Dhabi 2011-12
ODI debut	Sri Lanka v India at Colombo 2012
T20I debut	No T20Is yet

THE PROFILE Nuwan Pradeep didn't play with a proper cricket ball until he was 20 – but less than three years later he was in the Test squad. He won a pace contest at a soft-ball event in 2007, and was sent straight to Sri Lanka's Cricket's academy. He follows in the local tradition of unconventional bowlers: like Lasith Malinga, he has a slinging action, and has troubled many in domestic cricket with his speed, generated from a long run-up. "He's got raw pace, beautiful rhythm and consistency," says the national bowling coach Champaka Ramanayake. Pradeep's early international career, though, was stymied by injury. In May 2011 he took 4 for 29 against the England Lions at Derby, and looked set to feature in the Tests ... but was forced home with knee trouble. Then, at the end of the year, he had sent down just ten balls in a warm-up game in South Africa when he tore a hamstring, and was out for another three months. He had made his Test debut in Abu Dhabi a couple of months previously, but went wicketless as Pakistan amassed 511 for 6. When Pakistan toured Sri Lanka in mid-2012 Pradeep won two more caps, but managed only one wicket (the debutant Mohammad Ayub at Galle) and was promptly dropped again, nursing an embarrassing bowling average. An injury to Nuwan Kulasekara meant he was recalled for his first one-day internationals against India shortly afterwards: although he proved a little expensive he did produce a jaffa to castle Rohit Sharma at Pallekele. He improved his Test averages slightly with two wickets and a few runs at Sydney early in 2013 – then picked up another injury and didn't feature much for the rest of the year. "He's actually one of the fittest guys in the team," said Ramanayake, "but he needs bowling fitness."

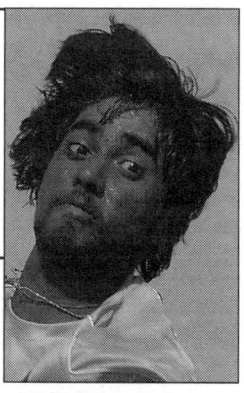

THE FACTS After three Tests Pradeep's bowling average (345.00) was 690 times higher than his batting one (0.50), an unprecedented figure ... He took 5 for 36 for Bloomfield against Ragama in December 2008 ... He was signed by Bangalore Royal Challengers for the 2011 IPL, but didn't actually play ...

THE FIGURES to 17.09.13   **espncricinfo.com**

Batting & Fielding	M	Inns	NO	Runs	HS	Avge	S/R	100	50	4s	6s	Ct	St
Tests	4	6	1	28	17*	5.60	47.45	0	0	5	0	0	0
ODIs	2	1	1	0	0*	–	–	0	0	0	0	0	0
T20Is	0	0	–	–	–	–	–	–	–	–	–	–	–
First-class	44	54	21	137	17*	4.15	42.54	0	0	19	3	17	0

Bowling	M	Balls	Runs	Wkts	BB	Avge	RpO	S/R	5i	10m
Tests	4	636	473	3	2-114	157.66	4.46	212.00	0	0
ODIs	2	108	115	3	2-63	38.33	6.38	36.00	0	0
T20Is	0	0	–	–	–	–	–	–	–	–
First-class	44	4150	2835	75	5-36	37.80	4.09	55.33	1	0

MATT **PRIOR**

Full name	**Matthew James Prior**
Born	**February 26, 1982, Johannesburg, South Africa**
Teams	**Sussex**
Style	**Right-hand bat, wicketkeeper**
Test debut	**England v West Indies at Lord's 2007**
ODI debut	**England v Zimbabwe at Bulawayo 2004-05**
T20I debut	**England v West Indies at The Oval 2007**

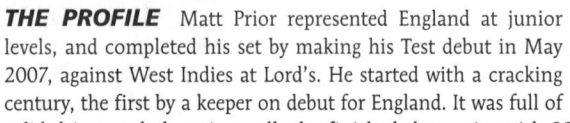

THE PROFILE Matt Prior represented England at junior levels, and completed his set by making his Test debut in May 2007, against West Indies at Lord's. He started with a cracking century, the first by a keeper on debut for England. It was full of solid drives and clumping pulls: he finished that series with 324 runs – but there were already rumbles about his wicketkeeping technique, which didn't seem to matter while England were winning. But then India arrived, and Prior's fumbles were magnified as the series slipped away: he dropped Tendulkar and Laxman as India ran up 664 at The Oval. The runs dried up, too, and suddenly Prior's footwork was called into question. He went back to Hove and sharpened up his technique, and was recalled late in 2008: Prior returned for the one-dayers against South Africa, and pouched six catches (one of them a one-handed flying stunner) at Trent Bridge. By 2009 he looked even more the part – and even more like his mentor, Alec Stewart – in the Ashes victory. More runs followed in 2010, including an important century against Pakistan at Trent Bridge: Prior was entrenched as England's Test keeper, contributing an Ashes century at Sydney in January 2011, two more tons in the home English summer that followed, and consistent runs after a slowish start in 2012. Oddly, he hasn't had the same success in limited-overs cricket, which ought to suit his attacking style. Early in 2013 his century saved the Auckland Test – and the series – although he had a poor time with the bat after that, failing to reach 50 in the Ashes series. Prior was born in South Africa, but moved to England at 11: he says he lost his accent within a week.

THE FACTS Prior was the 17th man to score a century on Test debut for England: he was the fifth to score a century on debut at Lord's, after Australia's Harry Graham, John Hampshire and Andrew Strauss of England, and India's Sourav Ganguly ... Prior equalled the ODI wicketkeeping record with six catches against South Africa at Nottingham in August 2008 ... He made 201* for Sussex v Loughborough University at Hove in May 2004 ...

THE FIGURES to 17.09.13   cricinfo.com

Batting & Fielding	M	Inns	NO	Runs	HS	Avge	S/R	100	50	4s	6s	Ct	St
Tests	72	110	20	3813	131*	42.36	62.20	7	26	456	15	207	13
ODIs	68	62	9	1282	87	24.18	76.76	0	3	141	6	71	8
T20Is	10	8	2	127	32	21.16	127.00	0	0	11	5	6	3
First-class	236	359	42	12673	201*	39.97	67.09	27	73	–	–	595	41

Bowling	M	Balls	Runs	Wkts	BB	Avge	RpO	S/R	5i	10m
Tests	72	0	–	–	–	–	–	–	–	–
ODIs	68	0	–	–	–	–	–	–	–	–
T20Is	10	0	–	–	–	–	–	–	–	–
First-class	236	0	–	–	–	–	–	–	–	–

CHETESHWAR **PUJARA**

Full name	Cheteshwar Arvind Pujara
Born	January 25, 1988, Rajkot, Gujarat
Teams	Saurashtra, Royal Challengers Bangalore
Style	Right-hand bat, occasional legspinner
Test debut	India v Australia at Bangalore 2010-11
ODI debut	India v Zimbabwe at Bulawayo 2013
T20I debut	No T20Is yet

THE PROFILE After years of prolific domestic runscoring, Cheteshwar Pujara finally got an opportunity in a Test, against Australia in October 2010. Coming in at No. 3 instead of Rahul Dravid in the second innings, he compiled an excellent 72 in a tricky run-chase. It looked as if Pujara had arrived ... but then a knee injury sidelined him for 18 months. But when he returned, runs again piled upon runs. The comeback started with 159 against New Zealand in August 2012, and Test double-centuries followed against England and Australia: in between he amassed 203 not out and 352 in successive Ranji Trophy games. All in all he made 1585 runs at 93 in the 2012-13 Indian season, just missing Chandu Borde's long-standing aggregate record (1604 in 1964-65, from eight more matches). Pujara's game-plan is simple, and his technique is classical: upright at the crease and confident on both sides of the wicket. So far he has not been thought of as a one-day player for India, but that is likely to change. The son of a former first-class player, Pujara was a mighty achiever at a young age, scoring a triple-century for Saurashtra's Under-14s and 211 in an Under-19 Test against England. In 2008-09 he embarked on a purple patch Don Bradman would have been hard-pushed to match: two triple-centuries for Saurashtra's Under-22s were followed by one in first-class cricket too, all in little more than a month. The figures couldn't be ignored and, after a double-century while captaining the A team in England, Pujara finally got that Test call. The *Times of India* likened him to Dravid, with added power: "He is like the Wall, but packs a wallop too."

THE FACTS Pujara scored 386 and 309 in successive matches for Saurashtra Under-22s in October 2008 ... The next month he made 302* in Saurashtra's Ranji Trophy match against Orissa at Rajkot, sharing a stand of 520 with Ravindra Jadeja ... Pujara made his first triple-century shortly before his 13th birthday, for Saurashtra's Under-14s in January 2001 ... Twelve of his 20 first-class hundreds have been scores of 150 or more ...

THE FIGURES to 17.09.13   espncricinfo.com

Batting & Fielding	M	Inns	NO	Runs	HS	Avge	S/R	100	50	4s	6s	Ct	St
Tests	13	22	4	1180	206*	65.55	52.63	4	3	145	2	10	0
ODIs	2	2	0	13	13	6.50	46.42	0	0	2	0	0	0
T20Is	0	0	–	–	–	–	–	–	–	–	–	–	–
First-class	79	130	23	6440	352	60.18	–	20	24	–	–	45	0

Bowling	M	Balls	Runs	Wkts	BB	Avge	RpO	S/R	5i	10m
Tests	13	0	–	–	–	–	–	–	–	–
ODIs	2	0	–	–	–	–	–	–	–	–
T20Is	0	0	–	–	–	–	–	–	–	–
First-class	79	153	83	5	2–4	16.60	3.25	30.60	0	0

RAHAT ALI

Full name	**Rahat Ali**
Born	**September 12, 1988, Multan, Punjab**
Teams	**Baluchistan, Khan Research Laboratories**
Style	**Right-hand bat, left-arm fast-medium bowler**
Test debut	**Pakistan v South Africa at Johannesburg 2012-13**
ODI debut	**Pakistan v Sri Lanka at Pallekele 2012**
T20I debut	**No T20Is yet**

THE PROFILE Rahat Ali was another left-arm quick bowler tried by Pakistan in the wake of the scandal which deprived them of the services of Mohammad Aamer. Rahat has a nice whippy action, quite like Aamer's, gets sideways-on at the crease in the classic manner – unlike, say, Wasim Akram with his bustle-through approach – and aims to swing the ball at a decent pace. Rahat started with his native Multan, but by 2011-12 was starring for Khan Research Laboratories and Baluchistan, taking 61 first-class wickets at 19.01, with a career-best 6 for 62 for KRL against Karachi Whites, when his victims included the first four of the innings. That earned him a call for the one-day leg of Pakistan's tour of Sri Lanka in mid-2012, and he made his one-day debut there, although it was a sobering one as he failed to take a wicket in four expensive overs that cost 34. Still, Rahat was retained for the South African tour early the following year, and made his Test debut at Johannesburg in February 2013. Again it was a chastening start: Rahat looked a little forlorn as he conceded 100 runs without taking a wicket in either innings, in between which Pakistan were shot out for 49. Things perked up in the next Test (apart from the end result) when he took 6 for 127 in South Africa's only innings at Centurion. That ensured Rahat was retained for the tour of Zimbabwe later in the year, and he looked much more the part there, being preferred to the more experienced Wahab Riaz and taking 5 for 52 in the second Test at Harare, which ended in an upset victory for the home side.

THE FACTS Rahat Ali took 6 for 62 for Khan Research Laboratories v Karachi Whites in October 2011 ... He took 6 for 127 in his second Test, against South Africa at Centurion in February 2013 ... Rahat took 5 for 52 against Zimbabwe at Harare in September 2013, the day after his 25th birthday ...

THE FIGURES to 17.09.13

Batting & Fielding	M	Inns	NO	Runs	HS	Avge	S/R	100	50	4s	6s	Ct	St
Tests	4	8	5	62	35*	20.66	69.66	0	0	8	3	2	0
ODIs	1	1	1	0	0*	–	–	0	0	0	0	0	0
T20Is	0	0	–	–	–	–	–	–	–	–	–	–	–
First-class	43	50	24	197	35*	7.57	46.57	0	0	20	6	14	0

Bowling	M	Balls	Runs	Wkts	BB	Avge	RpO	S/R	5i	10m
Tests	4	757	432	14	6–127	30.85	3.42	54.07	2	0
ODIs	1	24	34	0	–	–	8.50	–	0	0
T20Is	0	0	–	–	–	–	–	–	–	–
First-class	43	7155	3526	166	6–62	21.24	2.95	43.10	9	0

SURESH **RAINA**

Full name	**Suresh Kumar Raina**
Born	**November 27, 1986, Ghaziabad, Uttar Pradesh**
Teams	**Uttar Pradesh, Chennai Super Kings**
Style	**Left-hand bat, occasional offspinner**
Test debut	**India v Sri Lanka at Colombo 2010**
ODI debut	**India v Sri Lanka at Dambulla 2005**
T20I debut	**India v South Africa at Johannesburg 2006-07**

THE PROFILE In April 2005 Suresh Raina strolled in to bat in the domestic one-day final, spanked nine fours and a six in 48 from 33 balls as Uttar Pradesh tied with Tamil Nadu and shared the title, then left to catch the flight home for his school exams. The following season his 620 runs helped UP win the Ranji Trophy for the first time. Electric fielding added zing to India's one-day side, but eventually the runs dried up, and he was dropped early in 2007 after 16 innings without a half-century. A powerful left-hander, he was back a year later and hit two centuries in the Asia Cup in June 2008, against Hong Kong and Bangladesh, then made 53 and 76 in Sri Lanka as India fought back to win the one-day series there. In New Zealand at the start of 2009 he slammed 61 not out from 43 balls in a Twenty20 international then 66 from 39 in a one-dayer, but was underwhelming in the World Twenty20 in England in June. Test cricket seemed to have passed him by, but after 98 ODIs he finally made his debut in Sri Lanka the following month, and made up for lost time with a fine 120, adding 62 and 41 not out in the next match. He joined the 2011 World Cup party late, playing only the last four matches – but that included the joyous final, in which he didn't need to bat. After that, though, Raina had a tough time in the Tests in England, his ponderous technique against the short stuff being exposed. That eventually cost him his five-day place, but he remained a reliable one-day performer: at the start of 2013 he cracked four successive fifties against England, then later in the year was part of the unchanged team that won the 50-overs Champions Trophy.

THE FACTS Raina played 98 ODIs before his first Test in July 2010 – then promptly became the 12th Indian to score a century on debut ... He captained India in an ODI before he played in a Test ... Raina made 204 not out for Uttar Pradesh v Punjab in November 2011, and 203 for UP v Orrissa in November 2007 ... Raina made 520 runs in the third IPL in 2010, a number exceeded only by Sachin Tendulkar and Jacques Kallis ...

THE FIGURES to 17.09.13 espncricinfo.com

Batting & Fielding	M	Inns	NO	Runs	HS	Avge	S/R	100	50	4s	6s	Ct	St
Tests	17	29	2	768	120	28.44	53.29	1	7	100	4	22	0
ODIs	174	150	32	4305	116*	36.48	91.65	3	29	362	89	76	0
T20Is	36	32	7	840	101	33.60	136.14	1	3	76	30	16	0
First-class	81	135	9	5380	204*	42.69	60.48	11	35	–	–	91	0

Bowling	M	Balls	Runs	Wkts	BB	Avge	RpO	S/R	5i	10m
Tests	17	921	532	13	2–1	40.92	3.46	70.84	0	0
ODIs	174	1226	1032	21	2–17	49.14	5.05	58.38	0	0
T20Is	36	96	141	5	2–49	28.20	8.81	19.20	0	0
First-class	81	2447	1225	29	3–31	42.24	3.00	84.37	0	0

DENESH **RAMDIN**

Full name **Denesh Ramdin**
Born **March 13, 1985, Couva, Trinidad**
Teams **Trinidad & Tobago**
Style **Right-hand bat, wicketkeeper**
Test debut **West Indies v Sri Lanka at Colombo 2005**
ODI debut **West Indies v India at Dambulla 2005**
T20I debut **West Indies v New Zealand at Auckland 2005-06**

THE PROFILE Originally a fast bowler who kept wicket when he'd finished with the ball, at 13 Denesh Ramdin decided to concentrate on keeping. He led both the Trinidad and West Indies Under-19 sides before in 2005, still only 19 and with Ridley Jacobs retired, Ramdin went to Sri Lanka as the first-choice keeper. He impressed everyone with his work behind and in front of the stumps, and continued to do so in Australia later in 2005, especially with a plucky 71 at Hobart, where he shared a fine partnership of 182 with his fellow Trinidadian Dwayne Bravo. Carlton Baugh was preferred for some of the home one-dayers early in 2006, and it was a surprise when Ramdin returned for the Tests against India. But he justified his selection with some neat keeping on pitches on which the ball often died before it reached him, and a gritty unbeaten 62 that nearly brought victory in the deciding fourth Test in Jamaica. Early in 2009 he cashed in on a Bridgetown featherbed to make a seven-hour 166 against England, but then lost form with bat and gloves for a while, and the selectors went back to Baugh (then, when he was injured just before the 2011 World Cup, to Devon Thomas). But when Baugh also failed to provide enough runs, Ramdin returned for the 2012 tour of England – and silenced his critics with an unbeaten century at Edgbaston. Those critics had included Viv Richards, and Ramdin pointedly unfurled a message telling Sir Viv what he thought. He copped a fine for that – and the following year was banned for two matches after claiming a catch that he'd dropped during the Champions Trophy. But runs against Bangladesh and Zimbabwe ensured he kept his Test place.

THE FACTS Ramdin's 166 against England at Bridgetown in 2008-09 was the second-highest score by a West Indian wicketkeeper in a Test, after Clyde Walcott's 168* at Lord's in 1950 ... Ramdin also made 166* for Trinidad v Barbados in January 2010 ... He played in the side that won the Under-15 World Challenge in 2000, beating Pakistan in the Lord's final; four years later he captained in the Under-19 World Cup, when WI lost the final at Dhaka – to Pakistan ...

THE FIGURES to 17.09.13   espncricinfo.com

Batting & Fielding	M	Inns	NO	Runs	HS	Avge	S/R	100	50	4s	6s	Ct	St
Tests	51	85	10	1973	166	26.30	48.29	3	10	248	4	147	3
ODIs	101	75	18	1153	96	20.22	75.75	0	3	95	3	131	6
T20Is	35	22	6	237	44	14.81	114.49	0	0	28	2	26	8
First-class	112	183	24	4912	166*	30.89	–	11	22	–	–	294	25

Bowling	M	Balls	Runs	Wkts	BB	Avge	RpO	S/R	5i	10m
Tests	51	0	–	–	–	–	–	–	–	–
ODIs	101	0	–	–	–	–	–	–	–	–
T20Is	35	0	–	–	–	–	–	–	–	–
First-class	112	0	–	–	–	–	–	–	–	–

RAVI RAMPAUL

WEST INDIES

Full name	**Ravindranath Rampaul**
Born	**October 15, 1984, Preysal, Trinidad**
Teams	**Trinidad & Tobago, Royal Challengers Bangalore**
Style	**Left-hand bat, right-arm fast-medium bowler**
Test debut	**West Indies v Australia at Brisbane 2009-10**
ODI debut	**West Indies v Zimbabwe at Bulawayo 2003-04**
T20I debut	**West Indies v England at The Oval 2007**

THE PROFILE Ravi Rampaul is tall and well-built, but his career has been hamstrung by injuries and ill-luck. He made his Trinidad debut in 2002, and 18 wickets in six matches the following season – and an aggressive approach – propelled him to the verge of full international selection. Just 19, he made his ODI debut late in 2003: he was rarely collared, but hardly ran through sides either – in 14 matches he took nine wickets, only once managing more than one, a statistic that was echoed when his Test career eventually started. Nonetheless he was retained for the 2004 England tour, and played three more ODIs before he broke down and returned home ahead of the Tests. Sidelined by shin splints, Rampaul did not play another first-class match until 2006-07, taking 7 for 51 as T&T beat Barbados in the Carib Beer final. That won him another England tour but, restricted by a groin tear, he again missed the Tests, before helping to turn the one-day series around with 4 for 41 in the pivotal second match at Edgbaston. Rampaul finally made his Test debut in Australia late in 2009 – he'd been around so long it was a surprise he was still only 25 – but although he worked up a fair head of steam, success proved elusive at first. He took only four wickets in his first five Tests, but his strike-rate improved with 21 wickets against Pakistan and India in mid-2011, although the big hauls continued to elude him. Ten wickets in two Tests in Bangladesh late in 2012 helped improve his average and an already miserly economy-rate. Injuries to knee and ankle bothered him in 2013, but he remained a first choice when fit.

THE FACTS Rampaul scored 86* against India at Visakhapatnam in December 2011, the highest score by a No. 10 batsman in any ODI ... He took 7 for 51 as Trinidad & Tobago beat Barbados in the final of the Carib Beer Challenge at Pointe-à-Pierre in February 2007 ... In the World Under-15 Challenge in 2000, Rampaul took 7 for 11 against the Netherlands ... He played for Ireland in the Friends Provident Trophy in 2008 ...

THE FIGURES to 17.09.13   espncricinfo.com

Batting & Fielding	M	Inns	NO	Runs	HS	Avge	S/R	100	50	4s	6s	Ct	St
Tests	18	31	8	335	40*	14.56	53.25	0	0	40	10	3	0
ODIs	77	34	8	341	86*	13.11	78.39	0	1	32	12	12	0
T20Is	19	6	5	12	8	12.00	57.14	0	0	0	0	1	0
First-class	62	91	16	1031	64*	13.74	–	0	2	–	–	18	0

Bowling	M	Balls	Runs	Wkts	BB	Avge	RpO	S/R	5i	10m
Tests	18	3440	1705	49	4-48	34.79	2.97	70.20	0	0
ODIs	77	3309	2775	93	5-49	29.83	5.03	35.58	2	0
T20Is	19	418	597	25	3-16	23.88	8.56	16.72	0	0
First-class	62	9860	5485	182	7-51	30.13	3.33	54.17	7	1

SURAJ **RANDIV**

Full name	Hewa Kaluhalamullage Suraj Randiv Kaluhalamulla
Born	January 30, 1985, Matara
Teams	Bloomfield, Kandurata
Style	Right-hand bat, offspinner
Test debut	Sri Lanka v India at Colombo 2010
ODI debut	Sri Lanka v India at Nagpur 2009-10
T20I debut	Sri Lanka v Zimbabwe at Providence 2009-10

THE PROFILE Suraj Randiv – who changed his name from Mohamed Marshuk Mohamed Suraj in 2009, after converting to Buddhism – had the unenviable task of replacing Muttiah Muralitharan as Sri Lanka's offspinner. A consistent domestic performer, Randiv made his Test debut in July 2010 in the match immediately following Murali's retirement, and matched his predecessor's appetite for hard work by toiling through 73 overs in the first innings, taking 2 for 222. On a more sporting pitch for the third Test, at Colombo's Sara Oval, Randiv claimed nine wickets, including all five to fall in the second innings as India successfully chased 257. After that, though, he faded a little: he was not in the original 2011 World Cup squad, although he was summoned very late as a replacement and controversially played in the final. He had a quiet time in England in 2011, apart from 5 for 42 in the ODI at Old Trafford, and has rarely featured in the one-day side since. He briefly formed a useful spin partnership with left-armer Rangana Herath in Tests: Randiv took six wickets (to Herath's 12) as England were beaten at Galle in March 2012, and seven when Pakistan succumbed there three months later. But Randiv was dumped after proving expensive against New Zealand late in 2012. He continued to be a domestic force, taking 55 wickets in 2012-13, including 7 for 61 (and 11 in the match) as Bloomfield shot down the Air Force. Randiv actually started as a fast bowler, but switched to offspin at school. He is a tidy bowler – and a better batsman than Murali, with a first-class century as nightwatchman to his name – but doesn't possess the variety of his illustrious predecessor. He has twice taken nine wickets in an innings in domestic first-class cricket.

THE FACTS Randiv took 2 for 222 in his first Test innings, the most runs ever conceded by a debutant ... He claimed 9 for 62 for Sinhalese SC v Colombo CC in February 2006 ... Randiv took 9 for 109 (the other wicket was a run-out) for Bloomfield v Army in October 2009: earlier in the match he had scored his maiden century ...

THE FIGURES to 17.09.13 **cricinfo.com**

Batting & Fielding	M	Inns	NO	Runs	HS	Avge	S/R	100	50	4s	6s	Ct	St
Tests	12	17	1	147	39	9.18	30.62	0	0	16	0	1	0
ODIs	28	15	1	239	56	17.07	71.55	0	1	24	1	6	0
T20Is	7	2	0	8	6	4.00	133.33	0	0	1	0	0	0
First-class	99	139	23	2259	112	19.47	52.06	1	6	–	–	59	0

Bowling	M	Balls	Runs	Wkts	BB	Avge	RpO	S/R	5i	10m
Tests	12	3146	1613	43	5–82	37.51	3.07	73.16	1	0
ODIs	28	1269	1008	33	5–42	30.54	4.76	38.45	1	0
T20Is	7	126	139	7	3–20	19.85	6.61	18.00	0	0
First-class	99	19822	11424	445	9–62	25.67	3.45	44.54	29	9

BOYD **RANKIN**

Full name **William Boyd Rankin**
Born **July 5, 1984, Londonderry, Northern Ireland**
Teams **Warwickshire**
Style **Left-hand bat, right-arm fast-medium bowler**
Test debut **No Tests yet**
ODI debut **Ireland v Bermuda at Nairobi 2006-07**
T20I debut **Ireland v Bangladesh at Nottingham 2009**

THE PROFILE There were mixed feelings when Boyd Rankin took 4 for 46 in his first one-day international for England, in September 2013 – pleasure that another tall fast bowler (he's 6ft 7ins/201cm) was making his presence felt, but embarrassment that he was doing it against Ireland ... Rankin's native land, and, the side for which he played more than 50 limited-overs internationals before upsetting a few people back home by opting to throw in his lot with England, a path which offered him a shot at Test cricket. Early in 2013, as he was contemplating yet another injury, it looked as if Rankin's decision would be only theoretical – but a changed fitness regime (less gym, more swim) kept him fit for the rest of the summer and led to his call-up as England looked to restock their production line of lanky pacemen able to make the ball bounce and swerve around disconcertingly. Back in 2007 Rankin had made an impressive start in international cricket, taking 12 wickets on generally docile Caribbean tracks as Ireland fairytaled their way to the Super Eight stage. But it took him a while to find his feet in county cricket, spending time with Middlesex and Derbyshire before moving to Warwickshire in 2008. The following season he took 37 first-class wickets, and improved to 55 in 2011, by which time he was flitting between representative games for Ireland and England Lions. Late in 2012 he announced that he would no longer play for Ireland, a decision blamed in some (largely Irish) quarters on Ashley Giles, then Rankin's coach at Edgbaston ... and now the England one-day supremo, on whose watch he made his debut in his new colours.

THE FACTS Rankin's first 52 internationals (37 ODIs and 15 T20Is) were for Ireland: but in his first ODI for England Rankin took 4 for 46, his best figures, *against* Ireland ... He took 5 for 16 for Warwickshire v Essex at Edgbaston in August 2010 ... In the 2007 World Cup Rankin, playing for Ireland, dismissed Ed Joyce of England for 1: by 2013 they had swapped sides, and in Dublin Rankin of England dismissed Joyce of Ireland for 1 ...

THE FIGURES to 17.09.13   espncricinfo.com

Batting & Fielding	M	Inns	NO	Runs	HS	Avge	S/R	100	50	4s	6s	Ct	St
Tests	0	0	–	–	–	–	–	–	–	–	–	–	–
ODIs	42	18	12	40	7*	6.66	36.36	0	0	1	0	6	0
T20Is	17	3	2	13	7*	13.00	81.25	0	0	1	0	6	0
First-class	62	72	31	345	43	8.41	40.87	0	0	36	0	18	0

Bowling	M	Balls	Runs	Wkts	BB	Avge	RpO	S/R	5i	10m
Tests	0	0	–	–	–	–	–	–	–	–
ODIs	42	1929	1543	52	4–46	29.67	4.79	37.09	0	0
T20Is	17	378	388	18	3–20	21.55	6.15	21.00	0	0
First-class	62	9111	5594	203	5–16	27.55	3.68	44.88	6	0

KEMAR ROACH

Full name **Kemar Andre Jamal Roach**
Born **June 30, 1988, St Lucy, Barbados**
Teams **Barbados**
Style **Right-hand bat, right-arm fast-medium bowler**
Test debut **West Indies v Bangladesh at Kingstown 2009**
ODI debut **West Indies v Bermuda at King City 2008**
T20I debut **West Indies v Australia at Bridgetown 2008**

THE PROFILE A genuinely fast bowler with a free-flowing action, Kemar Roach was only 19, and had played only four first-class matches, when he was called into the squad for the third Test against Australia at Bridgetown in June 2008. Roach made his debut in the Twenty20 international shortly afterwards, and took two of the three wickets to fall, dismissing both Australian openers after starting with a nervous beamer. The following year he was one of West Indies' few successes after the senior players withdrew from the series against Bangladesh, taking 13 wickets in the two Tests. Floyd Reifer, his captain then, observed: "He does a lot, especially with the old ball." Roach hit trouble during the ODIs, when he let loose two beamers and was taken off and fined, but he still took ten wickets. When the seniors returned Roach retained his place, winning admirers in Australia in 2009-10 for his hostile pace. He unsettled Ricky Ponting, dismissing him in each of the three Tests, and also smashed him on the elbow at Perth, forcing him to retire hurt. But in 2011, after a World Cup hat-trick against the Netherlands, Roach struggled at home, eventually losing his place. He bounced back in 2012, with 19 wickets in the three home Tests against Australia, including ten in the second at Port-of-Spain. Later in the year he took 12 more as New Zealand lost both their Tests in the Caribbean, but he started 2013 poorly, not helped by the uncharacteristically spin-friendly pitches served up for Zimbabwe's Tests in the Caribbean. By July, though, Roach was looking more like his old self, blowing away Sri Lanka's middle order with 4 for 27 in an ODI in Trinidad.

THE FACTS Roach took 6 for 48 against Bangladesh at St George's in July 2009, and followed that with 5 for 44 in the first ODI at Roseau ... Roach took a hat-trick – West Indies' first in the World Cup, and only their second in all ODIs – against the Netherlands at Delhi in February 2011 ... He took 7 for 23 (five bowled and two lbw) for Barbados v Combined Colleges and Campuses in Nevis in January 2010 ...

THE FIGURES to 17.09.13   espncricinfo.com

Batting & Fielding	M	Inns	NO	Runs	HS	Avge	S/R	100	50	4s	6s	Ct	St
Tests	23	37	7	291	41	9.70	34.23	0	0	31	1	8	0
ODIs	61	41	25	216	34	13.50	52.17	0	0	17	3	14	0
T20Is	11	1	1	3	3*	–	150.00	0	0	0	0	1	0
First-class	54	75	14	644	52*	10.55	–	0	1	–	–	22	0

Bowling	M	Balls	Runs	Wkts	BB	Avge	RpO	S/R	5i	10m
Tests	23	4381	2356	85	6–48	27.71	3.22	51.54	5	1
ODIs	61	3067	2517	94	6–27	26.77	4.92	32.62	3	0
T20Is	11	234	284	10	2–25	28.40	7.28	23.40	0	0
First-class	54	8614	4965	172	7–23	28.86	3.45	50.08	8	1

CHRIS **ROGERS**

Full name	**Christopher John Llewellyn Rogers**
Born	**August 31, 1977, St George, Sydney**
Teams	**Victoria, Middlesex**
Style	**Left-hand bat**
Test debut	**Australia v India at Perth 2007-08**
ODI debut	**No ODIs yet**
T20I debut	**No ODIs yet**

THE PROFILE For five years the nuggety left-hand opener Chris Rogers seemed destined to be a one-cap wonder, never to play again after two low scores against India at Perth in January 2008, when he replaced the injured Matthew Hayden. Rogers remained prolific in first-class cricket, at home and in England, where he has averaged around 50 for four different counties, latterly Middlesex. By 2012-13, when he was 34, even Victoria were undecided about retaining him, but they did – albeit on reduced terms – and Rogers continued doing what he does best, chiselling out the runs. He made 742 at almost 50, and suddenly, with Ricky Ponting and Mike Hussey both retiring, began to be spoken of as a sticking-plaster solution for Australia's brittle batting. Even so, it was something of a surprise when he really was called up for the 2013 Ashes tour. But he did everything that could have been asked of him in England, regularly seeing off the new ball (he fell six times to Graeme Swann in the series, but only twice to Jimmy Anderson and once to Stuart Broad). Rogers made 52 in the first Test at Trent Bridge, and 84 in the third at Old Trafford, then bedded down for a six-hour 110 at Chester-le-Street. It was his 61st first-class hundred, and he was the oldest Australian to make a maiden Test century for 87 years. Rogers was inked in for the return Ashes series in the winter – not bad for someone who is short-sighted and colour-blind. His father John played for New South Wales and later became a respected administrator, notably as general manager at the WACA, where Chris played for a decade before moving to Melbourne.

THE FACTS Rogers made 319 for Northants v Gloucestershire in August 2006 ... At 35 in 2013, he was the second-oldest Australian to score a maiden Test century: Arthur Richardson was 37 at Headingley in July 1926 ... Rogers has made nine first-class double-centuries, including 209 *against* Australia for Leicestershire in July 2005 ... He and Marcus North put on 459 for WA's third wicket against Victoria in October 2006 ...

THE FIGURES to 17.09.13

cricinfo.com

Batting & Fielding	M	Inns	NO	Runs	HS	Avge	S/R	100	50	4s	6s	Ct	St
Tests	6	11	0	386	110	35.09	45.62	1	2	54	0	5	0
ODIs	0	0	–	–	–	–	–	–	–	–	–	–	–
T20Is	0	0	–	–	–	–	–	–	–	–	–	–	–
First-class	248	440	32	20425	319	50.06	–	62	94	–	–	212	0

Bowling	M	Balls	Runs	Wkts	BB	Avge	RpO	S/R	5i	10m
Tests	6	0	–	–	–	–	–	–	–	–
ODIs	0	0	–	–	–	–	–	–	–	–
T20Is	0	0	–	–	–	–	–	–	–	–
First-class	248	230	131	1	1–16	131.00	3.41	230.00	0	0

NEW ZEALAND

LUKE **RONCHI**

Full name **Luke Ronchi**
Born **April 23, 1981, Dannevirke, Manawatu**
Teams **Wellington**
Style **Right-hand bat, wicketkeeper**
Test debut **No Tests yet**
ODI debut **Australia v West Indies at St George's 2007-08**
T20I debut **Australia v West Indies at Bridgetown 2007-08**

THE PROFILE After a handful of one-day games for Australia in 2008, Luke Ronchi resurrected his career by moving back to his native New Zealand. He scored well for Wellington – four hundreds in 2012, and another in February 2013 – and became the first man to play official internationals for both Australia and New Zealand. His second career started with NZ's one-day team in England in 2013: there the fairytale stalled a little, because although he kept wicket well he struggled with the bat, starting with a third-ball duck at Lord's, and managing only 47 runs in six innings all told; he was left out for the Twenty20 games that followed the Champions Trophy. Possibly, at 32, it was too big an ask to expect him to open and keep wicket. Five years previously, Ronchi (it's pronounced "Ronky") had replaced the injured Brad Haddin for most of the limited-overs games on Australia's tour of the West Indies. He started in unique fashion, by taking a catch first ball – then, in just his second innings, spanked a 22-ball half-century. He had earned selection for that tour after several hard-hitting performances, including a run-a-ball century against New South Wales then, in 2007-08, a first-class hundred against Queensland in just 51 balls, the second fifty coming up from a scarcely believable 11 deliveries. But he mislaid his form as just the wrong moment, losing his WA place for a while during 2008-09: he had to watch Tim Paine and Matthew Wade move ahead of him in the national wicketkeeping queue. Eventually he decided to go back across the Tasman (his family had moved to Perth when he was seven), to try his luck there.

THE FACTS Ronchi was the first man to play international cricket for both Australia and New Zealand ... He reached 50 from only 22 balls in his second ODI innings (his fourth match) against West Indies in St Kitts in July 2008 ... He reached his hundred against NSW at Perth in February 2007 in just 56 balls, an Australian domestic one-day record at the time ... Ronchi hit 113 (with 88 in boundaries) and 108 (18 fours) for Wellington v Northern Districts in December 2012 (he also caught eight of the 12 ND wickets to fall) ...

THE FIGURES to 17.09.13   ESPNcricinfo.com

Batting & Fielding	M	Inns	NO	Runs	HS	Avge	S/R	100	50	4s	6s	Ct	St
Tests	0	0	–	–	–	–	–	–	–	–	–	–	–
ODIs	10	8	0	123	64	15.37	116.03	0	1	13	6	13	3
T20Is	3	2	0	47	36	23.50	174.07	0	0	8	1	0	0
First-class	71	115	12	3831	148	37.19	82.92	11	14	–	–	260	12

Bowling	M	Balls	Runs	Wkts	BB	Avge	RpO	S/R	5i	10m
Tests	0	0	–	–	–	–	–	–	–	–
ODIs	10	0	–	–	–	–	–	–	–	–
T20Is	3	0	–	–	–	–	–	–	–	–
First-class	71	0	–	–	–	–	–	–	–	–

JOE **ROOT**

Full name	**Joseph Edward Root**
Born	**December 30, 1990, Sheffield**
Teams	**Yorkshire**
Style	**Right-hand bat, offspinner**
Test debut	**England v India at Nagpur 2012-13**
ODI debut	**England v India at Rajkot 2012-13**
T20I debut	**England v India at Mumbai 2012-13**

THE PROFILE Almost from the start Joe Root, a calm, collected right-hander, drew comparisons with two of Yorkshire's finest: his patience and stubbornness at the crease had Geoffrey Boycott purring that he reminded him of himself, while Root is a product of the Sheffield Collegiate club, which also nurtured Michael Vaughan. And there are similarities between Root's batting style and Vaughan's, particularly when it comes to driving off the front foot. The baby-faced Root made his Yorkshire debut in 2010, and narrowly missed a thousand runs in his first season, although he was chosen for the England Lions. In 2011 he was one of the few bright spots in a miserable season for his relegated county: he made 937 runs in the Championship (only Jonny Bairstow hit more), and extended his maiden century – against Sussex at Scarborough – to 160. By now Root was being talked up as a future Test batsman, and was duly selected for the winter tours of India and New Zealand after Andrew Strauss retired. Once again he adapted quickly to his new environment: he scored 73 on Test debut at Nagpur, then his first six innings in ODIs all ranged between 31 and 79. After a prolific start to the home season in 2013 – which included three successive scores of more than 175 – Root added a maiden Test century against New Zealand in May, in front of appreciative home fans at Headingley, then – after Nick Compton was dropped – seemed to fulfil his destiny by moving up to open for England in the Ashes. He stroked a superb 180 at Lord's, but otherwise only once got past 30, suggesting that actually he did still have a bit to learn.

THE FACTS Root became only the fourth man to make three successive scores above 175, with 182 for Yorkshire v Durham, 236 v Derbyshire, and 179 for England Lions v New Zealanders in April/May 2013 ... Root scored 180 for England v Australia at Lord's in July 2013 ... He was the Cricket Writers' Club's young player of the year in 2012 ... Root hit 222* for Yorkshire v Hampshire at Southampton in July 2012 ...

THE FIGURES to 17.09.13   **cricinfo.com**

Batting & Fielding	M	Inns	NO	Runs	HS	Avge	S/R	100	50	4s	6s	Ct	St
Tests	11	21	2	763	180	40.15	41.71	2	3	80	3	6	0
ODIs	20	19	3	626	79*	39.12	82.15	0	4	51	4	10	0
T20Is	4	2	2	91	90*	–	182.00	0	1	13	1	3	0
First-class	51	88	10	3490	236	44.74	50.79	9	11	426	8	28	0

Bowling	M	Balls	Runs	Wkts	BB	Avge	RpO	S/R	5i	10m
Tests	11	180	71	3	2–9	23.66	2.36	60.00	0	0
ODIs	20	306	328	3	1–20	109.33	6.43	102.00	0	0
T20Is	4	36	67	2	1–15	33.50	11.16	18.00	0	0
First-class	51	1209	645	13	3–33	49.61	3.20	93.00	0	0

RUBEL HOSSAIN

Full name **Mohammad Rubel Hossain**
Born **January 1, 1990, Bagerhat**
Teams **Khulna**
Style **Right-hand bat, right-arm fast-medium bowler**
Test debut **Bangladesh v West Indies at Kingstown 2009**
ODI debut **Bangladesh v Sri Lanka at Mirpur 2008-09**
T20I debut **Bangladesh v South Africa at Johannesburg 2008-09**

THE PROFILE A right-arm fast bowler with a slingy action not unlike Lasith Malinga's, Rubel Hossain began by playing tape-ball cricket in his home town of Bagerhat (in Khulna), before he was discovered during a national search for fast bowlers after getting the highest reading on the speed-gun. He made his first-class debut in October 2007 against a Khulna side including his hero Mashrafe Mortaza – not that that stopped him letting Mashrafe have a few bouncers. He played in the Under-19 World Cup early in 2008, and in his first ODI, a rain-affected game against Sri Lanka at Mirpur in January 2009, he helped set up a rare Bangladesh victory with 4 for 33. He toured the Caribbean later in the year, playing in both Tests as Bangladesh pulled off a clean sweep against a depleted West Indian side. Once again he made a decent start: his three victims – Ryan Austin, Omar Phillips and Nikita Miller – were, like himself, making their Test debut. But Rubel didn't strike again in the Tests, and went for a few in the subsequent one-dayers: he was left out for a while, then returned to take five expensive wickets in a Test against New Zealand early in 2010, before looking the pick of the pacemen in home-and-away series against England. After a subdued World Cup – only five wickets on largely spin-friendly pitches – he showed his worth with 11 victims in five one-dayers in Zimbabwe later in 2011. However, just one wicket in three Tests after that meant his average stayed worryingly high: then he was sidelined by an injured shoulder, that needed surgery in mid-2012. He was back at the end of the year, though wickets remained elusive. Rubel's love of speed also runs to a fascination with motor-bikes.

THE FACTS Rubel Hossain took 5 for 60 for Chittagong at Sylhet in December 2008 ... He took 4 for 33 on his ODI debut as Bangladesh beat Sri Lanka at Mirpur in January 2009 ... Rubel took 5 for 166 (in 29 overs) against New Zealand at Hamilton in February 2010 ... He took 4 for 19 against the Netherlands and 5 for 16 against Scotland on successive days in warm-up games for the World Twenty20 in England in May 2009 ...

THE FIGURES to 17.09.13 **cricinfo.com**

Batting & Fielding	M	Inns	NO	Runs	HS	Avge	S/R	100	50	4s	6s	Ct	St
Tests	16	29	14	114	17	7.60	34.54	0	0	16	0	7	0
ODIs	40	20	12	39	15*	4.87	52.00	0	0	5	0	7	0
T20Is	7	2	2	8	8*	–	80.00	0	0	1	0	1	0
First-class	32	51	19	250	44	7.81	–	0	0	–	–	13	0

Bowling	M	Balls	Runs	Wkts	BB	Avge	RpO	S/R	5i	10m
Tests	16	2802	1849	25	5–166	73.96	3.95	112.08	1	0
ODIs	40	1801	1679	49	4–25	34.26	5.59	36.75	0	0
T20Is	7	146	245	6	2–63	40.83	10.06	24.33	0	0
First-class	32	4870	3259	53	5–60	61.49	4.01	91.88	2	0

JACQUES **RUDOLPH**

Full name	Jacobus Andries Rudolph
Born	May 4, 1981, Springs, Transvaal
Teams	Titans
Style	Left-hand bat, occasional legspinner
Test debut	South Africa v Bangladesh at Chittagong 2002-03
ODI debut	South Africa v India at Dhaka 2002-03
T20I debut	South Africa v Australia at Brisbane 2005-06

THE PROFILE Jacques Rudolph's debut double-century – and a record-breaking 429-run stand with Boeta Dippenaar – against Bangladesh in April 2003 came 18 months after he had forced his way into the squad through sheer weight of runs. Twice before he had been expecting to win his first cap, and twice politics intervened. At Centurion in November 2001 the Indians were in dispute with the ICC, who ruled the match unofficial. Then two months later he was named to face Australia at Sydney, but South Africa's board president vetoed his selection, saying there were not enough "players of colour" in the side. But once he finally got in Rudolph was a fixture for three years. An undemonstrative left-hander, he has neat footwork and balance, and favours the cover-drive. His long unbeaten 102 – a classic seven-hour rearguard – saved the Perth Test in December 2005. That was his fifth Test century, but his highest score in five more matches against the Aussies was only 41. After an indifferent run – not helped by a shoulder operation – he was left out for the 2007 World Cup, and threw in his lot with Yorkshire as a Kolpak player. He scored heavily there, and matured as a person, before returning home after the 2010 season for another crack at international cricket. He captained the A team in a triangular series in Zimbabwe in June 2011, and reached 90 three times in his five innings. Still only 30, Rudolph returned to the Test side – after more than five years – against Australia in November 2011. He made a century against New Zealand at Dunedin early the following year, but was otherwise underwhelming in a strong middle order, and eventually lost his place again.

THE FACTS Rudolph was the fifth man to score a double-century on Test debut, with 222* v Bangladesh at Chittagong in April 2003: he put on 429* for the third wicket with Boeta Dippenaar ... He scored 228* for Yorkshire v Durham in April 2010 ... Occasional legspinner Rudolph took a wicket with his second ball in Tests, dismissing Nasser Hussain for 42 at Headingley in 2003 ... His record includes two ODIs for the Africa XI ...

THE FIGURES to 17.09.13   espncricinfo.com

Batting & Fielding	M	Inns	NO	Runs	HS	Avge	S/R	100	50	4s	6s	Ct	St
Tests	48	83	9	2622	222*	35.43	43.81	6	11	362	7	29	0
ODIs	45	39	6	1174	81	35.57	68.05	0	7	109	5	11	0
T20Is	1	1	1	6	6*	–	85.71	0	0	0	0	0	0
First-class	234	400	26	16629	228*	44.46	–	46	77	–	–	205	0

Bowling	M	Balls	Runs	Wkts	BB	Avge	RpO	S/R	5i	10m
Tests	48	664	432	4	1–1	108.00	3.90	166.00	0	0
ODIs	45	24	26	0	–	–	6.50	–	0	0
T20Is	1	0	–	–	–	–	–	–	–	–
First-class	234	4523	2572	58	5–80	44.34	3.41	77.98	3	0

ANDRE **RUSSELL**

Full name **Andre Dwayne Russell**
Born **April 29, 1988, Jamaica**
Teams **Jamaica, Worcestershire, Delhi Daredevils**
Style **Right-hand bat, right-arm fast-medium bowler**
Test debut **West Indies v Sri Lanka at Galle 2010-11**
ODI debut **West Indies v Ireland at Mohali 2010-11**
T20I debut **West Indies v Pakistan at Gros Islet 2010-11**

THE PROFILE A bowler with a bit of nip and a big-hitting batsman, Andre Russell has showed signs of maturing into an international-class allrounder, something West Indies are badly in need of as Dwayne Bravo, Chris Gayle and Darren Sammy enter their thirties. Russell made his international debut against England during the 2011 World Cup. First he dismissed Matt Prior in his second over and Andrew Strauss in his third, finishing with 4 for 49; then, with West Indies struggling to keep up the chase, Russell spanked 49 from 46 balls from No. 8, and only when he and Ramnaresh Sarwan were out in successive overs could England breathe again. Two matches later, though, Russell was left out of the quarter-final against Pakistan, to general surprise. He was back for the home one-dayers that followed, and although he did little against Pakistan and was dropped, on his return he enlivened the third match of the India series by hammering 92 not out after entering at 96 for 7. "This was my biggest innings as it came on a big stage," said Russell, who cheerfully admits that he remains a bowling allrounder: "Bowling is my first choice. I bowl first in the nets and then have a hit. I want to have that balance and enjoy the success." Russell does have two first-class centuries to his name: the first was against Ireland, and included no fewer than ten sixes, nine of them as he sailed past three figures in just 62 balls. Russell has played in the IPL, while a T20 stint at Worcester in 2013 featured 77 from 42 balls against Somerset. He looks like one for the future, although his similarity in style to the current West Indies captain Darren Sammy might limit his opportunities in the short term.

THE FACTS Russell hit 92* against India in Antigua in June 2011, the highest score by a No. 9 in any ODI ... He reached his maiden first-class century, against Ireland at Spanish Town in April 2010, in just 62 balls, with nine sixes and seven fours ... He hit 128 for West Indies A v Bangladesh A in November 2011 ... Russell's first two first-class five-fors came in successive matches for West Indies A v India A in England in June 2010 ...

THE FIGURES to 17.09.13   ESPNcricinfo.com

Batting & Fielding	M	Inns	NO	Runs	HS	Avge	S/R	100	50	4s	6s	Ct	St
Tests	1	1	0	2	2	2.00	22.22	0	0	0	0	1	0
ODIs	34	27	5	660	92*	30.00	119.34	0	3	61	30	7	0
T20Is	15	10	4	81	23*	13.50	120.89	0	0	7	2	4	0
First-class	16	23	1	565	128	25.68	–	2	0	–	–	6	0

Bowling	M	Balls	Runs	Wkts	BB	Avge	RpO	S/R	5i	10m
Tests	1	138	104	1	1-73	104.00	4.52	138.00	0	0
ODIs	34	1427	1302	42	4-35	31.00	5.47	33.97	0	0
T20Is	15	126	214	1	1-14	214.00	10.19	126.00	0	0
First-class	16	1924	1044	50	5-36	20.88	3.25	38.48	3	0

HAMISH **RUTHERFORD**

NEW ZEALAND

Full name	**Hamish Duncan Rutherford**
Born	**April 27, 1989, Dunedin**
Teams	**Otago, Essex**
Style	**Left-hand bat**
Test debut	**New Zealand v England at Dunedin 2012-13**
ODI debut	**New Zealand v England at Napier 2012-13**
T20I debut	**New Zealand v England at Auckland 2012-13**

THE PROFILE Left-hand opener Hamish Rutherford made a dramatic entry into Test cricket by flogging 171 against England in his first match, at home in Dunedin in March 2013. It certainly trumped the Test debut of his father, Ken, who bagged a pair against West Indies in 1984-85 – although he recovered well enough to captain his country in due course. England's attack gave Rutherford junior too much room outside off stump, and he cut and carved away merrily: over 100 of his runs came in boundaries. The bowlers learned their lesson after that, and bowled much straighter: his next four Tests – at home and in England – produced a highest score of 42, although he baseball-batted a rapid 62 in a Twenty20 game at The Oval at the end of June. Little more than a year before, though, Rutherford had been contemplating the end of his professional career: dropped by Otago, he was working in a coffee shop. But then in March 2012 Aaron Redmond was dumped after a poor run, and the recalled Rutherford followed his maiden first-class hundred, 107 against Northern Districts, with 118 in the second innings. Shortly afterwards he hammered 239 against Wellington, with 36 fours. The following season Rutherford started with 99 against India A, and – with a Test place up for grabs as Martin Guptill was injured – made a copper-bottomed case for a call-up with 162 against ND, bookended by twin 90s against Wellington and the England tourists. Rutherford is short-sighted: "I'm blind as a bat without my contact lenses," he admitted after having to hold the game up for a while when he lost one during England's warm-up match at Queenstown shortly before his Test debut.

THE FACTS Rutherford scored 171 in his first Test, the highest by a New Zealander on debut against England ... He hit 239 for Otago v Wellington at Dunedin in March 2012, three weeks after scoring 107 and 118 against Northern Districts ... He made 84 from 43 balls for Essex v Sussex in the Twenty20 Cup at Hove in July 2013 ... His father, Ken Rutherford, captained New Zealand in 18 of his 56 Tests ...

THE FIGURES to 17.09.13   **ESPNcricinfo.com**

Batting & Fielding	M	Inns	NO	Runs	HS	Avge	S/R	100	50	4s	6s	Ct	St
Tests	5	9	0	328	171	36.44	65.73	1	0	41	5	6	0
ODIs	2	2	0	13	11	6.50	29.54	0	0	2	0	2	0
T20Is	5	4	0	131	62	32.75	157.83	0	1	11	8	1	0
First-class	29	51	0	2065	239	40.49	70.86	6	7	302	28	20	0

Bowling	M	Balls	Runs	Wkts	BB	Avge	RpO	S/R	5i	10m
Tests	5	0	–	–	–	–	–	–	–	–
ODIs	2	0	–	–	–	–	–	–	–	–
T20Is	5	0	–	–	–	–	–	–	–	–
First-class	29	0	–	–	–	–	–	–	–	–

JESSE **RYDER**

Full name **Jesse Daniel Ryder**
Born **August 6, 1984, Masterton, Wellington**
Teams **Wellington, Otago**
Style **Left-hand bat, right-arm medium-pacer**
Test debut **New Zealand v Bangladesh at Chittagong 2008-09**
ODI debut **New Zealand v England at Wellington 2007-08**
T20I debut **New Zealand v England at Auckland 2007-08**

THE PROFILE Jesse Ryder had a troubled childhood, and latterly battled with his weight and demons of his own: just after establishing himself in the one-day side early in 2008, he injured tendons in his hand when he smashed a window in a bar at 5.30am after a tight series victory over England. He missed the Tests, and the England tour which followed. Early in 2012, he lost his central contract and withdrew from international cricket, vowing to return "when the time was right". Then he suffered serious head injuries in a vicious assault in Christchurch in March 2013, just before he was supposed to be departing for the IPL. Thankfully he recovered, and such is his talent that fingers remain crossed – in New Zealand and elsewhere – that he will be able to return to international cricket soon. The NZ board had already forgiven him for snubbing their A team (he briefly threatened to try to qualify for England), and gave him several more chances despite continued concerns about his drinking. A chunky left-hander, Ryder gives the ball a good thump: he biffed 79 not out in the second game of that 2008 series against England, going run for run with Brendon McCullum in a rollicking opening stand of 165 which won the Hamilton encounter with half the overs unused. He finally made his Test debut in Bangladesh in November 2008, collecting 91 in his second match then three successive fifties against West Indies at home. A maiden Test century followed against India at Hamilton, then he went one better in the second Test at Napier with a superb 201, setting up a massive total of 619 after entering at 23 for 3.

THE FACTS Ryder scored 236 for Wellington v Central Districts at Palmerston North in March 2005 ... When he hit 201* against India at Napier in March 2009 it was the second time "J. Ryder" had made 201 in a Test – Jack of Australia made 201 not out against England at Adelaide in 1924-25 ... Ryder played two one-day games for Ireland in 2007 before being dumped after missing the plane to the next match ...

THE FIGURES to 17.09.13   **espncricinfo.com**

Batting & Fielding	M	Inns	NO	Runs	HS	Avge	S/R	100	50	4s	6s	Ct	St
Tests	18	33	2	1269	201	40.93	55.19	3	6	146	6	12	0
ODIs	39	33	1	1100	107	34.37	89.72	2	6	115	31	14	0
T20Is	20	19	1	412	62	22.88	122.98	0	3	42	16	5	0
First-class	71	119	7	4980	236	44.46	–	13	23	–	–	63	0

Bowling	M	Balls	Runs	Wkts	BB	Avge	RpO	S/R	5i	10m
Tests	18	492	280	5	2–7	56.00	3.41	98.40	0	0
ODIs	39	383	399	11	3–29	36.27	6.25	34.81	0	0
T20Is	20	60	68	2	1–2	34.00	6.80	30.00	0	0
First-class	71	3491	1702	48	4–23	35.45	2.92	72.72	0	0

SAEED AJMAL

Full name **Saeed Ajmal**
Born **October 14, 1977, Faisalabad, Punjab**
Teams **Faisalabad, Zarai Taraqiati Bank**
Style **Right-hand bat, offspinner**
Test debut **Pakistan v Sri Lanka at Galle 2009**
ODI debut **Pakistan v India at Karachi 2008**
T20I debut **Pakistan v Australia at Dubai 2009**

THE PROFILE Offspinner Saeed Ajmal had been a first-class cricketer for more than ten years when the selectors finally called. Given Pakistan's usual propensity for plucking teenagers from obscurity, he must have thought, at 30, that his chance had gone. However, another impressive domestic season earned him a place at the Asia Cup in Pakistan in mid-2008. He started with 1 for 47 against India, then strangled Bangladesh with two late strikes in his second match. Ajmal is very much a modern offspinner, tossing in a handy doosra to complement his stock offbreak. He received a jolting setback when his action was reported early in 2009 – he was also fined after he complained about being complained about – but tests found any elbow flexion was within the permitted 15-degree limit. He showed his delight by performing with guile and maturity as Pakistan swept to the World Twenty20 title in England in June, taking 12 wickets (only Umar Gul, with 13, took more) and often bottling up the middle overs. Then he embarked on Test cricket, with 14 wickets in three Tests in Sri Lanka, and two years later claimed 17 in two matches in the West Indies, although whispers about his action resurfaced (an occasional pause in delivery, to fox the batsman, keeps the doubters interested). Ajmal really came into his own in Tests in 2011-12, following 18 wickets against Sri Lanka in the UAE with nine in two games in Bangladesh, before orchestrating top-ranked England's embarrassing whitewash with 24 scalps in three Tests, including ten (seven of then lbw) in the first in Dubai. In 2013 he took ten more wickets in a narrow loss to South Africa at Cape Town, then claimed 11 to subdue Zimbabwe at Harare in September.

THE FACTS Saeed Ajmal took 7 for 55 (with five lbws) for Pakistan v England in Dubai in January 2012 ... He had unique match figures of 11 for 111 in a Test against West Indies in May 2011 ... Ajmal claimed 7 for 220 in 63 overs in only his second first-class match, for Faisalabad v Karachi Whites in November 1996 ... He was only the third bowler (after Clarrie Grimmett and Dilip Doshi) to take 100 wickets after making his Test debut when over 30 ...

THE FIGURES to 17.09.13   **cricinfo.com**

Batting & Fielding	M	Inns	NO	Runs	HS	Avge	S/R	100	50	4s	6s	Ct	St
Tests	28	42	10	377	50	11.78	42.17	0	1	39	4	9	0
ODIs	92	56	22	293	33	8.61	61.94	0	0	21	0	15	0
T20Is	54	19	11	63	21*	7.87	110.52	0	0	6	1	9	0
First-class	118	161	46	1381	53	12.00	–	0	3	–	–	38	0

Bowling	M	Balls	Runs	Wkts	BB	Avge	RpO	S/R	5i	10m
Tests	28	8851	3937	147	7–55	26.78	2.66	60.21	8	4
ODIs	92	4812	3347	146	5–24	22.92	4.17	32.95	0	0
T20Is	54	1200	1252	73	4–19	17.15	6.26	16.43	0	0
First-class	118	26494	12043	452	7–55	26.64	2.72	58.61	29	5

DARREN **SAMMY**

Full name	**Darren Julius Garvey Sammy**
Born	**December 20, 1983, Micoud, St Lucia**
Teams	**Windward Islands, Sunrisers Hyderabad**
Style	**Right-hand bat, right-arm medium-pacer**
Test debut	**West Indies v England at Manchester 2007**
ODI debut	**West Indies v New Zealand at Southampton 2004**
T20I debut	**West Indies v England at The Oval 2007**

THE PROFILE Darren Sammy was the surprise choice as captain when the West Indian board decided to dump Chris Gayle, a hard act to follow – especially for someone not a regular in the side before his elevation. Sammy did as well as could be expected during the 2011 World Cup, and probably better than that afterwards, squaring a home series with Pakistan (Sammy took 5 for 29 as the tourists slid to defeat in Guyana) then holding India to two draws, although victory in a low-scoring first Test at Kingston ultimately gave the visitors the series. Later in 2011 West Indies won in Bangladesh, and competed well with the Aussies at home early the following year, before predictably coming unstuck in early-season England. Then, in October 2012, West Indies joyously won the World Twenty20 in Sri Lanka. But although Sammy leads with a smile, fields like a panther, and has improved his always attacking batting – he smacked a maiden Test century at Trent Bridge in 2012 – several ex-players have questioned his place in the side on grounds of ability. He lost the ODI captaincy to Dwayne Bravo early in 2013, perhaps a sign of a change of tack by the selectors. Bowling is supposed to be his strongest suit, but it's a painful truth that his nagging medium-pace is not quite good enough – or quick enough – to make him a genuine third seamer at Test level: this despite a stunning debut, at Old Trafford in 2007, when he wobbled the ball around and finished up with seven wickets, three of them in one over. Sammy was the first Test cricketer from St Lucia, and is also thought to be Test cricket's only Seventh Day Adventist.

THE FACTS Sammy took 7 for 66 in his first Test, against England at Old Trafford in 2007: only Alf Valentine, with 8 for 104 against England at Old Trafford in 1950, has returned better figures on a Test debut for West Indies ... Sammy made 121 for Windward Islands v Barbados at Bridgetown in March 2009 ... He took 5 for 26 in a Twenty20 international against Zimbabwe at Port-of-Spain in February 2010 ...

THE FIGURES to 17.09.13   espncricinfo.com

Batting & Fielding	M	Inns	NO	Runs	HS	Avge	S/R	100	50	4s	6s	Ct	St
Tests	33	53	1	1164	106	22.38	69.65	1	4	132	31	54	0
ODIs	103	84	24	1313	84	21.88	99.09	0	5	95	61	56	0
T20Is	42	31	7	308	30	12.83	129.41	0	0	20	15	19	0
First-class	90	146	8	3372	121	24.43	–	2	21	–	–	125	0

Bowling	M	Balls	Runs	Wkts	BB	Avge	RpO	S/R	5i	10m
Tests	33	5608	2653	77	7–66	34.45	2.83	72.83	4	0
ODIs	103	4314	3253	74	4–26	43.95	4.52	58.29	0	0
T20Is	42	700	804	37	5–26	21.72	6.89	18.91	1	0
First-class	90	13041	5902	209	7–66	28.23	2.71	62.39	10	0

MARLON **SAMUELS**

Full name **Marlon Nathaniel Samuels**
Born **January 5, 1981, Kingston, Jamaica**
Teams **Jamaica, Pune Warriors**
Style **Right-hand bat, offspinner**
Test debut **West Indies v Australia at Adelaide 2000-01**
ODI debut **West Indies v Sri Lanka at Nairobi 2000-01**
T20I debut **West Indies v England at The Oval 2007**

THE PROFILE Marlon Samuels returned to international cricket in 2011 not long after completing a two-year ban for alleged involvement with bookmakers. He protested his innocence, but served his time. Samuels is a classy right-hander, whose composed start in Tests prompted comparisons with Viv Richards, and his return bolstered West Indies' suspect middle order – he made 57 in his first Test back, against Pakistan in St Kitts in May 2011, and 78 not out in his next one, against India. The rehabilitation continued with a defiant century at Trent Bridge in 2012 – in all he made 386 runs in the three Tests, at an average of 96.50 – and 123 and 52 at home in Kingston in August 2012, in a match that coincided with the 50th anniversary of Jamaican independence. Then he hammered 260 against Bangladesh at Khulna in November. He couldn't quite keep that up in 2013, although he ended a lean run with an ODI century against Pakistan in St Lucia in July. Samuels's international start was exceptional: he flew to Australia for the third Test of the 2000-01 series, only 19 and with just one first-class match under his belt, but showed a beautifully balanced technique, standing still at the crease and moving smoothly into his strokes off either foot. A combination of overconfidence and arrogance almost got him sent home from India late in 2002, after he defied a team curfew – but he survived, and responded with a disciplined maiden Test century at Kolkata (it was his first one in first-class cricket too). Samuels also bowls flattish offspin, having remodelled his action after being reported to the ICC on suspicion of throwing.

THE FACTS Samuels scored 257 and then took 5 for 87 for the West Indians v Queensland in Brisbane in October 2005 ... He scored his maiden first-class century in a Test – 104 v India at Kolkata in October 2002: he was the fifth West Indian to do this, following Clifford Roach, Clairmonte Depeiaza, Gerry Alexander and Bernard Julien ... His brother Robert, older by ten years, played six Tests and eight ODIs as a left-hand opener, and scored 125 against New Zealand in his second Test ...

THE FIGURES to 17.09.13   cricinfo.com

Batting & Fielding	M	Inns	NO	Runs	HS	Avge	S/R	100	50	4s	6s	Ct	St
Tests	46	80	6	2767	260	37.39	48.52	5	18	373	21	21	0
ODIs	154	144	22	3799	126	31.13	72.74	5	22	374	67	42	0
T20Is	25	23	3	610	85*	30.50	134.95	0	6	39	39	7	0
First-class	94	158	11	6012	260	40.89	–	12	33	–	–	60	0

Bowling	M	Balls	Runs	Wkts	BB	Avge	RpO	S/R	5i	10m
Tests	46	3093	1719	34	4–13	50.55	3.33	90.97	0	0
ODIs	154	4441	3531	80	3–25	44.13	4.77	55.51	0	0
T20Is	25	280	392	14	3–23	28.00	8.40	20.00	0	0
First-class	94	6133	3183	64	5–87	49.73	3.11	95.82	1	0

KUMAR **SANGAKKARA**

Full name	Kumar Chokshanada Sangakkara
Born	October 27, 1977, Matale
Teams	Nondescripts, Kandurata, Sunrisers Hyderabad
Style	Left-hand bat, wicketkeeper
Test debut	Sri Lanka v South Africa at Galle 2000
ODI debut	Sri Lanka v Pakistan at Galle 2000
T20I debut	Sri Lanka v England at Southampton 2006

SRI LANKA

THE PROFILE Within months of his debut at 22, Kumar Sangakkara was one of Sri Lanka's most influential players: a talented left-hand strokemaker with a sublime cut, a slick wicketkeeper, and a sharp-eyed strategist with an even sharper tongue. From the start his effortless batting oozed class: he possesses the grace of David Gower, but the attitude of an Aussie. He was briefly relieved of keeping duties after the 2003 World Cup: he made more runs, but soon got the gloves back. The extra burden had no obvious effect: he made 185 against Pakistan in March 2006. But there was a change of thinking after that, and Prasanna Jayawardene was given the gloves in Tests. Sangakkara responded with seven hundreds, three of them doubles, in his next nine Tests, including 287 as he and Mahela Jayawardene put on a world-record 624 against South Africa, successive double-centuries against Bangladesh, and a magnificent 192 against Australia at Hobart in November 2007. An astute thinker, he took over as captain early in 2009, and reached the final of the World Twenty20 in England. His batting seemed unaffected: he made five hundreds in his first ten Tests in charge, including three in successive matches against India in 2009 and 2010. Sangakkara relinquished the captaincy after defeat in the World Cup final, but stayed on as a player to complete 100 Tests later in 2011. He remained in prime form, scoring 199 not out and 192 in successive home Tests against Pakistan in June 2012, then in 2013 improving his one-day best to 169 against South Africa in Colombo, not long after an imperious century at England's expense in the Champions Trophy at The Oval.

THE FACTS Sangakkara scored 287, and put on a record 624 with Mahela Jayawardene against South Africa in Colombo in July 2006 ... He has scored eight Test double-centuries, behind only Don Bradman (12) and Brian Lara (9), plus three 190s ... Sangakkara averages 68.86 in Tests when not the designated wicketkeeper, but 40.48 when lumbered with the gloves ... His record includes three ODIs for the World XI and four for the Asia XI ...

THE FIGURES to 17.09.13   ESPNcricinfo.com

Batting & Fielding	M	Inns	NO	Runs	HS	Avge	S/R	100	50	4s	6s	Ct	St
Tests	117	200	16	10486	287	56.98	53.97	33	42	1292	36	169	20
ODIs	354	331	36	11798	169	39.99	76.63	16	79	1134	67	353	85
T20Is	45	43	6	1178	78	31.83	120.08	0	7	123	16	20	18
First-class	205	333	27	15075	287	49.26	–	42	66	–	–	330	33

Bowling	M	Balls	Runs	Wkts	BB	Avge	RpO	S/R	5i	10m
Tests	117	78	42	0	–	–	3.23	–	0	0
ODIs	354	0	–	–	–	–	–	–	–	–
T20Is	45	0	–	–	–	–	–	–	–	–
First-class	205	204	112	1	1-13	112.00	3.29	204.00	0	0

RAMNARESH **SARWAN**

Full name **Ramnaresh Ronnie Sarwan**
Born **June 23, 1980, Wakenaam Island, Essequibo, Guyana**
Teams **Guyana, Leicestershire**
Style **Right-hand batsman, legspinner**
Test debut **West Indies v Pakistan at Bridgetown 1999-2000**
ODI debut **West Indies v England at Nottingham 2000**
T20I debut **West Indies v South Africa at Johannesburg 2007-08**

THE PROFILE A light-footed artist, Ramnaresh Sarwan was brought up in the South American rainforest. After his first Test innings – 84 against Pakistan – the former England captain Ted Dexter was moved to predict a Test average of 50. And on his first tour, to England in 2000, Sarwan justified the hype: his footwork was strikingly confident and precise, and he topped the averages. It was a surprise when a horror run (three runs in five innings) followed in Australia. He soon put that behind him, although his first Test century took 28 matches. Good times followed, culminating in an unbeaten 261 against Bangladesh in June 2004. He started the 2007 England tour as captain, but injured his shoulder early on. Chris Gayle took over, but Sarwan was in peerless form at home against England in 2009, collecting 626 runs at 104.33, with three centuries, including a monumental 291 on a Bridgetown featherbed. Another silky hundred followed in the return series, before a back injury disrupted the early part of 2010, and he was summarily dropped after a run of indifferent form early the next year. He was dumped from the contracts list, but sued the board for defamation for remarks about his fitness and attitude. Sarwan won the case, and damages of $161,000. It seemed unlikely that he would play for West Indies again – he was enjoying playing for Leicestershire – but he was recalled after 18 months for the one-day series in Australia early in 2013 and, after starting with a couple of ducks, made a century against Zimbabwe in Grenada in February. A Test return is awaited.

THE FACTS Sarwan scored 291 at Bridgetown in 2008-09: only Brian Lara (twice) and Lawrence Rowe (302) have made higher Test scores for West Indies against England (Viv Richards also made 291, at The Oval in 1976) … Sarwan made 107, 94 and 106 in his previous three Test innings against England in the series … In ODIs Sarwan averages 58.90 v India – but only 23.76 v Australia … Sarwan made 100 and 111 for the West Indies Board President's XI v Zimbabwe at Pointe-à-Pierre in March 2000 …

THE FIGURES to 17.09.13   cricinfo.com

Batting & Fielding	M	Inns	NO	Runs	HS	Avge	S/R	100	50	4s	6s	Ct	St
Tests	87	154	8	5842	291	40.01	46.79	15	31	747	14	53	0
ODIs	181	169	33	5804	120*	42.67	75.74	5	38	480	58	45	0
T20Is	18	16	3	298	59	22.92	104.19	0	2	19	6	7	0
First-class	215	364	26	13221	291	39.11	–	33	70	–	–	152	0

Bowling	M	Balls	Runs	Wkts	BB	Avge	RpO	S/R	5i	10m
Tests	87	2022	1163	23	4–37	50.56	3.45	87.91	0	0
ODIs	181	581	586	16	3–31	36.62	6.05	36.31	0	0
T20Is	18	12	10	2	2–10	5.00	5.00	6.00	0	0
First-class	215	4368	2351	56	6–62	41.98	3.22	78.00	1	0

VIRENDER **SEHWAG**

Full name **Virender Sehwag**
Born **October 20, 1978, Delhi**
Teams **Delhi, Delhi Daredevils**
Style **Right-hand bat, offspinner**
Test debut **India v South Africa at Bloemfontein 2001-02**
ODI debut **India v Pakistan at Mohali 1998-99**
T20I debut **India v South Africa at Johannesburg 2006-07**

THE PROFILE Soon after his 2001 Test-debut century Virender Sehwag was being compared to Sachin Tendulkar. It is half-true: Sehwag is also short and square, and plays the straight drive, back-foot punch and whip off the hips identically – but he leaves even Sachin standing when it comes to audacity. He also bowls effective, loopy offspin. Opening in England in 2002, Sehwag proved an instant hit, and many pivotal innings followed, including India's first triple-century (brought up, characteristically, with a six), in Pakistan early in 2004. His fitness levels dropped for a while, and he struggled in ODIs – but continued to sparkle in Tests, making 254 at Lahore in January 2006. Dropped after the disastrous 2007 World Cup, Sehwag lost a stone, and the following March bounced back with another triple-century, against South Africa. Later that year he carried his bat for 201 at Galle, and overall scored 1462 Test runs in 2008, at a strike-rate (85.84) unprecedented for an opener. Sehwag started the 2011 World Cup with 175 against Bangladesh, although his desire to start every innings with a boundary saw productivity drop off after that. A shoulder injury bothered him for a while, although he exploded against West Indies in December 2011. People had long been wondering how many Sehwag might score if he batted through an ODI innings – and at Indore they found out: he carved 219 from 149 balls, with 25 fours and seven sixes (and was still out before the end, in the 47th over). He made 117 in the first Test against England in November 2012, but a poor run after that found him dropped in all three formats. Geoff Boycott was among those who dared to wonder whether India had seen the last of him.

THE FACTS Sehwag has made India's three highest Test scores (319, 309 and 293) ... He made 105 on his Test debut, v South Africa in November 2001 ... Sehwag carried his bat for 201* v Sri Lanka at Galle in mid-2008 ... He hit 219, the highest score in ODIs, v West Indies at Indore in December 2011 ... His record includes a Test and three ODIs for the World XI, and seven ODIs for the Asia XI ...

THE FIGURES to 17.09.13   ESPNcricinfo.com

Batting & Fielding	M	Inns	NO	Runs	HS	Avge	S/R	100	50	4s	6s	Ct	St
Tests	104	180	6	8586	319	49.34	82.23	23	32	1233	91	91	0
ODIs	251	245	9	8273	219	35.05	104.33	15	38	1132	136	93	0
T20Is	19	18	0	394	68	21.88	145.38	0	2	43	16	2	0
First-class	169	283	10	13223	319	48.43	–	38	50	–	–	150	0

Bowling	M	Balls	Runs	Wkts	BB	Avge	RpO	S/R	5i	10m
Tests	104	3731	1894	40	5–104	47.35	3.04	93.27	1	0
ODIs	251	4392	3853	96	4–6	40.13	5.26	45.75	0	0
T20Is	19	6	20	0	–	–	20.00	–	0	0
First-class	169	8470	4394	105	5–104	41.84	3.11	80.66	1	0

SHAFIUL ISLAM

Full name	Shafiul Islam
Born	October 6, 1989, Bogra
Teams	Rajshahi
Style	Right-hand bat, right-arm fast-medium bowler
Test debut	Bangladesh v India at Chittagong 2009-10
ODI debut	Bangladesh v Sri Lanka at Dhaka 2009-10
T20I debut	Bangladesh v New Zealand at Hamilton 2009-10

THE PROFILE An enthusiastic medium-pacer, Shafiul Islam's early marks in international cricket, oddly enough, came with bat in hand. Against India in January 2010 his first two scoring shots were big sixes smeared off the legspin of Amit Mishra (his next runs came when he was dropped on the boundary): Shafiul was the first to do this in Tests, although his team-mate Jahurul Islam followed suit against England at Mirpur two months later. During that match, "Suhas" again starred with the bat, making a forthright 53 (from 51 balls, with 11 fours) from No. 10 in a partnership of 74 with Naeem Islam as the total reached 419. Then, in the 2011 World Cup, Shafiul biffed a seemingly nerveless 24 not out in the ninth-wicket stand of 58 with Mahmudullah that spirited Bangladesh to an unlikely victory over England. This partly made up for an uninspiring tournament with the ball. Still, it is as a bowler that Shafiul is likely to make his mark long term. In 2008-09, his first full season, he took 23 wickets at 22.30 on Bangladesh's generally benign pitches, and received a national call-up after several senior bowlers were injured. He made his one-day debut in the Asia Cup at the start of 2010, and started promisingly – but he proved expensive later on, going for 95 in ten overs against Pakistan (with Shahid Afridi in full flow) in June 2010 and 97 off nine against England a month later. A foot problem kept him out when West Indies toured late in 2011, then he injured his side during the Asia Cup. But Shafiul was restored to the one-day team when fit, despite modest returns, and was boosted by chief selector Akram Khan describing him as "one of our first-choice pace bowlers".

THE FACTS Shafiul Islam's first two scoring shots in Test cricket were sixes, off Amit Mishra in two innings at Chittagong in January 2010: he was the first to achieve this in Tests (his team-mate Jahurul Islam soon emulated him) ... Shafiul took 4 for 21 against Ireland during the 2011 World Cup, while his best first-class figures of 4 for 38 came for Rajshahi at Khulna in November 2008 ...

THE FIGURES to 17.09.13   espncricinfo.com

Batting & Fielding	M	Inns	NO	Runs	HS	Avge	S/R	100	50	4s	6s	Ct	St
Tests	6	12	1	149	53	13.54	60.08	0	1	24	2	1	0
ODIs	49	27	8	109	24*	5.73	55.89	0	0	11	2	8	0
T20Is	11	4	1	18	16	6.00	75.00	0	0	1	1	1	0
First-class	26	40	8	500	53	15.62	71.63	0	1	62	16	8	0

Bowling	M	Balls	Runs	Wkts	BB	Avge	RpO	S/R	5i	10m
Tests	6	996	569	8	3–86	71.12	3.42	124.50	0	0
ODIs	49	2079	2013	58	4–21	34.70	5.80	35.84	0	0
T20Is	11	220	275	8	2–19	34.37	7.50	27.50	0	0
First-class	26	3865	1949	60	4–38	32.48	3.02	64.41	0	0

SHAHADAT HOSSAIN

Full name **Kazi Shahadat Hossain**
Born **August 7, 1986, Narayanganj, Dhaka**
Teams **Dhaka**
Style **Right-hand bat, right-arm fast-medium bowler**
Test debut **Bangladesh v England at Lord's 2005**
ODI debut **Bangladesh v Kenya at Bogra 2005-06**
T20I debut **Bangladesh v Zimbabwe at Khulna 2006-07**

THE PROFILE Shahadat Hossain was discovered at a talent-spotting camp, and whisked away to the Institute of Sports for refinement. "Rajib" has all the necessary attributes for a genuine fast bowler: he is tall and strong, and doesn't put unnecessary pressure on his body, with a slightly open-chested delivery position after a smooth run-up. He is naturally aggressive, and has raw pace. But his Test debut at Lord's in 2005 was a chastening experience, as his 12 overs disappeared for 101. He was just 18 then: after that he did well against Sri Lanka, taking four wickets in an innings twice before going one better in Bogra's inaugural Test in March 2006. Early in 2008 his 6 for 27 at Mirpur gave Bangladesh a rare first-innings lead over South Africa – and an even rarer (if illusory) sniff of victory. In one-day internationals, despite a hat-trick against Zimbabwe, he has been in and out of the side: he played only once in the 2007 World Cup (and was hit around in the sobering defeat by Ireland), and has since generally been viewed as too expensive and erratic for limited-overs games. In Tests, however, he played his part as Bangladesh won an overseas series for the first time, in the Caribbean in mid-2009, and in May 2010 he erased some of the memories of that painful Test debut with 5 for 98 at Lord's, although England still won comfortably in the end. Shahadat was set back by injury after that, and missed the 2011 World Cup – although 5 for 82 for Dhaka against Rajshahi (all but one of his victims a Test player) shortly afterwards suggested he was returning to his best, and indeed he was soon restored to the Test side, although success proved elusive – two matches in 2012-13 produced only two expensive wickets.

THE FACTS Shahadat Hossain's 6 for 27 against South Africa at Mirpur in February 2008 are the best figures by a Bangladesh fast bowler in Tests ... He took Bangladesh's first ODI hat-trick, against Zimbabwe at Harare in August 2006 ... Shahadat averages 26.75 with the ball in Tests against India, and 27.86 v South Africa – but 258.00 v Australia, and 221.00 v Pakistan ... He took only two wickets – both against Kenya – in his first six ODIs ...

THE FIGURES to 17.09.13　　　　　　　　　　　　　　　　　　　espncricinfo.com

Batting & Fielding	M	Inns	NO	Runs	HS	Avge	S/R	100	50	4s	6s	Ct	St
Tests	35	65	17	489	40	10.18	46.61	0	0	66	5	8	0
ODIs	51	27	17	79	16*	7.90	52.31	0	0	7	1	5	0
T20Is	6	5	3	8	4*	4.00	66.66	0	0	0	0	0	0
First-class	71	114	32	941	40	11.47	–	0	0	–	–	16	0

Bowling	M	Balls	Runs	Wkts	BB	Avge	RpO	S/R	5i	10m
Tests	35	5180	3633	70	6–27	51.90	4.20	74.00	4	0
ODIs	51	2198	2143	47	3–34	45.59	5.84	46.76	0	0
T20Is	6	120	198	4	2–22	49.50	9.90	30.00	0	0
First-class	71	10388	6868	179	6–27	38.36	3.96	58.03	9	0

SHAHID AFRIDI

Full name **Sahibzada Mohammad Shahid Khan Afridi**
Born **March 1, 1980, Khyber Agency**
Teams **Karachi, Habib Bank**
Style **Right-hand bat, legspinner**
Test debut **Pakistan v Australia at Karachi 1998-99**
ODI debut **Pakistan v Kenya at Nairobi 1996-97**
T20I debut **Pakistan v England at Bristol 2006**

THE PROFILE A flamboyant allrounder introduced to international cricket as a 16-year-old legspinner, Shahid Afridi astonished everyone except himself by pinch-hitting the fastest one-day hundred in his maiden innings. He's a compulsive shotmaker, and although initially that was too often his undoing, he eventually blossomed. A violent century against India in April 2005 came soon after he walloped 58 in 34 balls to square the Test series at Bangalore. Then came a Test ton against West Indies, important runs against England, and mayhem against India on some flat tracks early in 2006. A typical Afridi assault is laced with lofted drives and short-arm jabs over midwicket. He's at his best when forcing straight, and at his weakest pushing just outside off. With the ball he can get turn as well as lazy drift, but variety is the key: a vicious faster ball and an offbreak too. Afridi roared back to form in the World Twenty20 in England in 2009, and made a ferocious 51 as Pakistan bossed the final at Lord's. He had retired from Tests in 2006 but returned as captain four years later, only to quit dramatically after two irresponsible shots in a big defeat by Australia at Lord's. His slogging powers seemed to be waning, but his bowling remained a potent one-day weapon, as shown by 21 wickets in the 2011 World Cup. Not long after that Afridi fell out with the board and was dumped as one-day captain. He immediately retired again ... but was soon back, although his performances were fairly subdued. He was briefly dropped, and missed the Champions Trophy in England in 2013, but then ended a run of six wicketless matches with 7 for 12 – Pakistan's best figures in ODIs – to demolish West Indies in July.

THE FACTS In his second match (he didn't bat in the first) Shahid Afridi hit the fastest hundred in ODIs, from 37 balls, against Sri Lanka in October 1996 ... He took 7 for 12, Pakistan's best figures in ODIs, v West Indies at Providence in July 2013 ... Afridi has the highest strike-rate of anyone with more than 30 innings in ODIs, and has hit more sixes in ODIs than anyone else ... His record includes three ODIs for the Asia XI and two for the World XI ...

THE FIGURES to 17.09.13   espncricinfo.com

Batting & Fielding	M	Inns	NO	Runs	HS	Avge	S/R	100	50	4s	6s	Ct	St
Tests	27	48	1	1716	156	36.51	86.97	5	8	220	52	10	0
ODIs	362	335	22	7360	124	23.51	114.73	6	35	667	317	115	0
T20Is	63	59	7	939	54*	18.05	142.92	0	4	78	35	19	0
First-class	111	183	4	5631	164	31.45	–	12	30	–	–	75	0

Bowling	M	Balls	Runs	Wkts	BB	Avge	RpO	S/R	5i	10m
Tests	27	3194	1709	48	5–52	35.60	3.21	66.54	1	0
ODIs	362	15822	12184	359	7–12	33.93	4.62	44.07	9	0
T20Is	63	1385	1473	67	4–11	21.98	6.38	20.67	0	0
First-class	111	13493	7023	258	6–101	27.22	3.12	52.29	8	0

SHAHRIAR NAFEES

BANGLADESH

Full name	**Shahriar Nafees Ahmed**
Born	**January 25, 1986, Dhaka**
Teams	**Barisal**
Style	**Left-hand bat**
Test debut	**Bangladesh v Sri Lanka at Colombo 2005-06**
ODI debut	**Bangladesh v England at Nottingham 2005**
T20I debut	**Bangladesh v Zimbabwe at Khulna 2006-07**

THE PROFILE A talented left-hand opener, Shahriar Nafees went on Bangladesh's maiden tour of England in 2005, aged 19 and with just five first-class matches behind him. He hadn't fared too badly in those, making 350 runs at 35. That England trip was a case of watching and learning, but "Abir" did get an opportunity in the one-day series, and made 75 against Australia in the last game. A Test debut followed in Sri Lanka, and Shahriar made 51 in his second match. Then, in April 2006, he exploded in sensational fashion against the might of Australia, stroking his way to a brilliant hundred, his maiden first-class ton as well as his first in Tests, at Fatullah. His stunning 138, with 19 fours, set up a scarcely believable first-day total of 355 for 5 as the Aussies reeled, and a brisk 79 in the second Test showed this was no flash in the pan. There were also three one-day hundreds against Zimbabwe, and one against Bermuda, but he found life harder against the big boys, being dropped after six innings in the 2007 World Cup produced only 31 runs and a top score of 12. After that Shahriar seemed to have been lost to international cricket, copping a ten-year ban after signing up for the unauthorised Indian Cricket League, but he was the first to be welcomed back after an amnesty. He had another quiet World Cup in 2011, but then spanked 56 and 60 against his old friends Australia. After that he slipped out of the limited-overs teams, but 97 against Pakistan at Mirpur in December 2011 emphasised his Test credentials. But hundreds remained elusive, and he slipped out of the team in 2013.

THE FACTS Shahriar Nafees's 138 against Australia at Fatullah in 2005-06 was his maiden first-class century: his previous-best was 97, for the Board President's XI v Zimbabwe in January 2005 ... Shahriar hit four of Bangladesh's first seven ODI hundreds ... He averages 55.50 in ODIs against Zimbabwe, with three centuries, but only 5.50 v India (and 0 v Canada) ... His brother, Iftekhar Nayem, has also played first-class cricket ...

THE FIGURES to 17.09.13   **espncricinfo.com**

Batting & Fielding	M	Inns	NO	Runs	HS	Avge	S/R	100	50	4s	6s	Ct	St
Tests	24	48	0	1267	138	26.39	55.86	1	7	189	1	19	0
ODIs	75	75	5	2201	123*	31.44	69.49	4	13	277	7	13	0
T20Is	1	1	0	25	25	25.00	147.05	0	0	3	1	1	0
First-class	61	116	3	3615	138	31.99	58.98	5	23	–	–	39	0

Bowling	M	Balls	Runs	Wkts	BB	Avge	RpO	S/R	5i	10m
Tests	24	0	–	–	–	–	–	–	–	–
ODIs	75	0	–	–	–	–	–	–	–	–
T20Is	1	0	–	–	–	–	–	–	–	–
First-class	61	78	58	0	–	–	4.46	–	0	0

SHAKIB AL HASAN

Full name **Shakib Al Hasan**
Born **March 24, 1987, Magura, Jessore**
Teams **Khulna, Leicestershire, Kolkata Knight Riders**
Style **Left-hand bat, slow left-arm orthodox spinner**
Test debut **Bangladesh v India at Chittagong 2006-07**
ODI debut **Bangladesh v Zimbabwe at Harare 2006**
T20I debut **Bangladesh v Zimbabwe at Khulna 2006-07**

THE PROFILE A stylish left-hand batsman and flattish left-arm spinner, Shakib Al Hasan was earmarked for great things after starring for the Under-19s. His full debut duly arrived in August 2006: he took a wicket then strolled in at No. 4 to make 30 not out in the matchwinning partnership. From the start Shakib proved remarkably consistent, being dismissed in single figures only once in 18 one-dayers leading up to the 2007 World Cup. The heady start continued in the Caribbean with a half-century in the famous win over India, and another against England. After that came the inevitable dip – 17 runs in three innings in Sri Lanka – but he soon returned to form. He sealed Bangladesh's 2-0 triumph against West Indies in July 2009, finishing just short of a maiden Test ton in Grenada: by then he had taken over from the injured Mashrafe Mortaza as captain. Shakib's spin bowling – always effective and economical in ODIs – blossomed almost overnight in Tests. After only three wickets in his first six matches, he took 7 for 36 against New Zealand in October 2008, then 13 wickets in those two Tests in the West Indies. He also sailed past 100 one-day wickets in mid-2010, just before becoming the first Bangladeshi to play county cricket, for Worcestershire. By 2011 Shakib seemed entrenched as captain, his own successes contrasting with his team's often woeful performances. However, after a disheartening tour of Zimbabwe, Shakib was sacked as skipper. It didn't affect his performances, and he briefly sat atop the ICC's rankings for Test allrounders after scoring 144 – and taking seven wickets – against Pakistan in December 2011. A stress fracture of the shin kept him out for a while in 2012-13, but he was quickly restored when fit again.

THE FACTS Shakib Al Hasan took 7 for 36, Bangladesh's best Test bowling figures, against New Zealand at Chittagong in October 2008 ... He made 144 against Pakistan at Mirpur in December 2011, and a round 100 v New Zealand in February 2010 – and additionally has scored 96 in Tests three times ... Shakib hit 134* v Canada in Antigua in February 2007 ... He averages 59.66 with the bat in Tests against New Zealand – but 15.12 v South Africa ...

THE FIGURES to 17.09.13   cricinfo.com

Batting & Fielding	M	Inns	NO	Runs	HS	Avge	S/R	100	50	4s	6s	Ct	St
Tests	30	57	2	1984	144	36.07	59.79	2	13	246	8	13	0
ODIs	129	124	19	3688	134*	35.12	78.18	5	25	323	25	36	0
T20Is	26	26	0	528	84	20.30	125.71	0	3	58	10	7	0
First-class	65	120	9	3886	144	35.00	–	5	23	–	–	36	0

Bowling	M	Balls	Runs	Wkts	BB	Avge	RpO	S/R	5i	10m
Tests	30	7242	3476	106	7–36	32.79	2.87	68.32	9	0
ODIs	129	6578	4729	161	4–16	29.37	4.31	40.85	0	0
T20Is	26	582	684	33	4–21	19.81	6.74	17.63	0	0
First-class	65	13296	6202	205	7–32	30.25	2.79	64.85	14	0

ISHANT SHARMA

Full name **Ishant Sharma**
Born **September 2, 1988, Delhi**
Teams **Delhi, Sunrisers Hyderabad**
Style **Right-hand bat, right-arm fast-medium bowler**
Test debut **India v Bangladesh at Dhaka 2006-07**
ODI debut **India v South Africa at Belfast 2007**
T20I debut **India v Australia at Melbourne 2007-08**

THE PROFILE Tall fast bowlers have always been a much-prized rarity in India. Their earliest Tests featured Mohammad Nissar, a few years ago Abey Kuruvilla shone briefly ... and now there's Ishant Sharma, a lofty 6ft 4ins (193cm). He's regularly above 80mph, with a sharp and deceptive bouncer, delivered from a high arm action. After starting the game seriously at 14, he was playing one-dayers for Delhi only three years later in 2005-06. The following season he took 4 for 65 from 34 overs on first-class debut, and finished his first term with 29 wickets at 20.10. Early in 2007 he was on the verge of reinforcing the national team in South Africa – flights had been booked and visa arrangements made – but in the end he was left to concentrate on domestic cricket and a youth tour. However, when Munaf Patel was injured again in Bangladesh in May, Sharma finally did get on the plane, and took a wicket in a landslide victory at Dhaka. In Australia at the end of 2007 he looked the real deal, especially in the Perth Test, where he dismissed Ricky Ponting during a sensational spell, and again in the one-dayers as India ambushed the hosts to snaffle the series. In 2011 he took 22 wickets in three Tests in the Caribbean, including ten at Bridgetown, but then blew hot and cold in England – listless in the first innings at Lord's, magnificent in the second – before missing the one-day series with an ankle injury. That eventually needed an operation, but he was back to face England and Australia at home in 2012-13. Wickets remained elusive, though, and an undistinguished Test bowling average kept on climbing.

THE FACTS Ishant Sharma took 7 for 24 (11 for 51 in the match) for Delhi v Orissa at Delhi in November 2008 ... He took 22 wickets in three Tests in the West Indies in 2011, including 6 for 55 at Bridgetown ... His bowling average in ODIs against Australia is 25.13, but 52.00 v South Africa ... In 2006-07, his first season of first-class cricket, Sharma took 29 wickets at 20.10 for Delhi, then made his Test debut in only his seventh match ...

THE FIGURES *to 17.09.13*   **espncricinfo.com**

Batting & Fielding	M	Inns	NO	Runs	HS	Avge	S/R	100	50	4s	6s	Ct	St
Tests	51	74	28	450	31*	9.78	28.57	0	0	50	0	12	0
ODIs	65	22	9	65	13	5.00	35.32	0	0	6	0	15	0
T20Is	13	3	2	8	5*	8.00	88.88	0	0	1	0	3	0
First-class	77	99	40	540	31*	9.15	28.21	0	0	61	0	18	0

Bowling	M	Balls	Runs	Wkts	BB	Avge	RpO	S/R	5i	10m
Tests	51	9849	5471	144	6–55	37.99	3.33	68.39	3	1
ODIs	65	3025	2822	94	4–38	30.02	5.59	32.18	0	0
T20Is	13	254	348	8	2–34	43.50	8.22	31.75	0	0
First-class	77	14608	7758	238	7–24	32.59	3.18	61.37	5	2

ROHIT SHARMA

Full name **Rohit Gurunathan Sharma**
Born **April 30, 1987, Bansod, Nagpur, Maharashtra**
Teams **Mumbai, Mumbai Indians**
Style **Right-hand bat, offspinner**
Test debut **No Tests yet**
ODI debut **India v Ireland at Belfast 2007**
T20I debut **India v England at Durban 2007-08**

THE PROFILE Rohit Sharma made a great start to his first-class career, making 205 against Gujarat in only his fourth match for Mumbai. Earlier in 2006 he had made his first-class debut for India A, and also exuded class in the Under-19 World Cup. Sharma is an adaptable batsman, strong off the back foot, equally happy as accumulator or aggressor. He finished 2006-07 with 600 runs at 40, plus 356 in one-dayers and a 49-ball Twenty20 century against Gujarat, which earned him a national call as the dust settled on India's disastrous World Cup campaign. He had a couple of useful innings in the inaugural World Twenty20 in South Africa later in 2007. Then, during the second season of the IPL in 2009, Sharma's Deccan Chargers entered the last over against Kolkata needing 21 to win – and he hit 26, including a six off the final ball, off Bangladesh's Mashrafe Mortaza. A few matches previously Sharma's seldom-seen offspin had claimed an unlikely hat-trick to derail the Mumbai Indians. In 2009-10 he followed a triple-century for Mumbai with successive one-day hundreds against Zimbabwe and Sri Lanka. He would have had that elusive Test cap, too, except he twisted his ankle during the warm-up before the first match against South Africa at Nagpur in February 2010. He missed the 2011 World Cup, but returned in the Caribbean shortly afterwards and passed 50 in three of his five innings. He remained a one-day fixture, and during a successful run at the top of the order in 2013 reached a century of 50-overs caps ... but was still missing a Test one.

THE FACTS Rohit Sharma was the first man from a Test-playing country to appear in 100 ODIs before playing in a Test ... He extended his maiden first-class century to 205, for Mumbai v Gujarat in December 2006 ... Sharma scored 309* for Mumbai v Gujarat in December 2009: in his next innings he was out for a duck ... He took a hat-trick (and four wickets in five balls) against Mumbai Indians in the IPL at Centurion in May 2009 ...

THE FIGURES to 17.09.13   cricinfo.com

Batting & Fielding	M	Inns	NO	Runs	HS	Avge	S/R	100	50	4s	6s	Ct	St
Tests	0	0	–	–	–	–	–	–	–	–	–	–	–
ODIs	102	97	18	2558	114	32.37	75.61	2	18	196	29	34	0
T20Is	35	28	10	531	79*	29.50	127.64	0	5	42	20	15	0
First-class	57	86	8	4683	309*	60.03	–	15	20	–	–	41	0

Bowling	M	Balls	Runs	Wkts	BB	Avge	RpO	S/R	5i	10m
Tests	0	0	–	–	–	–	–	–	–	–
ODIs	102	527	450	8	2-27	56.25	5.12	65.87	0	0
T20Is	35	68	113	1	1-22	113.00	9.97	68.00	0	0
First-class	57	1548	822	20	4-41	41.10	3.18	77.40	0	0

SHANE **SHILLINGFORD**

Full name	Shane Shillingford
Born	February 22, 1983, Dominica
Teams	Windward Islands
Style	Right-hand bat, offspinner
Test debut	West Indies v South Africa at Port-of-Spain 2010
ODI debut	No ODIs yet
T20I debut	No T20Is yet

THE PROFILE Offspinner Shane Shillingford certainly experienced the highs and lows of international cricket in 2012. Recalled for his first Tests for 18 months after whispers about his bowling action, Shillingford took four wickets against Australia in Port-of-Spain then, at home in Dominica, claimed ten wickets in the match – enough to earn him a diplomatic passport from the island's government as their ambassador for sport. But he sat out the very next Test, in supposedly seam-friendly conditions at Lord's a couple of weeks later. Restored at Trent Bridge, Shillingford took only one wicket, and was replaced by the new wonder boy Sunil Narine. But Shillingford was preferred for the Tests against Zimbabwe in March 2013, and after warming up with nine wickets in Barbados again took ten at home at Roseau – although the modest nature of the opposition precluded any more governmental honours. Shillingford had started with a bang back in January 2001, taking 7 for 66 on his first-class debut, for Windward Islands against Jamaica at Kingston. It was always going to be difficult to live up to such a start, and his career received what might have been a terminal setback later the same month when he was called for throwing by Steve Bucknor. But the new rules which permitted a 15-degree elbow-bend quietened the talk about his action, and Shillingford returned with 31 wickets in 2007-08, adding 56 at 19.05 in the following season. In 2010 he became only the fifth Dominican to play Test cricket. Two of his predecessors share his surname, but they are not related: "Shillingford is a very common name in Dominica," says the veteran West Indian journalist Tony Cozier. "The original Mr Shillingford must have been quite a man."

THE FACTS Shillingford took 7 for 66 on first-class debut, for Windward Islands v Jamaica at Kingston in January 2001 ... He took 6 for 119 (and 4 for 100) against Australia at Roseau in April 2010: he was the first West Indian spinner to take ten in a Test since Lance Gibbs in 1966 ... He was the fifth Dominican to play a Test for West Indies, after Grayson and Irvine Shillingford (no relations), Norbert Phillip and Adam Sanford ...

THE FIGURES to 17.09.13   espncricinfo.com

Batting & Fielding	M	Inns	NO	Runs	HS	Avge	S/R	100	50	4s	6s	Ct	St
Tests	10	14	3	121	31*	11.00	38.41	0	0	17	2	5	0
ODIs	0	0	–	–	–	–	–	–	–	–	–	–	–
T20Is	0	0	–	–	–	–	–	–	–	–	–	–	–
First-class	82	133	23	1485	63	13.50	–	0	4	–	–	44	0

Bowling	M	Balls	Runs	Wkts	BB	Avge	RpO	S/R	5i	10m
Tests	10	3029	1499	48	6–49	31.22	2.96	63.10	4	2
ODIs	0	0	–	–	–	–	–	–	–	–
T20Is	0	0	–	–	–	–	–	–	–	–
First-class	82	19067	8327	361	8–33	23.06	2.62	52.81	21	7

VUSI SIBANDA

Full name	**Vusimuzi Sibanda**
Born	**October 10, 1983, Highfields, Harare**
Teams	**Mid West Rhinos**
Style	**Right-hand bat, occasional medium-pacer**
Test debut	**Zimbabwe v West Indies at Harare 2003-04**
ODI debut	**Zimbabwe v West Indies at Bulawayo 2003-04**
T20I debut	**Zimbabwe v Australia at Cape Town 2007-08**

THE PROFILE Vusi Sibanda comes from the Harare black township of Highfield, as did Hamilton Masakadza and Tatenda Taibu. An opening batsman, Sibanda was one of a clutch of young players promoted to the national team in 2004 before they were ready, as the dispute that cost Zimbabwe several senior players rumbled on. He was retained despite modest returns, his continued selection down to outstanding potential rather than actual performance. Sibanda has always been a superb timer of the ball, predominantly off the front foot, but was slow to learn how to build a big innings. He made 78 and 116 against Bermuda in the tri-series in Trinidad in May 2006, but continued to struggle against top-class opposition – and fought a similar long battle to get used to contact lenses. It all came right in 2009-10, when he kicked off a record-breaking domestic season with four centuries in two matches, and went on to score nine in all, a world record. He played only twice in the 2011 World Cup, making 61 against Kenya, but hit form when Bangladesh came calling in August for a tour that included Zimbabwe's first Test for six years. Sibanda started that with an elegant 78, and continued his good form in the one-day series, hitting 96 and 67 in the first two matches. Innings of 45 and 93 followed in the home Tests against Pakistan and New Zealand, but he missed the NZ tour early in 2012 as the board was angry that he had gone off to play club cricket in Australia. But Zimbabwe could not afford to ignore such a classy player, and Sibanda returned late in 2012. The following year a fine century at Bulawayo anchored a one-day series victory over Bangladesh, and he added 54 against Pakistan in August before struggling again in the Tests.

THE FACTS Sibanda hit nine centuries in Zimbabwe in 2009-10, the most by any batsman in an overseas season, breaking the record of Don Bradman (eight in Australia in 1947-48): the run included four centuries in two successive matches, and seven in nine innings overall … The sequence began with 209 (and 116*) for Zimbabwe v Kenya at Kwekwe in October 2009, and included a career-best 215 for Mid West Rhinos v Mountaineers …

THE FIGURES to 17.09.13   ESPNcricinfo.com

Batting & Fielding	M	Inns	NO	Runs	HS	Avge	S/R	100	50	4s	6s	Ct	St
Tests	12	24	0	526	93	21.91	50.96	0	2	76	5	13	0
ODIs	111	110	3	2706	116	25.28	63.59	2	20	299	31	39	0
T20Is	13	13	0	189	32	14.53	91.74	0	0	25	2	4	0
First-class	105	195	8	5785	215	30.93	–	14	23	–	–	116	0

Bowling	M	Balls	Runs	Wkts	BB	Avge	RpO	S/R	5i	10m
Tests	12	0	–	–	–	–	–	–	–	–
ODIs	111	141	149	2	1-12	74.50	6.34	70.50	0	0
T20Is	13	0	–	–	–	–	–	–	–	–
First-class	105	2001	1294	22	4-30	58.81	3.88	90.95	0	0

PETER SIDDLE

Full name **Peter Matthew Siddle**
Born **November 25, 1984, Traralgon, Victoria**
Teams **Victoria**
Style **Right-hand bat, right-arm fast bowler**
Test debut **Australia v India at Mohali 2008-09**
ODI debut **Australia v New Zealand at Brisbane 2008-09**
T20I debut **Australia v New Zealand at Sydney 2008-09**

AUSTRALIA

THE PROFILE Peter Siddle was long considered one of the most dangerous fast bowlers in Australia – but also one of the most fragile. A shoulder reconstruction sidelined him for most of 2006-07, then he dislocated the joint at the start of the following season, and aggravated it again later on. He still finished 2007-08 with 33 wickets in just five matches. He emerged from reconstructive surgery fitter than ever, and was a surprise inclusion for the Indian tour in October 2008: his first Test wicket was the plum one of Sachin Tendulkar. The burly Siddle has echoes of two illustrious predecessors: the run-up is reminiscent of Craig McDermott's, while the bustling delivery reminds some of Merv Hughes – and he has a touch of the old Hughes banter, too. In England in 2009 he moved the ball at a lively pace and finished up with 20 wickets. That included a decisive first-day spell of 5 for 21 to put England on the ropes at Headingley, where Australia won easily. He looked to have booked a spot – but then a stress fracture ruled him out for most of 2010. He returned for the Ashes, and started with a sensational first-day hat-trick on the way to 6 for 54, although he took only eight more wickets in that depressing series. Back trouble intruded again in 2012, sending him home early from a West Indian tour. The following year – by now a vegan – he toiled manfully in India then claimed 17 wickets in the 2013 Ashes series. Siddle grew up in Morwell in rural Victoria, and was a promising competitive wood-chopper before concentrating on cricket at 14. "I thought if I was going to play competitive sport I should give it away because I didn't want to chop any toes off!"

THE FACTS Siddle took a Test hat-trick – on his birthday – on the first day of the 2010-11 Ashes series at Brisbane: he finished with a Test-best 6 for 54 ... Siddle took 5 for 21 v England at Headingley in 2009 ... He was the first No. 9 ever to score two half-centuries in the same Test, with 51 and 50 against India at Delhi in March 2013 ... He hit 103* for Australia A v Scotland in June 2013 ...

THE FIGURES to 17.09.13   **ESPNcricinfo.com**

Batting & Fielding	M	Inns	NO	Runs	HS	Avge	S/R	100	50	4s	6s	Ct	St
Tests	46	66	8	872	51	15.03	46.95	0	2	92	3	16	0
ODIs	17	4	2	21	9*	10.50	116.66	0	0	1	0	1	0
T20Is	2	1	1	1	1*	–	100.00	0	0	0	0	0	0
First-class	84	112	17	1634	103*	17.20	48.74	1	4	177	7	33	0

Bowling	M	Balls	Runs	Wkts	BB	Avge	RpO	S/R	5i	10m
Tests	46	9791	4863	167	6–54	29.11	2.98	58.62	8	0
ODIs	17	751	581	15	3–55	38.73	4.64	50.06	0	0
T20Is	2	48	58	3	2–24	19.33	7.25	16.00	0	0
First-class	84	16333	8232	300	6–43	27.44	3.02	54.44	15	0

SIKANDAR RAZA

ZIMBABWE

Full name	**Sikandar Raza Butt**
Born	**April 24, 1986, Sialkot, Pakistan**
Teams	**Mashonaland Eagles**
Style	**Left-hand bat, occasional offspinner**
Test debut	**Zimbabwe v Pakistan at Harare 2013-14**
ODI debut	**Zimbabwe v Bangladesh at Bulawayo 2012-13**
T20I debut	**Zimbabwe v Bangladesh at Bulawayo 2012-13**

THE PROFILE Sikandar Raza is not your typical international cricketer. He wasn't a teenage prodigy, and didn't have an all-consuming ambition to play for his country: actually what he really wanted to be, from the age of about 11, was a fighter pilot. Born in Pakistan, Sikandar made it into Air Force college, coming in the top 60 of some 60,000 applicants – but a routine eye test in his third year uncovered a problem which spelt the end of that particular dream. He had started playing cricket again, almost stumbling across a game he'd tried occasionally as a child, and discovered he was rather good at it. At university in Scotland he began playing as a semi-professional, then returned to Zimbabwe, where his parents had moved in 2002. An aggressive left-hander, Sikandar made his first-class debut for Northerns in April 2007, and made 84 in his fourth match. But then he returned to his studies, and it was three years before he played again – but he came back with a bang, making 51 in his first match, for Southern Rocks in September 2010, then 145 and 60 not out in the second. In July 2011 he opened for a Zimbabwe XI against the touring Bangladeshis, and when they returned in 2013 Sikandar made his full one-day international debut. In July he made 82 in an ODI against India, and when Pakistan arrived in September 2013 he won his first five-day cap when Brendan Taylor pulled out for the birth of his son. Sikandar applied himself well to make 60 and 24, and was unfortunate to lose his place when Taylor returned. He might not be a test pilot, but he is now a Test player.

THE FACTS Sikandar Raza scored 145 for Southern Rocks v Matabeleland Tuskers at Bulawayo in September 2010 ... He was the first Pakistan-born player to represent Zimbabwe ... Sikandar was the 12th to score a half-century on Test debut for Zimbabwe (only two of them – Dave Houghton and Hamilton Masakadza – went on to 100) ... He played club cricket in Scotland in 2012, and made two centuries for Prestwick ...

THE FIGURES to 17.09.13

cricinfo.com

Batting & Fielding	M	Inns	NO	Runs	HS	Avge	S/R	100	50	4s	6s	Ct	St
Tests	1	2	0	84	60	42.00	48.83	0	1	12	0	0	0
ODIs	8	8	0	179	82	22.37	64.62	0	1	17	2	3	0
T20Is	2	2	0	45	31	22.50	102.27	0	0	1	2	2	0
First-class	31	58	3	1611	145	29.29	53.57	1	9	213	21	31	0

Bowling	M	Balls	Runs	Wkts	BB	Avge	RpO	S/R	5i	10m
Tests	1	0	–	–	–	–	–	–	–	–
ODIs	8	0	–	–	–	–	–	–	–	–
T20Is	2	0	–	–	–	–	–	–	–	–
First-class	31	717	466	8	3-26	58.25	3.89	89.62	0	0

LENDL SIMMONS

Full name **Lendl Mark Platter Simmons**
Born **January 25, 1985, Port-of-Spain, Trinidad**
Teams **Trinidad & Tobago**
Style **Right-hand bat, occasional medium-pacer**
Test debut **West Indies v England at Port-of-Spain 2008-09**
ODI debut **West Indies v Pakistan at Faisalabad 2006-07**
T20I debut **West Indies v England at The Oval 2007**

THE PROFILE Lendl Simmons, the nephew of the former Test opener Phil, made a steady rise through the junior ranks, playing in the Under-19 World Cups of 2002 and 2004. An opener, and a fine fielder who can keep wicket, Simmons – named after the top 1980s tennis player Ivan Lendl – made his first-class debut six weeks after his 17th birthday. After passing 500 runs in the previous two domestic seasons, he toured England with West Indies A in 2006. He stepped up to the full one-day side in Pakistan later that year, collecting a duck in his first match but a mature 70 in his second. He struggled after that – only 42 runs in four innings – but retained his place for the 2007 World Cup, although he made only one appearance in that. A massive 282 against the England tourists early in 2009 finally earned him a Test place, but he failed to set the world alight. Later he hammered 77 off 50 balls against South Africa in the World Twenty20 in England (he had earlier taken four wickets against Sri Lanka), but was then surprisingly dropped again. After nearly two years on the sidelines (save for a forgettable one-day series in Australia early in 2010), Simmons regained his place when new coach Ottis Gibson shuffled the pack after the 2011 World Cup. He has done well in limited-overs matches since: seven fifties in 12 games against Pakistan and India in mid-2011 were followed by 122, his first century, in Bangladesh in October. Simmons added 80 in the next match, and 78 against India shortly afterwards, but although he remained a one-day regular – he made 75 in a thrilling tie against Pakistan in St Lucia in July 2013 – he hasn't played a Test since October 2011.

THE FACTS Simmons made 282 for West Indies A v England in St Kitts in January 2009 ... He made 200 (his maiden century) for Trinidad & Tobago v Jamaica in Tobago in February 2006, after being out for 0 in the first innings: in March 2011 he made 204* for Trinidad v Guyana at Providence ... His uncle, Phil Simmons, won 26 Test caps for West Indies between 1988 and 1997 ...

THE FIGURES to 17.09.13   **espn**cricinfo.com

Batting & Fielding	M	Inns	NO	Runs	HS	Avge	S/R	100	50	4s	6s	Ct	St
Tests	8	16	0	278	49	17.37	46.88	0	0	28	4	5	0
ODIs	48	47	3	1385	122	31.47	70.23	1	12	112	36	21	0
T20Is	18	18	3	439	77	29.26	116.13	0	3	41	15	8	0
First-class	88	155	10	4848	282	33.43	–	10	22	–	–	92	4

Bowling	M	Balls	Runs	Wkts	BB	Avge	RpO	S/R	5i	10m
Tests	8	192	147	1	1–60	147.00	4.59	192.00	0	0
ODIs	48	90	82	1	1–3	82.00	5.46	90.00	0	0
T20Is	18	36	55	6	4–19	9.16	9.16	6.00	0	0
First-class	88	1032	555	17	3–6	32.64	3.22	60.70	0	0

GRAEME **SMITH**

SOUTH AFRICA

Full name	**Graeme Craig Smith**
Born	**February 1, 1981, Johannesburg, Transvaal**
Teams	**Cape Cobras, Surrey**
Style	**Left-hand bat, occasional offspinner**
Test debut	**South Africa v Australia at Cape Town 2001-02**
ODI debut	**South Africa v Australia at Bloemfontein 2001-02**
T20I debut	**South Africa v New Zealand at Johannesburg 2005-06**

THE PROFILE Graeme Smith became South Africa's youngest captain at 22, when Shaun Pollock was dumped after a disastrous World Cup. A tall, aggressive left-hand opener, Smith had few leadership credentials – and only a handful of caps – but the selectors' faith was instantly justified: in England in 2003 he collected back-to-back double-centuries. Reality bit back the following year, with Test-series defeats in Sri Lanka and India. There was also a run of 11 losses in 12 ODIs, a mixed time in New Zealand, and the start of an ultimately fruitless series against England. Yet Smith continued to crunch runs aplenty: his 125 to square the New Zealand series was a minor epic. He yields to no-one physically, but for a while he struggled against inswing, frequently fumbling around his front pad. But he roared back in the Caribbean in 2005, with hundreds in three successive Tests. A baton-charge to 85 squared the home Test series against West Indies at the start of 2008, and later that year Smith achieved what he narrowly missed in 2003 – winning a Test series in England, his unbeaten 154 in a stiff run-chase at Edgbaston being one of the great captain's innings. In 2008-09 he presided over South Africa's first Test-series victory in Australia. He stood down as one-day captain after the 2011 World Cup, but remains firmly at the helm in Tests, and led South Africa to the top of the rankings in August 2012, after another victory in England – a series he started with a century at The Oval in his 100th Test. He supervised another win over Australia in November, but missed much of 2013 after an ankle operation, which cut short a high-profile stint as Surrey's new captain.

THE FACTS Smith followed 277 at Edgbaston in July 2003 with 259 in the next Test, the highest Test score by a visiting player at Lord's, beating Don Bradman's 254 in 1930 ... He has captained in a record 102 Test matches, beating Allan Border's 93 ... Smith scored 311 for Somerset v Leicestershire at Taunton in July 2005 ... His record includes one Test for the World XI (as captain) and one ODI for the Africa XI ...

THE FIGURES to 17.09.13   **ESPNcricinfo.com**

Batting & Fielding	M	Inns	NO	Runs	HS	Avge	S/R	100	50	4s	6s	Ct	St
Tests	110	192	12	8753	277	48.62	59.61	26	37	1110	23	160	0
ODIs	193	190	10	6942	141	38.56	81.05	10	47	785	44	103	0
T20Is	33	33	2	982	89*	31.67	127.53	0	5	123	26	18	0
First-class	153	263	18	12141	311	49.55	–	35	49	–	–	222	0

Bowling	M	Balls	Runs	Wkts	BB	Avge	RpO	S/R	5i	10m
Tests	110	1418	885	8	2-145	110.62	3.74	177.25	0	0
ODIs	193	1026	951	18	3-30	52.83	5.56	57.00	0	0
T20Is	33	24	57	0	–	–	14.25	–	0	0
First-class	153	1786	1132	11	2-145	102.90	3.80	162.36	0	0

STEVEN **SMITH**

Full name	**Steven Peter Devereux Smith**
Born	**June 2, 1989, Sydney**
Teams	**New South Wales, Pune Warriors**
Style	**Right-hand bat, legspinner**
Test debut	**Australia v Pakistan at Lord's 2010**
ODI debut	**Australia v West Indies at Melbourne 2009-10**
T20I debut	**Australia v Pakistan at Melbourne 2009-10**

THE PROFILE Steven Smith was initially seen as a possible new Warne, but as his legspin has regressed he has come to depend more on his batting. By the time he was 21 Smith was in all of Australia's senior squads. There were words of caution about his early elevation, but there was no hiding the excitement about a player who gives the ball air, hits it hard, and catches it well. Smith became an international player in 2009-10 after starring with New South Wales, striking four Sheffield Shield centuries and finishing the season with career-best figures of 7 for 64. After only 13 first-class matches he was picked for the Test tour of New Zealand, but didn't get to play. He had already been tried in the limited-overs sides, impressing with his attitude, and was used more as a legspinner than a batsman. His maiden Test series, against Pakistan in England in 2010, was encouraging: there were three wickets in the two games, and a muscular 77 at Headingley. But then he played three Tests in the 2010-11 Ashes without achieving much, and was similarly anonymous in the World Cup, although his fielding stood out. Despite making 92 in a Test in India in March, he was originally left out of the 2013 Ashes squad. He was called up when Michael Clarke's back was causing concern – and played throughout the series, making 53 in the first Test and 89 in the third, before silencing the doubters with a superb undefeated 138 in the final Test at The Oval, where he reached his maiden ton with a straight six. Smith started his state career in 2007-08, making his biggest impact in the Twenty20 Big Bash, in which he took nine wickets at the remarkable average of 5.33.

THE FACTS Smith's first four first-class hundreds – including his highest of 177 for NSW v Tasmania at Hobart – came during the 2009-10 Australian season ... He made 138* – reaching his maiden Test hundred with a six off Jonathan Trott – at The Oval in August 2013 ... Smith took 7 for 64 for NSW v South Australia at Adelaide in March 2010, after scoring 100 in the first innings ...

THE FIGURES to 17.09.13   **ESPNcricinfo.com**

Batting & Fielding	M	Inns	NO	Runs	HS	Avge	S/R	100	50	4s	6s	Ct	St
Tests	12	24	2	765	138*	34.77	49.86	1	5	77	10	3	0
ODIs	33	22	4	380	46*	21.11	86.75	0	0	27	3	14	0
T20Is	20	15	4	165	34	15.00	108.55	0	0	12	3	16	0
First-class	50	88	10	3365	177	43.14	56.26	8	18	415	33	60	0

Bowling	M	Balls	Runs	Wkts	BB	Avge	RpO	S/R	5i	10m
Tests	12	618	389	8	3–18	48.62	3.77	77.25	0	0
ODIs	33	899	780	22	3–33	35.45	5.20	40.86	0	0
T20Is	20	285	373	17	3–20	21.94	7.85	16.76	0	0
First-class	50	4109	2795	51	7–64	54.80	4.08	80.56	1	0

SOHAG GAZI

Full name	**Sohag Gazi**
Born	**August 5, 1991, Khulna**
Teams	**Barisal**
Style	**Right-hand bat, offspinner**
Test debut	**Bangladesh v West Indies at Mirpur 2012-13**
ODI debut	**Bangladesh v West Indies at Khulna 2012-13**
T20I debut	**Bangladesh v West Indies at Mirpur 2012-13**

THE PROFILE Sohag Gazi, a rare offspinner in a land famous for its slow left-arm production line, had a stunning introduction to Test cricket. Called up to face West Indies in October 2012 – not long after his action was cleared following misgivings about a kink in the delivery – Sohag was handed the new ball for the first over of his debut at Mirpur. Chris Gayle duly monstered the first delivery for six – a unique start to any Test – and cleared the ropes again shortly afterwards. But Sohag stuck to his task, and eventually removed Gayle for 24. Two more wickets followed, then six in the second innings. He snared Gayle in his first ODI, too, finishing with 4 for 29 to cement a place in the Bangladesh attack at 21, often opening the bowling despite his modest pace. His run-up is short, but the action is a brisk whir, followed by a tight follow-through. Sohag grew up right by the Bay of Bengal, but had to move around to find recognition. He shuttled around the south, playing in the leagues in his native Khulna and Barisal. He first grabbed attention for Orient, one of Dhaka's second-tier clubs, before making his first-class debut in 2009-10, starting with 5 for 63 against Chittagong. The wickets kept coming – often from metronomic Muralitharan-like long spells – and the following season he claimed more victims (41) in the National Cricket League than anyone else, which led to a stint at the Bangladesh academy. And a Test cap was just around the corner: it came shortly after he kicked off the 2012-13 season with a century for Barisal against Khulna, then added a seven-wicket haul that included a hat-trick.

THE FACTS Sohag Gazi bowled the first over on his Test debut, in November 2012: uniquely, the first ball of the match was hit for six, by Chris Gayle ... Gazi was only the 13th man to score a century and take a hat-trick in the same first-class match, with 119 and a career-best 7 for 79 for Barisal at Khulna in October 2012 ...

THE FIGURES to 17.09.13

Batting & Fielding	M	Inns	NO	Runs	HS	Avge	S/R	100	50	4s	6s	Ct	St
Tests	6	11	0	145	32	13.18	53.50	0	0	13	4	3	0
ODIs	8	5	1	72	30	18.00	85.71	0	0	11	0	3	0
T20Is	4	3	2	19	9	19.00	105.55	0	0	2	0	1	0
First-class	28	46	1	1163	140	25.84	84.09	2	4	151	33	15	0

Bowling	M	Balls	Runs	Wkts	BB	Avge	RpO	S/R	5i	10m
Tests	6	1964	968	26	6-74	37.23	2.95	75.53	1	0
ODIs	8	382	254	11	4-29	23.09	3.98	34.72	0	0
T20Is	4	96	130	3	1-28	43.33	8.12	32.00	0	0
First-class	28	7672	3636	137	7-79	26.54	2.84	56.00	11	1

TIM SOUTHEE

NEW ZEALAND

Full name	**Timothy Grant Southee**
Born	**December 11, 1988, Whangarei**
Teams	**Northern Districts**
Style	**Right-hand bat, right-arm fast-medium bowler**
Test debut	**New Zealand v England at Napier 2007-08**
ODI debut	**New Zealand v England at Chester-le-Street 2008**
T20I debut	**New Zealand v England at Auckland 2007-08**

THE PROFILE Few players have made such a remarkable Test debut as 19-year-old Tim Southee in March 2008. First, swinging the ball at a healthy pace, he took 5 for 55 as England were restricted to 253, his victims including Andrew Strauss for 0 and Kevin Pietersen for 129. Later, with New Zealand in a hopeless position, he strolled in and smashed 77 not out from just 40 balls, with nine sixes, five of them off an unamused Monty Panesar. His second Test, at Lord's in May 2008, was rather more mundane – one run, no wickets. A few months later he shook up the Aussies with three wickets in his first four overs at Brisbane, but further Test success proved elusive until he grabbed 7 for 64 to take his side close to a rare Test victory over India. In the second innings in Bangalore he castled Sachin Tendulkar. By then Southee had become a consistent one-day force: he took 18 wickets in New Zealand's march to the semi-finals of the 2011 World Cup. Two years later he did well against England – taking ten wickets in the Lord's Test – but then suffered a barren Champions Trophy. Southee made his first-class debut for Northern Districts at 18 in February 2007, and the following season claimed 6 for 68 in a particularly impressive effort against Auckland. He was chosen for the Under-19 World Cup, but had to interrupt his preparations when he was drafted into the senior set-up for the Twenty20 games against England early in 2008. He ended the Under-19 World Cup as the Player of the Tournament and barely had time to unpack before the Test call came.

THE FACTS Southee hit nine sixes in his first Test innings, a number only ever exceeded by four players, none of whom was making his debut: he had earlier become only the sixth New Zealander to take a five-for on Test debut ... He hit 156 – with six sixes and 18 fours – for Northern Districts at Wellington in December 2012 ... Southee took 8 for 27 from 25 overs for ND v Wellington at Hamilton in November 2009 ...

THE FIGURES to 17.09.13   **ESFIcricinfo.com**

Batting & Fielding	M	Inns	NO	Runs	HS	Avge	S/R	100	50	4s	6s	Ct	St
Tests	26	43	5	729	77*	19.18	84.18	0	2	68	36	14	0
ODIs	70	40	15	274	32	10.96	88.38	0	0	18	10	12	0
T20Is	31	12	4	73	23	9.12	112.30	0	0	6	3	13	0
First-class	55	76	8	1337	156	19.66	83.04	1	4	131	54	21	0

Bowling	M	Balls	Runs	Wkts	BB	Avge	RpO	S/R	5i	10m
Tests	26	5406	2850	83	7–64	34.33	3.16	65.13	4	1
ODIs	70	3374	2921	94	5–33	31.07	5.19	35.89	1	0
T20Is	31	654	917	36	5–18	25.47	8.41	18.16	1	0
First-class	55	10897	5541	195	8–27	28.41	3.05	55.88	11	1

MITCHELL **STARC**

Full name **Mitchell Aaron Starc**
Born **January 30, 1990, Baulkham Hills, Sydney**
Teams **New South Wales**
Style **Left-hand bat, left-arm fast-medium bowler**
Test debut **Australia v New Zealand at Brisbane 2011-12**
ODI debut **Australia v India at Visakhapatnam 2010-11**
T20I debut **Australia v Pakistan at Dubai 2012-13**

THE PROFILE One of several promising fast bowlers who have emerged in New South Wales in recent years, Mitchell Starc has a couple of advantages: he's very tall (6ft 4½ ins/194 cm), and he's a left-armer, a readymade replacement for when the other Mitchell, Johnson, goes walkabout. Starc turned heads with his speed and bounce during 2009-10, his first full season, during which he took 21 wickets – but he was restricted by injury the following summer, so missed the Ashes embarrassment, which might have been a blessing. He did make his ODI debut in October 2010, and took 4 for 27 in his second match, against Sri Lanka at Brisbane, before picking up a side strain. Starc was back in 2011-12, taking 27 wickets and earning a first Test cap against New Zealand after injuries to others. He looked slightly diffident in his early Tests, but a pep talk from Wasim Akram early in 2012 worked wonders: Starc even moved the ball around in unhelpful conditions in the UAE during a limited-overs series in September, taking 5 for 42 in the first match and 4 for 51 in the third one. "He bowled with good pace," enthused Michael Clarke. "He's such a tall guy and he swung the ball beautifully in conditions where there wasn't much there for the fast bowlers." Starc continued the good work with 6 for 154 against South Africa at Perth in December 2012, and 5 for 63 v Sri Lanka at Hobart a fortnight later. But he was ineffective in India early in 2013, then blew hot and cold in the Ashes series in England. He did look menacing in the final Test, with six wickets at The Oval ... but then went home with a stress fracture of the back.

THE FACTS Starc took 6 for 154 against South Africa at Perth in December 2012 ... He took 5 for 20 and 5 for 32 in consecutive ODIs against West Indies at Perth in February 2013 ... Starc joined Yorkshire in 2012, but a visa problem meant he had to return to Australia immediately on arrival in the UK ...

THE FIGURES to 17.09.13   **ESPN**cricinfo.com

Batting & Fielding	M	Inns	NO	Runs	HS	Avge	S/R	100	50	4s	6s	Ct	St
Tests	12	20	6	431	99	30.78	70.65	0	3	51	4	4	0
ODIs	19	7	4	122	52*	40.66	100.82	0	1	14	0	4	0
T20Is	10	2	1	3	2	3.00	37.50	0	0	0	0	1	0
First-class	39	47	17	742	99	24.73	63.96	0	4	90	8	19	0

Bowling	M	Balls	Runs	Wkts	BB	Avge	RpO	S/R	5i	10m
Tests	12	2450	1378	41	6–154	33.60	3.37	59.75	2	0
ODIs	19	874	737	37	5–20	19.91	5.05	23.62	3	0
T20Is	10	235	246	15	3–11	16.40	6.28	15.66	0	0
First-class	39	6505	3700	117	6–154	31.62	3.41	55.59	4	0

DALE **STEYN**

SOUTH AFRICA

Full name	**Dale Willem Steyn**
Born	**June 27, 1983, Phalaborwa, Limpopo Province**
Teams	**Cape Cobras, Sunrisers Hyderabad**
Style	**Right-hand bat, right-arm fast bowler**
Test debut	**South Africa v England at Port Elizabeth 2004-05**
ODI debut	**Africa XI v Asia XI at Centurion 2005-06**
T20I debut	**South Africa v New Zealand at Johannesburg 2007-08**

THE PROFILE Dale Steyn's rise to the South African side was as rapid as his bowling: he was picked for his first Test little more than a year after his first-class debut. A rare first-class cricketer from the Limpopo province close to the Kruger National Park and the Zimbabwe border, Steyn is genuinely fast, and moves the ball away. He played three Tests against England in 2004-05 before returning to domestic cricket, but was recalled in April 2006 and claimed 5 for 47 as New Zealand were routed at Centurion. He rattled a few helmets for Warwickshire in 2007, and really came of age the following winter, taking 40 wickets in five home Tests against New Zealand and West Indies, then 14 on Bangladesh's traditionally slow tracks. Finally he blew India away with 5 for 23 as they subsided to 76 all out and defeat at Ahmedabad. After a subdued time in England in 2008, Steyn claimed 34 victims in the home-and-away series against Australia, including ten wickets – and a rollicking 76 during a match-turning stand of 180 with J-P Duminy – in the Melbourne win that sealed South Africa's first-ever series win Down Under. He had a quiet 2009, but roared back the following year: after 13 wickets in the last two Tests against England in January, his 7 for 51 helped sink India at Nagpur. In 2012 Steyn took 15 wickets in the three Tests in England which lifted South Africa to the top of the rankings – and roared past 300 wickets, at a phenomenal strike-rate, as New Zealand were humbled for 45 at Cape Town in January 2013. Then, at the Wanderers the following month, he demolished Pakistan for 49 with 6 for 8 – and added five more in the second innings.

THE FACTS Steyn's strike-rate in Tests has been bettered only by the 19th-century bowlers George Lohmann (34.19 balls per wicket) and John Ferris (37.73), Shane Bond of New Zealand (38.75) and his current team-mate Vernon Philander (36.84) ... Steyn took 8 for 41 (14 for 110 in the match) for Titans v Eagles in December 2007 ... Steyn made his ODI debut for the Africa XI, and his record includes two matches for them ...

THE FIGURES to 17.09.13   espncricinfo.com

Batting & Fielding	M	Inns	NO	Runs	HS	Avge	S/R	100	50	4s	6s	Ct	St
Tests	65	80	18	866	76	13.96	42.68	0	1	86	21	18	0
ODIs	73	29	7	159	35	7.22	66.80	0	0	10	4	20	0
T20Is	29	5	3	8	5	4.00	80.00	0	0	0	0	10	0
First-class	108	127	30	1374	82	14.16	47.72	0	3	–	–	24	0

Bowling	M	Balls	Runs	Wkts	BB	Avge	RpO	S/R	5i	10m
Tests	65	13666	7523	332	7–51	22.65	3.30	41.16	21	5
ODIs	73	3615	2966	102	5–50	29.07	4.92	35.44	1	0
T20Is	29	618	649	39	4–9	16.64	6.30	15.84	0	0
First-class	108	21386	11633	491	8–41	23.69	3.26	43.55	29	7

GRAEME **SWANN**

Full name **Graeme Peter Swann**
Born **March 24, 1979, Northampton**
Teams **Nottinghamshire**
Style **Right-hand bat, offspinner**
Test debut **England v India at Chennai 2008-09**
ODI debut **England v South Africa at Bloemfontein 1999-2000**
T20I debut **England v New Zealand at Auckland 2007-08**

THE PROFILE Self-confident and gregarious, Graeme Swann is an aggressive offspinner, not afraid to give the ball a real tweak, and also a hard-hitting lower-order batsman. He toured South Africa in 1999-2000, but found life outside the Test side frustrating, although he bravely continued to give the ball a rip. However, he was less impressive off the field – what some saw as confidence, others interpreted as arrogance or cheek – and slid out of the reckoning. After marking time with Northamptonshire for a while, not helped by Monty Panesar's rise, Swann moved to Nottinghamshire in 2005 – and immediately helped them win the Championship. He was recalled for the Sri Lankan tour late in 2007, and took 4 for 34 in a one-day win at Dambulla. He finally won his first Test cap in India in December 2008, making up for lost time by dismissing Gambhir and Dravid in his first over. He soon developed a reputation for troubling left-handers: nearly half his 248 Test wickets to date have been lefties. He also continued his enviable knack of taking wickets in the first over of a spell. Swann was underwhelming in the 2009 Ashes, but played his part in the stunning 2010-11 victory Down Under with 5 for 91 at Adelaide, and spun England to their 2011 whitewash over India with nine wickets at The Oval. By then he was ranked the No. 3 bowler in the world in Tests – and top in ODIs, although he slipped a little during a patchy 2012, when he was dropped for one of the home Tests against South Africa. He recovered from elbow surgery to take 26 wickets in the 3-0 triumph over Australia in 2013 – the most by an England offspinner in a home Ashes series since Jim Laker in 1956.

THE FACTS Swann took two wickets in his first over in Test cricket: the only other bowler to do this was England's Richard Johnson (v Zimbabwe at Chester-le-Street in 2003) ... 118 of Swann's 248 Test wickets have been left-handers ... Swann took 7 for 33 for Northamptonshire v Derbyshire in June 2003 ... He made 183 for Northants v Gloucestershire at Bristol in August 2002 ...

THE FIGURES to 17.09.13

Batting & Fielding	M	Inns	NO	Runs	HS	Avge	S/R	100	50	4s	6s	Ct	St
Tests	57	70	13	1334	85	23.40	76.93	0	5	176	19	50	0
ODIs	79	48	12	500	34	13.88	90.41	0	0	48	4	29	0
T20Is	39	16	11	104	34	20.80	116.85	0	0	9	1	5	0
First-class	247	336	36	7764	183	25.88	–	4	37	–	–	190	0

Bowling	M	Balls	Runs	Wkts	BB	Avge	RpO	S/R	5i	10m
Tests	57	14497	7082	248	6–65	28.55	2.93	58.45	17	3
ODIs	79	3809	2888	104	5–28	27.76	4.54	36.62	1	0
T20Is	39	810	859	51	3–14	16.84	6.36	15.88	0	0
First-class	247	46359	23019	729	7–33	31.57	2.97	63.59	32	6

TAMIM IQBAL

BANGLADESH

Full name	**Tamim Iqbal Khan**
Born	**March 20, 1989, Chittagong**
Teams	**Chittagong**
Style	**Left-hand bat**
Test debut	**Bangladesh v New Zealand at Dunedin 2007-08**
ODI debut	**Bangladesh v Zimbabwe at Harare 2006-07**
T20I debut	**Bangladesh v Kenya at Nairobi 2007-08**

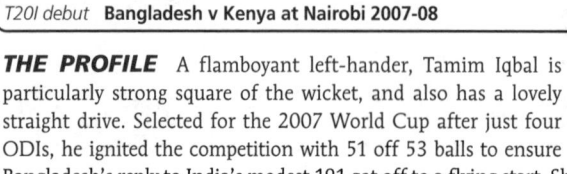

THE PROFILE A flamboyant left-hander, Tamim Iqbal is particularly strong square of the wicket, and also has a lovely straight drive. Selected for the 2007 World Cup after just four ODIs, he ignited the competition with 51 off 53 balls to ensure Bangladesh's reply to India's modest 191 got off to a flying start. Shrugging off a blow on the neck from Zaheer Khan, Tamim jumped down the track and smashed him over midwicket for six ... all this three days before his 18th birthday. He struggled to reproduce this form afterwards: it wasn't until his 18th match, in July 2007, that he reached 50 again. But the following year he made a hundred against Ireland, then in August 2009 rounded off a consistent run by hammering 154 – still a national one-day record – against Zimbabwe. It was a similar story in Tests: great start (53 and 84 v New Zealand), quieter phase (17 innings with a best of 47), exciting flowering (128 as West Indies were beaten in St Vincent in July 2009). And by 2010 Tamim was clearly Bangladesh's star batsman: a superb 151 forced India to bat again at Mirpur in January, then twin eighties at home against England were followed by centuries in both Tests of the return series, at Lord's and Old Trafford. He was rewarded by becoming the first Bangladeshi to be named as one of *Wisden's* Five Cricketers of the Year. Tamim started the 2011 World Cup with another cameo against India, although this time his 70 could not bring victory. He continued to fire fitfully, but apart from 112 in an ODI against Sri Lanka in March 2013, he kept getting out when seemingly well set. Still, the opposition's celebrations whenever he departs cheaply speak volumes for the danger he poses.

THE FACTS Tamim Iqbal scored 154, Bangladesh's highest in ODIs, against Zimbabwe at Bulawayo in August 2009 ... He made 192 for Chittagong against Dhaka at Bogra in October 2012 ... Only Sachin Tendulkar and Mohammad Ashraful reached 1000 Test runs at a younger age than Tamim (a week short of his 21st birthday in 2010) ... His brother, Nafees Iqbal, and their uncle, Akram Khan, both played for Bangladesh too ...

THE FIGURES to 17.09.13   ESPNcricinfo.com

Batting & Fielding	M	Inns	NO	Runs	HS	Avge	S/R	100	50	4s	6s	Ct	St
Tests	28	54	0	2010	151	37.22	60.57	4	12	269	15	8	0
ODIs	122	122	1	3639	154	30.07	78.61	4	24	409	49	33	0
T20Is	26	26	2	576	88*	24.00	109.50	0	3	70	6	7	0
First-class	51	94	2	3981	192	43.27	–	9	24	–	–	20	0

Bowling	M	Balls	Runs	Wkts	BB	Avge	RpO	S/R	5i	10m
Tests	28	30	20	0	–	–	4.00	–	0	0
ODIs	122	6	13	0	–	–	13.00	–	0	0
T20Is	26	0	–	–	–	–	–	–	–	–
First-class	51	156	96	0	–	–	3.69	–	0	0

BRENDAN **TAYLOR**

ZIMBABWE

Full name	**Brendan Ross Murray Taylor**
Born	**February 6, 1986, Harare**
Teams	**Mid West Rhinos, Wellington**
Style	**Right-hand bat, occasional wicketkeeper**
Test debut	**Zimbabwe v Sri Lanka at Harare 2004**
ODI debut	**Zimbabwe v Sri Lanka at Bulawayo 2004**
T20I debut	**Zimbabwe v Bangladesh at Khulna 2006-07**

THE PROFILE Brendan Taylor was fast-tracked into the national team at 18 after the withdrawal of several senior players. He shot to international prominence at Cape Town on September 12, 2007, when his ice-cool 60 not out carried Zimbabwe to victory over Australia in the inaugural World Twenty20. Taylor marshalled a tense run-chase with the sort of sang froid few had ever credited him with. But actually it wasn't the first time he had displayed a calm head in a pressure situation: in August 2006 he smoked 17 from the last over – including a six to win off the last ball – to beat Bangladesh. Early on, Taylor had often showed the ability to build an innings, but was frustratingly dismissed trying to play too aggressively: he passed 90 three times in ODIs before finally reaching 100. In Tests he made 77 against New Zealand in August 2005 when he was 19, but shortly after that Zimbabwe withdrew from Test cricket for six years. When they returned in August 2011, Taylor was captain, having put a chequered disciplinary record behind him. He had been Zimbabwe's outstanding batsman at the 2011 World Cup, his uppercut to third man one of the tournament's enduring images. He celebrated his elevation in style by scoring his first century – and leading Zimbabwe to victory – in their comeback Test, against Bangladesh at Harare. Another century followed soon afterwards against New Zealand, then in April 2013 he hit two in the match against Bangladesh to set up another Test victory. He may be more disciplined now, but still produces the trademark full-blooded front-foot cover-drives which make him an attractive batsman to watch. Taylor had a spell as wicketkeeper, and is now a reliable slip fielder.

THE FACTS Taylor hit 217 for Mid West Rhinos v Southern Rocks at Masvingo in February 2010 ... He scored 171 and 102* against Bangladesh at Harare in April 2013: he was the third Zimbabwean, after Andy and Grant Flower, to score twin hundreds in a Test ... Taylor made his first Test century in his first match as captain, against Bangladesh at Harare in August 2011 ... He averages 74 in ODIs against New Zealand, but only 13 against England ...

THE FIGURES to 17.09.13   espncricinfo.com

Batting & Fielding	M	Inns	NO	Runs	HS	Avge	S/R	100	50	4s	6s	Ct	St
Tests	19	38	2	1260	171	35.00	50.48	4	6	125	13	18	0
ODIs	146	145	14	4414	145*	33.69	72.21	6	27	372	59	86	19
T20Is	23	23	5	471	75*	26.16	121.39	0	4	42	13	9	1
First-class	79	146	8	5702	217	41.31	–	19	21	–	–	98	4

Bowling	M	Balls	Runs	Wkts	BB	Avge	RpO	S/R	5i	10m
Tests	19	42	38	0	–	–	5.42	–	0	0
ODIs	146	396	406	9	3–54	45.11	6.15	44.00	0	0
T20Is	23	30	17	1	1–16	17.00	3.40	30.00	0	0
First-class	79	366	213	4	2–36	53.25	3.49	91.50	0	0

JAMES **TAYLOR**

ENGLAND

Full name	**James William Arthur Taylor**
Born	**January 6, 1990, Nottingham**
Teams	**Nottinghamshire**
Style	**Right-hand bat, occasional legspinner**
Test debut	**England v South Africa at Leeds 2012**
ODI debut	**England v Ireland at Dublin 2011**
T20I debut	**No T20Is yet**

THE PROFILE A compact and correct batsman who is only 5ft 6ins (167cm) tall – his father was a jockey – James Taylor was long tipped for stardom. Unfazed by short-pitched bowling despite his small stature, he scored more than 1200 runs in 2009, his first full season, at an average of 57: that included a double-century against Surrey, and earned him the Cricket Writers' Club's young player of the year award. There was little drop-off in the often-significant second season – 1095 runs at 43, and another double-ton – which resulted in an England Lions tour to the West Indies, where he took 186 off Barbados's Test new-ball pairing of Pedro Collins and Fidel Edwards. In 2011 Taylor didn't make a Championship century till August, but he had scored 168 not out against Sri Lanka A for the Lions, which led to a one-day debut in Dublin. Taylor started the 2012 home season indifferently – by now he'd followed Stuart Broad and moved from lowly Leicestershire to Nottinghamshire. But another Lions century, against the West Indians, ushered in a run of better form, and when Jonny Bairstow was dropped for the start of the South African series after looking vulnerable to the short stuff, Taylor made his Test debut at Headingley. He made a composed 34, batting for two and a half hours and sharing a stand of 147 with Kevin Pietersen, but was outshone by the returning Bairstow at Lord's, not helped by a calamitous run-out. He missed the ensuing tour of India, where Joe Root annexed a place, but consistent domestic runs – including another double-century – kept Taylor in the selectors' thoughts. He was around the squad during the 2013 Ashes, and had another ODI outing against Ireland in September.

THE FACTS Taylor scored 237 for Leicestershire v Loughborough University in April 2011, after coming in at 2 for 2 ... In 2008 he was the second winner of the *Wisden* Schools Cricketer of the Year Award, following Jonny Bairstow ... Taylor made 207* for Leicestershire v Surrey at The Oval in July 2009, 206* v Middlesex at Leicester in May 2010, and 204* for Nottinghamshire v Sussex at Trent Bridge in June 2013 ...

THE FIGURES to 17.09.13

Batting & Fielding	M	Inns	NO	Runs	HS	Avge	S/R	100	50	4s	6s	Ct	St
Tests	2	3	0	48	34	16.00	31.57	0	0	6	0	2	0
ODIs	2	2	0	26	25	13.00	52.00	0	0	3	0	0	0
T20Is	0	0	–	–	–	–	–	–	–	–	–	–	–
First-class	97	155	22	6415	237	48.23	–	16	28	–	–	65	0

Bowling	M	Balls	Runs	Wkts	BB	Avge	RpO	S/R	5i	10m
Tests	2	0	–	–	–	–	–	–	–	–
ODIs	2	0	–	–	–	–	–	–	–	–
T20Is	0	0	–	–	–	–	–	–	–	–
First-class	97	228	176	0	–	–	4.63	–	0	0

ROSS **TAYLOR**

Full name	**Luteru Ross Poutoa Lote Taylor**
Born	**March 8, 1984, Lower Hutt, Wellington**
Teams	**Central Districts, Pune Warriors**
Style	**Right-hand bat, offspinner**
Test debut	**New Zealand v South Africa at Johannesburg 2007-08**
ODI debut	**New Zealand v West Indies at Napier 2005-06**
T20I debut	**New Zealand v Sri Lanka at Wellington 2006-07**

THE PROFILE Ross Taylor was spotted at an early age – he captained New Zealand in the 2001-02 Under-19 World Cup – but it was some time before he made the big breakthrough. In March 2005 he extended his maiden first-class century to 184, then began the following season with five sixes in a century against Otago. He then cracked 121 against Wellington, then 114 v Otago in the semi, then 50 in the final against Canterbury, and rounded off the season with 106 as CD won the State Championship final at Wellington. It all led to a call-up for the final two ODIs of West Indies' tour early in 2006, and a regular place the following season. Taylor flogged Sri Lanka – Murali and all – for an unbeaten 128 in only his third match, and added an equally muscular 117 against Australia at Auckland in February 2007. A belated Test debut followed in November, and he scored 120 against England in his third match, before entrancing Old Trafford with an unbeaten 154 in the return series in 2008, during which he also took some fine slip catches. Highlights since have included 151 against India at Napier in March 2009, and a defiant 138 against Australia at Hamilton a year later. He also entertained IPL crowds with some big hitting. Taylor scored consistently in the 2011 World Cup, the highlight coming against Pakistan – on his 27th birthday – when he clattered 55 from his last 13 deliveries to reach 131. After the tournament he was appointed New Zealand's captain: he made a brace of 76s in his first Test in charge, in Zimbabwe, then late in 2012 stroked a superb 113 at Bangalore and 142 in Colombo. But soon after that he was demoted by NZ's new coach, and withdrew – pride injured – for a while before returning against England and slamming a cathartic century in a one-dayer at Napier in February 2013.

THE FACTS Only Martin Donnelly and Bevan Congdon (twice) have made higher Test scores for New Zealand in England than Taylor's 154* at Manchester in 2008 ... He and Jesse Ryder put on 271, a record for NZ's fourth wicket, against India at Napier in March 2009 ... Taylor made 217 for Central Districts v Otago at Napier in December 2006 ...

THE FIGURES to 17.09.13 — ESPNcricinfo.com

Batting & Fielding	M	Inns	NO	Runs	HS	Avge	S/R	100	50	4s	6s	Ct	St
Tests	48	88	5	3504	154*	42.21	57.70	8	19	445	30	75	0
ODIs	125	113	15	3755	131*	38.31	81.66	7	24	304	96	86	0
T20Is	52	47	9	908	63	23.89	120.58	0	4	57	38	34	0
First-class	101	172	7	6708	217	40.65	–	14	38	–	–	127	0

Bowling	M	Balls	Runs	Wkts	BB	Avge	RpO	S/R	5i	10m
Tests	48	90	43	2	2–4	21.50	2.86	45.00	0	0
ODIs	125	42	35	0	–	–	5.00	–	0	0
T20Is	52	–	–	–	–	–	–	–	–	–
First-class	101	660	359	6	2–4	59.83	3.26	110.00	0	0

SACHIN **TENDULKAR**

Full name **Sachin Ramesh Tendulkar**
Born **April 24, 1973, Bombay (now Mumbai)**
Teams **Mumbai, Mumbai Indians**
Style **Right-hand bat, occasional medium-pace/legspin**
Test debut **India v Pakistan at Karachi 1989-90**
ODI debut **India v Pakistan at Gujranwala 1989-90**
T20I debut **India v South Africa at Johannesburg 2006-07**

THE PROFILE You only have to attend a one-dayer at the Wankhede Stadium, and watch the lights flicker and the floor tremble as the applause echoes around the ground when he comes in, to realise what Sachin Tendulkar means to Mumbai ... and India. Age, and niggling injuries, have dimmed the light a little – he's now retired from one-dayers, and a similar Test decision can't be far off – but he is still light-footed with bat in hand, the nearest thing to Bradman, as The Don himself recognised. Sachin seems to have been around for ever: he made his Test debut at 16, shrugging off a blow on the head against Pakistan, captivated England in 1990, with a maiden Test century, and similarly enchanted Australia in 1991-92. Two more big hundreds lit up the 2007-08 series Down Under, and Tendulkar now has 11 Test tons against the Aussies. He leads the list of ODI runscorers by a country mile, and owns the records for most runs, centuries and appearances in Tests too. Early in 2010 he stroked the first ODI double-century, then most of the talk after an immensely satisfying victory in the 2011 World Cup was of his quest for 100 international hundreds, a landmark he finally reached in March 2012. Until he throttled back in his thirties, Tendulkar usually looked to attack: latterly he is more circumspect, but no less destructive when in form. Small, steady at the crease before a decisive move forward or back, he has been a master, the whipped flick to fine leg an object of wonder. He could have starred as a bowler: he can do offbreaks, leggies or dobbly medium-pacers, although he doesn't bowl much these days.

THE FACTS Tendulkar passed his childhood idol Sunil Gavaskar's record of 34 Test centuries in December 2005 ... No-one is close to his 100 international centuries (Ricky Ponting is next with 71) ... Tendulkar hit 11 Test centuries against Australia, and nine in ODIs ... His first mention in *Wisden* came when he was 14, after a stand of 664* in a school game with another future Test batsman, Vinod Kambli ...

THE FIGURES to 17.09.13   espncricinfo.com

Batting & Fielding	M	Inns	NO	Runs	HS	Avge	S/R	100	50	4s	6s	Ct	St
Tests	198	327	33	15837	248*	53.86	–	51	67	2044	69	115	0
ODIs	463	452	41	18426	200*	44.83	86.23	49	96	2016	195	140	0
T20Is	1	1	0	10	10	10.00	83.33	0	0	2	0	1	0
First-class	307	486	50	25228	248*	57.86	–	81	114	–	–	186	0

Bowling	M	Balls	Runs	Wkts	BB	Avge	RpO	S/R	5i	10m
Tests	198	4198	2461	45	3-10	54.68	3.51	93.28	0	0
ODIs	463	8054	6850	154	5-32	44.48	5.10	52.29	2	0
T20Is	1	15	12	1	1-12	12.00	4.80	15.00	0	0
First-class	307	7563	4353	70	3-10	62.18	3.45	108.04	0	0

UPUL THARANGA

Full name	**Warushavithana Upul Tharanga**
Born	**February 2, 1985, Balapitiya**
Teams	**Nondescripts, Kandurata**
Style	**Left-hand bat, occasional wicketkeeper**
Test debut	**Sri Lanka v India at Ahmedabad 2005-06**
ODI debut	**Sri Lanka v West Indies at Dambulla 2005-06**
T20I debut	**Sri Lanka v England at Southampton 2006**

THE PROFILE Upul Tharanga's international call-up in July 2005 brightened a year marred by the Indian Ocean tsunami, which washed away his family home in Ambalangoda, a fishing town on the west coast. Tharanga, a wispy left-hander blessed with natural timing, had played premier-league cricket at 15 and passed seamlessly through the national age-group squads. He hit 105 against Bangladesh in only his fifth match – he celebrated modestly, aware that stiffer challenges lay ahead – then pummelled 165 against them in his third Test. During 2006 he lit up Lord's with 120 in the first of five successive defeats of England: he added 109 in the last of those, at Headingley, sharing a record opening stand of 286 with Sanath Jayasuriya. The feature of those innings was the way he made room to drive through the off side. In the 2007 World Cup Tharanga made 73 in the semi-final, but struggled the following season and lost his place. But in August 2009 he scored 76 against New Zealand (his first international fifty for more than two years), celebrated with 80 in the next game, and has been a 50-overs regular ever since. He scored World Cup centuries against England and Zimbabwe in 2011, but made only 2 in the final, and was then hit with a three-month ban after taking a herbal remedy for a shoulder injury which contained a banned drug. He was back later in the year, stroked another ODI hundred against Australia at Hambantota, and scored consistently during 2012 too. Then, in July 2013, he ended an indifferent run by whooshing to 174 against India in Jamaica. It was his 13th ODI hundred, and – at a time when the Test openers were struggling – made it seem odd that Tharanga had not played a five-day game since December 2007.

THE FACTS Tharanga and Sanath Jayasuriya put on 286 (in 31.5 overs) against England at Leeds in July 2006, a first-wicket record for all ODIs ... There have been 24 opening stands of 200-plus in ODIs: Tharanga has been involved in a record six of them ... He averages 57.80 in ODIs against England, but 0 v Ireland ... Tharanga carried his bat for 265 for Ruhuna v Basnahira South in March 2009 ... His record includes one ODI for the Asia XI ...

THE FIGURES to 17.09.13   **cricinfo.com**

Batting & Fielding	M	Inns	NO	Runs	HS	Avge	S/R	100	50	4s	6s	Ct	St
Tests	15	26	1	713	165	28.52	49.51	1	3	99	5	11	0
ODIs	171	163	9	5228	174*	33.94	73.86	13	28	603	28	33	0
T20Is	10	10	0	131	37	13.10	113.91	0	0	12	3	1	0
First-class	92	152	6	5526	265*	37.84	–	13	21	–	–	64	1

Bowling	M	Balls	Runs	Wkts	BB	Avge	RpO	S/R	5i	10m
Tests	15	0	–	–	–	–	–	–	–	–
ODIs	171	0	–	–	–	–	–	–	–	–
T20Is	10	0	–	–	–	–	–	–	–	–
First-class	92	18	4	0	–	–	1.33	–	0	0

LAHIRU **THIRIMANNE**

SRI LANKA

Full name	Hettige Don Rumesh Lahiru Thirimanne
Born	September 8, 1989, Moratuwa
Teams	Ragama
Style	Left-hand bat, occ. right-arm medium-pacer
Test debut	Sri Lanka v England at Southampton 2011
ODI debut	Sri Lanka v India at Dhaka 2010-11
T20I debut	Sri Lanka v Pakistan at Hambantota 2012

THE PROFILE Left-hander Lahiru Thirimanne was long considered one of the best young batsmen in Sri Lanka, and it was no great surprise when he was named in the senior team for a tri-series in Bangladesh early in 2010. He made 22 in his first match, opening against India's experienced new-ball attack of Zaheer Khan and Ashish Nehra, but slipped out of the team after two more outings and missed the 2011 World Cup. He was back for the England tour that followed, and when Tillekeratne Dilshan broke a finger in the second Test, the match against Essex boiled down to a shootout between Thirimanne and Dinesh Chandimal for the vacant opening spot for the third Test at the Rose Bowl. Chandimal was out for 16 – but Thirimanne booked his place with a fine 104. In *The Guardian*, David Hopps observed: "Thirimanne's hundred was his first outside Sri Lanka, but his application against the moving ball suggested that it will not be the last." On his Test debut at 21 he survived an hour for 10 in the first innings, then applied himself well for 38 in the second as Sri Lanka – nearly 200 behind – dug in for the draw. Dilshan naturally displaced him when the Australians toured later in 2011, but when Thilan Samaraweera was dropped it was Thirimanne who replaced him. He scored 68 in his third Test, against Pakistan in Abu Dhabi, but lost his place early in 2012 after a couple of failures. He had better luck in ODIs, though, making 47 and 77 in successive matches against India later in the year. And he came of age in 2013, following a fighting 91 in the Sydney Test with a maiden ODI century against the Aussies a few days later. Then, in March, he extended his first Test century, against Bangladesh at Galle, to 155 not out.

THE FACTS Thirimanne made 148 (one of four centuries in a total of 720) for Basnahira South against Ruhuna in Colombo in May 2010 ... He scored 108 for Sri Lanka Under-19s against England (whose opening bowler was Steven Finn) in a one-day international in Kuala Lumpur in February 2007 ...

THE FIGURES to 17.09.13   espncricinfo.com

Batting & Fielding	M	Inns	NO	Runs	HS	Avge	S/R	100	50	4s	6s	Ct	St
Tests	10	20	4	526	155*	32.87	42.59	1	2	47	1	4	0
ODIs	52	38	4	990	102*	29.11	67.71	1	6	68	8	19	0
T20Is	16	11	1	143	30	14.30	110.85	0	0	14	1	5	0
First-class	57	99	12	3644	155*	41.88	49.28	10	18	370	26	51	0

Bowling	M	Balls	Runs	Wkts	BB	Avge	RpO	S/R	5i	10m
Tests	10	18	20	0	–	–	6.66	–	0	0
ODIs	52	50	41	1	1–25	41.00	4.92	50.00	0	0
T20Is	16	0	–	–	–	–	–	–	–	–
First-class	57	78	69	0	–	–	5.30	–	0	0

JAMES **TREDWELL**

Full name	**James Cullum Tredwell**
Born	**February 27, 1982, Ashford, Kent**
Teams	**Kent**
Style	**Left-hand bat, offspinner**
Test debut	**England v Bangladesh at Mirpur 2009-10**
ODI debut	**England v Bangladesh at Mirpur 2009-10**
T20I debut	**England v India at Pune 2012-13**

THE PROFILE James "Pingu" Tredwell made steady progress after making his Kent debut in 2001. Initially seen as a containing offspinner in one-day cricket, it took him a while to establish himself in the Championship side. After he did that, in 2007, he was soon making his way steadily up the batting order: pushed up to No. 4, he made a maiden century against Yorkshire at Tunbridge Wells. He made another hundred against the New Zealand tourists from first drop the following year and is now settled in the middle order. Tredwell had a place at the ECB National Academy in 2003-04, and made the Performance Programme in the winter of 2007. The following year he was part of the one-day squad in New Zealand, although he didn't get a game, but 69 Championship wickets in 2009 kept him in the frame. He was called up as cover for Graeme Swann during that winter's South African tour, and although again he did not feature in the internationals, his consistent performances booked him a place on the trip to Bangladesh which followed. Finally he won an England cap: after a quiet one-day debut he played in the second Test at Mirpur, dismissed the danger men Tamim Iqbal and Shakib Al Hasan in the first innings, and followed that with four more wickets in the second. However, with Swann firmly entrenched, chances were limited after that, although Tredwell continues to feature in England's one-day plans. He took 4 for 44 against India at Rajkot in January 2013, and later in the year even captained England's Twenty20 team – although his first match in charge lasted only two balls before it rained.

THE FACTS Tredwell took 8 for 66 for Kent v Glamorgan at Canterbury in May 2009 ... On his World Cup debut, against West Indies at Chennai in March 2011, Tredwell took 4 for 48 ... He scored 123* for Kent v New Zealand at Canterbury in April 2008 ... Tredwell took 7 for 22, including a hat-trick, as Kent beat Yorkshire at Leeds in September 2010 ...

THE FIGURES to 17.09.13   **ESPNcricinfo.com**

Batting & Fielding	M	Inns	NO	Runs	HS	Avge	S/R	100	50	4s	6s	Ct	St
Tests	1	1	0	37	37	37.00	58.73	0	0	6	0	1	0
ODIs	24	13	7	57	16	9.50	47.89	0	0	3	0	8	0
T20Is	7	3	2	23	22	23.00	191.66	0	0	3	1	2	0
First-class	138	194	24	3809	123*	22.40	43.57	3	14	–	–	142	0

Bowling	M	Balls	Runs	Wkts	BB	Avge	RpO	S/R	5i	10m
Tests	1	390	181	6	4–82	30.16	2.78	65.00	0	0
ODIs	24	1076	896	36	4–44	24.88	4.99	29.88	0	0
T20Is	7	108	165	3	1–20	55.00	9.16	36.00	–	–
First-class	138	24119	12346	348	8–66	35.47	3.07	69.30	12	3

CHRIS **TREMLETT**

ENGLAND

Full name **Christopher Timothy Tremlett**
Born **September 2, 1981, Southampton**
Teams **Surrey**
Style **Right-hand bat, right-arm fast bowler**
Test debut **England v India at Lord's 2007**
ODI debut **England v Bangladesh at Nottingham 2005**
T20I debut **England v India at Durban 2007-08**

THE PROFILE Chris Tremlett has the silent, simmering looks of a baddie in a spaghetti western, and bangs the ball down from an impressive height at an impressive speed. He has a fine cricket pedigree: grandfather captained Somerset, and father played for Hampshire. But this Tremlett needed no nepotism: he took 4 for 16 on his Hampshire debut in 2000, and has since been halted only by niggling injuries (growing pains, perhaps: he's now 6ft 7ins/201cm). In 2005 he almost marked his ODI debut with a hat-trick – the vital ball fell on the stumps without dislodging a bail – then was 12th man in the first four Tests of the epic Ashes series. As England's pacemen hit the treatment table in 2007 Tremlett finally got the call. Using his height well, he collected 13 wickets in three Tests against India, including Laxman three times, Dravid and Tendulkar. A side strain forced him home early from New Zealand that winter, after which he lost form. But a move to Surrey in 2010 was revitalising, and he claimed a place on that winter's Ashes tour: when Stuart Broad broke down Tremlett immediately looked the part, taking 5 for 87 at Perth then 4 for 26 as Australia were routed for 98 on Boxing Day at Melbourne. A six-for followed against Sri Lanka in June 2011, but then back and hamstring injuries impinged. It looked as if his international career was over – but a resurgence in 2013 found him restored to the Ashes squad. He looked likely to play at The Oval, but Chris Woakes was preferred: Tremlett showed what he thought of that by driving up to Durham and taking a career-best 8 for 96.

THE FACTS Tremlett's grandfather, Maurice, played three Tests for England in 1948: his father, Tim, played for Hampshire ... Chris took two wickets in successive balls in his first ODI, against Bangladesh in June 2005: the hat-trick ball bounced on top of the stumps but didn't dislodge the bails ... Tremlett took 8 for 96 for Surrey v Durham in August 2013 after being released from the England squad for the final Ashes Test ...

THE FIGURES to 17.09.13   ESPNcricinfo.com

Batting & Fielding	M	Inns	NO	Runs	HS	Avge	S/R	100	50	4s	6s	Ct	St
Tests	11	13	4	98	25*	10.88	42.42	0	0	10	0	4	0
ODIs	15	11	4	50	19*	7.14	56.17	0	0	2	2	4	0
T20Is	1	0	–	–	–	–	–	–	–	–	–	0	0
First-class	129	164	42	2089	64	17.12	–	0	8	–	–	35	0

Bowling	M	Balls	Runs	Wkts	BB	Avge	RpO	S/R	5i	10m
Tests	11	2686	1311	49	6–48	26.75	2.92	54.81	2	0
ODIs	15	784	705	15	4–32	47.00	5.39	52.26	0	0
T20Is	1	24	45	2	2–45	22.50	11.25	12.00	0	0
First-class	129	22633	11819	422	8–96	28.00	3.13	53.63	11	0

JONATHAN **TROTT**

Full name	**Ian Jonathan Leonard Trott**
Born	**April 22, 1981, Cape Town, South Africa**
Teams	**Warwickshire**
Style	**Right-hand bat, right-arm medium-pacer**
Test debut	**England v Australia at The Oval 2009**
ODI debut	**England v Ireland at Belfast 2009**
T20I debut	**England v West Indies at The Oval 2007**

THE PROFILE The story sounds familiar: aggressive right-hander, born in South Africa, reputation for cockiness on the county circuit. But no, we're not talking Kevin Pietersen here, rather Jonathan Trott, who moved to England in 2003. His grandparents were British, which meant he could play as a non-overseas player for Warwickshire, although he didn't actually become eligible for England until 2006. He was consistent from the start, following up 763 runs from ten matches in 2003 with 1000 in each of the next three seasons. His form dipped in 2007, although he was a left-field pick for that summer's two Twenty20s against West Indies. But when he continued to make eye-catchingly forthright runs in 2009, he was called up for the final Test against Australia at The Oval, the first to make his England debut in an Ashes decider since 1896. He duly silenced the doubters with a seemingly nerveless century. Trott added 226 against Bangladesh in May 2010, and against Pakistan later in the summer made 184, sharing a record eighth-wicket stand of 332 with Stuart Broad. And the runs just kept coming: 445 in the Ashes success, including two fine hundreds, then England's leading batsman in the ODI series there and in the World Cup. Another double-century followed against Sri Lanka at Cardiff, before a shoulder injury kept him out for a while. Trott was the ICC's cricketer of the year for 2011, and continued to do well the following year, although big scores were more elusive – he went through two home summers with a highest Test score of 76, although he did make important centuries at Nagpur and Wellington in between in 2012-13. Michael Clarke restricted him by placing two shortish midwickets in the 2013 Ashes, and the rematch Down Under should make interesting viewing.

THE FACTS Trott was the 18th batsman to score a century on Test debut for England ... Trott made 226 against Bangladesh at Lord's in May 2010, and 203 v Sri Lanka at Cardiff a year later ... At Lord's in 2010 Trott shared a Test-record eighth-wicket stand of 332 with Stuart Broad ... Trott took 7 for 39 for Warwickshire v Kent at Canterbury in September 2003 ...

THE FIGURES to 17.09.13   **espncricinfo.com**

Batting & Fielding	M	Inns	NO	Runs	HS	Avge	S/R	100	50	4s	6s	Ct	St
Tests	48	85	6	3744	226	47.39	47.32	9	18	441	0	29	0
ODIs	68	65	10	2819	137	51.25	77.06	4	22	216	3	14	0
T20Is	7	7	1	138	51	23.00	95.83	0	1	9	3	0	0
First-class	205	344	37	13796	226	44.93	–	32	69	–	–	183	0

Bowling	M	Balls	Runs	Wkts	BB	Avge	RpO	S/R	5i	10m
Tests	48	702	398	5	1–5	79.60	3.40	140.40	0	0
ODIs	68	183	166	2	2–31	83.00	5.44	91.50	0	0
T20Is	7	0	–	–	–	–	–	–	–	–
First-class	205	5198	2928	61	7–39	48.00	3.37	85.21	1	0

LONWABO **TSOTSOBE**

SOUTH AFRICA

Full name	Lonwabo Lopsy Tsotsobe
Born	March 7, 1984, Port Elizabeth
Teams	Dolphins
Style	Right-hand bat, left-arm fast-medium
Test debut	South Africa v West Indies at Port-of-Spain 2010
ODI debut	South Africa v Australia at Perth 2008-09
T20I debut	South Africa v Australia at Melbourne 2008-09

THE PROFILE A tall left-arm swing bowler, Lonwabo Tsotsobe had a dream start to his ODI career in January 2009, when after removing Shaun Marsh he had Ricky Ponting caught behind. Later on he nabbed Mike Hussey and Mitchell Johnson as well, to finish with debut figures of 4 for 50 as South Africa romped to a 4-1 series victory. This put him in the frame for a Test cap when the Australians toured shortly afterwards, but a knee injury kept him out, allowing his Warriors team-mate Wayne Parnell – quicker through the air and a better batsman – to take his chance. But in the West Indies early in 2010, with Parnell injured, Tsotsobe did well in the one-dayers and played two of the Tests. Three more caps followed against India in 2010-11: he took five wickets in the second game. He remains in the one-day mix – a superb yorker accounted for Alastair Cook second ball at the Rose Bowl in August 2012 – but others are ahead in the Test queue. Tsotsobe made his first-class debut for Eastern Province in 2004-05, taking 7 for 44 in his first match. Moving to the Warriors, he took 49 wickets in 2007-08, then 12 in two matches against Sri Lanka A in September 2008 earned him that trip to Australia. But he had an unhappy spell at Essex in 2011, being dropped to the second team before a Twitter outburst resulted in him being sent home. He is seen in South Africa as a talisman for the black population – the natural successor to Makhaya Ntini – but it remains to be seen whether Tsotsobe is worth his place in the side on merit. Late in 2013 he was taken to Sri Lanka despite Russell Domingo, SA's new coach, admitting he had "massive concerns about his form, fitness, and possibly his work ethic".

THE FACTS Tsotsobe took 7 for 44 (9 for 96 in the match) on his first-class debut for Eastern Province against Boland at Paarl in November 2004, and took 10 for 72 in the match for EP v South Western Districts in Port Elizabeth in October 2006 ... He took 7 for 39 for Warriors v Lions at Johannesburg in October 2007 ... Tsotsobe's first victim in both Twenty20 internationals and ODIs was the Australian batsman Shaun Marsh ...

THE FIGURES to 17.09.13   espncricinfo.com

Batting & Fielding	M	Inns	NO	Runs	HS	Avge	S/R	100	50	4s	6s	Ct	St
Tests	5	5	2	19	8*	6.33	35.84	0	0	2	0	1	0
ODIs	51	17	10	37	9	5.28	59.67	0	0	5	0	8	0
T20Is	15	2	1	1	1	1.00	12.50	0	0	0	0	0	0
First-class	56	74	30	268	27*	6.09	29.94	0	0	35	3	13	0

Bowling	M	Balls	Runs	Wkts	BB	Avge	RpO	S/R	5i	10m
Tests	5	870	448	9	3–43	49.77	3.08	96.66	0	0
ODIs	51	2483	2007	83	4–22	24.18	4.84	29.91	0	0
T20Is	15	312	337	14	3–16	24.07	6.48	22.28	0	0
First-class	56	9423	5040	185	7–39	27.24	3.20	50.93	5	1

UMAR AKMAL

Full name	**Mohammad Umar Akmal**
Born	**May 26, 1990, Lahore, Punjab**
Teams	**Lahore Shalimar, Sui Northern Gas**
Style	**Right-hand batsman, occasional wicketkeeper**
Test debut	**Pakistan v New Zealand at Dunedin 2009-10**
ODI debut	**Pakistan v Sri Lanka at Dambulla 2009**
T20I debut	**Pakistan v Sri Lanka at Colombo 2009**

THE PROFILE Umar Akmal, the brother of Pakistan's wicketkeepers Kamran and Adnan Akmal, started his international career with a flourish. Only 19, he hit a run-a-ball 66 in only his second one-dayer, in Sri Lanka in August 2009, and bettered that with a superb century in the next match. He entered with Pakistan a wobbly 130 for 4 in the 26th over, and hurtled to his hundred from just 70 balls: he outscored Younis Khan in a stand of 176, and looked comfortable from the start. He refused to be tied down, swinging his seventh delivery – from Ajantha Mendis – over long-on for the first of four sixes. In November 2009 Akmal marked his Test debut, in New Zealand, with 129 and 75, and he continued to look the part throughout 2010, scoring consistently in all three formats, although impetuosity often got the better of him. People started to lose patience, though, as he kept trying the big shots too soon and the tall scores refused to come: in 15 further Tests after his debut he reached 30 on 11 occasions but never progressed beyond 79, and eventually that cost him his place. He remained a one-day regular, scoring well in the West Indies in July 2013, but had to pull out of the Zimbabwe tour which followed after suffering a seizure on an aeroplane: a neurologist later cleared him. Akmal's international start mirrored his domestic one. In 2007-08, he amassed 855 runs at 77.72 in nine Quaid-e-Azam Trophy matches, at an impressive strike-rate of 90.18. He extended his maiden century – in his sixth match – to 248 (off 225 balls) against Karachi Blues, and two matches later clattered 186 not out from 170 balls against Quetta.

THE FACTS Umar Akmal made 129 and 75 on his Test debut, against New Zealand in November 2009: only KS Ranjitsinhji, with 216 for England v Australia in 1896, scored more runs in his debut Test yet finished on the losing side ... Umar made 248 for Sui Northern Gas v Karachi Blues in December 2007 ... He hit a century, from only 70 balls, in his fourth ODI, against Sri Lanka in Colombo in August 2009 ... His brothers Kamran and Adnan Akmal have also kept wicket for Pakistan, as Umar has occasionally done ...

THE FIGURES to 17.09.13   **cricinfo.com**

Batting & Fielding	M	Inns	NO	Runs	HS	Avge	S/R	100	50	4s	6s	Ct	St
Tests	16	30	2	1003	129	35.82	65.98	1	6	117	17	12	0
ODIs	76	67	11	2176	102*	38.85	85.73	1	17	179	35	39	4
T20Is	45	42	8	929	64	27.32	118.19	0	4	71	24	33	2
First-class	60	101	8	4552	248	48.94	71.83	10	27	580	60	50	0

Bowling	M	Balls	Runs	Wkts	BB	Avge	RpO	S/R	5i	10m
Tests	16	0	–	–	–	–	–	–	–	–
ODIs	76	0	–	–	–	–	–	–	–	–
T20Is	45	0	–	–	–	–	–	–	–	–
First-class	60	180	143	3	2–24	47.66	4.76	60.00	0	0

UMAR GUL

Full name **Umar Gul**
Born **April 14, 1984, Peshawar, North-Western Frontier Province**
Teams **Habib Bank**
Style **Right-hand bat, right-arm fast-medium bowler**
Test debut **Pakistan v Bangladesh at Karachi 2003-04**
ODI debut **Pakistan v Zimbabwe at Sharjah 2002-03**
T20I debut **Pakistan v Kenya at Nairobi 2007-08**

THE PROFILE Umar Gul was called up by Pakistan at 19, after their miserable 2003 World Cup. He usually keeps a good line, and obtains appreciable outswing with the new ball, while he can also nip the ball back in. His first real challenge in Tests came against India at Lahore in April 2004. Disparaged by some as the "Peshawar Rickshaw" to Shoaib Akhtar's "Rawalpindi Express", Gul tore through India's imposing top order, moving the ball both ways off the seam at a sharp pace. His 5 for 31 gave Pakistan the early initiative, and they went on to level the series. Stress fractures in the back then kept him out for two years, but he did well in England in 2006. Nine wickets followed against West Indies at Lahore, but then he injured his knee. He was back for the 2007 World Cup, and was one of the few to return with reputation intact, but injuries intruded again before he started 2009 with a superb six-for against Sri Lanka on a Lahore batting paradise. Gul has proved a Twenty20 star, usually coming on after the initial overs and firing in yorkers on demand. He was the leading wicket-taker in the first two World Twenty20s, and it was a blow when a shoulder injury ruled him out of the third one in 2010. But in England later that year he revealed unexpected talent with the bat and bowled with his old fire, then led the attack well at the 2011 World Cup. In 2012 he took 11 wickets on spin-friendly tracks against England in the UAE, and remained a regular in all three formats until injuring his knee again in South Africa in March 2013, soon after demolishing them with his second Twenty20 haul of 5 for 6. After an operation, Gul hoped to be firing again in 2013-14.

THE FACTS Umar Gul took 5 for 6 in a Twenty20 international against New Zealand at The Oval in June 2009: he did it again at South Africa's expense at Centurion in March 2013 ... He took 6 for 42 in an ODI against England at The Oval in September 2010 ... Gul claimed 8 for 78 for Peshawar v Karachi Urban in October 2005 ...

THE FIGURES to 17.09.13   **ESPNcricinfo.com**

Batting & Fielding	M	Inns	NO	Runs	HS	Avge	S/R	100	50	4s	6s	Ct	St
Tests	47	67	9	577	65*	9.94	47.92	0	1	63	20	11	0
ODIs	116	58	16	414	39	9.85	69.57	0	0	34	11	15	0
T20Is	52	24	8	160	32	10.00	109.58	0	0	11	10	18	0
First-class	84	111	15	1156	65*	12.04	–	0	1	–	–	20	0

Bowling	M	Balls	Runs	Wkts	BB	Avge	RpO	S/R	5i	10m
Tests	47	9599	5553	163	6–135	34.06	3.47	58.88	4	0
ODIs	116	5407	4604	161	6–42	28.59	5.10	33.58	2	0
T20Is	52	1050	1217	74	5–6	16.44	6.95	14.18	2	0
First-class	84	16456	9335	327	8–78	28.54	3.40	50.32	16	1

PROSPER **UTSEYA**

ZIMBABWE

Full name	**Prosper Utseya**
Born	**March 26, 1985, Harare**
Teams	**Mountaineers**
Style	**Right-hand bat, offspinner**
Test debut	**Zimbabwe v Sri Lanka at Harare 2004**
ODI debut	**Zimbabwe v Sri Lanka at Bulawayo 2004**
T20I debut	**Zimbabwe v Bangladesh at Khulna 2006-07**

THE PROFILE A diminutive offspinner, Prosper Utseya was unexpectedly thrust into the national team in 2004, aged 19, after several senior players withdrew as a damaging dispute rumbled on. Utseya made 45 in his first Test, but failed to take a wicket, and he was soon pigeonholed as a one-day specialist. He was given a long run in the 50-overs side, but struggled for consistency with either bat or ball ... until the West Indian tour early in 2006, when his mature bowling was a rare highlight. His flight was widely praised, and at times his economy-rate was remarkable, which became a trademark. Utseya stifled the runs in the middle overs, and provided two of the series highlights – comprehensively beating Brian Lara with successive deliveries in the first match in Trinidad, and taking a remarkable diving, juggling boundary catch in the second. In 2006 Utseya took over as captain, and at first continued to keep the runs down. But as opponents grew used to his flattish delivery that economy-rate rose a little, and after a disappointing World Twenty20 campaign in May 2010 he resigned as skipper. Ironically, as his bowling had lost its sparkle his batting improved, to the point where he made a dozen successive double-figure scores in ODIs in 2010-11. In 2013 he finally got back in the Test side, and teased out five Pakistanis in the first Test at Harare in September. He might struggle to take wickets at international level, but Utseya is a force to be reckoned with in domestic cricket, and his spin partnership with Timycen Maruma has brought their teams several titles: in 2008-09 his ten-wicket haul helped Easterns clinch the Logan Cup with a thrilling one-wicket victory against Northerns.

THE FACTS Utseya took his first Test wicket in March 2013, almost nine years after his debut – a record for any specialist bowler ... He took 7 for 56 (11 for 110 in the match) for Easterns v Centrals in Harare in April 2009: in his next game he had match figures of 10 for 93 against Northerns in the Logan Cup final ... Utseya made 115* from No. 9 for Zimbabwe against a South African XI at Potchefstroom in November 2007 ...

THE FIGURES to 17.09.13   ESPNcricinfo.com

Batting & Fielding	M	Inns	NO	Runs	HS	Avge	S/R	100	50	4s	6s	Ct	St
Tests	4	8	1	107	45	15.28	46.72	0	0	12	1	2	0
ODIs	151	122	46	1319	68*	17.35	58.28	0	4	81	16	46	0
T20Is	26	17	6	66	13*	6.00	70.96	0	0	4	0	5	0
First-class	79	134	9	2725	115*	21.80	42.35	1	15	–	–	30	0

Bowling	M	Balls	Runs	Wkts	BB	Avge	RpO	S/R	5i	10m
Tests	4	753	410	10	3–60	41.00	3.26	75.30	0	0
ODIs	151	7857	5691	119	4–38	47.82	4.34	66.02	0	0
T20Is	26	563	617	22	3–25	28.04	6.57	25.59	0	0
First-class	79	13927	6358	211	7–56	30.13	2.73	66.00	8	2

DANIEL **VETTORI**

NEW ZEALAND

Full name	**Daniel Luca Vettori**
Born	**January 27, 1979, Auckland**
Teams	**Northern Districts, Royal Challengers Bangalore**
Style	**Left-hand bat, left-arm orthodox spinner**
Test debut	**New Zealand v England at Wellington 1996-97**
ODI debut	**New Zealand v Sri Lanka at Christchurch 1996-97**
T20I debut	**New Zealand v Kenya at Durban 2007-08**

THE PROFILE Daniel Vettori, the first slow left-armer to take 300 Test wickets, has been arguably the best bowler of his type in international cricket for almost a decade – an assessment reinforced by his selection for the World XI in Australia late in 2005 – and the only cloud on his horizon is a susceptibility to injury. He seemed to have recovered from one stress fracture, which led to a dip in form in 2003, but after a couple of matches for Warwickshire in 2006 he was on the plane home nursing another one. After a number of back injuries, he had trouble with his Achilles tendon, which kept him largely on the sidelines in 2013 until an operation in June. His presence before that was just as well for New Zealand, as for years he carried a huge burden as captain (until standing down after the 2011 World Cup), key batsman and senior bowler. His early Tests in charge were notable for some superb personal performances: two fifties and nine wickets to stave off an embarrassing defeat by Bangladesh in October 2008, and two similar allround efforts which could not prevent defeat in Sri Lanka the following August. Vettori still has the enticing flight and guile that made him New Zealand's youngest Test player at 18 in 1996-97, and he remains economical in limited-over-games. After his mini-slump he returned to form in England in 2004, then butchered Bangladesh with 20 wickets in two Tests. He has improved his batting – after starting at No. 11, blinking nervously through his glasses – to the point that his six centuries include New Zealand's fastest in Tests, an 82-ball effort against the admittedly hopeless Zimbabweans at Harare in August 2005.

THE FACTS Vettori made his first-class debut at 17 in 1996-97, for Northern Districts against the England tourists: his maiden first-class victim was Nasser Hussain ... Three weeks later Vettori became NZ's youngest-ever Test player, at 18 years 10 days: his first wicket was Hussain again ... Vettori averages 23.62 with the ball in Tests against Sri Lanka, but 73.28 v South Africa ... His record includes a Test and four ODIs for the World XI ...

THE FIGURES to 17.09.13   ESPNcricinfo.com

Batting & Fielding	M	Inns	NO	Runs	HS	Avge	S/R	100	50	4s	6s	Ct	St
Tests	112	173	23	4516	140	30.10	58.10	6	23	553	17	58	0
ODIs	275	173	51	2110	83	17.29	81.62	0	4	156	14	78	0
T20Is	33	21	6	205	38	13.66	109.62	0	0	14	2	9	0
First-class	169	249	31	6531	140	29.95	–	9	33	–	–	94	0

Bowling	M	Balls	Runs	Wkts	BB	Avge	RpO	S/R	5i	10m
Tests	112	28670	12392	360	7–87	34.42	2.59	79.63	20	3
ODIs	275	13029	8946	284	5–7	31.50	4.11	45.87	2	0
T20Is	33	769	720	37	4–20	19.45	5.61	20.78	0	0
First-class	169	40130	17549	552	7–87	31.79	2.62	72.69	32	3

MURALI **VIJAY**

Full name	**Murali Vijay Krishna**
Born	**April 1, 1984, Chennai**
Teams	**Tamil Nadu, Chennai Super Kings**
Style	**Right-hand bat, occasional offspinner**
Test debut	**India v Australia at Nagpur 2008-09**
ODI debut	**India v West Indies at Roseau 2011**
T20I debut	**India v Afghanistan at Gros Islet 2008-09**

THE PROFILE All batsmen want to go in to their first Test in good form, and Murali Vijay was in better nick than most: when Gautam Gambhir was banned against Australia in November 2008, Vijay was hoicked out of a Ranji Trophy match in which he'd just scored 243. He made a sound debut, sharing useful opening stands of 98 and 116 with Virender Sehwag as India set about what became a series-clinching 172-run victory. Vijay helped in the field too, running out Matthew Hayden and Michael Hussey, and taking a catch at short leg. Once Gambhir returned Vijay sat out the Tests in New Zealand early in 2009, but later that year made 87 in an opening stand of 221 with Sehwag against Sri Lanka in Mumbai. His next five Tests did not produce anything special, but he remained a consistent runscorer for Tamil Nadu – and upped his short game too, especially in the IPL. After what seemed like an age being the opener-in-waiting behind Sehwag and Gambhir, Vijay finally got a chance when they lost form in 2012-13. And he made people wonder whether that dynamic duo were a thing of the past, running up 167 and 153 in successive Tests against Australia, not long after a career-best 266 in the Irani Cup. Tall and solid, Vijay was an instant success in first-class cricket, despite being a late starter (he only switched to "proper" cricket from the soft-ball variety at 17). He hit 179 against Andhra in his second match, and finished his first season (2006-07) with 628 runs at 52 – only two others made more. There was no second-season dip, either: 667 runs, including a double-century against Saurashtra.

THE FACTS Vijay made 243 for Tamil Nadu v Maharashtra in November 2008, sharing an opening stand of 462 with Abhinav Mukund (300*) ... Vijay also scored 230* for Tamil Nadu v Saurashtra in December 2007: this time the opening stand with Mukund was worth 256 ... He made 266 for the Rest of India v Rajasthan in September 2012 ... Vijay made 179 against Andhra in his second first-class match, at Chennai in December 2006 ...

THE FIGURES to 17.09.13 **ESPNcricinfo.com**

Batting & Fielding	M	Inns	NO	Runs	HS	Avge	S/R	100	50	4s	6s	Ct	St
Tests	16	27	0	1039	167	38.48	48.80	3	3	127	9	12	0
ODIs	14	13	0	253	33	19.46	66.40	0	0	30	1	8	0
T20Is	7	7	0	122	48	17.42	98.38	0	0	8	6	3	0
First-class	64	106	5	4891	266	48.42	50.81	13	18	598	69	61	0

Bowling	M	Balls	Runs	Wkts	BB	Avge	RpO	S/R	5i	10m
Tests	16	0	–	–	–	–	–	–	–	–
ODIs	14	0	–	–	–	–	–	–	–	–
T20Is	7	0	–	–	–	–	–	–	–	–
First-class	64	330	212	3	1-8	70.66	3.85	110.00	0	0

VINAY KUMAR

Full name	Ranganath Vinay Kumar
Born	February 12, 1984, Davanagere, Karnataka
Teams	Karnataka, Royal Challengers Bangalore
Style	Right-hand bat, right-arm fast-medium bowler
Test debut	India v Australia at Perth 2011-12
ODI debut	India v Zimbabwe at Bulawayo 2010
T20I debut	India v Sri Lanka at Gros Islet 2010

THE PROFILE Vinay Kumar is a bowler in the mould of the former Indian stalwart Venkatesh Prasad, relying more on outswingers, legcutters and accuracy than outright speed. For a while, this lack of pace threatened to stymie his international ambitions, but eventually he made it to the full Indian side. "Vinay Kumar is one of the hardest-working cricketers I have worked with," said coach Eric Simons. "You get guys with natural skill, and you get guys who just do it through really hard work. He is one of those." Vinay, who is also a fine outfielder, made his Ranji Trophy debut in 2004-05, and soon established himself as a key part of Karnataka's attack, taking more than 20 wickets in each of his first three seasons. He added an inducker to his stock outswinger, resulting in a superb 2007-08 season, when he was the country's leading wicket-taker with 47 at a shade over 20. Vinay improved that to 53 wickets in 2009-10, and also mentored Karnataka's young fast bowlers, Abhimanyu Mithun and Sreenath Aravind, as they reached the Ranji final for the first time for 11 years. Finally the national call came: after a successful start to the 2010 IPL, Vinay was named in the squad for the World Twenty20 in the Caribbean later in the year. He played only once there, but the highlight among some consistent performances afterwards was 4 for 30 against England at Delhi in October 2011. His Test debut at Perth, which followed injuries to others, was forgettable – 13-0-73-1 – but it didn't stop Royal Challengers Bangalore from shelling out a cool million dollars to secure his services for IPL5. He remained in the one-day mix throughout 2013, and was part of the squad that won the Champions Trophy in England, although he didn't actually play as India fielded an unchanged side in all their five matches.

THE FACTS Vinay Kumar took 8 for 32 (11 for 102 in the match) for Karnataka against Delhi in November 2009 ... He took 7 for 58 (and 3 for 31) for Karnataka against Orissa at Bangalore in November 2012 ... His fourth ball in Test cricket was hit for six by Australia's David Warner ...

THE FIGURES to 17.09.13 — espncricinfo.com

Batting & Fielding	M	Inns	NO	Runs	HS	Avge	S/R	100	50	4s	6s	Ct	St
Tests	1	2	0	11	6	5.50	45.83	0	0	2	0	0	0
ODIs	26	11	4	75	27*	10.71	59.52	0	0	4	2	5	0
T20Is	8	1	1	2	2*	–	50.00	0	0	0	0	0	0
First-class	77	101	18	1453	61	17.50	45.09	0	7	–	–	29	0

Bowling	M	Balls	Runs	Wkts	BB	Avge	RpO	S/R	5i	10m
Tests	1	78	73	1	1–73	73.00	5.61	78.00	0	0
ODIs	26	1175	1078	30	4–30	35.93	5.50	39.17	0	0
T20Is	8	165	221	7	3–24	31.57	8.03	23.57	0	0
First-class	77	13878	6637	271	8–32	24.49	2.86	51.21	12	3

SRI LANKA

KITHURUWAN **VITHANAGE**

Full name	**Kasun Disi Kithuruwan Vithanage**
Born	**February 26, 1991, Colombo**
Teams	**Tamil Union, Basnahira**
Style	**Left-hand bat, legspinner**
Test debut	**Sri Lanka v Bangladesh at Galle 2012-13**
ODI debut	**No ODIs yet**
T20I debut	**No T20Is yet**

THE PROFILE A left-hand batsman at home opening or in the middle order, Kithuruwan Vithanage made a seamless transition from youth cricket into the first-class game. In February 2011, in his first senior match, going in first against two Test newball bowlers in Dammika Prasad and Thilan Thushara, he made 105 for Colombo Cricket Club. Next season he moved to Tamil Union, and the runs kept coming: 121 against Bloomfield was followed by 125 against Chilaw Marians. And in 2012-13 he averaged 83, including a superb undefeated 168 for Sri Lanka Emerging Players against the touring Bangladeshis at Matara. It came at better than a run a ball, and he showed his confidence by batting in a cap to start with. He swept the spinners well, although he did keep them interested when they pitched up by moving away to leg to play the ball. That innings got him into the side for the first Test against Bangladesh a few days later. On a batsman's paradise at Galle he didn't get to the crease in the first innings, but cashed in with 59 in the second. He made only 12 in the second Test, then toured the West Indies with the A team. Vithanage will doubtless make way when Mahela Jayawardene returns – he missed the Bangladesh Tests with a broken finger – but has done enough to show he is one for the future. He attended the famous Royal College in Colombo, and played age-group cricket at international level. His 25 ODIs for the Under-19 team included the vice-captaincy at the 2010 Youth World Cup in New Zealand, where Sri Lanka lost to the eventual winners Australia in the semi-final despite Vithanage's 40.

THE FACTS Vithanage scored 105 on his first-class debut, for Colombo CC v Sinhalese Sports Club in February 2011 ... He made 168* for Sri Lanka Emerging Players against the Bangladesh tourists at Matara in March 2013 ... In January-February 2012 Vithanage had successive increasing first-class innings of 0, 38, 53, 69, 98 and 121 (and then 1) ...

THE FIGURES to 17.09.13   ESPNcricinfo.com

Batting & Fielding	M	Inns	NO	Runs	HS	Avge	S/R	100	50	4s	6s	Ct	St
Tests	2	2	0	71	59	35.50	81.60	0	1	9	1	1	0
ODIs	0	0	–	–	–	–	–	–	–	–	–	–	–
T20Is	0	0	–	–	–	–	–	–	–	–	–	–	–
First-class	28	44	2	1781	168*	42.40	82.30	5	8	185	42	16	0

Bowling	M	Balls	Runs	Wkts	BB	Avge	RpO	S/R	5i	10m
Tests	2	0	–	–	–	–	–	–	–	–
ODIs	0	0	–	–	–	–	–	–	–	–
T20Is	0	0	–	–	–	–	–	–	–	–
First-class	28	330	253	2	2–24	126.50	4.60	165.00	0	0

BRIAN **VITORI**

ZIMBABWE

Full name	**Brian Vitalis Vitori**
Born	**February 22, 1990, Masvingo**
Teams	**Southern Rocks**
Style	**Left-hand bat, left-arm fast-medium bowler**
Test debut	**Zimbabwe v Bangladesh at Harare 2011**
ODI debut	**Zimbabwe v Bangladesh at Harare 2011**
T20I debut	**Zimbabwe v Sri Lanka at Hambantota 2012-13**

THE PROFILE Like his near-namesake Daniel Vettori, Brian Vitori is a left-hander: unlike the New Zealander, though, this Vitori likes to bowl fast, and can move the ball in to the right-hander at a decent pace. He is a stocky youngster from the southern province of Masvingo: "I started playing street cricket when I was eight, at primary school," he says. He played a few one-day matches early in 2006 with mixed results – hardly surprising given that he was barely 16 – but the new franchise system, created in 2008, offered him an opportunity to improve under the guidance of the former Surrey batsman Monte Lynch, who recommended him for a national training camp early in 2011. Vitori had just taken 25 wickets in the season for Southern Rocks – a reasonable return, although his average (37.16) was nothing to write home about. But Alan Butcher, Zimbabwe's then coach and an old county colleague of Lynch's, was also impressed: "I knew we had found someone special." Butcher kept Vitori under wraps until Bangladesh toured in August 2011, for a series that included Zimbabwe's first Test for six years. He made an immediate impact, taking five wickets in a joyous victory, moving the ball around at a waspish pace. Vitori then grabbed five wickets in each of his first two ODIs, a unique feat. He struggled a little in New Zealand early in 2012, before doing well for the A team. He was a regular choice for the limited-overs teams in 2013, with unspectacular results, but returned to the Test side in September, taking 5 for 61 in the surprise victory over Pakistan at Harare.

THE FACTS Vitori took five wickets in each of his first two ODIs, an unprecedented feat (Ryan Harris of Australia took two in his first three): he had ten wickets after two ODIs, another record (previously eight) ... Only six bowlers had previously taken a five-for on ODI debut ... Vitori conceded 105 runs in nine overs v New Zealand at Napier in February 2012: only Mick Lewis of Australia had conceded more (115) in an ODI innings ... He took 6 for 55 for Southern Rocks against Mountaineers at Masvingo in March 2011 ...

THE FIGURES to 17.09.13   **cricinfo.com**

Batting & Fielding	M	Inns	NO	Runs	HS	Avge	S/R	100	50	4s	6s	Ct	St
Tests	4	7	2	52	19*	10.40	61.90	0	0	7	1	2	0
ODIs	13	7	1	32	17	5.33	68.08	0	0	2	2	1	0
T20Is	6	2	2	8	7*	–	114.28	0	0	0	0	1	0
First-class	27	41	14	256	71	9.48	53.78	0	1	26	7	6	0

Bowling	M	Balls	Runs	Wkts	BB	Avge	RpO	S/R	5i	10m
Tests	4	833	464	12	5–61	38.66	3.34	69.41	1	0
ODIs	13	668	600	22	5–20	27.27	5.38	30.36	2	0
T20Is	6	126	165	2	1–24	82.50	7.85	63.00	0	0
First-class	27	3753	2298	70	6–55	32.82	3.67	53.61	4	0

MATTHEW **WADE**

Full name **Matthew Scott Wade**
Born **December 26, 1987, Hobart**
Teams **Victoria**
Style **Right-hand bat, wicketkeeper**
Test debut **Australia v West Indies at Bridgetown 2011-12**
ODI debut **Australia v India at Melbourne 2011-12**
T20I debut **Australia v South Africa at Cape Town 2011-12**

THE PROFILE Everything Matthew Wade achieves in his cricket career will be a bonus after the shocking diagnosis, when he was just 16, that he had testicular cancer. He underwent chemotherapy to beat the disease, and by the time he was 19 was playing first-class cricket – for Victoria, rather than his native Tasmania, as too many keepers were spoiling the broth there. Wade was an instant hit in Melbourne, scoring 83 and taking six catches on debut against South Australia. The following season he made 57 dismissals – a Victorian record – then in 2009-10 scored 677 Sheffield Shield runs, including a vital 96 in the final. He still looked a fair way off the international side, with his childhood mate Tim Paine proving a capable understudy to Brad Haddin, but then Paine broke a finger, and Wade played the Twenty20 internationals in South Africa. An innings of 72 from 43 balls in a T20 match against India in February 2012 meant Wade stayed in when Haddin missed some of the 50-overs games shortly afterwards – and then he got his big break, in unfortunate circumstances, after Haddin returned home from the Caribbean when his daughter was stricken with cancer. Wade grabbed his chance with a century in the third Test at Roseau in April, and added another against Sri Lanka in the New Year Test at Sydney in January 2013. But a quiet time in India – plus some occasionally sloppy glovework – Haddin reclaimed the gloves for the 2013 Ashes, where he took a record 29 catches to keep Wade waiting a little longer for an automatic place.

THE FACTS Wade hit 106 against West Indies at Roseau in his third Test: he was only the sixth Australian wicketkeeper to score a Test hundred, after Rod Marsh, Wayne Philips, Ian Healy, Adam Gilchrist and Brad Haddin ... Wade made 57 dismissals in 2008-09, a record for Victoria ... He was a talented junior Aussie Rules footballer (his father Scott played in the AFL for Hawthorn) but at 170cm decided he was too short to make a career out of it and pursued cricket instead ...

THE FIGURES to 17.09.13   **ESPNcricinfo.com**

Batting & Fielding	M	Inns	NO	Runs	HS	Avge	S/R	100	50	4s	6s	Ct	St
Tests	12	22	4	623	106	34.61	50.08	2	3	59	6	33	3
ODIs	40	36	2	738	75	21.70	69.55	0	4	47	11	41	6
T20Is	19	12	3	183	72	20.33	113.66	0	1	10	7	12	1
First-class	68	106	20	3403	113*	39.56	49.64	6	22	390	40	238	8

Bowling	M	Balls	Runs	Wkts	BB	Avge	RpO	S/R	5i	10m
Tests	12	6	0	0	–	–	0.00	–	0	0
ODIs	40	0	–	–	–	–	–	–	–	–
T20Is	19	0	–	–	–	–	–	–	–	–
First-class	68	6	0	0	–	–	0.00	–	0	0

NEIL **WAGNER**

NEW ZEALAND

Full name	**Neil Wagner**
Born	**March 13, 1986, Pretoria, South Africa**
Teams	**Otago**
Style	**Left-hand bat, left-arm fast-medium bowler**
Test debut	**New Zealand v West Indies at North Sound 2012**
ODI debut	**No ODIs yet**
T20I debut	**No T20Is yet**

THE PROFILE One of several South African-born imports currently plying their trade in New Zealand domestic cricket, left-arm seamer Neil Wagner was immediately called up to the national squad once his four-year qualification period was completed in 2012. He's not the quickest or tallest of bowlers, but does have the precious ability to swing the ball. He can reverse it, too, which made him a more complete bowler in all conditions. Wagner learnt his cricket in Pretoria, and made a splash on his first-class debut for the local Northerns side in 2005-06, with four wickets in each innings. He then toured Zimbabwe and Bangladesh with the National Academy, and even fielded as South Africa's 12th man in two Tests at Centurion. In 2006-07 he was the leading wicket-taker in the Provincial Challenge, but decided to look elsewhere as opportunities seemed limited. He came close to a county contract with Sussex, but eventually decided to try his luck in New Zealand. After 21 wickets in his first season with Otago, he topped the domestic wicket-taking charts in 2010-11 – when his 51 scalps uniquely included five, all bowled, in the same over against Wellington – and 2011-12. A national call was soon seen as inevitable, and it came as soon as his eligibility was confirmed. "He brings a lot of aggression," said an admiring Daniel Vettori. "He runs in hard all day and wants to compete the whole time – I think he's a welcome addition to our side." The early results weren't spectacular – four wickets in two Tests in the West Indies – but he chugged in with some success against England in 2013, taking seven wickets in the match at Dunedin, and seven in the two early-season Tests in England.

THE FACTS Wagner took five wickets in an over – unique in first-class cricket – including four in four balls, for Otago v Wellington at Queenstown in April 2011: all of them were bowled … For Otago against Wellington in the 2011-12 season Wagner took 7 for 96 at the Basin Reserve in November and a career-best 7 for 46 at Dunedin in March 2012 …

THE FIGURES to 17.09.13 **cricinfo.com**

Batting & Fielding	M	Inns	NO	Runs	HS	Avge	S/R	100	50	4s	6s	Ct	St
Tests	8	13	4	106	27	11.77	31.45	0	0	15	0	4	0
ODIs	0	0	–	–	–	–	–	–	–	–	–	–	–
T20Is	0	0	–	–	–	–	–	–	–	–	–	–	–
First-class	73	93	26	1411	70	20.15	49.47	0	6	–	29	21	0

Bowling	M	Balls	Runs	Wkts	BB	Avge	RpO	S/R	5i	10m
Tests	8	1806	1000	24	4–42	41.66	3.32	75.25	0	0
ODIs	0	0	–	–	–	–	–	–	–	–
T20Is	0	0	–	–	–	–	–	–	–	–
First-class	73	14148	7707	309	7–46	24.94	3.26	45.78	13	1

MALCOLM **WALLER**

ZIMBABWE

Full name **Malcolm Noel Waller**
Born **September 28, 1984, Harare**
Teams **Mid West Rhinos**
Style **Right-hand bat, offspinner**
Test debut **Zimbabwe v New Zealand at Bulawayo 2011-12**
ODI debut **Zimbabwe v Bangladesh at Mirpur 2008-09**
T20I debut **Zimbabwe v New Zealand at Harare 2011-12**

THE PROFILE A hard-hitting batsman and a handy offspinner, Malcolm Waller – whose father Andy, now the national coach, captained Zimbabwe in pre-Test days – played for Zimbabwe under-15s in 2000, and four years later appeared for Mashonaland in the domestic one-day competition. His appearances were sporadic until he finally broke into first-class cricket in 2007-08, although even then his performances – except for some eye-catching Twenty20 displays – were hardly spectacular. But good club form for Harare Sports Club helped win him selection for the tour of Bangladesh in 2008-09, and soon after that he hit 63 in a thumping win over Kenya in Mombasa. His offbreaks, though, proved unpenetrative at international level (and still are). Waller missed out on initial selection when Zimbabwe returned to the Test arena in August 2011, but he anchored a rare one-day victory over New Zealand a couple of months later with a mature 99 not out at Bulawayo: "I decided to take the team home rather than get a hundred," he said after Zimbabwe ran down a daunting target of 329 with a ball to spare. That ensured him a Test debut the following week, after which he boasted a batting average of 101 – he followed a battling 72 not out with 29 – but that took a bit of a knock in New Zealand early in 2012, when a technique tailored to Zimbabwe's usually trustworthy pitches came unstuck on seaming surfaces. The horror continued at home until mid-2012, but he emerged from that with a maiden double-century in November. He kept up the good work with 55 in a Test victory over Bangladesh in April 2013, and a few months later added a fine 70 in the first Test against Pakistan.

THE FACTS Waller became only the 11th batsman (and the third Zimbabwean after Andy Flower and Alistair Campbell) to be stranded on 99* in an ODI, against New Zealand at Bulawayo in October 2011 ... Waller made 208* for Mid West Rhinos v Matabeleland Tuskers at Kwekwe in November 2012 ... His father, Andy "Bundu" Waller, also scored a half-century on his Test debut, against England at Bulawayo in 1996-97 ...

THE FIGURES to 17.09.13   **ESF∩cricinfo.com**

Batting & Fielding	M	Inns	NO	Runs	HS	Avge	S/R	100	50	4s	6s	Ct	St
Tests	8	16	1	386	72*	25.73	46.56	0	3	48	1	6	0
ODIs	38	35	3	753	99*	23.53	76.52	0	4	77	6	11	0
T20Is	11	10	2	159	49	19.87	131.40	0	0	14	6	4	0
First-class	53	93	9	3223	208*	38.36	56.56	6	17	397	20	38	0

Bowling	M	Balls	Runs	Wkts	BB	Avge	RpO	S/R	5i	10m
Tests	8	18	8	0	–	–	2.66	–	0	0
ODIs	38	252	254	3	1-17	84.66	6.04	84.00	0	0
T20Is	11	6	4	0	–	–	4.00	–	0	0
First-class	53	2713	1504	35	5-48	42.97	3.32	77.50	1	0

DAVID **WARNER**

Full name **David Andrew Warner**
Born **October 27, 1986, Paddington, Sydney**
Teams **New South Wales, Delhi Daredevils**
Style **Left-hand bat, occasional legspinner**
Test debut **Australia v New Zealand at Brisbane 2011-12**
ODI debut **Australia v South Africa at Hobart 2008-09**
T20I debut **Australia v South Africa at Melbourne 2008-09**

THE PROFILE David Warner, a diminutive and dangerous opener, exploded onto the international scene in January 2009. His astonishing 89 from 43 balls, wielding the bat more like a club, on his Twenty20 debut at the MCG was all the more remarkable as he was the first man to play for the full Australian side before playing first-class cricket since the inaugural Test back in 1877. This was after he smashed nine sixes in 165 not out – a NSW one-day record – against Tasmania in Sydney. After that jet-propelled start, things predictably slowed down: Warner was tried in 50-overs ODIs, without much success, although he did finally play a first-class match for NSW. For a couple of years he was pigeonholed as a Twenty20 blaster, but all that changed in 2011. After making a 7½-hour double-century for Australia A in Zimbabwe, Warner made his Test debut later in the year. He still looked to attack, but treated decent balls with some respect and – playing a brand of cricket described by Greg Baum in *Wisden* as "Test20" – carried his bat in only his second Test, almost conjuring a victory over New Zealand at Hobart, then caned India for a majestic 180 shortly afterwards at Perth. There was another hundred against South Africa at Adelaide in November 2012, but the following year was a tester. He did little during the Test whitewash in India, then missed the start of the 2013 Ashes after a late-night incident when he slapped the England batsman Joe Root in a pub. Warner made 41 in the third Test and 71 in the fourth – but was then jettisoned from the one-day side for poor form. He is an excellent fielder, and a handy legspinner too (as he should be with a name like his).

THE FACTS Warner was the first man since John Hodges and Tom Kendall in the first Test of all in 1876-77 to represent Australia in a full international without having previously played first-class cricket: Warner won the match award for his 89 from 43 balls (seven fours and six sixes) v South Africa in January 2009 ... He finally made his first-class debut for NSW in March 2009 ... He carried his bat for 123 in his second Test, against New Zealand at Hobart in December 2011 ... Warner hit 211 for Australia A v Zimbabwe A at Harare in July 2011 ...

THE FIGURES to 17.09.13   ESPNcricinfo.com

Batting & Fielding	M	Inns	NO	Runs	HS	Avge	S/R	100	50	4s	6s	Ct	St
Tests	22	40	2	1401	180	36.86	68.87	3	8	168	14	18	0
ODIs	39	38	0	1133	163	29.81	80.58	2	6	114	13	11	0
T20Is	46	46	2	1260	90*	28.63	138.00	0	10	117	57	27	0
First-class	36	63	3	2645	211	44.08	70.21	7	11	330	30	27	0

Bowling	M	Balls	Runs	Wkts	BB	Avge	RpO	S/R	5i	10m
Tests	22	264	205	4	2–45	51.25	4.65	66.00	0	0
ODIs	39	6	8	0	–	–	8.00	–	0	0
T20Is	46	0	–	–	–	–	–	–	–	–
First-class	36	499	370	6	2–45	61.66	4.44	83.16	0	0

B-J WATLING

Full name **Bradley-John Watling**
Born **July 9, 1985, Durban, South Africa**
Teams **Northern Districts**
Style **Right-hand bat, wicketkeeper**
Test debut **New Zealand v Pakistan at Napier 2009-10**
ODI debut **New Zealand v Sri Lanka at Dambulla 2010**
T20I debut **New Zealand v Pakistan at Dubai 2009-10**

THE PROFILE A perky right-hand batsman and an improving wicketkeeper, Bradley-John (usually known just by his initials) Watling spent his early years in South Africa before his family moved to New Zealand when he was ten. He was part of the squad for the Under-19 World Cup in Bangladesh in 2003-04 before making it to the Northern Districts team, but in 2006-07 – his third season – he made 564 runs at 37.60, and passed 500 again in 2009-10 and 2010-11. He also did well in one-dayers, and was rewarded with a place in New Zealand's squad against Pakistan in November 2009. He made his first appearances in the Twenty20 games in Dubai – a slight surprise, since he is not regarded at home as a terribly fast scorer. However, that didn't bother Daniel Vettori: "He plays pace well, lets the ball come to him, and in the middle overs he is very adept at turning the strike over against spin." When Pakistan toured New Zealand later in 2009 Watling made his debut in the third Test at Napier, making an undefeated 60 in the second innings, and later resisted the Australian attack for more than two hours in making 46 at Hamilton. But he slipped out of the national side after a modest Indian tour late in 2010: he missed the following year's World Cup, although another good domestic season rescued his national contract. Watling was entrusted with the wicketkeeping gloves for the Test against Zimbabwe at Napier in January 2012: he took four catches, and also made a maiden century. After a dalliance with Kruger van Wyk, the new coach Mike Hesson installed Watling as the regular keeper, and he responded with some polished performances, plus half-centuries against South Africa and England.

THE FACTS Watling made 164* as Northern Districts chased down 384 to beat Wellington by nine wickets at Whangarei in March 2011, after conceding a first-innings lead of 175 ... His first three first-class hundreds all came at Otago's expense ... Watling made 145* in the final of New Zealand's one-day competition in February 2010 ...

THE FIGURES to 17.09.13 espncricinfo.com

Batting & Fielding	M	Inns	NO	Runs	HS	Avge	S/R	100	50	4s	6s	Ct	St
Tests	14	25	3	657	102*	29.86	44.63	1	4	91	1	32	0
ODIs	22	20	2	528	96*	29.33	68.83	0	5	54	3	16	0
T20Is	3	3	0	37	22	12.33	66.07	0	0	3	0	2	0
First-class	74	132	15	4361	164*	37.27	42.90	8	26	–	–	117	0

Bowling	M	Balls	Runs	Wkts	BB	Avge	RpO	S/R	5i	10m
Tests	14	0	–	–	–	–	–	–	–	–
ODIs	22	0	–	–	–	–	–	–	–	–
T20Is	3	0	–	–	–	–	–	–	–	–
First-class	74	47	39	2	2–31	19.50	4.97	23.50	0	0

SHANE **WATSON**

Full name **Shane Robert Watson**
Born **June 17, 1981, Ipswich, Queensland**
Teams **New South Wales, Rajasthan Royals**
Style **Right-hand bat, right-arm fast-medium bowler**
Test debut **Australia v Pakistan at Sydney 2004-05**
ODI debut **Australia v South Africa at Centurion 2001-02**
T20I debut **Australia v South Africa at Johannesburg 2005-06**

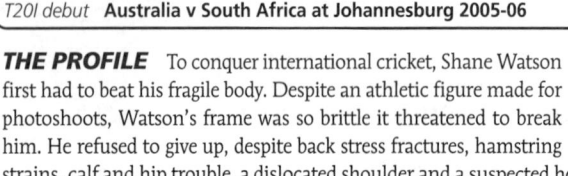

THE PROFILE To conquer international cricket, Shane Watson first had to beat his fragile body. Despite an athletic figure made for photoshoots, Watson's frame was so brittle it threatened to break him. He refused to give up, despite back stress fractures, hamstring strains, calf and hip trouble, a dislocated shoulder and a suspected heart attack that turned out to be food poisoning. He changed his training, and gave up alcohol, but not his dream. It finally paid off when he was promoted to open in the middle of the 2009 Ashes. In his first eight Tests in the new role he scored seven fifties and a 120. His first Test century was a long time coming, but after two nineties (and an 89) he finally reached three figures against Pakistan at the MCG in December 2009. Watson retained the opening slot until the 2012 West Indian tour, usually getting started without cashing in. He had a topsy-turvy tour in India in 2013, being disciplined for insubordination but then finding himself captain when Michael Clarke's back gave out. Watson was then shovelled around the order in the Ashes, finishing up at No. 3 at The Oval – where he unfurled a superb Test-best 176, his first century for 48 innings since November 2010. At the crease he is an aggressive brute with a broad chest, a right-handed disciple of Matthew Hayden. He's had some purple patches in ODIs: successive centuries in the semi and final of the 2009 Champions Trophy, and an astonishing undefeated 185 – with a record 15 sixes – to bully Bangladesh three months later. As a bowler he is willing and speedy, if not quite as good as he thinks he is, and does pick up handy wickets – 11 of them in two Tests against Pakistan in England in 2010, and 5 for 17 against South Africa at Johannesburg the following November.

THE FACTS Watson made 185*, Australia's highest score in ODIs, v Bangladesh at Mirpur in April 2011: the innings included an ODI-record 15 sixes ... He hit 201 in the 2005-06 Pura Cup final demolition of Victoria before retiring hurt: uniquely, four batsmen passed 150 in Queensland's 900 for 6 ... Watson played for Hampshire, alongside Shane Warne: in 2005 he scored 203* for them v Warwickshire at the Rose Bowl ...

THE FIGURES to 17.09.13 — espncricinfo.com

Batting & Fielding	M	Inns	NO	Runs	HS	Avge	S/R	100	50	4s	6s	Ct	St
Tests	46	85	2	2998	176	36.12	51.37	3	20	395	19	30	0
ODIs	165	144	24	5019	185*	41.82	89.43	8	29	499	108	57	0
T20Is	38	37	3	1024	81	30.11	150.14	0	10	79	64	13	0
First-class	119	211	18	8477	203*	43.92	–	19	47	–	–	92	0

Bowling	M	Balls	Runs	Wkts	BB	Avge	RpO	S/R	5i	10m
Tests	46	4419	2043	64	6–33	31.92	2.77	69.04	3	0
ODIs	165	5808	4633	159	4–36	29.13	4.78	36.52	0	0
T20Is	38	632	781	36	4–15	21.69	7.41	17.55	0	0
First-class	119	10830	5690	198	7–69	28.73	3.15	54.69	7	1

CHANAKA **WELAGEDARA**

SRI LANKA

Full name	**Uda Walawwe Mahim Bandaralage Chanaka Asanga Welagedara**
Born	**March 20, 1981, Matale**
Teams	**Tamil Union**
Style	**Right-hand bat, left-arm fast-medium bowler**
Test debut	**Sri Lanka v England at Galle 2007-08**
ODI debut	**Sri Lanka v India at Rajkot 2009-10**
T20I debut	**Sri Lanka v New Zealand at Providence 2009-10**

THE PROFILE Chanaka Welagedara is a brisk left-armer with a sturdy action, who was seen as a like-for-like replacement for Chaminda Vaas. Welagedara, whose array of initials outdoes even Vaas's, swings the ball in nicely, and traps a lot of batsmen lbw. He had problems at first with consistency – against India at home in mid-2010 he sprayed the ball around and proved expensive. A few months earlier, he had reduced India to 31 for 3 at Ahmedabad without the aid of a fielder. Shortly afterwards Welagedara took 5 for 66 in a one-dayer against India, again removing the top three before proving costly later on. He was dropped after only three wickets in four Tests following nine in his first two, but returned for the 2011 England tour. He added spark to the attack in the second Test at Lord's, dismissing Andrew Strauss early on and finishing with five wickets in the match. Later that year he took 5 for 87 against Pakistan in Sharjah, then 5 for 52 against South Africa at Durban, but missed much of 2012 with injuries to groin and shoulder. At the end of the year he took six wickets in the match at Hobart – but then tore a hamstring early in the next Test at Melbourne. After recovering from that, he injured his foot just before the Champions Trophy in England. Welagedara was a late starter to cricket, not playing seriously until he was 17. When he came to Colombo from Matale (a hill-country town not far from Kandy) in 2000 he was soon chosen for the national Pace Academy, headed by former Test paceman Rumesh Ratnayake. Welagedara bowled Moors to the Premier League title in 2002-03, with 34 wickets at 24.14. He made his Test debut against England in December 2007, and took four wickets, three of them top-five batsmen.

THE FACTS Welagedara took 5 for 34 (10 for 95 in the match) for a Sri Lanka Cricket XI v Tamil Nadu in the Gopalan Trophy match in Colombo in September 2007 ... He took 5 for 52 in a Test against South Africa at Durban in December 2011 ... Welagedara scored 76 for Moors v Sinhalese SC in Colombo in October 2009 ...

THE FIGURES to 17.09.13   **ESPNcricinfo.com**

Batting & Fielding	M	Inns	NO	Runs	HS	Avge	S/R	100	50	4s	6s	Ct	St
Tests	20	28	5	191	48	8.30	48.84	0	0	25	4	4	0
ODIs	10	3	2	4	2*	4.00	44.44	0	0	0	0	2	0
T20Is	2	1	1	2	2*	–	66.66	0	0	0	0	0	0
First-class	101	122	42	813	76	10.16	44.71	0	1	–	–	22	0

Bowling	M	Balls	Runs	Wkts	BB	Avge	RpO	S/R	5i	10m
Tests	20	3637	2186	54	5–52	40.48	3.60	67.35	2	0
ODIs	10	457	433	15	5–66	28.86	5.68	30.46	1	0
T20Is	2	36	61	1	1–21	61.00	10.16	36.00	0	0
First-class	101	14498	8623	281	5–34	30.68	3.56	51.59	8	1

SEAN **WILLIAMS**

ZIMBABWE

Full name	Sean Colin Williams
Born	September 26, 1986, Bulawayo
Teams	Matabeleland Tuskers
Style	Left-hand bat, slow left-arm orthodox spinner
Test debut	Zimbabwe v West Indies at Roseau 2012-13
ODI debut	Zimbabwe v South Africa at Johannesburg 2004-05
T20I debut	Zimbabwe v Pakistan at Harare 2013-14

THE PROFILE Sean Williams was long seen as one of Zimbabwe's most promising youngsters – but his career has constantly been interrupted by off-field dramas. A flowing left-hander and useful left-arm spinner, Williams was the pick of Zimbabwe's batsmen in the Under-19 World Cup in 2004, and even though he was only 17 was widely expected to make the full team shortly afterwards when an acrimonious dispute with the board stripped the squad of many experienced players. But Williams's father Collin – a former first-class cricketer himself, and the national hockey coach – insisted his son should concentrate on his studies. Sean did tour South Africa early the following year, and made a classy undefeated 33 in his second one-day international. But after skippering in the Under-19 World Cup in 2006 – and leading his side to a satisfying victory over England – Williams turned down a national contract and skipped off to play club cricket in Britain. By the end of 2006 he was back, scoring 61 and 68 in Bangladesh, but was then injured. Fast-forward to 2008, and he quit again to try his luck in South Africa, only to return a few weeks later. The on-off saga continued until the 2011 World Cup, in which he played only twice: after that he disappeared for personal reasons. Finally, in 2013, aged 26 and eight years after his one-day debut, he took the field in a Test for Zimbabwe, in the West Indies, and made a breezy 31. Still the drama wasn't quite done: when the cash-strapped Zimbabwean board was late paying the players, Williams opted out of the home Tests against Pakistan in September 2013 after doing well in earlier one-dayers against Bangladesh and India.

THE FACTS Williams hit 178 for a Zimbabwe XI in an ICC Intercontinental Cup match against Ireland at Harare in September 2010: in his next match, for Matabeleland Tuskers v Mashonaland Eagles, he made 127 ... Williams captained Zimbabwe in the Under-19 World Cup in February 2006, leading to them to victory over England in the group stage ... Williams made his ODI debut aged 18, but won his first Test cap more than eight years later ...

THE FIGURES to 17.09.13   **cricinfo.com**

Batting & Fielding	M	Inns	NO	Runs	HS	Avge	S/R	100	50	4s	6s	Ct	St
Tests	1	2	0	37	31	18.50	34.25	0	0	4	0	1	0
ODIs	58	57	10	1483	78*	31.55	76.83	0	14	120	11	18	0
T20Is	5	5	0	94	38	18.80	105.61	0	0	7	3	1	0
First-class	37	65	5	2586	178	43.10	–	6	15	–	–	35	0

Bowling	M	Balls	Runs	Wkts	BB	Avge	RpO	S/R	5i	10m
Tests	1	6	9	0	–	–	9.00	–	0	0
ODIs	58	1011	862	12	3–23	71.83	5.11	84.25	0	0
T20Is	5	60	77	1	1–28	77.00	7.70	60.00	0	0
First-class	37	1451	713	20	3–37	35.65	2.94	72.55	0	0

KANE WILLIAMSON

Full name	**Kane Stuart Williamson**
Born	**August 8, 1990, Tauranga**
Teams	**Northern Districts, Yorkshire**
Style	**Right-hand bat, offspinner**
Test debut	**New Zealand v India at Ahmedabad 2010-11**
ODI debut	**New Zealand v India at Dambulla 2010**
T20I debut	**New Zealand v Zimbabwe at Harare 2011-12**

THE PROFILE Well balanced, with an enviably perpendicular bat in defence, Kane Williamson is the most exciting batting talent New Zealand have unearthed since Martin Crowe in the early 1980s. He's also an improving offspinner, who took 4 for 44 against England at Auckland in March 2013. He had a smooth ride through age-group cricket, and made his first-class debut at 17 in December 2007. A slow start (2 and 0) was followed next season by innings of 82, 73 and 98, and the seemingly inevitable maiden century came up in his tenth match. He finished 2008-09 with 812 runs at 50.75, and collected 614 more the following season, with two eye-catching big scores, 170 against Wellington and 192 against Auckland. All this propelled him into the squad for the second Test against Australia at Hamilton in March 2010, and although he didn't play in the end it was a clear sign that his entry would not be long delayed. He made a quiet start in one-day internationals – a ninth-ball duck, courtesy of a peach from Praveen Kumar, and another blob in his next match before finally getting off the mark in his third. But then he made 108 against Bangladesh, before marking his Test debut with a seemingly nerveless 131 against India at Ahmedabad in November 2010. He looked set for another in his second Test, too, before being cut off by an unlucky lbw for 69 in Hyderabad. He did well in the 2011 World Cup, then saved the Wellington Test against South Africa in March 2012 with an unbeaten century after coming in at 1 for 2. Another fine century in Sri Lanka preceded a consistent showing against England as Williamson, still only 23, matured into a fine Test batsman.

THE FACTS Williamson is the youngest of eight New Zealanders to score a century on Test debut, with 131 v India at Ahmedabad in November 2010, when he was 20 ... He made 284* for Northern Districts v Wellington at Lincoln in November 2011 ... He hit 75 and 151 v England in an Under-19 Test at Worcester in August 2008 ... Williamson scored more first-class runs before he had turned 20 than Martin Crowe (1428 to 1127) ...

THE FIGURES to 17.09.13   **ESPNcricinfo.com**

Batting & Fielding	M	Inns	NO	Runs	HS	Avge	S/R	100	50	4s	6s	Ct	St
Tests	25	46	2	1385	135	31.47	40.33	3	8	148	1	17	0
ODIs	45	41	6	1267	145*	36.20	77.77	3	6	102	8	13	0
T20Is	13	11	2	206	48	22.88	118.39	0	0	19	3	5	0
First-class	69	121	6	4646	284*	40.40	50.17	12	21	555	17	61	0

Bowling	M	Balls	Runs	Wkts	BB	Avge	RpO	S/R	5i	10m
Tests	25	1171	659	20	4–44	32.95	3.37	58.55	0	0
ODIs	45	618	560	17	4–22	32.94	5.43	36.35	0	0
T20Is	13	40	70	2	1–6	35.00	10.50	20.00	–	–
First-class	69	4616	2614	65	5–75	40.21	3.39	71.01	1	0

CHRIS **WOAKES**

Full name	Christopher Roger Woakes
Born	March 2, 1989, Birmingham
Teams	Warwickshire
Style	Right-hand bat, right-arm fast-medium bowler
Test debut	England v Australia at The Oval 2013
ODI debut	England v Australia at Sydney 2010-11
ODI debut	England v Australia at Adelaide 2010-11

THE PROFILE A tall quick bowler and a handy batsman, Chris Woakes hit the headlines in his first international, a Twenty20 game at Adelaide, when he kept his cool to hit the winning run off the last ball, after earlier striking the pacy Shaun Tait for a big six: not for nothing did the England coach Andy Flower describe him beforehand as "a serious batter". He almost did it again in the next game, keeping England in touch by hammering Brett Lee over long-on for six in the final over, but history didn't quite repeat itself there. Then, in only his second ODI, Woakes ripped through Australia's middle order to take 6 for 45 at Brisbane – although, just to ruin the fairytale, England eventually lost by 51 runs. It looked as if a star had been born – but, rather perplexingly, Woakes soon slid from view. He missed out on selection for the World Cup, and had only three limited-overs outings at home in 2011, although he remained an England Lions regular. At county level Woakes is a considerable force. He seems to like playing Hampshire: his first two first-class hundreds came at their expense, then in August 2011 he took a career-best 7 for 20 against them at Edgbaston as Warwickshire continued their ultimately unsuccessful bid for the Championship title. Woakes played a big part in that campaign, with 56 wickets, and starred again as they *did* win the pennant in 2012, although he missed the first part of the season with an ankle injury. He made more regular England one-day appearances during 2013, then was a rather surprising debutant in the final Ashes Test at The Oval. He batted with some style, square-driving his first ball for four, but his bowling proved unthreatening.

THE FACTS Woakes took 6 for 45 against Australia at Brisbane in his second ODI, in January 2011: only Paul Collingwood (6 for 31 v Bangladesh at Trent Bridge in 2005) has recorded better figures for England ... Woakes took 5 for 18, including a hat-trick, for England Lions v Guyana at Providence in March 2011 ... He scored 136* against Hampshire in April 2010, and the following August took 7 for 20 against them, also at Edgbaston ...

THE FIGURES to 17.09.13   **espncricinfo.com**

Batting & Fielding	M	Inns	NO	Runs	HS	Avge	S/R	100	50	4s	6s	Ct	St
Tests	1	2	1	42	25	42.00	50.60	0	0	6	0	0	0
ODIs	13	10	4	141	36	23.50	73.43	0	0	10	0	5	0
T20Is	4	3	2	37	19*	37.00	123.33	0	0	1	2	1	0
First-class	84	115	30	3155	136*	37.11	–	6	13	–	–	37	0

Bowling	M	Balls	Runs	Wkts	BB	Avge	RpO	S/R	5i	10m
Tests	1	144	96	1	1-96	96.00	4.00	144.00	0	0
ODIs	13	590	557	15	6-45	37.13	5.66	39.33	1	0
T20Is	4	66	113	2	1-29	56.50	10.27	33.00	0	0
First-class	84	14417	7348	286	7-20	25.69	3.05	50.40	13	3

UMESH **YADAV**

Full name **Umeshkumar Tilak Yadav**
Born **October 25, 1987, Nagpur, Maharashtra**
Teams **Vidarbha, Delhi Daredevils**
Style **Right-hand bat, right-arm fast-medium bowler**
Test debut **India v West Indies at Delhi 2011-12**
ODI debut **India v Zimbabwe at Bulawayo 2010**
T20I debut **India v Sri Lanka at Pallekele 2012**

THE PROFILE Less than two seasons after Umesh Yadav first bowled with a leather ball, he was up against the likes of Rahul Dravid and VVS Laxman in the Duleep Trophy. What makes his ascent even more remarkable is that he plays for unglamorous Vidarbha, which had never produced a Test cricketer before. Yadav is the son of a coalmine worker, and had been thinking of becoming a policeman before his cricket started to get him noticed. A fast bowler with a fine flowing action, he nudges 90mph, moves the ball both ways, and has an effective bouncer. These qualities helped him take 20 wickets in four matches in 2008-09, his first season. That made a few local headlines, but he really caught the eye with some pacy spells for Delhi Daredevils in the IPL: he was flown to the West Indies as a replacement for the injured Praveen Kumar during the World Twenty20 in May 2010, and toured South Africa later that year. A Test cap had to wait until the following November, when West Indies visited, but Yadav made his mark with 3 for 23 and 4 for 80 in the second Test at Kolkata, wrapping up victory by taking the last two wickets with successive balls. In the otherwise miserable Australian trip that followed, Yadav was "the find of the tour" according to Gautam Gambhir, after a five-for to stall Australia's progress in the Perth Test in January 2012 and some fine displays in the one-day series. Later in the year he took five wickets in two spin-dominated victories at home against New Zealand. He was then sidelined by a stress fracture of the back, which kept him out of the home series against Australia early in 2013. But he was fit again for the Champions Trophy in England, and played throughout India's successful campaign after shaking up the Aussies with 5 for 18 in one of the warm-up games.

THE FACTS Yadav took 7 for 74 for Vidarbha against Maharashtra at Nasik in November 2010 ... He is the first Test cricketer to emerge from Vidarbha, and claimed 5 for 93 against Australia at Perth in January 2012 ... Yadav took 6 for 40 for Vidarbha against Jharkhand at Ranchi in November 2009 ...

THE FIGURES to 17.09.13   **ESFN cricinfo.com**

Batting & Fielding	M	Inns	NO	Runs	HS	Avge	S/R	100	50	4s	6s	Ct	St
Tests	9	11	5	36	21	6.00	33.33	0	0	5	1	2	0
ODIs	26	9	8	26	11*	–	61.90	0	0	4	0	4	0
T20Is	1	0	–	–	–	–	–	–	–	–	–	0	0
First-class	31	37	21	173	24*	10.81	46.88	0	0	22	2	15	0

Bowling	M	Balls	Runs	Wkts	BB	Avge	RpO	S/R	5i	10m
Tests	9	1485	1040	32	5–93	32.50	4.20	46.40	1	0
ODIs	26	1202	1206	29	3–32	41.58	6.01	41.44	0	0
T20Is	1	18	24	1	1–24	24.00	8.00	18.00	0	0
First-class	31	5299	3028	113	7–74	26.79	3.42	46.89	7	0

YOUNIS KHAN

PAKISTAN

Full name	**Mohammad Younis Khan**
Born	**Nov 29, 1977, Mardan, North-West Frontier Province**
Teams	**NWFP, Peshawar, Habib Bank**
Style	**Right-hand bat, occasional legspinner**
Test debut	**Pakistan v Sri Lanka at Rawalpindi 1999-2000**
ODI debut	**Pakistan v Sri Lanka at Karachi 1999-2000**
T20I debut	**Pakistan v England at Bristol 2006**

THE PROFILE Younis Khan is a fearless middle-order batsman, as befits his Pathan ancestry. He plays with a flourish, and is especially strong in the arc from backward point to extra cover; he is prone to getting down on one knee and driving extravagantly. But this flamboyance is coupled with grit. He started with a century on Test debut, early in 2000, and soon added 153 against West Indies in Sharjah. He lost his place shortly after the 2003 World Cup following a modest run, but was soon back in favour. He remained a heavy runmaker, especially against India: in March 2005 he hit 147 and 267 in successive Tests, then early the following year made 199, 83, 194, 0 and 77, before doing well in England too, with 173 at Leeds. He flirted with the captaincy – theatrically resigning more than once – and started his reign as fulltime skipper with 313 in 760 minutes against Sri Lanka on a Karachi featherbed early in 2009. Later that year he led Pakistan to victory in the World Twenty20 in England ... but retired from 20-over cricket immediately afterwards. A short-lived ban for unspecified offences in Australia meant he missed the disastrous 2010 England tour, but scored a century against South Africa in his first Test back. He had a quiet World Cup in 2011, then missed the West Indian tour after his brother died. But Younis was soon back in the runs, making 122 against Sri Lanka in Sharjah in November, caning Bangladesh for 200 a few weeks later, and rounding off the whitewash of England early in 2012 with 127 in Dubai. His one-day form dropped off after that, and he was left out early in 2013 – but he answered questions about his Test place with a superb undefeated 200 against Zimbabwe in September, and glided past 7000 runs in the next match.

THE FACTS Younis Khan scored 313, Pakistan's third Test triple-century, against Sri Lanka at Karachi in February 2009 ... He averages 88.06 in Tests against India – and more than 31 against everyone else ... Younis was the seventh Pakistani to score a century on Test debut, with 107 v Sri Lanka in February 2000 ... Against India at home early in 2006 he shared successive stands of 319, 142, 242, 0 and 158 with Mohammad Yousuf ...

THE FIGURES to 17.09.13   espncricinfo.com

Batting & Fielding	M	Inns	NO	Runs	HS	Avge	S/R	100	50	4s	6s	Ct	St
Tests	84	148	12	7058	313	51.89	52.04	22	27	799	43	92	0
ODIs	253	243	23	7014	144	31.88	75.36	6	48	560	53	131	0
T20Is	25	23	3	442	51	22.10	121.42	0	2	31	12	12	0
First-class	181	298	34	13269	313	50.26	–	42	53	–	–	186	0

Bowling	M	Balls	Runs	Wkts	BB	Avge	RpO	S/R	5i	10m
Tests	84	804	491	9	2–23	54.55	3.66	89.33	0	0
ODIs	253	272	271	3	1–3	90.33	5.97	90.66	0	0
T20Is	25	22	18	3	3–18	6.00	4.90	7.33	0	0
First-class	181	3444	1997	43	4–52	46.44	3.47	80.09	0	0

YUVRAJ SINGH

Full name **Yuvraj Singh**
Born **December 12, 1981, Chandigarh**
Teams **Punjab, Pune Warriors**
Style **Left-hand bat, left-arm orthodox spinner**
Test debut **India v New Zealand at Mohali 2003-04**
ODI debut **India v Kenya at Nairobi 2000-01**
T20I debut **India v Scotland at Durban 2007-08**

THE PROFILE Yuvraj Singh had swatted fast bowling all over the place – in the first World Twenty20 he collared Stuart Broad for six sixes in an over – but in 2012 he faced his biggest battle ... cancer. He conquered a rare germ-cell disorder with the aid of chemotherapy, his recovery crowned by inclusion in India's squad for the World Twenty20 in Sri Lanka in September. He made an emotional return, and even made 72 in a Test against England at Ahmedabad in November. But 14 further international innings produced only two fifties, and by February 2013 Yuvraj was back on the sidelines, looking to recapture the form that once made him an automatic one-day choice. Yuvraj had made a lordly entry into international cricket at 18, toppling Australia in the ICC Knockout of October 2000 with a blistering 84 and some scintillating fielding. He supplements those skills with loopy left-arm spin, with which he took two IPL hat-tricks in 2009. While his ability to hit the ball long and clean was instantly recognised, at first he was troubled by quality spin, and temporarily lost his place. But in 2002 his stand with Mohammad Kaif set up a memorable victory over England at Lord's. It still took another 15 months, and an injury to Sourav Ganguly, for Yuvraj to get a Test look-in. But in his third match, on a Lahore greentop, he stroked a stunning first-day century off 110 balls. A scintillating 169 against Pakistan at Bangalore in December 2007 seemed to have nailed down a Test place at last ... but a string of modest scores followed. He remained a fearsome sight (for bowlers, at least) in limited-overs games – and was a star with bat and ball as the 2011 World Cup was won, lifting four match awards.

THE FACTS Yuvraj hit England's Stuart Broad for six sixes in an over during the World Twenty20 at Durban in September 2007 ... He played 73 ODIs before winning his first Test cap ... He averages 63.55 in Tests against Pakistan, but 9.14 v Australia ... Yuvraj hit 358 for Punjab Under-19s against Bihar's in December 1999 ... His father, fast bowler Yograj Singh, played one Test in 1980-81 ... Yuvraj's record includes three ODIs for the Asia XI ...

THE FIGURES *to 17.09.13*   espncricinfo.com

Batting & Fielding	M	Inns	NO	Runs	HS	Avge	S/R	100	50	4s	6s	Ct	St
Tests	40	62	6	1900	169	33.92	57.97	3	11	260	22	31	0
ODIs	282	260	38	8211	139	36.98	87.64	13	50	850	145	91	0
T20Is	33	31	5	791	72	30.42	148.68	0	6	45	54	8	0
First-class	105	168	18	6756	209	45.04	–	20	32	–	–	96	0

Bowling	M	Balls	Runs	Wkts	BB	Avge	RpO	S/R	5i	10m
Tests	40	931	547	9	2–9	60.77	3.52	103.44	0	0
ODIs	282	4904	4137	109	5–31	37.95	5.06	44.99	1	0
T20Is	33	316	373	23	3–17	16.21	7.08	13.73	0	0
First-class	105	2424	1390	26	5–94	53.46	3.44	93.23	1	0

AFGHANISTAN

Mohammad Nabi   *Asghar Stanikzai*   *Mohammad Shahzad*

The improbable rise of war-torn Afghanistan as a cricket power was one of the great feelgood stories of recent years. Starting in the lowly backwaters of world cricket's fifth division in May 2008, they won in Jersey to progress up the ladder a notch. They topped Division Four, too, in Tanzania, then emerged from Division Three, in Argentina at the end of January 2009. That put them into the World Cup qualifying series in South Africa, where they finished just one win short of a fairytale appearance in the main event itself in 2011. The decision to reduce the number of associate nations in the World Cup from six in 2007 to four next time ultimately cost Afghanistan a place, as they finished sixth – but that did bring the considerable consolation (and considerable funding) of official one-day international status for the next four years. They celebrated by walloping Scotland in their first ODI, and later in the year shared a short series in the unfamiliar surroundings of the Netherlands. They were also holding their own in the ICC's first-class Intercontinental Cup competition: also in Holland, Noor Ali became only the fourth man – after Test players in Arthur Morris of Australia, India's Nari Contractor and Aamer Malik of Pakistan – to score two centuries on his first-class debut. They qualified for the World Twenty20 in the West Indies early in 2010, and did not look out of place despite losing to India and South Africa, and qualified again in 2012, when they came within 24 runs of upsetting India. Some more impressive Intercontinental Cup performances followed, and soon the players were starting to bemoan their lack of opportunities against the senior Test nations in 50-overs matches. That's still the case, although they did play (and avoided embarrassment) against Australia late in 2012, not long before the ICC upgraded them to Associate membership. Afghanistan's cricketers still have hurdles to overcome, but they have coped admirably with everything that has been thrown at them so far.

Afghanistan's ODI records as at 17.09.13

Highest total	295-8	v Scotland at Benoni 2008-09
Lowest total	88	v Kenya at Nairobi 2010-11
Most runs	810	Mohammad Shahzad (avge. 36.81)
Highest score	118	Moh'd Shahzad v Canada at Sharjah 2009-10
Most wickets	31	Samiullah Shenwari (avge. 26.67)
Best bowling	4-24	Shapoor Zadran v Netherlands at Amstelveen 2009
Most matches	25	Mohammad Nabi, Samiullah Shenwari (2009-13)
World Cup record	Have not qualified yet	
Overall ODI record	Played 25: Won 14, Lost 11	

AFGHANISTAN

ASGHAR STANIKZAI, Mohammad December 22, 1987, Kabul
RHB, RFM: 24 ODIs, 499 runs at 24.95, HS 66; 2 wickets at 42.00, BB 1-22.
Middle-order batsman who scored 66 against Australia at Sharjah in August 2012.

DAWLAT ZADRAN March 19, 1988, Khost
RHB, RFM: 8 ODIs, 36 runs at 7.20, HS 12; 12 wickets at 25.91, BB 3-49.
Hit for two sixes in his first ODI over - v Canada in 2011 - but took a wicket in his next one.

GULBADIN NAIB March 16, 1991, Peshawar, Pakistan
RHB, RFM: 8 ODIs, 70 runs at 14.00, HS 22; 5 wicket at 24.40, BB 4-31.
Medium-pacer who took 4-31 against Scotland in Sharjah in March 2013.

HAMID HASSAN June 1, 1987, Bati Kot, Nangrahar
RHB, RFM: 16 ODIs, 42 runs at 7.00, HS 17; 24 wickets at 22.48, BB 4-26.
Fast bowler who took 5-23 against Ireland in World Cup qualifier in South Africa in April 2009.

HAMZA HOTAK August 15, 1991, Nangrahar
LHB, SLA: 4 ODIs, 3 runs at 3.00, HS 3*; 2 wickets at 56.00; BB 2-18.
Young spinner, with an action like Daniel Vettori's, who took 2-18 v Ireland in July 2012.

KARIM SADIQ Khan February 18, 1984, Nangrahar
RHB, OB, WK: 21 ODIs, 458 runs at 25.44, HS 114*, 1x100: 4 wickets at 38.75, BB 2-22.
Scored 114 against Scotland at Ayr in August 2010.*

MIRWAIS ASHRAF June 30, 1988, Kunduz
RHB, RFM: 11 ODIs, 83 runs at 11.85, HS 17; 11 wickets at 29.81, BB 4-35.
Medium-pacer who took 4-35 v Kenya in Nairobi in October 2010.

MOHAMMAD NABI Eisakhil March 7, 1985, Loger
RHB, OB: 25 ODIs, 609 runs at 33.83, HS 62; 21 wickets at 38.71, BB 4-31.
Hard-hitting batsman who spent some time on the MCC cricket staff at Lord's.

MOHAMMAD SHAHZAD Mohammadi July 15, 1991, Nangrahar
RHB, WK: 23 ODIs, 810 runs at 36.81, HS 118, 3x100; 25 ct, 6 st.
Scored Afghanistan's first ODI hundred, and later made 214 v Canada in a fc match.*

MOHIBULLAH ORYAKHEL Paak October 12, 1992, Afghanistan
RHB, RFM: 2 ODIs, has not batted.
Batsman who hit 58 v Papua New Guinea in the Under-19 World Cup in 2012.*

NAWROZ MANGAL, Khan July 15, 1984, Kabul
RHB, OB: 24 ODIs, 582 runs at 32.33, HS 112*, 1x100; 7 wickets at 27.85, BB 3-35.
Afghanistan's captain throughout their storybook rise. Scored 112 v Scotland in March 2013.*

NOOR ALI Zadran July 10, 1988, Khost
RHB, RM: 14 ODIs, 371 runs at 28.53, HS 114, 1x100.
Made 130 and 100 on first-class debut, for Afghanistan v Zimbabwe A in August 2009.*

RAHMAT SHAH Zurmatai July 6, 1993, Paktia
RHB, LBG: 2 ODIs, 38 runs at 19.00, HS 35; 0 wickets for 32.
Allrounder who scored 67 on first-class debut against Scotland in Abu Dhabi in 2013.*

SAMIULLAH SHENWARI February 3, 1987, Nangrahar
RHB, LBG: 25 ODIs, 461 runs at 32.92, HS 82; 31 wickets at 26.67, BB 4-31.
Legspinner who took 4-28 v Bermuda in World Cup qualifier in 2009.

SHAPOOR ZADRAN July 8, 1987, Loger
LHB, LFM: 16 ODIs, 21 runs at 4.20, HS 17; 22 wickets at 27.27, BB 4-24.
Left-armer who took 4-24 - including 3 for 1 in 8 balls - on ODI debut v Netherlands in Aug 2009.

CANADA

Jimmy Hansra   *Nitish Kumar*   *Henry Osinde*

Cricket has long been played in Canada: the first-ever international match was not England v Australia but Canada v the United States, in New York in 1844. But although the series continued fitfully over the years, cricket never quite took hold in north America – although the States had several handy teams around the turn of the 20th century, and the Canadians have long hosted visits by strong touring sides. Don Bradman made one such trip in the 1930s, and nominated the Brockton Point ground in Vancouver as the most beautiful he'd ever seen. In 1954 a Canadian side toured England, playing several first-class matches. In a portent of things to come, that team included several players who had moved to Canada from the West Indies for better job prospects. After a quiet period, Canadian cricket received a shot in the arm when they qualified for the 1979 World Cup in England, although the inexperienced team was embarrassed by the hosts, being hustled out for 45 at Old Trafford. Canada missed out on World Cup qualification until 2002-03, when a side largely made up of expats – and a few journeymen who happened to have been born in Canada – gave a decent account of themselves. John Davison, who had hovered on the fringes of the Victoria and South Australia sides, returned for the land of his birth and shocked everyone by hammering a century in 67 balls – the fastest in the World Cup at the time – against West Indies. Sri Lanka proved rather more ruthless, bowling them out for 36. Canada qualified again in 2007 and 2011, without upsetting any apple-carts. Their administration has been striving hard to become more professional, and in 2009 the first central contracts were introduced. Whether to accept them was simple for some, like the hard-hitting batsman Rizwan Cheema, who was serving behind the counter in a fast-food joint. But results since then have been dire, not helped by administrative squabbles. The shortage of home-grown talent remains a worry, so the next few years are vital.

Canada's ODI records as at 17.09.13

Highest total	312-4	v Ireland at Nairobi 2006-07
Lowest total	36	v Sri Lanka at Paarl 2002-03
Most runs	1961	A Bagai (avge. 38.45)
Highest score	137*	A Bagai v Scotland at Nairobi 2006-07
Most wickets	45	H Osinde (avge. 30.86)
Best bowling	5-27	A Codrington v Bangladesh at Durban 2002-03
Most matches	60	A Bagai (2003–2011)
World Cup record	\multicolumn{2}{l}{First phase 1979, 2002-03, 2006-07, 2010-11}
Overall ODI record	\multicolumn{2}{l}{Played 73: Won 17, Lost 55, No result 1}

CANADA

BAIDWAN, Harvir Singh   July 31, 1987, Chandigarh, India
RHB, RM: 28 ODIs, 215 runs at 17.91, HS 33; 43 wickets at 28.39, BB 3-19.
Tidy medium-pacer who has a good economy-rate (just above five an over) in ODIs.

DAESRATH, Damodar   July 4, 1981, Berbice, Guyana
RHB, OB: 2 ODIs, 64 runs at 32.00, HS 40; 2 wickets at 24.00, BB 1-13.
Former Guyana captain: scored 111 for Canada v UAE in August 2013.

GUNASEKERA, Ruvindu   July 20, 1991, Colombo, Sri Lanka
LHB: 15 ODIs, 400 runs at 26.66, HS 72.
Batsman who played his first ODI at 17: in 2010 hit 71 and 59 v Ireland on successive days.

HAMZA TARIQ   July 21, 1990, Karachi, Pakistan
RHB, WK: 5 ODIs, 45 runs at 9.00, HS 24; 4 ct.
Wicketkeeper/batsman who scored 52 against Afghanistan in 2011.

HANSRA, Amarbhir Singh ("Jimmy")   December 29, 1984, Ludhiana, India
RHB, OB: 20 ODIs, 419 runs at 27.93, HS 70*; 7 wickets at 51.71, BB 3-27.
Scored 70 v Kenya and 70 v New Zealand in successive World Cup matches in 2011.*

JUNAID SIDDIQUI   March 25, 1985, Karachi, Pakistan
RHB, LBG: 6 ODIs, 50 runs at 16.66, HS 25; 3 wickets at 73.00, BB 1-35.
Pakistan-born allrounder who played fc cricket in Sri Lanka in 2010-11.

KHURRAM CHOHAN   February 22, 1980, Lahore, Pakistan
RHB, RFM: 23 ODIs, 142 runs at 12.90, HS 35*; 31 wickets at 29.90, BB 4-26.
Medium-pacer who took eight wickets in successive matches against Afghanistan in 2010.

KUMAR, Nitish Roenik   May 21, 1994, Scarborough, Ontario
RHB: 12 ODIs, 150 runs at 13.63, HS 38.
Precocious batsman, nicknamed "Tendulkar", who made his ODI debut at 15.

OSINDE, Henry   October 17, 1978, Uganda
RHB, RFM: 42 ODIs, 64 runs at 4.26, HS 21*; 45 wickets at 30.86, BB 4-26.
Experienced opening bowler who took 4-26 v Kenya in the 2011 World Cup.

PATEL, Hiral   August 10, 1991, Ahmedabad, India
RHB, SLA: 21 ODIs, 434 runs at 20.66, HS 62; 10 wickets at 35.30, BB 4-28.
Aggressive batsman who hit 54 against Australia in the 2011 World Cup.

PATHAN, Rayyan Khan   December 6, 1991, Toronto, Ontario
RHB, RFM: 1 ODI, 2 runs at 2.00, HS 2; 2 wickets at 25.00, BB 2-50.
Bowler from Toronto whose brother, Riyaz, has played for Canada Under-19s.

RAZA-UR-REHMAN   November 5, 1985, Bulawayo, Zimbabwe
RHB, LFM: 2 ODIs, 121 runs at 60.50, HS 70; 0 wicket for 37.
Attacking batsman who hit 70 and 51 in his first two ODIs, against Kenya in March 2013.

RIZWAN CHEEMA   August 15, 1978, Pakistan
RHB, RM: 33 ODIs, 764 runs at 24.64, HS 94; 32 wickets at 34.21, BB 3-25.
Big-hitting batsman with an ODI strike-rate of 111.53 - and 35 sixes.

USMAN LIMBADA   October 2, 1989, Scarborough, Ontario
RHB, RM: 10 ODIs, 170 runs at 18.88, HS 50.
Young batsman who scored 50 against Ireland in September 2011.

IRELAND

George Dockrell   *Paul Stirling*   *Ed Joyce*

Cricket in Ireland was once so popular that Oliver Cromwell banned it in 1656. Since then, it has been something of a minority sport, although there were occasional big days, as in 1969 when the West Indians were skittled for 25 on a boggy pitch at Sion Mills in County Tyrone (rumours that the visitors enjoyed lavish hospitality at a nearby Guinness brewery the night before are thought to be unfounded). Cricket continued as an amateur pastime until the 1990s, when the Irish board left the auspices of the English one and attained independent ICC membership. Ireland became eligible to play in the World Cup, and narrowly missed out on the 1999 tournament, when they lost a playoff to Scotland. They made no mistake for 2007, though, winning the ICC Trophy (handily, it was played in Ireland) to ensure qualification. A change of captain to the Australian-born Trent Johnston ushered in a new, more professional set-up, and Ireland travelled to the Caribbean hopeful of making a mark. No-one, though, was quite prepared for what happened – except maybe Johnston himself, who packed enough for a seven-week stay when most were expecting a quiet return home in a week or two. In their first World Cup match, Ireland tied with Zimbabwe, then went one better on a Sabina Park greentop on St Patrick's Day, hanging on to beat Pakistan. Ireland sailed on to the Super Eights, where they beat Bangladesh too. In 2011, the highlight of several good performances was a stunning victory over England, thanks to Kevin O'Brien's 50-ball hundred. But the better Irish players are already with English counties – England's ODI win over Ireland in 2013 featured a century from Eoin Morgan and four wickets from Boyd Rankin, both former Ireland internationals – and the others struggle to fit in ever-increasing international commitments around a steady job. Irish cricket is striving to build on World Cup success by planning a proper first-class structure, and is dreaming of Test status by 2020.

Ireland's ODI records *as at 17.09.13*

Highest total	329-7	v England at Bangalore 2010-11
Lowest total	77	v Sri Lanka at St George's 2006-07
Most runs	2060	WTS Porterfield (avge. 32.18)
Highest score	177	PR Stirling v Canada at Toronto 2010
Most wickets	66	DT Johnston (avge. 32.04)
Best bowling	5-14	DT Johnston v Canada at Centurion 2008-09
Most matches	75	KJ O'Brien (2006-2013)
World Cup record		Super Eights 2006-07, first phase 2010-11
Overall ODI record		Played 81: Won 37, Lost 37, Tied 3, No result 4

IRELAND

CUSACK, Alex Richard   October 29, 1980, Brisbane, Australia
RHB, RFM: 50 ODIs, 679 runs at 22.63, HS 71; 52 wickets at 22.40, BB 5-20.
Man of the Match on ODI debut for 36* and 3-15 v South Africa at Belfast in June 2007.

DOCKRELL, George Henry   July 22, 1992, Dublin
RHB, SLA: 37 ODIs, 88 runs at 11.00, HS 19; 44 wickets at 27.65, BB 4-24.
Precocious slow left-armer who now plays for Somerset: took 4-24 v Scotland at Belfast in Sept 2013.

JOHNSTON, David Trent   April 29, 1974, Wollongong, NSW, Australia
RHB, RFM: 67 ODIs, 743 runs at 19.55, HS 45*; 66 wickets at 32.04, BB 5-14.
Inspirational captain (and innovative chicken dancer) during Ireland's 2007 World Cup run.

JOYCE, Edmund Christopher   September 22, 1978, Dublin
LHB: 39 ODIs (17 for England), 1252 runs at 34.77, HS 116*, 2×100.
Played for England in the 2006-07 World Cup, and Ireland in 2010-11; 116* v Pakistan in May 2013.

MOONEY, John Francis   February 10, 1982, Dublin
LHB, RM: 48 ODIs, 737 runs at 23.77, HS 55; 35 wickets at 29.60, BB 4-27.
Left-hander with a mean reverse-sweep; his brother Paul played for Ireland too.

MURTAGH, Timothy James   August 2, 1981, London
LHB, RFM: 8 ODIs, 48 runs at 16.00, HS 23*; 7 wickets for 38.71, BB 3-33.
Bustling Middlesex seamer with Irish grandparents: 3-33 v England at Dublin in Sept. 2013.

O'BRIEN, Kevin Joseph   March 4, 1984, Dublin
RHB, RFM: 75 ODIs, 1933 runs at 33.32, HS 142, 2×100; 62 wickets at 28.03, BB 4-13.
Well-built allrounder whose 50-ball century led to victory over England at the 2011 World Cup.

O'BRIEN, Niall John   November 8, 1981, Dublin
LHB, WK: 58 ODIs, 1469 runs at 28.25, HS 72; 39 ct, 7 st.
Feisty keeper who has played for Kent, Northants and Leics: made 72 in World Cup win v Pakistan.

PORTERFIELD, William Thomas Stuart   September 6, 1984, Londonderry
RHB: 67 ODIs, 2060 runs at 32.18, HS 112*, 6×100.
Solid opener: made two ODI hundreds in three days early in 2007; took over as captain in 2008.

RICHARDSON, Edward James   July 22, 1990, Louth
RHB, RM: 2 ODIs, 12 runs at 12.00, HS 12; 2 wickets at 27.00, BB 2-39.
Young medium-pacer who plays for Dublin's North County club: cousin of John Mooney.

SHANNON, James Norman Knight   February 12, 1990, Belfast
RHB, OB: 1 ODI, 2 runs at 2.00, HS 2.
Handy middle-order batsman from Instonians, whose brother Sam is also a useful prospect.

SORENSEN, Max Christian   November 18, 1985, Johannesburg, South Africa
RHB, RFM: 3 ODIs, 55 runs at 55.00, HS 31; 5 wickets at 19.40, BB 3-36.
Fast bowler from The Hills club in Dublin: took 5-50 v Australia A in 2013.

STIRLING, Paul Robert   September 3, 1990, Belfast
RHB: 45 ODIs, 1654 runs at 37.59, HS 177, 5×100; 25 wickets at 34.76, BB 4-11.
Batsman on Middlesex's books who slammed 177 against Canada in September 2010.

WHITE, Andrew Roland   July 3, 1980, Newtownards, Co. Down
RHB, OB: 58 ODIs, 769 runs at 18.75, HS 79; 25 wickets at 26.56, BB 4-44.
Offspinner, formerly with Northants, who hit 152* on first-class debut, for Ireland v Holland in 2004.

WILSON, Gary Craig   February 5, 1986, Dundonald, Northern Ireland
RHB, WK: 46 ODIs, 1014 runs at 25.35, HS 113, 1×100; 29 ct, 8 st.
Handy keeper-batsman who also plays for Surrey; scored 113 v Holland in Dublin in 2010.

KENYA

Collins Obuya   *Maurice Ouma*   *Tanmay Mishra*

The British Empire spread cricket to Kenya: the first notable match was played there in 1899, and English-style country clubs still flourish in Nairobi, which can claim one cricket record – six different grounds there have staged official one-day internationals, more than any other city. Strong MCC teams have made several visits to East Africa – one of them, in the early 1960s, unearthed Basharat Hassan, who went on to enjoy a long career with Nottinghamshire. Kenyan players formed the backbone of the East African side in the first World Cup, in 1975, but soon after that they struck out on their own, joining the ICC in their own right in 1981. Kenyan cricket continued to improve quietly until they qualified for the World Cup in 1995-96, where they amazed everyone by upsetting West Indies in a group game. Players reared on hard pitches struggled in early-season England at the 1999 Cup, but the 2003 version was different: it was held in Africa, and some of the matches were played in Kenya. Helped by outside events (England refused to go to Zimbabwe, while New Zealand boycotted Nairobi for security reasons), the Kenyans progressed to the semi-finals. It seemed like the start of a golden era: instead it ushered in a depressing time, marked by player strikes and arguments about administration. Peace broke out in time for the 2007 World Cup, but with several players approaching the veteran stage the results were poor, and Ireland comfortably usurped them as the leading non-Test nation: others have passed them since. More haggling over money intruded in 2010, before a resolution in time for the following year's World Cup. But more dreadful results there led to a clearout of the old guard, meaning farewells to stalwarts like Steve Tikolo – once seen as the best batsman outside Test cricket – and the chunky allrounder Thomas Odoyo, the first bowler from a non-Test nation to take 100 wickets in one-day internationals. Now a new young side is struggling to compete in international 50- and 20-overs cricket.

Kenya's ODI records *as at 17.09.13*

Highest total	347-3	v Bangladesh at Nairobi 1997-98
Lowest total	69	v New Zealand at Chennai 2010-11
Most runs	3362	SO Tikolo (avge. 29.49)
Highest score	144	KO Otieno v Bangladesh at Nairobi 1997-98
Most wickets	137	TM Odoyo (avge. 29.71)
Best bowling	5-24	CO Obuya v Sri Lanka at Nairobi 2002-03
Most matches	130	SO Tikolo (1996-2011)
World Cup record		Semi-finalists 2002-03; first phase 1995-96, 1999, 2006-07, 2010-11
Overall ODI record		Played 150: Won 41, Lost 104, No result 5

KENYA

AGA, Ragheb Gul July 10, 1984, Nairobi
RHB, RFM: 8 ODIs, 25 runs at 5.00, HS 12; 6 wickets at 38.00, BB 2-17.
Allrounder who reappeared after almost eight years in 2012: has played for Sussex.

ALLAN, Duncan Iain October 14, 1991, Brisbane, Australia
RHB, RFM: 5 ODIs, 71 runs at 14.20, HS 27; 2 wickets at 40.00, BB 1-22.
Promising allrounder: player of the tournament at the 2011 Under-19 World Cup qualifier.

KARIM, Irfan Ali September 25, 1992, Kenya
LHB, OB: 5 ODIs, 260 runs at 52.00, HS 112, 1x100.
Opening batsman who scored 65 and 112 in successive ODIs against Canada in March 2013.

MISHRA, Tanmay December 22, 1986, Mumbai, India
RHB, RM: 42 ODIs, 1128 runs at 34.18, HS 72; 1 wicket for 12.00, BB 1-6.
Talented batsman who returned to Kenya in 2010 after studying in India: played in the IPL in 2012.

NGOCHE, James Otieno January 29, 1988, Nairobi
RHB, OB: 17 ODIs, 35 runs at 5.00, HS 21*; 20 wickets at 28.45, BB 3-18.
Offspinner who took 3-18 v Scotland in 2010: three brothers and two sisters also played for Kenya.

NGOCHE, Shem Obado June 6, 1989, Kenya
RHB, SLA: 11 ODIs, 46 runs at 5.75, HS 28; 9 wickets at 36.66, BB 2-28.
Slow left-armer who faced three balls at the 2011 World Cup – and was dismissed by all three.

OBANDA, Alex Ouma December 25, 1987, Nairobi
RHB: 46 ODIs, 1209 runs at 30.22, HS 96*.
Strokeplaying batsman who was stranded four short of a century against Zimbabwe in Feb 2009.

OBUYA, Collins Omondi July 27, 1981, Nairobi
RHB, LB: 100 ODIs, 1976 runs at 26.00, HS 98*; 35 wickets at 46.77, BB 5-24.
Made 98 v Australia in the 2011 World Cup – and took over as captain afterwards.*

ODHIAMBO, Nelson Mandela March 21, 1989, Nairobi
RHB, RFM: 7 ODIs, 54 runs at 10.80, HS 29; 8 wickets at 32.00, BB 3-48.
Medium-pacer who opened the bowling in two ODIs in 2010 with his uncle, Thomas Odoyo.

ODHIAMBO, Nehemiah Ngoche August 7, 1983, Nairobia
RHB, RFM: 65 ODIs, 516 runs at 12.58, HS 66; 70 wickets at 35.32, BB 4-61.
Fast bowler who took 5-20 in T20 v Scotland in Feb 2010; three brothers have played for Kenya.

OTIENO, Elijah Asoyo January 3, 1988, Nairobi
RHB, RFM: 24 ODIs, 40 runs at 4.44, HS 11; 21 wickets at 40.95, BB 4-33.
Promising young seamer – but with the bat collected five ducks in his first seven first-class innings.

OUMA, Maurice Akumu November 8, 1982, Kiambli
RHB, WK: 76 ODIs, 1433 runs at 20.76, HS 61; 48 ct, 10 st.
Handy striker who often opens: took over as captain in 2009 but resigned in 2010.

PATEL, Rakep Rajendra July 12, 1989, Nairobi
RHB, OB: 35 ODIs, 552 runs at 20.44, HS 92; 2 wickets at 65.00, BB 1-14.
Promising batsman who hit 92 against the Netherlands in February 2010.

VARAIYA, Hiren Ashok April 9, 1984, Mumbai, India
RHB, SLA: 59 ODIs, 228 runs at 12.66, HS 34; 65 wickets at 29.47, BB 4-25.
Canny spinner who struck with his first ball in ODIs (v Canada in 2006).

THE NETHERLANDS

Edgar Schiferli   *Peter Borren*   *Daan van Bunge*

Cricket was brought to The Netherlands by British soldiers during the Napoleonic War: by 1881 there was a Dutch team, and two years later a national board was set up, comprising 18 clubs, four of which still exist. A league system has long flourished, and there has been a tradition of foreign players coming over to coach. Dutch cricket received a boost in 1964 when Australia visited after an Ashes tour and lost by three wickets, and more noses were tweaked in 1989, with a win over England A. West Indies (1991) and South Africa (1994) also succumbed – it's safe to say they were more relaxed than they might have been for an official international – and another strongish England side was beaten in 1993. The Netherlands qualified for their first World Cup three years later, and weren't disgraced, and they were there again in 2003, when they beat Namibia. They just scraped in to the 2007 tournament, winning a playoff against the UAE, but again managed a consolation win, this time over Scotland, which made up for being pummelled by South Africa and Australia. Perhaps their biggest moment, though, came in the first match of the World Twenty20 in 2009, when they embarrassed England – at Lord's, too. Standout performers in recent years – as the local board has cast its net far and wide for players with Dutch connections – have included Roland Lefebvre, who played for Somerset and Glamorgan, and Bas Zuiderent, who had a spell with Sussex. Essex's Ryan ten Doeschate hammered four centuries in three ICC Intercontinental Cup games in 2006, while the Australian Tom Cooper, whose mother is Dutch, made a stunning start in 2010. Ten Doeschate hit two fine centuries in the 2011 World Cup, including 119 as the Netherlands nearly embarrassed England again. The local players are very keen, but there are not that many of them, fans are thin on the ground, and there's really no prospect of a proper first-class competition. But the men in orange brighten up any tournament they play in.

The Netherlands' ODI records as at 17.09.13

Highest total	315-8	v Bermuda at Rotterdam 2007
Lowest total	80	v West Indies at Dublin 2007
Most runs	1541	RN ten Doeschate (avge. 67.00)
Highest score	134*	KJJ van Noortwijk v Namibia at Bloemfontein 2002-03
Most wickets	55	RN ten Doeschate (avge. 24.12)
Best bowling	4-23	E Schiferli v Kenya at Potchefstroom 2008-09
Most matches	57	B Zuiderent (1996-2011)
World Cup record		Eliminated in first round 1995-96, 2002-03, 2006-07 and 2010-11
Overall ODI record		Played 76: Won 26, Lost 43, Tied 1, No result 2

THE NETHERLANDS

AHSAN MALIK Jamil Ahmed August 29, 1989, Rotterdam
RHB, RFM: 8 ODIs, 13 runs without dismissal, HS 10*; 4 wickets at 45.00, BB 3-38.
Energetic medium-pacer who took 4-24 against Lancashire in 2012.

BARRESI, Wesley May 3, 1984, Johannesburg, South Africa
RHB, WK: 24 ODIs, 609 runs at 29.00, HS 67; 10 ct, 8 st.
Hard-hitting batsman who formerly played for Easterns in South Africa: 64 v Sussex in August 2013.

BORREN, Peter William August 21, 1983, Christchurch, New Zealand
RHB, RM: 54 ODIs, 913 runs at 21.23, HS 96; 46 wickets at 33.69, BB 4-32.
Combative allrounder who made 105 and 96 v Canada in 2006: appointed captain in 2010.

BUKHARI, Mudassar December 26, 1983, Gujrat, Pakistan
RHB, RFM: 42 ODIs, 494 runs at 17.64, HS 71; 53 wickets at 27.60, BB 3-17.
Primarily a bowler, he scored 71 (after opening) and took 3-24 against Ireland in July 2007.

COOPER, Tom Lexley William November 26, 1986, Wollongong, NSW, Australia
RHB, OB: 23 ODIs, 976 runs at 48.80, HS 101, 1×100; 13 wickets at 33.69, BB 3-11.
Hard-hitting batsman who uniquely passed 50 in his first three ODIs, then made 101 in his fifth.

de GROOTH, Tom Nico May 14, 1979, The Hague
RHB, OB: 34 ODIs, 480 runs at 17.14, HS 97; 1 wicket at 2.00, BB 1-2.
Made 98 (v Scotland), 196 and 97 (v Bermuda) in successive matches in August 2007.

KERVEZEE, Alexei Nicolaas September 11, 1989, Walvis Bay, Namibia
RHB, RM: 39 ODIs, 924 runs at 28.00, HS 92; 0 wickets for 34.
World Cup debut at 17, later made 98 v Canada, and joined Worcestershire in 2007.

MYBURGH, Stephanus Johannes February 28, 1984, Pretoria, South Africa
LHB, OB: 7 ODIs, 173 runs at 24.71, HS 56.
Import who scored 77, 74, 66 and 34 in successive CB40 matches in 2012.*

RIPPON, Michael James Grattan September 14, 1991, Cape Town, South Africa
RHB, SLC: 2 ODIs, 17 runs at 17.00, HS 14*; 1 wicket at 52.00, BB 1-30.
Unorthodox spinner who was on the Sussex staff in 2013.

SCHIFERLI, Edgar May 17, 1976, The Hague
RHB, RFM: 29 ODIs, 158 runs at 10.53, HS 41; 33 wickets at 30.18, BB 4-23.
Long-serving fast bowler (ODI debut in 2002-03) who emerged from retirement in 2013.

SEELAAR, Pieter Marinus July 2, 1987, Schiedam
RHB, SLA: 34 ODIs, 97 runs at 8.81, HS 34*; 36 wickets at 34.63, BB 3-22.
Tidy spinner who took 5-57 in Intercontinental Cup match v Kenya at Amstelveen in 2008.

SWART, Michael Richard October 1, 1982, Subiaco, Perth, Australia
RHB, OB: 8 ODIs, 142 runs at 20.28, HS 52; 3 wickets at 74.00, BB 1-21.
Batsman with a Sheffield Shield hundred: made 89 in T20 international v Kenya in 2013.

SZWARCZYNSKI, Eric Stefan February 13, 1983, Vanderbijlpark, South Africa
RHB: 38 ODIs, 970 runs at 27.71, HS 98.
Batsman whose favourite player is Allan Donald: run out for 98 in ODI v South Africa in May 2013.

ten DOESCHATE, Ryan Neil June 30, 1980, Port Elizabeth, South Africa
RHB, RFM: 33 ODIs, 1541 runs at 67.00, HS 119, 5×100; 55 wickets at 24.12, BB 4-31.
Allrounder who reached 1000 ODI runs quicker than anyone bar Viv Richards and Gordon Greenidge.

van BUNGE, Daan Lodewijk Samuel October 19, 1982, Leidschendam, Voorburg
RHB, LB: 35 ODIs, 623 runs at 21.48, HS 80; 11 wickets at 29.90, BB 3-16.
Stylish batsman and legspinner hit for 36 in over by Herschelle Gibbs in 2007 World Cup.

SCOTLAND

Kyle Coetzer   *Matt Machan*   *Richie Berrington*

Cricket crept over the border from England in the mid-18th century: soldiers played it near Perth in 1750, although the first recorded match in Scotland was not till 1785. More recently there has long been a strong amateur league system in the country, although – just as in Ireland – international aspirations have always been handicapped by the absence of a proper professional set-up, which has meant that the better players have always migrated south. One of them, the Ayr-born Mike Denness, captained England, while one of the few bowlers to trouble Don Bradman in 1930 was the Scottish legspinner Ian Peebles. More recently, offspinner Peter Such (born in Helensburgh) played for England, while Gavin Hamilton (born in Broxburn) also won an England Test cap after doing well for Scotland at the 1999 World Cup. Unfortunately, Hamilton bagged a pair, and was soon back playing for Scotland: he hit his maiden one-day international century in 2008. At the 2007 World Cup, Hamilton appeared alongside another former England player in Dougie Brown, the combative allrounder who had a long career with Warwickshire and played nine ODIs for England in 1997-98. Scotland left the auspices of the English board and joined the ICC in 1994, but they failed to win a match – or reach 200 – in any of their World Cup games in 1999 or 2007. They also competed in the English counties' limited-overs league for many years, without managing more than the occasional upset, and the team failed to qualify for the World Twenty20 in 2010 or the following year's World Cup. The main problem lying in the way of Scotland's advancement – apart from the legendarily poor weather – remains the lack of a sound domestic structure which might support first-class cricket; local support is also patchy, despite the sterling efforts of a few diehards. Until this is addressed – if it ever can be – Scotland, like Ireland, will continue to suffer from a player drain to English counties.

Scotland's ODI records *as at 17.09.13*

Highest total	323-5	v Ireland at Edinburgh 2011
Lowest total	68	v West Indies at Leicester 1999
Most runs	1231	GM Hamilton (avge. 35.17)
Highest score	133	KJ Coetzer v Afghanistan at Sharjah 2012-13
Most wickets	49	RM Haq (avge. 30.65)
Best bowling	5-9	JH Davey v Afghanistan at Ayr 2010
Most matches	43	NFI McCallum (2006-2011)
World Cup record		Eliminated in first round 1999 and 2006-07
Overall ODI record		Played 63: Won 21, Lost 39, No result 3

SCOTLAND

BERRINGTON, Richard Douglas　　　　　　　　April 3, 1987, Pretoria, South Africa
RHB, RFM: 29 ODIs, 521 runs at 21.70, HS 84; 11 wickets at 47.90, BB 2-14.
Handy allrounder who made a Twenty20 international hundred against Bangladesh in 2012.

CARTER, Neil Miller　　　　　　　　January 29, 1975, Cape Town, South Africa
LHB, LFM: 3 ODIs, 0 runs at 0.00, HS 0; 5 wickets at 26.40, BB 3-27.
Much-travelled allrounder who opened both batting and bowling on ODI debut v Pakistan in 2012.

COETZER, Kyle James　　　　　　　　April 14, 1984, Aberdeen
RHB, RM: 15 ODIs, 670 runs at 47.85, HS 133, 1 x100; 1 wicket at 125.00, BB 1-35.
Attractive batsman who plays for Northants: 133 v Afghanistan in ODI in Sharjah in 2013.

COLEMAN, Frederick Robert John　　　　　　　　December 15, 1991, Edinburgh
RHB: 5 ODIs, 28 runs at 5.60, HS 10.
Young batsman who scored 110 for Oxford MCCU v Worcestershire in 2012.

DAVEY, Joshua Henry　　　　　　　　August 3, 1990, Aberdeen
RHB, RM: 11 ODIs, 254 runs at 25.40, HS 64; 15 wickets at 21.33, BB 5-9.
Batsman on Middlesex's books: took 5-9 v Afghanistan at Ayr in August 2010.

DRUMMOND, Gordon David　　　　　　　　April 21, 1980, Meigle, Perthshire
RHB, RFM: 30 ODIs, 240 runs at 18.46, HS 35*; 25 wickets at 37.28, BB 4-41.
Watsonians fast bowler who took 4-41 v Canada in July 2009: captain 2010-13.

HAQ Khan, Rana Majid　　　　　　　　February 11, 1983, Paisley
LHB, OB: 40 ODIs, 477 runs at 16.44, HS 71; 49 wickets at 30.65, BB 4-28.
Hard-hitting allrounder, who plays for Ferguslie: took 4-28 v West Indies at Clontarf in 2007.

IQBAL, Moneeb Mohammed　　　　　　　　February 28, 1986, Glasgow
RHB, LBG: 12 ODIs, 192 runs at 24.00, HS 63; 4 wickets at 67.50, BB 2-35.
Allrounder who first played for Scotland aged 16: scored 63 v Netherlands in 2010.

MacLEOD, Calum Scott　　　　　　　　November 15, 1988, Glasgow
RHB, RFM: 16 ODIs, 285 runs at 21.92, HS 99*; 7 wickets at 33.71, BB 2-26.
Stranded on 99 in ODI against Canada at Ayr in 2012. Formerly with Warwickshire.*

MACHAN, Matthew William　　　　　　　　February 15, 1991, Brighton
LHB, OB: 8 ODIs, 289 runs at 36.12, HS 114, 1x100; 7 wickets at 30.00, BB 3-31.
Sussex batsman with Scottish mother: 114 in ODI v Kenya at Aberdeen in June 2013.

MOMMSEN, Preston Luke　　　　　　　　October 14, 1987, Durban, South Africa
RHB, OB: 19 ODIs, 408 runs at 24.00, HS 91*; 6 wickets at 21.66, BB 3-26.
Prolific schoolboy batsman who qualified for Scotland in 2010. 91 v Ireland in September 2013.*

MURPHY, David　　　　　　　　June 24, 1989, Welwyn Garden City
RHB, WK: 8 ODIs, 58 runs at 11.60, HS 20*; 8 ct, 3 st.
County wicketkeeper with Scottish parentage: 81 for Northants v Hampshire in 2013.

SHARIF, Safyaan Mohammed　　　　　　　　May 24, 1991, Huddersfield
RHB, RFM: 6 ODIs, 49 runs at 24.50, HS 26; 6 wickets at 39.83, BB 4-27.
Clydesdale fast bowler who took 4-27 on ODI debut v Netherlands at Aberdeen in 2011.

TAYLOR, Robert Meadows Lombe　　　　　　　　December 21, 1989, Northampton
LHB, LFM: 5 ODIs, 49 runs at 12.25, HS 16; 7 wickets at 32.71, BB 3-39.
Northants allrounder with Scottish mother: 101 for Loughborough MCCU v Leics in 2011.*

WARDLAW, Iain　　　　　　　　June 29, 1985, Dewsbury,
RHB, RFM: 8 ODIs, 13 runs at 13.00, HS 7*; 15 wickets at 27.26, BB 4-43.
Yorkshire seamer with Scottish father: took 4-43 v Kenya at Aberdeen in June 2013.

OFFICIALS

ALEEM DAR

UMPIRE

Aleem Dar played 17 first-class matches as an offspinning allrounder, but never surpassed the 39 he scored in his first innings, for Railways in February 1987. He took up umpiring in 1998-99, and stood in his first ODI the following season. He officiated at the 2003 World Cup, and a year later was the first Pakistani to join the ICC's elite panel. Calm and unobtrusive, he soon established a good reputation, and it was no surprise when he was chosen to stand in the 2007 World Cup final. What was a surprise was his part in the chaos in the dark at the end, for which all the officials were excluded from the World Twenty20 later in the year. But he was soon back in favour, and stood in the World Twenty20 final in Barbados in 2010 and the World Cup final in Mumbai in April 2011. He was the ICC's umpire of the year three times running from 2009.

Born *June 6, 1968, Jhang, Pakistan.* **Tests** *84,* **ODIs** *159,* **T20Is** *26*

DAVID **BOON**

REFEREE

David Boon, and his trademark bushy moustache, were Australian legends: he scored 7,422 runs in more than 100 Tests between 1984 and 1996, and was also a feared presence at short leg. He soon became a national selector, and also worked in cricket administration in his native Tasmania before replacing his fellow Aussie Alan Hurst as a match referee in 2011.

Born *December 29, 1960, Launceston, Tasmania, Australia.* **Tests** *18,* **ODIs** *33,* **T20Is** *6*

CHRIS **BROAD**

REFEREE

It was a classic case of poacher turned gamekeeper when Chris Broad became a match referee: he had several jousts with authority during a 25-Test career in the 1980s. A tall, angular left-hander, Broad did well in Australia, scoring four Test hundreds there. After a back injury hastened his retirement, he tried his hand at TV commentary, then in 2003 became a match referee keen on enforcing the Code of Conduct. His son, Stuart, made his England debut in 2006, and his freqent brushes with authority cause occasional embarrassment for his Dad.

Born *September 29, 1957, Knowle, Bristol, England.* **Tests** *60,* **ODIs** *227,* **T20Is** *48*

JEFF **CROWE**

Jeff Crowe might have played for Australia – he had several successful Sheffield Shield seasons in Adelaide – but he eventually returned to New Zealand, winning 39 Test caps, six as captain. Although he was often overshadowed by his younger brother Martin, Jeff managed three Test centuries of his own. After retirement he had a spell as New Zealand's manager, before becoming a referee in 2003. He oversaw the World Cup finals of 2007 and 2011.

Born *September 14, 1958, Auckland, New Zealand.* **Tests** *62,* **ODIs** *178,* **T20Is** *45*

STEVE **DAVIS**

Steve Davis played club cricket in Adelaide before turning to umpiring. He had a rapid rise: appointed to the Australian first-class list in 1990-91, he joined the national panel two years later and stood in his first ODI the same season. He stood in three matches in the 2007 World Cup, and in the final two Tests in his native England in 2008, against South Africa, shortly after being elevated to the elite panel. He was one of the umpires in Lahore early the following year, and was lucky to survive the terrorist attack on the Sri Lankan team coach.

Born *April 9, 1952, London, England.* **Tests** *48,* **ODIs** *120,* **T20Is** *19*

KUMAR **DHARMASENA**

Kumar Dharmasena played 31 Tests for Sri Lanka as a brisk offspinner who could bat a bit. Although he was, almost inevitably overshadowed by the amazing feats of Muttiah Muralitharan, he still took 69 wickets, with a best of 6 for 72 against New Zealand at Galle in 1998, and also claimed 138 wickets in 141 one-day internationals. After retiring in 2006 he was fast-tracked into umpiring, standing in his first ODI less than three years later. He joined the ICC's elite panel in 2011, and was named Umpire of the Year in 2012.

Born *April 24, 1971, Colombo, Sri Lanka.* **Tests** *18,* **ODIs** *49,* **T20Is** *11*

RUSSELL **DOMINGO**

After realising he was unlikely to make it in first-class cricket as a player, admitting he was "a very average batsman", Russell Domingo turned to coaching, earning his first certificates when just 22. He revitalised the Warriors franchise, taking them to both limited-overs titles in 2009-10, and then joined the national coaching set-up. After a spell as Gary Kirsten's assistant, Domingo took over the top job in May 2013: he was only 38, and South Africa's first coach from a non-white background.

Born *Port Elizabeth, South Africa, August 30, 1974. Appointed South Africa coach in 2013*

OFFICIALS

MARAIS **ERASMUS**

UMPIRE

The solidly built Marais Erasmus was a handy allrounder for Boland in South African domestic cricket, averaging just under 30 with the bat and also taking 131 wickets with some energetic medium-pace. That included 6 for 22 as the New Zealanders were bundled out for an embarrassing 86 on a sporting Paarl pitch in December 1994. Erasmus turned to umpiring on retirement and was speedily promoted: he stood in his first ODI in Kenya in 2007. Three years later he was appointed to the ICC's elite panel, although his standing took a knock in a 2013 Ashes series dominated by disputes about umpiring decisions.

Born *February 27, 1964, George, Cape Province, South Africa.* **Tests** *20,* **ODIs** *47,* **T20Is** *15*

DUNCAN **FLETCHER**

COACH

Duncan Fletcher was a gutsy allrounder for Zimbabwe in pre-Test days – he scored 69 not out and took four wickets when they upset Australia in the 1983 World Cup – and after a successful coaching career had a mixed time in charge of England, when the euphoric 2005 Ashes victory was followed by the 2006-07 whitewash Down Under. Fletcher replaced Gary Kirsten as India's coach after the 2011 World Cup. He was the first international coach to be in charge for 100 Tests, and helped orchestrate the 4-0 whitewash of Australia early in 2013.

Born *September 27, 1948, Salisbury (now Harare), Zimbabwe. Appointed India's coach in 2011*

ANDY **FLOWER**

COACH

Andy Flower was often a lone beacon of class in an underpowered Zimbabwe side. A compact left-hander strong on the sweep, Flower scored 4,794 Test runs at 51, and nearly 7,000 in ODIs. But he was hounded out of Zimbabwe after he and Henry Olonga wore black armbands mourning the "death of democracy" there during the 2003 World Cup. Flower moved to England, where he did well for Essex, then joined the national coaching set-up, taking over as fulltime team director in time for the successful 2009 Ashes series and – iron fist evident beneath the velvet glove – oversaw England's climb to No. 1 in the world Test rankings, and two more Ashes triumphs.

Born *April 28, 1968, Cape Town, South Africa. Appointed England coach in 2009*

GRAHAM **FORD**

COACH

A batsman who played a few matches for Natal B, Graham Ford has had a long coaching career, including spells at Natal (who won the Currie Cup under his stewardship) and Kent. He was South Africa's assistant coach at the 1999 World Cup, and replaced Bob Woolmer in the hot seat shortly afterwards, staying in charge until two series defeats cost him his job in 2002. After turning down an offer to coach India in 2009, he took on the Sri Lankan post in January 2012.

Born November 16, 1960, Pietermaritzburg, South Africa. Appointed Sri Lanka's coach in 2012

OTTIS **GIBSON**

COACH

Fast bowler Ottis Gibson was unlucky that his best years coincided with the pomp of Curtly Ambrose and Courtney Walsh: Gibson played only two Tests. Still, he carved out a successful county career with Glamorgan, Leicestershire and latterly Durham, for whom he took all ten wickets in an innings against Hampshire in 2007. That winter he joined the England coaching staff, but early in 2010 Gibson was persuaded to return home and take on the big task of returning West Indies to Test cricket's top table. Victory in the World Twenty20 early in 2013 suggested things were moving in the right direction.

Born March 16, 1969, Sion Hill, St Peter, Barbados. Appointed West Indies coach in 2010

IAN **GOULD**

UMPIRE

Ian "Gunner" Gould was a combative wicketkeeper/batsman who scored nearly 9000 runs and made more than 700 dismissals in first-class cricket. He started with Middlesex, then moved to Sussex, who he captained to the NatWest Trophy in 1986. Although he never won a Test cap, he did appear in 18 ODIs, all of them in 1983, including that year's World Cup in England. He joined the English first-class umpires' panel in 2002, was promoted to the international list in April 2006, joined the elite panel three years later, and immediately looked at home.

Born August 19, 1957, Taplow, Buckinghamshire, England. **Tests** 34, **ODIs** 86, **T20Is** 20

MIKE **HESSON**

COACH

Mike Hesson took up coaching at the unusually early age of 22. He became Otago's head coach in 2004, and in six years converted a previously struggling team into one which regularly challenged for titles. He took over as Kenya's coach after their disappointing 2011 World Cup, then in July 2012, still only 37, replaced John Wright as New Zealand's coach. Hesson had a turbulent start, falling out with then captain Ross Taylor, but matters improved with a strong showing at home to England early in 2013.

Born October 30, 1974, Dunedin, New Zealand. Appointed New Zealand's coach in 2012

OFFICIALS

TONY HILL

UMPIRE

Tony Hill came into umpiring without any background in first-class cricket, but soon established himself, being appointed to the ICC's international panel in 1998 and to the full elite list in 2009, although he had umpired the occasional Test since 2001-02. His reputation took a knock during a 2013 Ashes series dominated by controversy about umpiring decisions. A keen golfer, he is a regional training officer and mentor for umpires in the Northern Districts.

Born June 26, 1951, Auckland, New Zealand. **Tests** 40, **ODIs** 96, **T20Is** 17

RICHARD ILLINGWORTH

UMPIRE

A parsimonious left-arm spinner who toiled away for Worcestershire (and briefly Derbyshire), Richard Illingworth took the wicket of West Indies batsman Phil Simmons with his first ball in Test cricket, in 1991, and the following year played in the World Cup final at Melbourne, when England lost to Pakistan. He joined the English umpires' list in 2006, and soon developed a reputation as a calm, attentive official. He stood in his first internationals in 2010, and his first Test in 2012-13, not long before being elevated to the elite panel.

Born August 23, 1963, Greengates, Bradford, Yorkshire, England. **Tests** 4, **ODIs** 19, **T20Is** 9

RICHARD KETTLEBOROUGH

UMPIRE

Richard Kettleborough had an unspectacular career as a batsman with Yorkshire and Middlesex, the highlight 108 for his native county against Essex in 1996. He became a first-class umpire in 2006, when only 33, and soon made a mark as a calm official who usually got things right. He stood in his first internationals in 2009, and joined the ICC's elite panel in 2011.

Born March 15, 1973, Sheffield, Yorkshire, England. **Tests** 14, **ODIs** 37, **T20Is** 9

SHANE JURGENSEN

COACH

Shane Jurgensen played a few Sheffield Shield matches for Western Australia and Tasmania, before finally having a run with his native Queensland. He took a hat-trick for Tasmania against NSW in March 2002, then took 11 wickets in vain in the Shield final against Queensland. He retired after the 2006-07 season, aged only 31, and turned to coaching: he was New Zealand's bowling coach from 2008-10, and next year joined the Bangladesh set-up in a similar role. After Richard Pybus quit late in 2012, Jurgensen was appointed interim coach, and got the job fulltime early the following year.

Born April 28, 1976, Redcliffe, Queensland, Australia. Appointed Bangladesh coach in 2013

DARREN **LEHMANN**

COACH

Pugnacious and prolific, bullet-headed Darren Lehmann would have played more than 27 Tests but for Australia's batting riches in the 1990s. As it was he made five Test centuries, won two World Cups, and became a folk hero in Yorkshire, for whom he averaged 68 in first-class matches. After retiring he moved seamlessly into coaching, with Queensland and Kings XI Punjab in the IPL, before taking on the Australian job when Mickey Arthur was sensationally sacked halfway through the 2013 England tour. The Ashes drifted away, though, and Lehmann got into trouble for comments about Stuart Broad in a radio interview.

Born *February 5, 1970, Gawler, South Australia. Appointed Australia coach in 2013*

NIGEL **LLONG**

UMPIRE

A tall left-hander and part-time offspinner, Nigel Llong played for Kent throughout the 1990s, scoring six centuries. He joined the English umpires' panel in 2002, and in 2005 stood in the first Twenty20 international in England. Quiet and undemonstrative, with a disarming smile that seems to calm the players, Llong stood in a few international matches, including the odd Test, before replacing Billy Doctrove on the ICC's elite panel in 2012.

Born *February 11, 1969, Ashford, Kent, England.* **Tests** *18,* **ODIs** *70,* **T20Is** *17*

RANJAN **MADUGALLE**

REFEREE

A stylish right-hander, Ranjan Madugalle won 21 Test caps, the first of them in Sri Lanka's inaugural Test, against England in 1981-82, when he top-scored with 65. He also made 103 against India in Colombo in 1985, and captained Sri Lanka twice. Not long after retiring, he became one of the first match refs, and was appointed the ICC's chief referee in 2001. His easygoing exterior and charming personality are a mask for someone who has a reputation as a strict disciplinarian.

Born *April 22, 1959, Kandy, Sri Lanka.* **Tests** *144,* **ODIs** *271,* **T20Is** *56*

ROSHAN **MAHANAMA**

REFEREE

Roshan Mahanama was part of the winning team in the 1996 World Cup, and the following year made 225 as he and Sanath Jayasuriya put on 576, then a record Test partnership, as Sri Lanka ran up 952 for 6 (another record) against India in Colombo. An attacking right-hander who made four Test centuries, he was also a fine fielder. He was jettisoned after the 1999 World Cup and quit not long afterwards. He joined the ICC's referees panel in 2003.

Born *May 31, 1966, Colombo, Sri Lanka.* **Tests** *45,* **ODIs** *188,* **T20Is** *28*

OFFICIALS

BRUCE **OXENFORD**

UMPIRE

A legspinner who played eight times for Queensland, taking 5 for 91 against New South Wales at Sydney in January 1992 in only his third match, Bruce Oxenford soon turned to umpiring, and by 2001-02 was overseeing some of his former team-mates in the Sheffield Shield. He umpired his first Test in Sri Lanka late in 2010, and two years later was elevated to the elite panel when Simon Taufel retired to become the ICC's umpire performance and training manager.

Born March 5, 1960, Southport, Queensland, Australia. **Tests** 13, **ODIs** 47, **T20Is** 12

ANDY **PYCROFT**

REFEREE

A fine batsman, especially strong off the back foot, Andy Pycroft was a Zimbabwe regular throughout the 1980s, although he was slightly past his peak when they gained Test status in 1992-93. Still, he played in their first three Tests, scoring 60 against New Zealand at Harare in the last of them. The first and last of his 20 ODIs produced famous wins: over Australia in the 1983 World Cup and England in the 1991-92 one. He also found time to fit in the occasional spot of commentary. Outside cricket he was an attorney-at-law for 17 years, which stood him in good stead when he joined the ICC's referees' panel in 2009.

Born June 6, 1956, Salisbury (now Harare), Zimbabwe. **Tests** 22, **ODIs** 92, **T20Is** 27

PAUL **REIFFEL**

UMPIRE

An under-rated seamer who took 104 wickets in 35 Tests (and 106 in ODIs as well), Paul "Pistol" Reiffel was an unsung member of the powerful Australian side of the 1990s. He was also a handy batsman, falling just short of 1000 Test runs. He went out at the top, retiring from international cricket after the 1999 World Cup victory. Reiffel soon became a rare former player to turn to umpiring in Australia. He stood in his first state games in 2004-05, and his first internationals early in 2009. In 2013 he was elevated to the elite panel after Asad Rauf and Billy Bowden were demoted.

Born April 19, 1966, Box Hill, Victoria, Australia. **Tests** 4, **ODIs** 33, **T20Is** 9

JAVAGAL **SRINATH**

REFEREE

Arguably the fastest bowler India has ever produced, Javagal Srinath took 236 wickets in Tests, and 315 more in ODIs. Unusually for a quick bowler, he did better in India than overseas, his bowling average of 26 at home being four runs lower than his overall one. He went out at the top: his last international match was the 2003 World Cup final. Sadly, there was no fairytale farewell – Srinath was caned (0 for 87) as Australia ran out easy winners. After a spell as a commentator he joined the referees' panel in 2006: "I'll have to concentrate more than I did during my playing days," he observed wryly.

Born *August 31, 1969, Mysore, Karnataka, India.* **Tests** *26,* **ODIs** *130,* **T20Is** *31*

ROD **TUCKER**

UMPIRE

Allrounder Rod Tucker played 100 first-class matches for Tasmania over ten years from 1988-89. His seven hundreds included a satisfying 165 against his native NSW in March 1991. He was also a handy medium-pacer who took 123 wickets. On his first morning as a first-class umpire, in December 2004, South Australia were bowled out for 29, but by January 2009 Tucker was standing in his first ODI. He officiated in the World Twenty20s of 2009 and 2010, in between making his Test debut in New Zealand, and was appointed to the ICC's elite panel in 2010.

Born *August 28, 1964, Auburn, Sydney, Australia.* **Tests** *25,* **ODIs** *33,* **T20Is** *14*

ANDY **WALLER**

COACH

Andy "Bundu" Waller was a hard-hitting batsman who played for – and captained – Zimbabwe in pre-Test days when he could get away from the family tobacco farm. He did manage to squeeze in two Test appearances, against England late in 1996, when he was 37, and made an uncharacteristically slow 50 on his debut. After Alan Butcher stepped down as Zimbabwe's head coach early in 2013, Waller took over, and oversaw the thrilling Test defeat of Pakistan a few months later. Among his charges in the national squad is his son Malcolm (see page 195), an exciting batting prospect.

Born *September 25, 1959, Salisbury (now Harare, Rhodesia). Appointed Zimbabwe coach in 2013*

DAV **WHATMORE**

COACH

Stocky Dav (it's short for Davenell) Whatmore was a popular figure around the MCG, after scoring prolifically for Victoria in the Sheffield Shield. He won seven caps for Australia, with modest results, during the Packer schism. On turning to coaching he had two spells with Sri Lanka, and was in charge when they won the World Cup in 1996. He also won trophies with Lancashire, before the harder challenge of coaching Bangladesh (2003-07). Early in 2012 he took on the Pakistan job, starting with a flourish as his side won the Asia Cup.

Born *March 16, 1954, Colombo, Ceylon (now Sri Lanka). Appointed Pakistan's coach in 2012*

OVERALL RECORDS *Test Matches*

Most appearances

198	SR Tendulkar *I*	
168	RT Ponting *A*	
168	SR Waugh *A*	
164	R Dravid *I**	
162	JH Kallis *SA**	
156	AR Border *A*	
148	S Chanderpaul *WI*	
147	MV Boucher *SA**	
145	SK Warne *A*	
138	DPMD Jayawardene *SL*	

*The records for Boucher, Dravid and Kallis include one Test for the World XI

Most runs

			Avge
15837	SR Tendulkar *I*		53.86
13378	RT Ponting *A*		51.85
13288	R Dravid *I**		52.31
13128	JH Kallis *SA**		56.10
11953	BC Lara *WI**		52.88
11174	AR Border *A*		50.56
10927	SR Waugh *A*		51.06
10830	S Chanderpaul *WI*		51.81
10806	DPMD J'wardene *SL*		49.56
10486	KC Sangakkara *SL*		56.98

*Dravid, Kallis and Lara played one Test for the World XI. SM Gavaskar (I; 10122) also passed 10000

Most wickets

			Avge
800	M Muralitharan *SL**		22.72
708	SK Warne *A*		25.41
619	A Kumble *I*		29.65
563	GD McGrath *A*		21.64
519	CA Walsh *WI*		24.44
434	Kapil Dev *I*		29.64
431	RJ Hadlee *NZ*		22.29
421	SM Pollock *SA*		23.11
414	Wasim Akram *P*		23.62
413	Harbhajan Singh *I*		32.37

*Muralitharan's record includes one Test (5 wickets) for the World XI. CEL Ambrose (WI; 405) also passed 400

Highest scores

400*	BC Lara	WI v Eng at St John's	2003-04
380	ML Hayden	Aust v Zim at Perth	2003-04
375	BC Lara	WI v Eng at St John's	1993-94
374	DPMD Jayawardene	SL v SA at Colombo	2006
365*	GS Sobers	WI v Pak at Kingston	1957-58
364	L Hutton	Eng v Aust at The Oval	1938
340	ST Jayasuriya	SL v India at Colombo	1997-98
337	Hanif Mohammad	Pak v WI at Bridgetown	1957-58
336*	WR Hammond	Eng v NZ at Auckland	1932-33
334*	MA Taylor	Aust v Pak at Peshawar	1998-99
334	DG Bradman	Aust v Eng at Leeds	1930

In all 26 scores of 300 or more have been made in Tests

Best innings bowling

10-53	JC Laker	Eng v Aust at Manchester	1956
10-74	A Kumble	India v Pak at Delhi	1998-99
9-28	GA Lohmann	Eng v SA at Jo'burg	1895-96
9-37	JC Laker	Eng v Aust at Manchester	1956
9-51	M Muralitharan	SL v Zim at Kandy	2001-02
9-52	RJ Hadlee	NZ v Aust at Brisbane	1985-86
9-56	Abdul Qadir	Pak v Eng at Lahore	1987-88
9-57	DE Malcolm	Eng v SA at The Oval	1994
9-65	M Muralitharan	SL v Eng at The Oval	1998
9-69	JM Patel	India v Aust at Kanpur	1959-60

There have been seven further instances of a bowler taking nine wickets in an innings

Record wicket partnerships

1st	415	ND McKenzie (226) and GC Smith (232)	South Africa v Bangladesh at Chittagong	2007-08
2nd	576	ST Jayasuriya (340) and RS Mahanama (225)	Sri Lanka v India at Colombo	1997-98
3rd	624	KC Sangakkara (287) and DPMD Jayawardene (374)	Sri Lanka v South Africa at Colombo	2006
4th	437	DPMD Jayawardene (240) and TT Samaraweera (231)	Sri Lanka v Pakistan at Karachi	2008-09
5th	405	SG Barnes (234) and DG Bradman (234)	Australia v England at Sydney	1946-47
6th	351	DPMD Jayawardene (275) and HAPW Jayawardene (154*)	Sri Lanka v India at Ahmedabad	2009-10
7th	347	DS Atkinson (219) and CC Depeiaza (122)	West Indies v Australia at Bridgetown	1954-55
8th	332	IJL Trott (184) and SCJ Broad (169)	England v Pakistan at Lord's	2010
9th	195	MV Boucher (78) and PL Symcox (108)	South Africa v Pakistan at Johannesburg	1997-98
10th	163	PJ Hughes (81*) and AC Agar (98)	Australia v England at Nottingham	2013

Figures to 17.09.13. Updated records can be found at **www.cricinfo.com/ci/engine/records**

Test Matches — OVERALL RECORDS

Most catches

Fielders

210	R Dravid	I/World
196	RT Ponting	A
194	DPMD Jayawardene	SL
194	JH Kallis	SA
181	ME Waugh	A

Most dismissals

Wicketkeepers — Ct/St

555	MV Boucher SA	532/23
416	AC Gilchrist A	379/37
395	IA Healy A	366/29
355	RW Marsh A	343/12
270	PJL Dujon WI	265/5

Highest team totals

952-6d	**Sri Lanka** v India at Colombo	1997-98
903-7d	**Eng** v Australia at The Oval	1938
849	**Eng** v WI at Kingston	1929-30
790-3d	**WI** v Pakistan at Kingston	1957-58
765-6d	**Pak** v Sri Lanka at Karachi	2008-09
760-7d	**SL** v India at Ahmedabad	2009-10
758-8d	**Aust** v WI at Kingston	1954-55
756-5d	**Sri Lanka** v SA at Colombo	2006
751-5d	**WI** v England at St John's	2003-04
749-9d	**WI** v England at Bridgetown	2008-09

There have been 10 further totals of more than 700, three by Australia and India, and one each by England, Pakistan, Sri Lanka and West Indies

Lowest team totals

Completed innings

26	**NZ** v Eng at Auckland	1954-55
30	**SA** v Eng at Pt Elizabeth	1895-96
30	**SA** v Eng at Birmingham	1924
35	**SA** v Eng at Cape Town	1898-99
36	**Aust** v Eng at B'ham	1902
36	**SA** v Aust at M'bourne	1931-32
42	**Aust** v Eng at Sydney	1887-88
42	**NZ** v Aust at W'ton	1945-46
42*	**India** v England at Lord's	1974
43	**SA** v Eng at Cape Town	1888-89

* One batsmen absent hurt. There have been ten further totals of less than 50, the most recent Pakistan's 49 v S Africa at Jo'burg in 2012-13

Best match bowling

19-90	JC Laker	Eng v Aust at Manchester	1956
17-159	SF Barnes	Eng v SA at Jo'burg	1913-14
16-136	ND Hirwani	India v WI at Madras	1987-88
16-137	RAL Massie	Aust v England at Lord's	1972
16-220	M Muralitharan	SL v England at The Oval	1998
15-28	J Briggs	Eng v SA at Cape Town	1888-89
15-45	GA Lohmann	Eng v SA at Pt Elizabeth	1895-96
15-99	C Blythe	Eng v SA at Leeds	1907
15-104	H Verity	England v Aust at Lord's	1934
15-123	RJ Hadlee	NZ v Aust at Brisbane	1985-86

Hirwani and Massie were making their Test debuts. W Rhodes (15-124) and Harbhajan Singh (15-217) also took 15 wickets in a match

Most centuries

		Tests
51	SR Tendulkar *India*	198
44	JH Kallis *South Africa/World XI*	162
41	RT Ponting *Australia*	168
36	R Dravid *India/World XI*	164
34	SM Gavaskar *India*	125
34	BC Lara *West Indies/World XI*	131
33	KC Sangakkara *Sri Lanka*	117
32	SR Waugh *Australia*	168
31	DPMD Jayawardene *Sri Lanka*	138
30	ML Hayden *Australia*	94

DG Bradman (Australia) scored 29 hundreds in 52 Test matches between 1928-29 and 1948

Test match results

	Played	Won	Lost	Drawn	Tied	% win
Australia	759	353	202	202	2	46.50
Bangladesh	79	4	67	8	0	5.06
England	940	336	268	336	0	35.74
India	472	119	149	203	1	25.21
New Zealand	384	72	158	154	0	18.75
Pakistan	375	116	105	154	0	30.93
South Africa	377	137	126	114	0	36.33
Sri Lanka	222	66	80	76	0	29.72
West Indies	490	160	162	167	1	32.65
Zimbabwe	93	11	56	26	0	11.82
World XI	1	0	1	0	0	0.00
TOTAL	2096	1374	1374	720	2	

OVERALL RECORDS *One-day Internationals*

Most appearances

463	SR Tendulkar *I*	
445	ST Jayasuriya *SL*	
404	DPMD Jayawardene *SL*	
378	Inzamam-ul-Haq *P*	
375	RT Ponting *A*	
362	Shahid Afridi *P*	
356	Wasim Akram *P*	
354	KC Sangakkara *SL*	
350	M Muralitharan *SL*	
344	R Dravid *I*	

Seven further men have played in more than 300 ODIs, while BC Lara appeared in 299

Most runs

		Avge
18426	SR Tendulkar *I*	44.83
13704	RT Ponting *A*	42.03
13430	ST Jayasuriya *SL*	32.36
11798	KC Sangakkara *SL*	39.99
11739	Inzamam-ul-Haq *P*	39.52
11498	JH Kallis *SA*	45.26
11363	SC Ganguly *I*	41.02
11354	DPMD Jayawardene *SL*	33.39
10889	R Dravid *I*	39.16
10405	BC Lara *WI*	40.48

Mohammad Yousuf (9720), AC Gilchrist (9619), M Azharuddin (9378) and PA de Silva (9284) also reached 9000 runs

Most wickets

		Avge
534	M Muralitharan *SL*	23.08
502	Wasim Akram *P*	23.52
416	Waqar Younis *P*	23.84
400	WPUJC Vaas *SL*	27.53
393	SM Pollock *SA*	24.50
381	GD McGrath *A*	22.02
380	B Lee *A*	23.36
359	Shahid Afridi *P*	33.69
337	A Kumble *I*	30.89
323	ST Jayasuriya *SL*	36.75

J Srinath (315) also took 300 wickets. Eleven further bowlers have taken more than 250

Highest scores

219	V Sehwag	India v WI at Indore	2011-12
200*	SR Tendulkar	India v SA at Gwalior	2009-10
194*	CK Coventry	Zim v Bangladesh at Bulawayo	2008-09
194	Saeed Anwar	Pakistan v India at Chennai	1996-97
189*	IVA Richards	W Indies v England at Manchester	1984
189*	MJ Guptill	NZ v Eng at Southampton	2013
189	ST Jayasuriya	Sri Lanka v India at Sharjah	2000-01
188*	G Kirsten	SA v UAE at Rawalpindi	1995-96
186*	SR Tendulkar	India v NZ at Hyderabad	1999-2000
185*	SR Watson	Aust v Bangladesh at Mirpur	2010-11

SR Tendulkar scored 49 ODI centuries, RT Ponting 30, ST Jayasuriya 28, SC Ganguly 22, CH Gayle and HH Gibbs 21

Best innings bowling

8-19	WPUJC Vaas	SL v Zimbabwe at Colombo	2001-02
7-12	Shahid Afridi	Pakistan v WI at Providence	2013
7-15	GD McGrath	Aust v Namibia at P'stroom	2002-03
7-20	AJ Bichel	Aust v Eng at Port Elizabeth	2002-03
7-30	M Muralitharan	Sri Lanka v India at Sharjah	2000-01
7-36	Waqar Younis	Pakistan v England at Leeds	2001
7-37	Aqib Javed	Pakistan v India at Sharjah	1991-92
7-51	WW Davis	West Indies v Australia at Leeds	1983
6-12	A Kumble	India v West Indies at Calcutta	1993-94
6-13	BAW Mendis	Sri Lanka v India at Karachi	2008

Waqar Younis took five in an innings 13 times, M Muralitharan 10, B Lee and Shahid Afridi 9

Record wicket partnerships

1st	286	WU Tharanga (109) and ST Jayasuriya (152)	Sri Lanka v England at Leeds	2006
2nd	331	SR Tendulkar (186*) and R Dravid (153)	India v New Zealand at Hyderabad	1999-2000
3rd	238	HM Amla (122) and AB de Villiers (128)	South Africa v Pakistan at Johannesburg	2012-13
4th	275*	M Azharuddin (153*) and A Jadeja (116*)	India v Zimbabwe at Cuttack	1997-98
5th	226*	EJG Morgan (124*) and RS Bopara (101*)	England v Ireland at Dublin	2013
6th	218	DPMD Jayawardene (107) and MS Dhoni (139*)	Asia XI v Africa XI at Chennai	2007
7th	130	A Flower (142*) and HH Streak (56)	Zimbabwe v England at Harare	2001-02
8th	138*	JM Kemp (110*) and AJ Hall (56*)	South Africa v India at Cape Town	2006-07
9th	132	AD Mathews (77*) and SL Malinga (56)	Sri Lanka v Australia at Melbourne	2010-11
10th	106*	IVA Richards (189*) and MA Holding (12*)	West Indies v England at Manchester	1984

*Figures to 17.09.13. Updated records can be found at **www.cricinfo.com/ci/engine/records***

One-day Internationals **OVERALL RECORDS**

Most catches

Fielders
201	DPMD Jayawardene *SL*	
160	RT Ponting *A*	
156	M Azharuddin *I*	
140	SR Tendulkar *I*	
133	SP Fleming *NZ*	

Most dismissals

Wicketkeepers
		Ct/St
472	AC Gilchrist *A*	417/55
424	MV Boucher *SA*	402/22
419	KC Sangakkara *SL*	334/85
287	MS Dhoni *I*	212/75
287	Moin Khan *P*	214/73

Highest team totals

443-9	**SL** v N'lands at Amstelveen	2006
438-9	**SA** v Aust at Johannesburg	2005-06
434-4	**Australia** v SA at Jo'burg	2005-06
418-5	**SA** v Zim at P'stroom	2006-07
418-5	**India** v WI at Indore	2011-12
414-7	**India** v SL at Rajkot	2009-10
413-5	**Ind** v Bermuda at P-o-Spain	2006-07
411-8	**SL** v India at Rajkot	2009-10
402-2	**NZ** v Ireland at Aberdeen	2008
401-3	**India** v SA at Gwalior	2009-10

All these totals were made in 50 overs except SA's 438-9, when the winning run came off the fifth ball of the 50th over

Lowest team totals

Completed innings
35	**Zim** v SL at Harare	2003-04
36	**Canada** v SL at Paarl	2002-03
38	**Zim** v SL at Colombo	2001-02
43	**Pak** v WI at Cape Town	1992-93
43	**SL** v SA at Paarl	2011-12
44	**Zim** v B'desh at Ch'gong	2009-10
45	**Can** v Eng at Manchester	1979
45	**Nam** v Aust at P'stroom	2002-03
54	**India** v SL at Sharjah	2000-01
54	**WI** v SA at Cape Town	2003-04

The lowest total successfully defended in a non-rain-affected ODI is 125, by India v Pakistan (87) at Sharjah in 1984-85

Most sixes

317	Shahid Afridi *P*	
270	ST Jayasuriya *SL*	
204	CH Gayle *WI*	
195	SR Tendulkar *I*	
190	SC Ganguly *I*	
162	RT Ponting *A*	
154	MS Dhoni *I*	
153	CL Cairns *NZ*	
149	AC Gilchrist *A*	
147	BB McCullum *NZ*	

Twelve others have hit 100 sixes

Best strike rate

Runs per 100 balls — Runs
114.73	Shahid Afridi *P*	7360
104.33	V Sehwag *I*	8273
99.43	IDS Smith *NZ*	1055
99.09	DJG Sammy *WI*	1313
96.94	AC Gilchrist *A*	9619
96.66	RL Powell *WI*	2085
95.07	Kapil Dev *I*	3783
94.35	PR Stirling *Ire*	1654
93.78	DR Smith *WI*	1102
93.71	JR Hopes *A*	1326

Qualification: 1000 runs

Most economical bowlers

Runs per over — Wkts
3.09	J Garner *WI*	146
3.28	RGD Willis *E*	80
3.30	RJ Hadlee *NZ*	158
3.32	MA Holding *WI*	142
3.37	SP Davis *A*	44
3.40	AME Roberts *WI*	87
3.48	CEL Ambrose *WI*	225
3.53	MD Marshall *WI*	157
3.54	ARC Fraser *E*	47
3.55	MR Whitney *A*	46

Qualification: 2000 balls bowled

One-day international results

	Played	Won	Lost	Tied	No result	% win
Australia	819	503	278	9	29	64.24
Bangladesh	273	77	193	0	3	28.51
England	608	296	284	7	21	51.02
India	832	418	373	6	35	52.82
Kenya	150	41	104	0	5	28.27
New Zealand	641	275	327	5	34	45.71
Pakistan	799	428	346	8	17	55.24
South Africa	493	303	171	6	13	63.75
Sri Lanka	698	327	337	4	30	49.25
West Indies	702	360	310	8	24	53.68
Zimbabwe	421	110	297	5	9	27.30
Others (see below)	396	130	248	4	14	34.55
TOTAL	**3416**	**3268**	**3268**	**31**	**117**	

Others: Afghanistan (P25, W14, L11), Africa XI (P6, W1, L4, NR1), Asia XI (P7, W4, L2, NR1), Bermuda (P35, W7, L28), Canada (P75, W17, L56, NR2), East Africa (P3, L3), Hong Kong (P4, L4), Ireland (P81, W37, L37, T3, NR4), Namibia (P6, L6), Netherlands (P74, W27, L43, T1, NR3), Scotland (P63, W21, L39, NR3), UAE (P11, W1, L10), USA (P2, L2), World XI (P4, W1, L3).

OVERALL RECORDS *Twenty20 Internationals*

Most appearances

63	Shahid Afridi	P
62	BB McCullum	NZ
54	Saeed Ajmal	P
53	Shoaib Malik	P
52	LRPL Taylor	NZ
52	Umar Gul	P
50	TM Dilshan	SL
50	Kamran Akmal	P
48	SCJ Broad	E
48	AB de Villiers	SA
48	DPMD Jayawardene	SL

The first Twenty20 international was played in New Zealand in February 2005

Most runs

			Avge
1882	BB McCullum	NZ	35.50
1332	DPMD Jayawardene	SL	32.48
1260	DA Warner	A	28.63
1203	TM Dilshan	SL	29.34
1178	KC Sangakkara	SL	31.88
1176	KP Pietersen	E	37.93
1168	MJ Guptill	NZ	35.39
1093	Mohammad Hafeez	P	24.84
1084	JP Duminy	SA	34.96
1024	SR Watson	A	30.11

The highest batting average (min. 200 runs) is 51.33, by ML Hayden (Aust)

Most wickets

			Avge
74	Umar Gul	P	16.44
73	Saeed Ajmal	P	17.15
67	Shahid Afridi	P	21.98
58	BAW Mendis	SL	12.84
57	SCJ Broad	E	22.43
51	GP Swann	E	16.84
51	SL Malinga	SL	22.62
43	M Morkel	SA	19.93
42	Mohammad Hafeez	P	19.76
42	NL McCullum	NZ	21.47

Twelve further bowlers have taken 30 or more wickets

Highest Scores

156	AJ Finch	Aust v Eng at Southampton	2013
123	BB McCullum	NZ v Bang at Pallekele	2012-13
117*	RE Levi	SA v NZ at Hamilton	2011-12
117	CH Gayle	WI v SA at Johannesburg	2007-08
116*	BB McCullum	NZ v Aust at Christchurch	2009-10
104*	TM Dilshan	SL v Aust at Pallekele	2011
101*	MJ Guptill	NZ v SA at East London	2012-13
101	SK Raina	India v SA at Gros Islet	2010
100	RD Berrington	Scot v Bang at The Hague	2012
100	DPMD J'wardene	SL v Zim at Providence	2010

Finch's innings included a record 14 sixes; Levi's, on debut, included 13

Best innings bowling

6-8	BAW Mendis	SL v Zim at Hambantota	2012-13
6-16	BAW Mendis	SL v Australia at Pallekele	2011
5-6	Umar Gul	Pakistan v NZ at The Oval	2009
5-6	Umar Gul	Pakistan v SA at Centurion	2012-13
5-13	Elias Sunny	Bang v Ireland at Belfast	2012
5-18	TG Southee	NZ v Pakistan at Auckland	2010-11
5-19	R McLaren	SA v WI at N Sound	2010
5-20	NN Odhiambo	Ken v Scot at Nairobi	2009-10
5-26	DJG Sammy	WI v Zim at P-of-Spain	2009-10
5-31	SL Malinga	SL v England at Pallekele	2012-13

Umar Gul has taken four wickets in an innings six times, BAW Mendis five, Saeed Ajmal four and Shahid Afridi three

Record wicket partnerships

1st	170	GC Smith (88) and LL Bosman (94)	South Africa v England at Centurion	2009-10
2nd	166	DPMD Jayawardene (98*) and KC Sangakkara (68)	Sri Lanka v West Indies at Bridgetown	2010
3rd	137	MJ Guptill (91*) and KS Williamson (48)	New Zealand v Zimbabwe at Auckland	2011-12
4th	112*	KP Pietersen (43*) and EJG Morgan (67*)	England v Pakistan at Dubai	2009-10
5th	119*	Shoaib Malik (52*) and Misbah-ul-Haq (66*)	Pakistan v Australia at Johannesburg	2007-08
6th	101*	CL White (85*) and MEK Hussey (39*)	Australia v Sri Lanka at Bridgetown	2010
7th	91	PD Collingwood (79) and MH Yardy (23*)	England v West Indies at The Oval	2007
8th	64*	WD Parnell (29*) and J Theron (31*)	South Africa v Australia at Johannesburg	2011-12
9th	47*	GC Wilson (41*) and MC Sorensen (12*)	Ireland v Bangladesh at Belfast	2012
10th	31*	Wahab Riaz (30*) and Shoaib Akhtar (8*)	Pakistan v New Zealand at Auckland	2010-11

Figures to 17.09.13. Updated records can be found at **www.cricinfo.com/ci/engine/records**

Twenty20 Internationals **OVERALL RECORDS**

Most catches

Fielders

34	**LRPL Taylor** *NZ*	
27	**DA Warner** *A*	
26	**AB de Villiers** *SA*	
24	**DJ Hussey** *A*	
24	**Shoaib Malik** *P*	

Most dismissals

Wicketkeepers — *Ct/St*

54	**Kamran Akmal** *P*	24/30
38	**KC Sangakkara** *SL*	20/18
34	**D Ramdin** *WI*	26/8
32	**BB McCullum** *NZ*	24/8
29	**MS Dhoni** *I*	21/8

Highest team totals

260-6	**Sri Lanka** v Kenya at Jo'burg	2007-08
248-6	**Aust** v Eng at Southampton	2013
241-6	**SA** v England at Centurion	2009-10
221-5	**Aust** v England at Sydney	2006-07
219-4	**SA** v India at Johannesburg	2011-12
218-4	**India** v England at Durban	2007-08
215-5	**Sri Lanka** v India at Nagpur	2009-10
214-4	**Aust** v NZ at Christchurch	2009-10
214-5	**Aust** v NZ at Auckland	2004-05
214-6	**NZ** v Aust at Christchurch	2009-10
214-7	**England** v NZ at Auckland	2012-13

There have been 17 further totals of 200+

Lowest team totals

Completed innings

67	**Kenya** v Ireland at Belfast	2008
68	**Ireland** v WI at Providence	2010
70	**Bermuda** v Can at Belfast	2008
71	**Kenya** v Ire at Dubai	2011-12
73	**Kenya** v NZ at Durban	2007-08
74	**India** v Aus at M'bourne	2007-08
74	**Pak** v Aus at Dubai	2012-13
75	**Can** v Zim at King City	2008-09
78	**B'desh** v NZ at Hamilton	2009-10
78	**Kenya** v Scot at Aberdeen	2013

West Indies scored 79-7 in 20 overs v Zimbabwe at Port-of-Spain in 2009-10

Most sixes

75	**BB McCullum** *NZ*	
64	**SR Watson** *A*	
60	**CH Gayle** *WI*	
57	**DA Warner** *A*	
54	**Yuvraj Singh** *I*	
48	**MJ Guptill** *NZ*	
39	**MN Samuels** *WI*	
38	**CL White** *A*	
38	**LRPL Taylor** *NZ*	
35	**Shahid Afridi** *P*	

Yuvraj's sixes included 6 in one over

Best strike rate

Runs per 100 balls — *Runs*

181.04	**AJ Finch** *A*	277
169.34	**A Symonds** *A*	337
159.82	**CD McMillan** *NZ*	187
154.78	**NLTC Perera** *SL*	291
150.14	**SR Watson** *A*	1024
149.73	**KA Pollard** *WI*	569
149.61	**E Chigumbura** *Z*	389
148.95	**JC Buttler** *E*	286
148.68	**Yuvraj Singh** *I*	791
147.48	**LE Bosman** *SA*	323

Qualification: 100 balls faced

Meanest bowlers

Runs per over — *Wkts*

4.88	**TM Odoyo** *Kenya*	6
5.40	**JAR Blain** *Scot*	6
5.41	**AC Botha** *Ire*	21
5.45	**JD Nel** *Scot*	12
5.49	**HA Varaiya** *Ken*	15
5.61	**SMSM Senanayake** *SL*	8
5.61	**DL Vettori** *NZ*	37
5.70	**S Dhaniram** *Can*	6
5.75	**GH Dockrell** *Ire*	27
5.76	**Junaid Siddiqui** *Can*	7

Qualification: 120 balls bowled

Twenty20 international results

	Played	Won	Lost	Tied	No Result	% win
Australia	63	31	29	2	1	51.61
Bangladesh	30	9	21	0	0	30.00
England	62	31	27	0	4	53.44
India	45	24	19	1	1	55.68
New Zealand	67	29	31	5	2	48.46
Pakistan	71	44	25	2	0	63.38
South Africa	59	36	22	0	1	62.06
Sri Lanka	55	32	21	1	1	60.18
West Indies	51	23	24	3	1	49.00
Zimbabwe	28	4	23	1	0	16.07
Others (see below)	127	50	71	1	5	41.39
TOTAL	**329**	**313**	**313**	**8**	**8**	

Other teams: Afghanistan (P15, W8, L7), Bermuda (P3, L3), Canada (P17, W4, L12, T1), Ireland (P30, W15, L12, NR3),
Kenya (P23, W7, L16), Netherlands (P18, W9, L8, NR1), Scotland (P21, W7, L13, NR1). Matches decided by bowlouts are shown as tied

AUSTRALIA *Test Match Records*

Most appearances

168	RT Ponting	
168	SR Waugh	
156	AR Border	
145	SK Warne	
128	ME Waugh	
124	GD McGrath	
119	IA Healy	
107	DC Boon	
105	JL Langer	
104	MA Taylor	

ML Hayden (103) also won more than 100 caps

Most runs

		Avge
13378	RT Ponting	51.85
11174	AR Border	50.56
10927	SR Waugh	51.06
8625	ML Hayden	50.73
8029	ME Waugh	41.81
7696	JL Langer	45.27
7656	MJ Clarke	52.08
7525	MA Taylor	43.49
7422	DC Boon	43.65
7110	GS Chappell	53.86

DG Bradman scored 6996 runs in 52 Tests at an average of 99.94

Most wickets

		Avge
708	SK Warne	25.41
563	GD McGrath	21.64
355	DK Lillee	23.92
310	B Lee	30.81
291	CJ McDermott	28.63
259	JN Gillespie	26.13
248	R Benaud	27.03
246	GD McKenzie	29.78
228	RR Lindwall	23.03
216	CV Grimmett	24.21

MG Hughes took 212 wickets, SCG MacGill 208, MG Johnson 205 and JR Thomson 200

Highest scores

380	ML Hayden	v Zimbabwe at Perth	2003-04
334*	MA Taylor	v Pakistan at Peshawar	1998-99
334	DG Bradman	v England at Leeds	1930
329*	MJ Clarke	v India at Sydney	2011-12
311	RB Simpson	v England at Manchester	1964
307	RM Cowper	v England at Melbourne	1965-66
304	DG Bradman	v England at Leeds	1934
299*	DG Bradman	v South Africa at Adelaide	1931-32
270	DG Bradman	v England at Melbourne	1936-37
268	GN Yallop	v Pakistan at Melbourne	1983-84

At the time of his retirement in 1948 DG Bradman had made eight of Australia's highest ten Test scores

Best innings bowling

9-121	AA Mailey	v England at Melbourne	1920-21
8-24	GD McGrath	v Pakistan at Perth	2004-05
8-31	FJ Laver	v England at Manchester	1909
8-38	GD McGrath	v England at Lord's	1997
8-43	AE Trott	v England at Adelaide	1894-95
8-53	RAL Massie	v England at Lord's	1972
8-59	AA Mallett	v Pakistan at Adelaide	1972-73
8-61	MG Johnson	v South Africa at Perth	2008-09
8-65	H Trumble	v England at The Oval	1902
8-71	GD McKenzie	v West Indies at Melbourne	1968-69
8-71	SK Warne	v England at Brisbane	1994-95

Trott and Massie were making their Test debuts

Record wicket partnerships

1st	382	WM Lawry (210) and RB Simpson (205)	v West Indies at Bridgetown	1964-65
2nd	451	WH Ponsford (266) and DG Bradman (244)	v England at The Oval	1934
3rd	315	RT Ponting (206) and DS Lehmann (160)	v West Indies at Port-of-Spain	2002-03
4th	388	WH Ponsford (181) and DG Bradman (304)	v England at Leeds	1934
5th	405	SG Barnes (234) and DG Bradman (234)	v England at Sydney	1946-47
6th	346	JHW Fingleton (136) and DG Bradman (270)	v England at Melbourne	1936-37
7th	217	KD Walters (250) and GJ Gilmour (101)	v New Zealand at Christchurch	1976-77
8th	243	MJ Hartigan (116) and C Hill (160)	v England at Adelaide	1907-08
9th	154	SE Gregory (201) and JM Blackham (74)	v England at Sydney	1894-95
10th	163	PJ Hughes (81*) and AC Agar (98)	v England at Nottingham	2013

Figures to 17.09.13. Updated records can be found at **www.cricinfo.com/ci/engine/records**

Test Match Records — **AUSTRALIA**

Most catches

Fielders
196	RT Ponting	
181	ME Waugh	
157	MA Taylor	
156	AR Border	
128	ML Hayden	

Most dismissals

Wicketkeepers — Ct/St
416	AC Gilchrist	379/37
395	IA Healy	366/29
355	RW Marsh	343/12
198	BJ Haddin	193/5
187	ATW Grout	163/24

Highest team totals

758-8d	v West Indies at Kingston	1954-55
735-6d	v Zimbabwe at Perth	2003-04
729-6d	v England at Lord's	1930
701	v England at The Oval	1934
695	v England at The Oval	1930
674-6d	v England at Cardiff	2009
674	v India at Adelaide	1947-48
668	v West Indies at Bridgetown	1954-55
659-4d	v India at Sydney	2011-12
659-8d	v England at Sydney	1946-47

Australia have reached 600 on 31 occasions in all, 16 of them against England

Lowest team totals

Completed innings
36	v England at Birmingham	1902
42	v England at Sydney	1887-88
44	v England at The Oval	1896
47	v SA at Cape Town	2011-12
53	v England at Lord's	1896
58*	v England at Brisbane	1936-37
60	v England at Lord's	1888
63	v England at The Oval	1882
65	v England at The Oval	1912
66*	v England at Brisbane	1928-29

*One or more batsmen absent

Best match bowling

16-137	RAL Massie	v England at Lord's	1972
14-90	FR Spofforth	v England at The Oval	1882
14-199	CV Grimmett	v South Africa at Adelaide	1931-32
13-77	MA Noble	v England at Melbourne	1901-02
13-110	FR Spofforth	v England at Melbourne	1878-79
13-148	BA Reid	v England at Melbourne	1990-91
13-173	CV Grimmett	v South Africa at Durban	1935-36
13-217	MG Hughes	v West Indies at Perth	1988-89
13-236	AA Mailey	v England at Melbourne	1920-21
12-87	CTB Turner	v England at Sydney	1887-88

Massie was playing in his first Test, Grimmett (1935-36) in his last – he took ten or more wickets in each of his last three

Hat-tricks

FR Spofforth	v England at Melbourne	1878-79
H Trumble	v England at Melbourne	1901-02
H Trumble	v England at Melbourne	1903-04
TJ Matthews	v South Africa at Manchester	1912
TJ Matthews	v South Africa at Manchester	1912
LF Kline	v South Africa at Cape Town	1957-58
MG Hughes	v West Indies at Perth	1988-89
DW Fleming	v Pakistan at Rawalpindi	1994-95
SK Warne	v England at Melbourne	1994-95
GD McGrath	v West Indies at Perth	2000-01
PM Siddle	v England at Brisbane	2010-11

Fleming was playing in his first Test, Trumble (1903-04) in his last. Matthews took two in the same Test

Australia's Test match results

	Played	Won	Lost	Drawn	Tied	% win
v Bangladesh	4	4	0	0	0	100.00
v England	331	133	105	93	0	40.18
v India	86	38	24	23	1	44.18
v New Zealand	52	27	8	17	0	51.92
v Pakistan	57	28	12	17	0	49.12
v South Africa	88	48	20	20	0	54.54
v Sri Lanka	26	17	1	8	0	65.38
v West Indies	111	54	32	24	1	48.64
v Zimbabwe	3	3	0	0	0	100.00
v World XI	1	1	0	0	0	100.00
TOTAL	**759**	**353**	**202**	**202**	**2**	**46.50**

Figures to 17.09.13. Updated records can be found at **www.cricinfo.com/ci/engine/records**

AUSTRALIA *One-day International Records*

Most appearances

374	RT Ponting	
325	SR Waugh	
286	AC Gilchrist	
273	AR Border	
249	GD McGrath	
244	ME Waugh	
232	MG Bevan	
232	MJ Clarke	
221	B Lee	
208	DR Martyn	

A total of 25 Australians have played in more than 100 ODIs

Most runs

		Avge
13589	RT Ponting	41.81
9595	AC Gilchrist	35.93
8500	ME Waugh	39.35
7581	MJ Clarke	45.12
7569	SR Waugh	32.90
6912	MG Bevan	53.58
6524	AR Border	30.62
6131	ML Hayden	44.10
6068	DM Jones	44.61
5964	DC Boon	37.04

Five further batsmen scored more than 4000 runs

Most wickets

		Avge
380	GD McGrath	21.98
380	B Lee	23.36
291	SK Warne	25.82
203	CJ McDermott	24.71
200	MG Johnson	25.09
195	SR Waugh	34.67
174	NW Bracken	24.36
159	SR Watson	29.13
156	GB Hogg	26.84
142	JN Gillespie	25.42

Five further bowlers have taken 100 wickets in ODIs

Highest scores

185*	SR Watson	v Bangladesh at Mirpur	2010-11
181*	ML Hayden	v New Zealand at Hamilton	2006-07
173	ME Waugh	v West Indies at Melbourne	2000-01
172	AC Gilchrist	v Zimbabwe at Hobart	2003-04
164	RT Ponting	v South Africa at Johannesburg	2005-06
163	DA Warner	v Sri Lanka at Brisbane	2011-12
161*	SR Watson	v England at Melbourne	2010-11
158	ML Hayden	v West Indies at North Sound	2006-07
156	A Symonds	v New Zealand at Wellington	2005-06
154	AC Gilchrist	v Sri Lanka at Melbourne	1998-99

Ponting scored 29 hundreds, ME Waugh 18, Gilchrist 16, Hayden 10, GR Marsh 9, MJ Clarke and SR Watson 8

Best innings bowling

7-15	GD McGrath	v Namibia at Potchefstroom	2002-03
7-20	AJ Bichel	v England at Port Elizabeth	2002-03
6-14	GJ Gilmour	v England at Leeds	1975
6-31	MG Johnson	v Sri Lanka at Pallekele	2011
6-39	KH MacLeay	v India at Nottingham	1983
5-13	SP O'Donnell	v New Zealand at Christchurch	1989-90
5-14	GD McGrath	v West Indies at Manchester	1999
5-14	JR Hopes	v Ireland at Dublin	2010
5-15	GS Chappell	v India at Sydney	1980-81
5-16	CG Rackemann	v Pakistan at Adelaide	1983-84

DK Lillee took 5-34 against Pakistan at Leeds in the 1975 World Cup, the first five-wicket haul in ODIs

Record wicket partnerships

1st	246	AJ Finch (148) and SE Marsh (151)	v Scotland at Edinburgh	2013
2nd	252*	SR Watson (136*) and RT Ponting (111*)	v England at Centurion	2009-10
3rd	234*	RT Ponting (140*) and DR Martyn (88*)	v India at Johannesburg	2002-03
4th	237	RT Ponting (124) and A Symonds (151)	v Sri Lanka at Sydney	2005-06
5th	220	A Symonds (156) and MJ Clarke (82*)	v New Zealand at Wellington	2005-06
6th	165	MEK Hussey (109*) and BJ Haddin (70)	v West Indies at Kuala Lumpur	2006-07
7th	123	MEK Hussey (73) and B Lee (57)	v South Africa at Brisbane	2005-06
8th	119	PR Reiffel (58) and SK Warne (55)	v South Africa at Port Elizabeth	1993-94
9th	88	SE Marsh (110) and DE Bollinger (30)	v England at Hobart	2010-11
10th	63	SR Watson (35*) and AJ Bichel (28)	v Sri Lanka at Sydney	2002-03

Figures to 17.09.13. Updated records can be found at **www.cricinfo.com/ci/engine/records**

One-day International Records — AUSTRALIA

Most catches

Fielders

159	RT Ponting	
127	AR Border	
111	SR Waugh	
108	ME Waugh	
105	MEK Hussey	

Most dismissals

Wicketkeepers		Ct/St
470	AC Gilchrist	416/54
233	IA Healy	194/39
142	BJ Haddin	133/9
124	RW Marsh	120/4
49	WB Phillips	42/7

Highest team totals

434-4	v South Africa at Johannesburg	2005-06
377-6	v South Africa at Basseterre	2006-07
368-5	v Sri Lanka at Sydney	2005-06
362-3	v Scotland at Edinburgh	2013
361-8	v Bangladesh at Mirpur	2010-11
359-2†	v India at Johannesburg	2002-03
359-5	v India at Sydney	2003-04
358-5	v Netherlands at Basseterre	2006-07
350-4	v India at Hyderabad	2009-10
349-6	v New Zealand at St George's	2006-07

† In World Cup final. All scores made in 50 overs

Lowest team totals

Completed innings

70	v England at Birmingham	1977
70	v New Zealand at Adelaide	1985-86
74	v Sri Lanka at Brisbane	2012-13
91	v West Indies at Perth	1986-87
93	v S Africa at Cape Town	2005-06
101	v England at Melbourne	1978-79
101	v India at Perth	1991-92
107	v W Indies at Melbourne	1981-82
109	v England at Sydney	1982-83
120	v Pakistan at Hobart	1996-97

Australia scored 101-9 in a 30-overs match against West Indies at Sydney in 1992-93 – and won by 14 runs

Most sixes

159	RT Ponting*
148	AC Gilchrist*
108	SR Watson
103	A Symonds
87	ML Hayden
80	MEK Hussey
68	SR Waugh
64	DM Jones
57	BJ Haddin
57	ME Waugh

*Also hit sixes for the World XI

Best strike rate

Runs per 100 balls		Runs
96.89	AC Gilchrist	9595
93.71	JR Hopes	1326
93.36	MG Johnson	788
92.44	A Symonds	5504
90.70	DJ Hussey	1796
89.43	SR Watson	5019
88.16	IJ Harvey	715
87.81	AC Voges	721
87.51	BJ Hodge	516
87.16	MEK Hussey	5442

Qualification: 500 runs

Most economical bowlers

Runs per over		Wkts
3.37	SP Davis	44
3.55	MR Whitney	46
3.58	DK Lillee	103
3.65	GF Lawson	88
3.65	TM Alderman	88
3.87	GD McGrath	380
3.92	PR Reiffel	106
3.94	CG Rackemann	82
3.94	RM Hogg	85
4.03	CJ McDermott	203

Qualification: 2000 balls bowled

Australia's one-day international results

	Played	Won	Lost	Tied	No Result	% win
v Bangladesh	19	18	1	0	0	94.73
v England	122	69	48	2	3	58.82
v India	109	64	37	0	8	63.36
v New Zealand	125	85	34	0	6	71.42
v Pakistan	89	54	31	1	3	63.37
v South Africa	80	41	36	3	0	53.12
v Sri Lanka	90	55	31	0	4	63.95
v West Indies	135	70	59	3	3	54.16
v Zimbabwe	28	26	1	0	1	96.29
v others *(see below)*	22	21	0	0	1	100.00
TOTAL	**819**	**503**	**278**	**9**	**29**	**64.24**

Other teams: Afghanistan (P1, W1), Canada (P2, W2), Ireland (P3, W2, NR1), Kenya (P5, W5), Namibia (P1, W1), Netherlands (P2, W2), Scotland (P4, W4), USA (P1, W1), World XI (P3, W3).

BANGLADESH *Test Match Records*

Most appearances

61	Mohammad Ashraful	
50	Habibul Bashar	
44	Khaled Mashud	
40	Javed Omar	
36	Mashrafe Mortaza	
35	Shahadat Hossain	
34	Mushfiqur Rahim	
33	Mohammad Rafique	
30	Shakib Al Hasan	
28	Tamim Iqbal	

Habibul Bashar missed only two of Bangladesh's first 52 Tests

Most runs

		Avge
3026	Habibul Bashar	30.87
2737	Mohammad Ashraful	24.00
2010	Tamim Iqbal	37.22
1993	Mushfiqur Rahim	32.14
1984	Shakib Al Hasan	36.07
1720	Javed Omar	22.05
1409	Khaled Mashud	19.04
1267	Shahriar Nafees	26.39
1141	Rajin Saleh	25.93
1059	Mohammad Rafique	18.57

Habibul reached 2000 runs for Bangladesh before anyone else had made 1000

Most wickets

		Avge
106	Shakib Al Hasan	32.79
100	Mohammad Rafique	40.76
78	Mashrafe Mortaza	41.52
70	Shahadat Hossain	51.90
44	Enamul Haque jnr	40.61
36	Tapash Baisya	59.36
28	Mahmudullah	45.07
28	Manjural Islam	57.32
26	Sohag Gazi	37.23
25	Rubel Hossain	73.96

Moh'd Rafique completed the 1000-run 100-wicket double in his last Test

Highest scores

200	Mushfiqur Rahim	v Sri Lanka at Galle	2012-13
190	Moh'd Ashraful	v Sri Lanka at Galle	2012-13
158*	Moh'd Ashraful	v India at Chittagong	2004-05
151	Tamim Iqbal	v India at Mirpur	2009-10
145	Aminul Islam	v India at Dhaka	2000-01
144	Shakib Al Hasan	v Pakistan at Mirpur	2011-12
138	Shahriar Nafees	v Australia at Fatullah	2005-06
136	Moh'd Ashraful	v Sri Lanka at Chittagong	2005-06
129*	Moh'd Ashraful	v Sri Lanka at Colombo	2007
128	Tamim Iqbal	v West Indies at Kingstown	2009

Mohammad Ashraful scored six Test centuries, Tamim Iqbal four, Habibul Bashar three, Mushfiqur Rahim and Shakib Al Hasan two

Best innings bowling

7-36	Shakib Al Hasan	v NZ at Chittagong	2008-09
7-95	Enamul Haque jnr	v Zimbabwe at Dhaka	2004-05
6-27	Shahadat Hossain	v South Africa at Dhaka	2007-08
6-45	Enamul Haque jnr	v Zim at Chittagong	2004-05
6-71	Robiul Islam	v Zim at Harare	2012-13
6-74	Sohag Gazi	v WI at Mirpur	2012-13
6-77	Moh'd Rafique	v South Africa at Dhaka	2002-03
6-81	Manjural Islam	v Zim at Bulawayo	2000-01
6-82	Shakib Al Hasan	v Pakistan at Mirpur	2011-12
6-94	Elias Sunny	v WI at Chittagong	2011-12

Shakib Al Hasan has taken five wickets in an innings on nine occasions, Mohammad Rafique seven, Shahadat Hossain four, and Enamul Haque jnr three

Record wicket partnerships

1st	185	Tamim Iqbal (103) and Imrul Kayes (75)	v England at Lord's	2010
2nd	200	Tamim Iqbal (151) and Junaid Siddique (55)	v India at Mirpur	2009-10
3rd	130	Javed Omar (119) and Mohammad Ashraful (77)	v Pakistan at Peshawar	2003-04
4th	167	Naeem Islam (108) and Shakib Al Hasan (89)	v West Indies at Mirpur	2012-13
5th	267	Mohammad Ashraful (190) and Mushfiqur Rahim (200)	v Sri Lanka at Galle	2012-13
6th	191	Mohammad Ashraful (129*) and Mushfiqur Rahim (80)	v Sri Lanka at Colombo	2007
7th	145	Shakib Al Hasan (87) and Mahmudullah (115)	v New Zealand at Hamilton	2009-10
8th	113	Mushfiqur Rahim (79) and Naeem Islam (38)	v England at Chittagong	2009-10
9th	184	Mahmudullah (76) and Abul Hasan (113)	v West Indies at Khulna	2012-13
10th	69	Mohammad Rafique (65) and Shahadat Hossain (3*)	v Australia at Chittagong	2005-06

Figures to 17.09.13. Updated records can be found at **www.cricinfo.com/ci/engine/records**

Test Match Records — BANGLADESH

Most catches

Fielders
25	Mohammad Ashraful	
22	Habibul Bashar	
19	Shahriar Nafees	
16	Imrul Kayes	
15	Mahmudullah	

Most dismissals

Wicketkeepers — Ct/St
87	Khaled Mashud	78/9
65	Mushfiqur Rahim	56/9
4	Mohammad Salim	3/1
2	Mehrab Hossain	2/0

Highest team totals

638	v Sri Lanka at Galle	2012-13
556	v West Indies at Mirpur	2012-13
488	v Zimbabwe at Chittagong	2004-05
427	v Australia at Fatullah	2005-06
419	v England at Mirpur	2009-10
416	v West Indies at Gros Islet	2004
413	v Sri Lanka at Mirpur	2008-09
408	v New Zealand at Hamilton	2009-10
400	v India at Dhaka	2000-01
391	v Zimbabwe at Harare	2012-13

The 400 against India came in Bangladesh's inaugural Test

Lowest team totals

Completed innings
62	v Sri Lanka at Colombo	2007
86	v Sri Lanka at Colombo	2005-06
87	v West Indies at Dhaka	2002-03
89	v Sri Lanka at Colombo	2007
90	v Sri Lanka at Colombo	2001-02
91	v India at Dhaka	2000-01
96	v Pakistan at Peshawar	2003-04
97	v Australia at Darwin	2003
102	v South Africa at Dhaka	2002-03
104	v Eng at Chester-le-Street	2005

The lowest all-out total by the opposition is 154, by Zimbabwe at Chittagong in 2004-05 (Bangladesh's first Test victory)

Best match bowling

12-200	Enamul Haque jnr	v Zimbabwe at Dhaka	2004-05
9-97	Shahadat Hossain	v South Africa at Dhaka	2007-08
9-115	Shakib Al Hasan	v NZ at Chittagong	2008-09
9-155	Robiul Islam	v Zimbabwe at Harare	2012-13
9-160	Moh'd Rafique	v Australia at Fatullah	2005-06
9-129	Sohag Gazi	v W Indies at Mirpur	2012-13
8-110	Mahmudullah	v W Indies at Kingstown	2009
8-129	Shakib Al Hasan	v W Indies at St George's	2009
7-105	Khaled Mahmud	v Pakistan at Multan	2003-04
7-116	Moh'd Rafique	v Pakistan at Multan	2003-04

Khaled Mahmud took only six other wickets in 11 more Tests

Hat-tricks

Alok Kapali	v Pakistan at Peshawar	2003-04

Alok Kapali's figures were 2.1-1-3-3; he ended Pakistan's innings by dismissing Shabbir Ahmed, Danish Kaneria and Umar Gul. He took only three other Test wickets.

Two bowlers have taken hat-tricks against Bangladesh: AM Blignaut for Zimbabwe at Harare in 2003-04, and JEC Franklin for New Zealand at Dhaka in 2004-05.

Shahadat Hossain and Abdur Razzak have taken ODI hat-tricks for Bangladesh

Bangladesh's Test match results

	Played	Won	Lost	Drawn	Tied	% win
v Australia	4	0	4	0	0	0.00
v England	8	0	8	0	0	0.00
v India	7	0	6	1	0	0.00
v New Zealand	9	0	8	1	0	0.00
v Pakistan	8	0	8	0	0	0.00
v South Africa	8	0	8	0	0	0.00
v Sri Lanka	14	0	13	1	0	0.00
v West Indies	10	2	6	2	0	20.00
v Zimbabwe	11	2	6	3	0	18.18
TOTAL	79	4	67	8	0	5.06

Figures to 17.09.13. Updated records can be found at www.cricinfo.com/ci/engine/records

BANGLADESH One-day International Records

Most appearances

175	Mohammad Ashraful	
144	Abdur Razzak	
129	Shakib Al Hasan	
126	Khaled Mashud	
126	Mashrafe Mortaza	
123	Mohammad Rafique	
122	Tamim Iqbal	
119	Mushfiqur Rahim	
111	Habibul Bashar	
91	Mahmudullah	

Habibul Bashar captained in 69 ODIs, Shakib Al Hasan in 47, and Mohammad Ashraful in 38

Most runs

		Avge
3688	Shakib Al Hasan	35.12
3639	Tamim Iqbal	30.07
3468	Moh'd Ashraful	22.37
2326	Mushfiqur Rahim	25.84
2201	Shahriar Nafees	31.44
2168	Habibul Bashar	21.68
1954	Aftab Ahmed	24.73
1818	Khaled Mashud	21.90
1763	Mahmudullah	33.90
1315	Imrul Kayes	27.97

Seven further batsmen have scored 1000 runs in ODIs for Bangladesh

Most wickets

		Avge
201	Abdur Razzak	27.81
161	Mashrafe Mortaza	30.32
161	Shakib Al Hasan	29.37
119	Mohammad Rafique	38.75
67	Khaled Mahmud	42.76
61	Syed Rasel	33.62
59	Tapash Baisya	41.55
58	Shafiul Islam	34.70
54	Mahmudullah	43.09
49	Rubel Hossain	34.26

Mohammad Rafique completed the 1000-run/100-wicket double in ODIs as well as Tests

Highest scores

154	Tamim Iqbal	v Zimbabwe at Bulawayo	2009
134*	Shakib Al Hasan	v Canada at St John's	2006-07
129	Tamim Iqbal	v Ireland at Dhaka	2007-08
125	Tamim Iqbal	v England at Mlrpur	2009-10
123*	Shahriar Nafees	v Zimbabwe at Jaipur	2006
120	Anamul Haque	v W Indies at Khulna	2012-13
118*	Shahriar Nafees	v Zimbabwe at Harare	2006-07
115	Alok Kapali	v India at Karachi	2008
112	Tamim Iqbal	v SL at Hambantota	2012-13
109	Moh'd Ashraful	v UAE at Lahore	2008

Shakib Al Hasan has scored five ODI hundreds, Shahriar Nafees and Tamim Iqbal four, and Mohammad Ashraful three

Best bowling figures

6-26	Mashrafe Mortaza	v Kenya at Nairobi	2006
5-29	Abdur Razzak	v Zimbabwe at Mirpur	2009-10
5-30	Abdur Razzak	v Zimbabwe at Mirpur	2010-11
5-30	Ziaur Rahman	v Zim at Bulawayo	2012-13
5-31	Aftab Ahmed	v NZ at Dhaka	2004-05
5-33	Abdur Razzak	v Zimbabwe at Bogra	2006-07
5-42	Farhad Reza	v Ireland at Dhaka	2007-08
5-47	Moh'd Rafique	v Kenya at Fatullah	2005-06
5-62	Abdur Razzak	v Sri Lanka at Pallekele	2012-13
4-14	Abdur Razzak	v Zimbabwe at Mirpur	2010-11

Aftab Ahmed took only seven more wickets in 84 other ODIs

Record wicket partnerships

1st	170	Shahriar Hossain (68) and Mehrab Hossain (101)	v Zimbabwe at Dhaka	1998-99
2nd	160	Imrul Kayes (66) and Junaid Siddique (97)	v Pakistan at Dambulla	2010
3rd	174	Anamul Haque (120) and Mushfiqur Rahim (79)	v West Indies at Khulna	2012-13
4th	175*	Rajin Saleh (108*) and Habibul Bashar (64*)	v Kenya at Fatullah	2005-06
5th	119	Shakib Al Hasan (52) and Raqibul Hassan (63)	v South Africa at Dhaka	2007-08
6th	123*	Al Sahariar (62*) and Khaled Mashud (53*)	v West Indies at Dhaka	1999-2000
7th	101	Mushfiqur Rahim (86) and Naeem Islam (43)	v New Zealand at Dunedin	2009-10
8th	70*	Khaled Mashud (35*) and Mohammad Rafique (41*)	v New Zealand at Kimberley	2002-03
9th	97	Shakib Al Hasan (108) and Mashrafe Mortaza (38)	v Pakistan at Multan	2007-08
10th	54*	Khaled Mashud (39*) and Tapash Baisya (22*)	v Sri Lanka at Colombo	2005-06

Figures to 17.09.13. Updated records can be found at www.cricinfo.com/ci/engine/records

One-day International Records **BANGLADESH**

Most catches

Fielders

38	Mashrafe Mortaza	
36	Shakib Al Hasan	
35	Mohammad Ashraful	
33	Tamim Iqbal	
30	Abdur Razzak	

Highest team totals

320-8	v Zimbabwe at Bulawayo	2009
313-6	v Zimbabwe at Bulawayo	2009
301-7	v Kenya at Bogra	2005-06
300-8	v UAE at Lahore	2008
296-6	v India at Mirpur	2009-10
295-6	v Australia at Mirpur	2010-11
293-5	v India at Mirpur	2011-12
293-7	v Ireland at Dhaka	2007-08
292-6	v West Indies at Khulna	2012-13
285-7	v Pakistan at Lahore	2007-08

Bangladesh passed 300 for the first time in their 119th one-day international

Lowest team totals

Completed innings

58	v West Indies at Mirpur	2010-11
74	v Australia at Darwin	2008
76	v Sri Lanka at Colombo	2002
76	v India at Dhaka	2002-03
77	v NZ at Colombo	2002-03
78	v S Africa at Mirpur	2010-11
86	v NZ at Chittagong	2004-05
87*	v Pakistan at Dhaka	1999-2000
91	v Pakistan at Mirpur	2011-12
92	v Zimbabwe at Nairobi	1997-98

* One batsman absent hurt

Most dismissals

Wicketkeepers   Ct/St

126	Khaled Mashud	91/35
118	Mushfiqur Rahim	84/34
13	Dhiman Ghosh	9/4
4	Jahurul Islam	4/0

Most sixes

49	Aftab Ahmed
49	Tamim Iqbal
42	Mashrafe Mortaza
29	Mohammad Ashraful
29	Mohammad Rafique
26	Mushfiqur Rahim
25	Shakib Al Hasan
21	Abdur Razzak
16	Mahmudullah
12	Imrul Kayes
12	Naeem Islam

Best strike rate

Runs per 100 balls   *Runs*

86.76	Mashrafe Mortaza	1206
83.04	Aftab Ahmed	1954
80.56	Nasir Hossain	771
78.61	Tamim Iqbal	3639
78.18	Shakib Al Hasan	3688
76.02	Abdur Razzak	742
71.81	Mohammad Rafique	1190
71.78	Mahmudullah	1763
70.11	Mohammad Ashraful	3468
69.49	Shahriar Nafees	2201

Qualification: 500 runs

Most economical bowlers

Runs per over   *Wkts*

4.31	Shakib Al Hasan	161
4.39	Mohammad Rafique	119
4.42	Mushfiqur Rahman	19
4.47	Abdur Razzak	201
4.63	Mashrafe Mortaza	161
4.63	Syed Rasel	61
4.79	Naeem Islam	35
4.84	Manjural Islam	24
4.95	Naimur Rahman	10
5.04	Nazmul Hossain	44

Qualification: 1000 balls bowled

Bangladesh's one-day international results

	Played	Won	Lost	Tied	No Result	% win
v Australia	19	1	18	0	0	5.26
v England	15	2	13	0	0	13.33
v India	24	3	21	0	0	12.50
v New Zealand	21	5	16	0	0	23.80
v Pakistan	31	1	30	0	0	3.22
v South Africa	14	1	13	0	0	7.14
v Sri Lanka	33	4	28	0	1	12.50
v West Indies	25	7	16	0	2	30.43
v Zimbabwe	59	31	28	0	0	52.54
v others (see below)	32	22	10	0	0	68.75
TOTAL	**273**	**77**	**193**	**0**	**3**	**28.51**

Other teams: Bermuda (P2, W2), Canada (P2, W1, L1), Hong Kong (P1, W1), Ireland (P7, W5, L2), Kenya (P14, W8, L6), Netherlands (P2, W1, L1), Scotland (P3, W3), UAE (P1, W1).

ENGLAND
Test Match Records

Most appearances

133	AJ Stewart	
118	GA Gooch	
117	DI Gower	
115	MA Atherton	
114	MC Cowdrey	
108	G Boycott	
102	IT Botham	
100	AJ Strauss	
100	GP Thorpe	
99	KP Pietersen	

Cowdrey was the first man from any country to reach 100 Tests, in 1968

Most runs

		Avge
8900	GA Gooch	42.58
8463	AJ Stewart	39.54
8231	DI Gower	44.25
8114	G Boycott	47.72
7887	KP Pietersen	48.38
7801	AN Cook	47.85
7728	MA Atherton	37.69
7624	MC Cowdrey	44.06
7249	WR Hammond	58.45
7037	AJ Strauss	40.91

L Hutton (6971), KF Barrington (6806), GP Thorpe (6744) and IR Bell (6487) also passed 6000 runs

Most wickets

		Avge
383	IT Botham	28.40
329	JM Anderson	30.11
325	RGD Willis	25.20
307	FS Trueman	21.57
297	DL Underwood	25.83
252	JB Statham	24.84
248	GP Swann	28.55
248	MJ Hoggard	30.50
236	AV Bedser	24.89
234	AR Caddick	29.91

D Gough took 229 wickets, SJ Harmison 222, A Flintoff 219, SCJ Broad 217 and JA Snow 202

Highest scores

364	L Hutton	v Australia at The Oval	1938
336*	WR Hammond	v New Zealand at Auckland	1932-33
333	GA Gooch	v India at Lord's	1990
325	A Sandham	v West Indies at Kingston	1929-30
310*	JH Edrich	v New Zealand at Leeds	1965
294	AN Cook	v India at Birmingham	2011
287	RE Foster	v Australia at Sydney	1903-04
285*	PBH May	v West Indies at Birmingham	1957
278	DCS Compton	v Pakistan at Nottingham	1954
262*	DL Amiss	v West Indies at Kingston	1973-74

Foster was playing in his first Test, Sandham in his last

Best innings bowling

10-53	JC Laker	v Australia at Manchester	1956
9-28	GA Lohmann	v South Africa at Johannesburg	1895-96
9-37	JC Laker	v Australia at Manchester	1956
9-57	DE Malcolm	v South Africa at The Oval	1994
9-103	SF Barnes	v S Africa at Johannesburg	1913-14
8-7	GA Lohmann	v S Africa at Port Elizabeth	1895-96
8-11	J Briggs	v South Africa at Cape Town	1888-89
8-29	SF Barnes	v South Africa at The Oval	1912
8-31	FS Trueman	v India at Manchester	1952
8-34	IT Botham	v Pakistan at Lord's	1978

Botham also scored 108 in England's innings victory

Record wicket partnerships

1st	359	L Hutton (158) and C Washbrook (195)	v South Africa at Johannesburg	1948-49
2nd	382	L Hutton (364) and M Leyland (187)	v Australia at The Oval	1938
3rd	370	WJ Edrich (189) and DCS Compton (208)	v South Africa at Lord's	1947
4th	411	PBH May (285*) and MC Cowdrey (154)	v West Indies at Birmingham	1957
5th	254	KWR Fletcher (113) and AW Greig (148)	v India at Bombay	1972-73
6th	281	GP Thorpe (200*) and A Flintoff (137)	v New Zealand at Christchurch	2001-02
7th	197	MJK Smith (96) and JM Parks (101*)	v West Indies at Port-of-Spain	1959-60
8th	332	IJL Trott (184) and SCJ Broad (169)	v Pakistan at Lord's	2010
9th	163*	MC Cowdrey (128*) and AC Smith (69*)	v New Zealand at Wellington	1962-63
10th	130	RE Foster (287) and W Rhodes (40*)	v Australia at Sydney	1903-04

Figures to 17.09.13. Updated records can be found at www.cricinfo.com/ci/engine/records

Test Match Records — **ENGLAND**

Most catches

Fielders

121	AJ Strauss	
120	IT Botham	
120	MC Cowdrey	
110	WR Hammond	
105	GP Thorpe	

Most dismissals

Wicketkeepers — Ct/St

269	APE Knott	250/19
241	AJ Stewart	227/14
220	MJ Prior	207/13
219	TG Evans	173/46
174	RW Taylor	167/7

Highest team totals

903-7d	v Australia at The Oval	1938
849	v West Indies at Kingston	1929-30
710-7d	v India at Birmingham	2011
658-8d	v Australia at Nottingham	1938
654-5	v South Africa at Durban	1938-39
653-4d	v India at Lord's	1990
652-7d	v India at Madras	1984-85
644	v Australia at Sydney	2010-11
636	v Australia at Sydney	1928-29
633-5d	v India at Birmingham	1979

England have made nine other totals of 600 or more

Lowest team totals

Completed innings

45	v Australia at Sydney	1886-87
46	v WI at Port-of-Spain	1993-94
51	v WI at Kingston	2008-09
52	v Australia at The Oval	1948
53	v Australia at Lord's	1888
61	v Aust at Melbourne	1901-02
61	v Aust at Melbourne	1903-04
62	v Australia at Lord's	1888
64	v NZ at Wellington	1977-78
65*	v Australia at Sydney	1894-95

One batsman absent

Best match bowling

19-90	JC Laker	v Australia at Manchester	1956
17-159	SF Barnes	v S Africa at Johannesburg	1913-14
15-28	J Briggs	v S Africa at Cape Town	1888-89
15-45	GA Lohmann	v S Africa at Port Elizabeth	1895-96
15-99	C Blythe	v South Africa at Leeds	1907
15-104	H Verity	v Australia at Lord's	1934
15-124	W Rhodes	v Australia at Melbourne	1903-04
14-99	AV Bedser	v Australia at Nottingham	1953
14-102	W Bates	v Australia at Melbourne	1882-83
14-144	SF Barnes	v South Africa at Durban	1913-14

Barnes took ten or more wickets in a match a record seven times for England

Hat-tricks

W Bates	v Australia at Melbourne	1882-83
J Briggs	v Australia at Sydney	1891-92
GA Lohmann	v S Africa at Port Elizabeth	1895-96
JT Hearne	v Australia at Leeds	1899
MJC Allom	v New Zealand at Christchurch	1929-30
TWJ Goddard	v S Africa at Johannesburg	1938-39
PJ Loader	v West Indies at Leeds	1957
DG Cork	v West Indies at Manchester	1995
D Gough	v Australia at Sydney	1998-99
MJ Hoggard	v West Indies at Bridgetown	2003-04
RJ Sidebottom	v New Zealand at Hamilton	2007-08
SCJ Broad	v India at Nottingham	2011

England's Test match results

	Played	Won	Lost	Drawn	Tied	% win
v Australia	331	105	133	93	0	31.72
v Bangladesh	8	8	0	0	0	100.00
v India	107	40	20	47	0	37.38
v New Zealand	99	47	8	44	0	47.47
v Pakistan	74	22	16	36	0	29.72
v South Africa	141	56	31	54	0	39.71
v Sri Lanka	26	10	7	9	0	38.46
v West Indies	148	45	53	50	0	30.40
v Zimbabwe	6	3	0	3	0	50.00
TOTAL	**940**	**336**	**268**	**336**	**0**	**35.74**

Figures to 17.09.13. Updated records can be found at **www.cricinfo.com/ci/engine/records**

ENGLAND
One-day International Records

Most appearances

197	PD Collingwood	
174	JM Anderson	
170	AJ Stewart	
158	D Gough	
138	A Flintoff	
135	IR Bell	
134	KP Pietersen	
127	AJ Strauss	
125	GA Gooch	
123	ME Trescothick	

Seven further men have played 100 or more ODIs for England

Most runs

		Avge
5092	PD Collingwood	35.36
4677	AJ Stewart	31.60
4428	IR Bell	36.90
4422	KP Pietersen	41.32
4335	ME Trescothick	37.37
4290	GA Gooch	36.98
4205	AJ Strauss	35.63
4010	AJ Lamb	39.31
3846	GA Hick	37.33
3637	NV Knight	40.41

A Flintoff (3293) and DI Gower (3170) also passed 3000 runs in ODIs

Most wickets

		Avge
245	JM Anderson	29.11
234	D Gough	26.29
168	A Flintoff	23.61
160	SCJ Broad	28.13
145	IT Botham	28.54
115	PAJ DeFreitas	32.82
111	PD Collingwood	38.68
104	GP Swann	27.76
94	TT Bresnan	36.36
80	RGD Willis	24.60

Eleven further bowlers have taken 50 wickets in ODIs for England

Highest scores

167*	RA Smith	v Australia at Birmingham	1993
158	DI Gower	v New Zealand at Brisbane	1982-83
158	AJ Strauss	v India at Bangalore	2010-11
154	AJ Strauss	v Bangladesh at Birmingham	2010
152	AJ Strauss	v Bangladesh at Nottingham	2005
142*	CWJ Athey	v New Zealand at Manchester	1986
142	GA Gooch	v Pakistan at Karachi	1987-88
137	DL Amiss	v India at Lord's	1975
137	AN Cook	v Pakistan at Abu Dhabi	2011-12
137	ME Trescothick	v Pakistan at Lord's	2001
137	IJL Trott	v Australia at Sydney	2010-11

Trescothick scored 12 centuries in ODIs, KP Pietersen 9, Gooch 8, Gower 7, and Strauss 6

Best innings bowling

6-31	PD Collingwood	v B'desh at Nottingham	2005
6-45	CR Woakes	v Australia at Brisbane	2010-11
5-15	MA Ealham	v Zim at Kimberley	1999-2000
5-19	A Flintoff	v WI at Gros Islet	2008-09
5-20	VJ Marks	v NZ at Wellington	1983-84
5-21	C White	v Zim at Bulawayo	1999-2000
5-23	SCJ Broad	v S Africa at Nottingham	2008
5-23	JM Anderson	v SA at Port Elizabeth	2009-10
5-26	RC Irani	v India at The Oval	2002
5-28	GP Swann	v Aust at Chester-le-Street	2009

Collingwood also scored 112 in the same match.*
All Ealham's five wickets were lbw, an ODI record

Record wicket partnerships

1st	200	ME Trescothick (114*) and VS Solanki (106)	v South Africa at The Oval	2003
2nd	250	AJ Strauss (154) and IJL Trott (110)	v Bangladesh at Birmingham	2010
3rd	213	GA Hick (86*) and NH Fairbrother (113)	v West Indies at Lord's	1991
4th	226	AJ Strauss (100) and A Flintoff (123)	v West Indies at Lord's	2004
5th	226*	EJG Morgan (124*) and RS Bopara (101*)	v Ireland at Dublin	2013
6th	150	MP Vaughan (90*) and GO Jones (80)	v Zimbabwe at Bulawayo	2004-05
7th	110	PD Collingwood (100) and C White (48)	v Sri Lanka at Perth	2002-03
8th	99*	RS Bopara (43*) and SCJ Broad (45*)	v India at Manchester	2007
9th	100	LE Plunkett (56) and VS Solanki (39*)	v Pakistan at Lahore	2005-06
10th	53	JM Anderson (20*) and ST Finn (35)	v Australia at Brisbane	2010-11

Figures to 17.09.13. Updated records can be found at **www.cricinfo.com/ci/engine/records**

One-day International Records

ENGLAND

Most catches

Fielders
- **108** PD Collingwood
- **64** GA Hick
- **57** AJ Strauss
- **47** JM Anderson
- **46** A Flintoff

Most dismissals

Wicketkeepers		Ct/St
163	AJ Stewart	148/15
77	MJ Prior	69/8
72	GO Jones	68/4
64	C Kieswetter	52/12
47	RC Russell	41/6

Highest team totals

391-4	v Bangladesh at Nottingham	2005
363-7	v Pakistan at Nottingham	1992
347-7	v Bangladesh at Birmingham	2010
340-6	v New Zealand at Napier	2007-08
338-8	v India at Bangalore	2010-11
334-4	v India at Lord's	1975
333-6	v Australia at Sydney	2010-11
333-9	v Sri Lanka at Taunton	1983
328-7	v West Indies at Birmingham	2009
327-4	v Pakistan at Lahore	2005-06
327-8	v Ireland at Bangalore	2010-11

England have reached 300 on 17 other occasions in ODIs

Lowest team totals

Completed innings

86	v Australia at Manchester	2001
88	v SL at Dambulla	2003-04
89	v NZ at Wellington	2001-02
93	v Australia at Leeds	1975
94	v Aust at Melbourne	1978-79
101	v NZ at Chester-le-Street	2004
103	v SA at The Oval	1999
104	v SL at Colombo	2007-08
107	v Zim at Cape Town	1999-2000
110	v Aust at Melbourne	1998-99
110	v Aust at Adelaide	2006-07

The lowest totals against England are 45 by Canada (1979), and 70 by Australia (1977)

Most sixes

- **92** A Flintoff*
- **76** KP Pietersen*
- **74** PD Collingwood
- **47** EJG Morgan
- **44** IT Botham
- **41** GA Hick
- **41** ME Trescothick
- **32** C Kieswetter
- **30** RS Bopara
- **30** AJ Lamb

*Also hit one six for the World XI

Best strike rate

Runs per 100 balls		Runs
91.73	EJG Morgan	2421
90.41	GP Swann	500
90.19	TT Bresnan	773
89.93	C Kieswetter	1054
89.14	A Flintoff	3293
87.59	LJ Wright	706
86.70	KP Pietersen	4422
85.21	ME Trescothick	4335
83.83	PAJ DeFreitas	690
82.15	JE Root	626

Qualification: 500 runs

Most economical bowlers

Runs per over		Wkts
3.28	RGD Willis	80
3.54	ARC Fraser	47
3.79	GR Dilley	48
3.84	AD Mullally	63
3.96	IT Botham	145
3.96	PAJ DeFreitas	115
4.01	AR Caddick	69
4.08	MA Ealham	67
4.10	JE Emburey	76
4.17	GC Small	58

Qualification: 2000 balls bowled

England's one-day international results

	Played	Won	Lost	Tied	No result	% win
v Australia	122	48	69	2	3	41.17
v Bangladesh	15	13	2	0	0	86.66
v India	87	35	47	2	3	42.85
v New Zealand	77	33	38	2	4	46.57
v Pakistan	72	42	28	0	2	60.00
v South Africa	51	22	25	1	3	46.87
v Sri Lanka	51	26	25	0	0	50.98
v West Indies	85	40	41	0	4	49.38
v Zimbabwe	30	21	8	0	1	72.41
v others (see below)	18	16	1	0	1	94.11
TOTAL	**608**	**296**	**284**	**7**	**21**	**51.02**

Other teams: Canada (P2, W2), East Africa (P1, W1), Ireland (P6, W5, L1), Kenya (P2, W2), Namibia (P1, W1), Netherlands (P3, W3), Scotland (P2, W1, NR1), United Arab Emirates (P1, W1).

INDIA — Test Match Records

Most appearances

198	SR Tendulkar	
163	R Dravid	
134	VVS Laxman	
132	A Kumble	
131	Kapil Dev	
125	SM Gavaskar	
116	DB Vengsarkar	
113	SC Ganguly	
101	Harbhajan Singh	
99	M Azharuddin	

Gavaskar played 106 consecutive Tests between 1974-75 and 1986-87

Most runs

		Avge
15837	SR Tendulkar	53.86
13265	R Dravid	52.63
10122	SM Gavaskar	51.12
8781	VVS Laxman	45.97
8503	V Sehwag	49.43
7212	SC Ganguly	42.17
6868	DB Vengsarkar	42.13
6215	M Azharuddin	45.03
6080	GR Viswanath	41.74
5248	Kapil Dev	31.05

Tendulkar scored 51 centuries, Dravid 36, Gavaskar 34, Sehwag 23 and Azharuddin 22

Most wickets

		Avge
619	A Kumble	29.65
434	Kapil Dev	29.64
413	Harbhajan Singh	32.37
295	Z Khan	32.35
266	BS Bedi	29.74
242	BS Chandrasekhar	29.74
236	J Srinath	30.49
189	EAS Prasanna	30.38
162	MH Mankad	32.32
156	S Venkataraghavan	36.11

In all 19 Indians have taken 100 wickets in Tests

Highest scores

319	V Sehwag	v South Africa at Chennai	2007-08
309	V Sehwag	v Pakistan at Multan	2003-04
293	V Sehwag	v Sri Lanka at Mumbai	2009-10
281	VVS Laxman	v Australia at Kolkata	2000-01
270	R Dravid	v Pakistan at Rawalpindi	2003-04
254	V Sehwag	v Pakistan at Lahore	2005-06
248*	SR Tendulkar	v Bangladesh at Dhaka	2004-05
241*	SR Tendulkar	v Australia at Sydney	2003-04
239	SC Ganguly	v Pakistan at Bangalore	2007-08
236*	SM Gavaskar	v West Indies at Madras	1983-84

Sehwag and Tendulkar have scored six double-centuries, Dravid five, and Gavaskar four

Best innings bowling

10-74	A Kumble	v Pakistan at Delhi	1998-99
9-69	JM Patel	v Australia at Kanpur	1959-60
9-83	Kapil Dev	v WI at Ahmedabad	1983-84
9-102	SP Gupte	v W Indies at Kanpur	1958-59
8-52	MH Mankad	v Pakistan at Delhi	1952-53
8-55	MH Mankad	v England at Madras	1951-52
8-61	ND Hirwani	v W Indies at Madras	1987-88
8-72	S Venkataraghavan	v N Zealand at Delhi	1964-65
8-75	ND Hirwani	v W Indies at Madras	1987-88
8-76	EAS Prasanna	v NZ at Auckland	1975-76

Hirwani's two performances were in the same match, his Test debut

Record wicket partnerships

1st	413	MH Mankad (231) and P Roy (173)	v New Zealand at Madras	1955-56
2nd	370	M Vijay (167) and CA Pujara (204)	v Australia at Hyderabad	2012-13
3rd	336	V Sehwag (309) and SR Tendulkar (194*)	v Pakistan at Multan	2003-04
4th	353	SR Tendulkar (241*) and VVS Laxman (178)	v Australia at Sydney	2003-04
5th	376	VVS Laxman (281) and R Dravid (180)	v Australia at Calcutta	2000-01
6th	298*	DB Vengsarkar (164*) and RJ Shastri (121*)	v Australia at Bombay	1986-87
7th	259*	VVS Laxman (143*) and MS Dhoni (132*)	v South Africa at Kolkata	2009-10
8th	161	M Azharuddin (109) and A Kumble (88)	v South Africa at Calcutta	1996-97
9th	149	PG Joshi (52*) and RB Desai (85)	v Pakistan at Bombay	1960-61
10th	133	SR Tendulkar (248*) and Z Khan (75)	v Bangladesh at Dhaka	2004-05

Figures to 17.09.13. Updated records can be found at www.cricinfo.com/ci/engine/records

Test Match Records — INDIA

Most catches

Fielders		
209	R Dravid	
135	VVS Laxman	
115	SR Tendulkar	
108	SM Gavaskar	
105	M Azharuddin	

Most dismissals

Wicketkeepers		Ct/St
248	MS Dhoni	212/36
198	SMH Kirmani	160/38
130	KS More	110/20
107	NR Mongia	99/8
82	FM Engineer	66/16

Highest team totals

726-9d	v Sri Lanka at Mumbai	2009-10
707	v Sri Lanka at Colombo	2010
705-7d	v Australia at Sydney	2003-04
676-7	v Sri Lanka at Kanpur	1986-87
675-5d	v Pakistan at Multan	2003-04
664	v England at The Oval	2007
657-7d	v Australia at Kolkata	2000-01
644-7d	v West Indies at Kanpur	1978-79
643-6d	v South Africa at Kolkata	2009-10
642	v Sri Lanka at Kanpur	2009-10

India have reached 600 on 13 further occasions

Lowest team totals

Completed innings		
42*	v England at Lord's	1974
58	v Australia at Brisbane	1947-48
58	v England at Manchester	1952
66	v S Africa at Durban	1996-97
67	v Aust at Melbourne	1947-48
75	v West Indies at Delhi	1987-88
76	v SA at Ahmedabad	2007-08
81*	v NZ at Wellington	1975-76
81	v W Indies at Bridgetown	1996-97
82	v England at Manchester	1952

*One or more batsmen absent

Best match bowling

16-136	ND Hirwani	v West Indies at Madras	1987-88
15-217	Harbhajan Singh	v Australia at Chennai	2000-01
14-124	JM Patel	v Australia at Kanpur	1959-60
14-149	A Kumble	v Pakistan at Delhi	1998-99
13-131	MH Mankad	v Pakistan at Delhi	1952-53
13-132	J Srinath	v Pakistan at Calcutta	1998-99
13-181	A Kumble	v Australia at Chennai	2004-05
13-196	Harbhajan Singh	v Australia at Kolkata	2000-01
12-85	R Ashwin	v NZ at Hyderabad	2011-12
12-104	BS Chandrasekhar	v Australia at Melbourne	1977-78

Hirwani's feat was on his Test debut

Hat-tricks

Harbhajan Singh v Australia at Kolkata 2000-01

The wickets of RT Ponting, AC Gilchrist and SK Warne, as India fought back to win after following on.

IK Pathan v Pakistan at Karachi 2005-06

Salman Butt, Younis Khan and Mohammad Yousuf with the fourth, fifth and sixth balls of the match – Pakistan still won the match by 341 runs.

India had never conceded a hat-trick in a Test match until SCJ Broad took one for England at Nottingham in 2011.

India's Test match results

	Played	Won	Lost	Drawn	Tied	% win
v Australia	86	24	38	23	1	27.90
v Bangladesh	7	6	0	1	0	85.71
v England	107	20	40	47	0	18.69
v New Zealand	52	18	9	25	0	34.61
v Pakistan	59	9	12	38	0	15.25
v South Africa	27	7	12	8	0	25.92
v Sri Lanka	35	14	6	15	0	40.00
v West Indies	88	14	30	44	0	15.90
v Zimbabwe	11	7	2	2	0	63.63
TOTAL	**472**	**119**	**149**	**203**	**1**	**25.21**

Figures to 17.09.13. Updated records can be found at **www.cricinfo.com/ci/engine/records**

INDIA

One-day International Records

Most appearances

463	SR Tendulkar	
340	R Dravid	
334	M Azharuddin	
308	SC Ganguly	
279	Yuvraj Singh	
269	A Kumble	
251	V Sehwag	
229	J Srinath	
227	Harbhajan Singh	
225	Kapil Dev	

Robin Singh played 136 ODIs for India – but only one Test match

Most runs

		Avge
18426	SR Tendulkar	44.83
11221	SC Ganguly	40.95
10768	R Dravid	39.15
9378	M Azharuddin	36.92
8119	Yuvraj Singh	36.90
7995	V Sehwag	35.37
7184	MS Dhoni	50.95
5359	A Jadeja	37.47
5238	G Gambhir	39.68
4575	V Kohli	49.72

NS Sidhu (4413), SK Raina (4305) and K Srikkanth (4091) also scored more than 4000 runs

Most wickets

		Avge
334	A Kumble	30.83
315	J Srinath	28.08
288	AB Agarkar	27.85
269	Z Khan	30.11
255	Harbhajan Singh	33.52
253	Kapil Dev	27.45
196	BKV Prasad	32.30
173	IK Pathan	29.72
157	M Prabhakar	28.87
155	A Nehra	31.60

SR Tendulkar (154), RJ Shastri (129), Yuvraj Singh (108) and SC Ganguly (100) have also taken 100 wickets

Highest scores

219	V Sehwag	v West Indies at Indore	2011-12
200*	SR Tendulkar	v South Africa at Gwalior	2009-10
186*	SR Tendulkar	v N Zealand at Hyderabad	1999-2000
183*	MS Dhoni	v Sri Lanka at Jaipur	2005-06
183	SC Ganguly	v Sri Lanka at Taunton	1999
183	V Kohli	v Pakistan at Dhaka	2011-12
175*	Kapil Dev	v Zimbabwe at Tunbridge Wells	1983
175	SR Tendulkar	v Australia at Hyderabad	2009-10
175	V Sehwag	v Bangladesh at Mirpur	2010-11
163*	SR Tendulkar	v NZ at Christchurch	2008-09

Tendulkar scored 49 centuries, Ganguly 22, Kohli and Sehwag 15, Yuvraj Singh 13, R Dravid 12 and G Gambhir 11

Best bowling figures

6-12	A Kumble	v West Indies at Calcutta	1993-94
6-23	A Nehra	v England at Durban	2002-03
6-27	M Kartik	v Australia at Mumbai	2007-08
6-42	AB Agarkar	v Australia at Melbourne	2003-04
6-48	A Mishra	v Zimbabwe at Bulawayo	2013
6-55	S Sreesanth	v England at Indore	2005-06
6-59	A Nehra	v Sri Lanka at Colombo	2005
5-6	SB Joshi	v South Africa at Nairobi	1999-2000
5-15	RJ Shastri	v Australia at Perth	1991-92
5-16	SC Ganguly	v Pakistan at Toronto	1997-98

Agarkar took four wickets in an ODI innings 12 times, J Srinath and A Kumble 10

Record wicket partnerships

1st	258	SC Ganguly (111) and SR Tendulkar (146)	v Kenya at Paarl	2001-02
2nd	331	SR Tendulkar (186*) and R Dravid (153)	v New Zealand at Hyderabad	1999-2000
3rd	237*	R Dravid (104*) and SR Tendulkar (140*)	v Kenya at Bristol	1999
4th	275*	M Azharuddin (153*) and A Jadeja (116*)	v Zimbabwe at Cuttack	1997-98
5th	223	M Azharuddin (111*) and A Jadeja (119)	v Sri Lanka at Colombo	1997-98
6th	158	Yuvraj Singh (120) and MS Dhoni (67*)	v Zimbabwe at Harare	2005-06
7th	102	HK Badani (60*) and AB Agarkar (53)	v Australia at Melbourne	2003-04
8th	84	Harbhajan Singh (49) and P Kumar (40*)	v Australia at Vadodara	2009-10
9th	126*	Kapil Dev (175*) and SMH Kirmani (24*)	v Zimbabwe at Tunbridge Wells	1983
10th	64	Harbhajan Singh (41*) and L Balaji (18)	v England at The Oval	2004

Figures to 17.09.13. Updated records can be found at www.cricinfo.com/ci/engine/records

One-day International Records — INDIA

Most catches

Fielders

156	M Azharuddin	
140	SR Tendulkar	
124	R Dravid	
99	SC Ganguly	
90	V Sehwag/Yuvraj Singh	

Highest team totals

418-5	v West Indies at Indore	2011-12
414-7	v Sri Lanka at Rajkot	2009-10
413-5	v Bermuda at Port-of-Spain	2006-07
401-3	v South Africa at Gwalior	2009-10
392-4	v N Zealand at Christchurch	2008-09
387-5	v England at Rajkot	2008-09
376-2	v N Zealand at Hyderabad	1999-2000
374-4	v Hong Kong at Karachi	2008
373-6	v Sri Lanka at Taunton	1999
370-4	v Bangladesh at Mirpur	2010-11

All scored in 50 overs

Lowest team totals

Completed innings

54	v Sri Lanka at Sharjah	2000-01
63	v Australia at Sydney	1980-81
78	v Sri Lanka at Kanpur	1986-87
79	v Pakistan at Sialkot	1978-79
88	v NZ at Dambulla	2010
91	v South Africa at Durban	2006-07
100	v WI at Ahmedabad	1993-94
100	v Australia at Sydney	1999-2000
103	v Sri Lanka at Colombo	2008-09
103	v Sri Lanka at Dambulla	2010

The lowest score against India is Zimbabwe's 65 at Harare in 2005

Most dismissals

Wicketkeepers		Ct/St
281	MS Dhoni	209/72
154	NR Mongia	110/44
90	KS More	63/27
86	R Dravid	72/14
39	PA Patel	30/9

Most sixes

195	SR Tendulkar
189	SC Ganguly
147	MS Dhoni
143	Yuvraj Singh
131	V Sehwag
89	SK Raina
85	A Jadeja
77	M Azharuddin
67	Kapil Dev
44	NS Sidhu

Dhoni hit 10 sixes in one innings

Best strike rate

Runs per 100 balls		Runs
113.60	YK Pathan	810
104.44	V Sehwag	7995
95.07	Kapil Dev	3783
91.92	RV Uthappa	786
91.65	SK Raina	4305
89.43	SB Joshi	584
88.28	S Dhawan	776
87.54	MS Dhoni	7184
87.39	Yuvraj Singh	8119
86.64	V Kohli	4575

Qualification: 500 runs

Most economical bowlers

Runs per over		Wkts
3.71	Kapil Dev	253
3.95	Maninder Singh	66
4.05	Madan Lal	73
4.21	RJ Shastri	129
4.27	M Prabhakar	157
4.29	Harbhajan Singh	255
4.29	A Kumble	334
4.33	M Amarnath	46
4.36	SLV Raju	63
4.44	SB Joshi	69
4.44	J Srinath	315

Qualification: 2000 balls bowled

India's one-day international results

	Played	Won	Lost	Tied	No result	% win
v Australia	109	37	64	0	8	36.63
v Bangladesh	24	21	3	0	0	87.50
v England	87	47	35	2	3	57.14
v New Zealand	88	46	37	0	5	55.42
v Pakistan	125	50	71	0	4	41.32
v South Africa	67	25	40	0	2	38.46
v Sri Lanka	143	78	53	1	11	59.46
v West Indies	109	48	58	1	2	45.32
v Zimbabwe	56	44	10	2	0	78.43
v others (see below)	24	22	2	0	0	80.35
TOTAL	**832**	**418**	**373**	**6**	**35**	**52.82**

Other teams: Bermuda (P1, W1), East Africa (P1, W1), Hong Kong (P1, W1), Ireland (P2, W2), Kenya (P13, W11, L2), Namibia (P1, W1), Netherlands (P2, W2), Scotland (P1, W1), United Arab Emirates (P2, W2).

NEW ZEALAND *Test Match Records*

Most appearances

111	SP Fleming	
111	DL Vettori	
86	RJ Hadlee	
82	JG Wright	
81	NJ Astle	
78	AC Parore	
77	MD Crowe	
77	BB McCullum	
71	CS Martin	
63	IDS Smith	

Vettori also played for the World XI against Australia in October 2005

Most runs

		Avge
7172	SP Fleming	40.06
5444	MD Crowe	45.36
5334	JG Wright	37.82
4702	NJ Astle	37.02
4508	DL Vettori	30.25
4459	BB McCullum	35.38
3504	LRPL Taylor	42.21
3448	BE Congdon	32.22
3428	JR Reid	33.28
3320	CL Cairns	33.53

RJ Hadlee (3124) and CD McMillan (3116) also scored more than 3000 runs in Tests

Most wickets

		Avge
431	RJ Hadlee	22.29
359	DL Vettori	34.20
233	CS Martin	33.81
218	CL Cairns	29.40
160	DK Morrison	34.68
130	BL Cairns	32.92
123	EJ Chatfield	32.17
116	RO Collinge	29.25
111	BR Taylor	26.60
102	JG Bracewell	35.81

RC Motz took exactly 100 Test wickets. Vettori also took one wicket for the World XI

Highest scores

299	MD Crowe	v Sri Lanka at Wellington	1990-91
274*	SP Fleming	v Sri Lanka at Colombo	2002-03
267*	BA Young	v Sri Lanka at Dunedin	1996-97
262	SP Fleming	v South Africa at Cape Town	2005-06
259	GM Turner	v West Indies at Georgetown	1971-72
239	GT Dowling	v India at Christchurch	1967-68
230*	B Sutcliffe	v India at Delhi	1955-56
225	BB McCullum	v India at Hyderabad	2010-11
224	L Vincent	v Sri Lanka at Wellington	2004-05
223*	GM Turner	v West Indies at Kingston	1971-72

There have been six other double-centuries, two by MS Sinclair and one each by NJ Astle, MP Donnelly, SP Fleming and JD Ryder

Best innings bowling

9-52	RJ Hadlee	v Australia at Brisbane	1985-86
7-23	RJ Hadlee	v India at Wellington	1975-76
7-27	CL Cairns	v West Indies at Hamilton	1999-2000
7-52	C Pringle	v Pakistan at Faisalabad	1990-91
7-53	CL Cairns	v Bangladesh at Hamilton	2001-02
7-64	TG Southee	v India at Bangalore	2012-13
7-65	SB Doull	v India at Wellington	1998-99
7-74	BR Taylor	v West Indies at Bridgetown	1971-72
7-74	BL Cairns	v England at Leeds	1983
7-87	SL Boock	v Pakistan at Hyderabad	1984-85
7-87	DL Vettori	v Australia at Auckland	1999-2000

Hadlee took five or more wickets in an innings 36 times

Record wicket partnerships

1st	387	GM Turner (259) and TW Jarvis (182)	v West Indies at Georgetown	1971-72
2nd	241	JG Wright (116) and AH Jones (143)	v England at Wellington	1991-92
3rd	467	AH Jones (186) and MD Crowe (299)	v Sri Lanka at Wellington	1990-91
4th	271	LRPL Taylor (151) and JD Ryder (201)	v India at Napier	2008-09
5th	222	NJ Astle (141) and CD McMillan (142)	v Zimbabwe at Wellington	2000-01
6th	339	MJ Guptill (189) and BB McCullum (185)	v Bangladesh at Hamilton	2009-10
7th	225	CL Cairns (158) and JDP Oram (90)	v South Africa at Auckland	2003-04
8th	256	SP Fleming (262) and JEC Franklin (122*)	v South Africa at Cape Town	2005-06
9th	136	IDS Smith (173) and MC Snedden (22)	v India at Auckland	1989-90
10th	151	BF Hastings (110) and RO Collinge (68*)	v Pakistan at Auckland	1972-73

Figures to 17.09.13. Updated records can be found at **www.cricinfo.com/ci/engine/records**

Test Match Records — NEW ZEALAND

Most catches

Fielders

171	SP Fleming	
75	LRPL Taylor	
71	MD Crowe	
70	NJ Astle	
64	JV Coney	

Most dismissals

Wicketkeepers — Ct/St

201	AC Parore	194/7
178	BB McCullum	167/11
176	IDS Smith	168/8
96	KJ Wadsworth	92/4
59	WK Lees	52/7

Highest team totals

671-4	v Sri Lanka at Wellington		1990-91
630-6d	v India at Chandigarh		2003-04
619-9d	v India at Napier		2008-09
595	v South Africa at Auckland		2003-04
593-8d	v South Africa at Cape Town		2005-06
586-7d	v Sri Lanka at Dunedin		1996-97
563	v Pakistan at Hamilton		2003-04
561	v Sri Lanka at Napier		2004-05
553-7d	v Australia at Brisbane		1985-86
553-7d	v Bangladesh at Hamilton		2009-10

671-4 is the record score in any team's second innings in a Test match

Lowest team totals

Completed innings

26	v England at Auckland	1954-55
42	v Australia at Wellington	1945-46
45	v SA at Cape Town	2012-13
47	v England at Lord's	1958
54	v Australia at Wellington	1945-46
65	v England at Christchurch	1970-71
67	v England at Leeds	1958
67	v England at Lord's	1978
68	v England at Lord's	2013
70	v Pakistan at Dacca	1955-56

26 is the lowest all-out total by any team in a Test match

Best match bowling

15-123	RJ Hadlee	v Australia at Brisbane	1985-86
12-149	DL Vettori	v Australia at Auckland	1999-2000
12-170	DL Vettori	v Bangladesh at Chittagong	2004-05
11-58	RJ Hadlee	v India at Wellington	1975-76
11-102	RJ Hadlee	v West Indies at Dunedin	1979-80
11-152	C Pringle	v Pakistan at Faisalabad	1990-91
11-155	RJ Hadlee	v Australia at Perth	1985-86
11-169	DJ Nash	v England at Lord's	1994
11-180	CS Martin	v South Africa at Auckland	2003-04
10-88	RJ Hadlee	v India at Bombay	1988-89

Hadlee took 33 wickets at 12.15 in the three-Test series in Australia in 1985-86

Hat-tricks

PJ Petherick	v Pakistan at Lahore		1976-77
JEC Franklin	v Bangladesh at Dhaka		2004-05

*Petherick's hat-trick was on Test debut: he dismissed Javed Miandad (who had made 163 on **his** debut), Wasim Raja and Intikhab Alam. Petherick won only five more Test caps.*

Franklin is one of only seven men to have scored a century and taken a hat-trick in Tests: the others are J Briggs and SCJ Broad of England, Abdul Razzaq and Wasim Akram of Pakistan, and Harbhajan Singh and IK Pathan of India

New Zealand's Test match results

	Played	Won	Lost	Drawn	Tied	% win
v Australia	52	8	27	17	0	15.38
v Bangladesh	9	8	0	1	0	88.88
v England	99	8	47	44	0	8.08
v India	52	9	18	25	0	17.30
v Pakistan	50	7	23	20	0	14.00
v South Africa	40	4	23	13	0	10.00
v Sri Lanka	28	10	8	10	0	35.71
v West Indies	39	9	12	18	0	23.07
v Zimbabwe	15	9	0	6	0	60.00
TOTAL	384	72	158	154	0	18.75

Figures to 17.09.13. Updated records can be found at www.cricinfo.com/ci/engine/records

NEW ZEALAND One-day International Records

Most appearances

279	SP Fleming	
271	DL Vettori	
250	CZ Harris	
223	NJ Astle	
218	BB McCullum	
214	CL Cairns	
197	CD McMillan	
188	SB Styris	
179	AC Parore	
160	JDP Oram	

Fleming (1), Vettori (4) and Cairns (1) also played in official ODIs for the World XI

Most runs

		Avge
8007	SP Fleming	32.41
7090	NJ Astle	34.92
4952	BB McCullum	30.75
4881	CL Cairns	29.22
4707	CD McMillan	28.18
4704	MD Crowe	38.55
4483	SB Styris	32.48
4379	CZ Harris	29.00
3891	JG Wright	26.46
3755	LRPL Taylor	38.31

AC Parore (3314) and KR Rutherford (3143) also passed 3000. Fleming also scored 30 runs and Cairns 69 for the World XI

Most wickets

		Avge
276	DL Vettori	31.76
222	KD Mills	26.29
203	CZ Harris	37.50
200	CL Cairns	32.78
173	JDP Oram	28.92
158	RJ Hadlee	21.56
147	SE Bond	20.88
140	EJ Chatfield	25.84
137	SB Styris	35.32
126	DK Morrison	27.53

MC Snedden (114), GR Larsen (113), DR Tuffey (110) and C Pringle (103) also took 100 wickets. Vettori also took 8 wickets, and Cairns 1, for the World XI

Highest scores

189*	MJ Guptill	v England at Southampton	2007-08
172	L Vincent	v Zimbabwe at Bulawayo	2005-06
171*	GM Turner	v East Africa at Birmingham	1975
166	BB McCullum	v Ireland at Aberdeen	2008
161	JAH Marshall	v Ireland at Aberdeen	2008
146	RJ Nicol	v Zimbabwe at Whangarei	2011-12
145*	NJ Astle	v USA at The Oval	2004
145*	KS Williamson	v SA at Kimberley	2012-13
141	SB Styris	v Sri Lanka at Bloemfontein	2002-03
140	GM Turner	v Sri Lanka at Auckland	1982-83

Turner's 171 was the highest score in the first World Cup*

Best bowling figures

6-19	SE Bond	v India at Bulawayo	2005-06
6-23	SE Bond	v Australia at Port Elizabeth	2002-03
6-25	SB Styris	v West Indies at Port-of-Spain	2001-02
5-7	DL Vettori	v Bangladesh at Queenstown	2007-08
5-22	MN Hart	v West Indies at Margao	1994-95
5-22	AR Adams	v India at Queenstown	2002-03
5-23	RO Collinge	v India at Christchurch	1975-76
5-23	SE Bond	v Australia at Wellington	2006-07
5-25	RJ Hadlee	v Sri Lanka at Bristol	1983
5-25	SE Bond	v Australia at Adelaide	2001-02
5-25	KD Mills	v South Africa at Durban	2007-08

In all Hadlee took five wickets in an ODI on five occasions

Record wicket partnerships

1st	274	JAH Marshall (161) and BB McCullum (166)	v Ireland at Aberdeen	2008
2nd	157	MJ Guptill (105) and BB McCullum (87)	v Zimbabwe at Harare	2011-12
3rd	180	AC Parore (96) and KR Rutherford (108)	v India at Baroda	1994-95
4th	190	LRPL Taylor (95) and SB Styris (89)	v India at Dambulla	2010
5th	195	LRPL Taylor (119) and KS Williamson (100*)	v Zimbabwe at Bulawayo	2011-12
6th	165	CD McMillan (117) and BB McCullum (86*)	v Australia at Hamilton	2006-07
7th	123	NT Broom (71) and JDP Oram (83)	v Bangladesh at Napier	2009-10
8th	94	JEC Franklin (72*) and NL McCullum (43)	v India at Vadodara	2010-11
9th	83	KD Mills (54) and TG Southee (32)	v India at Christchurch	2008-09
10th	65	MC Snedden (40) and EJ Chatfield (19*)	v Sri Lanka at Derby	1983

Figures to 17.09.13. Updated records can be found at www.cricinfo.com/ci/engine/records

One-day International Records NEW ZEALAND

Most catches

Fielders

132	SP Fleming	
96	CZ Harris	
86	LRPL Taylor	
83	NJ Astle	
76	DL Vettori	

Most dismissals

Wicketkeepers   *Ct/St*

238	BB McCullum	223/15
136	AC Parore	111/25
85	IDS Smith	80/5
37	TE Blain	36/1
30	LK Germon	21/9
30	WK Lees	28/2

Highest team totals

402-2	v Ireland at Aberdeen	2008
397-5	v Zimbabwe at Bulawayo	2005-06
373-8	v Zimbabwe at Napier	2011-12
372-6	v Zimbabwe at Whangarei	2011-12
363-5	v Canada at St Lucia	2006-07
359-3	v England at Southampton	2013
358-6	v Canada at Mumbai	2010-11
350-9	v Australia at Hamilton	2006-07
349-9	v India at Rajkot	1999-2000
348-8	v India at Nagpur	1995-96

The 397-5 came from 44 overs; all the others were from 50, except 350-9 (49.3)

Lowest team totals

Completed innings

64	v Pakistan at Sharjah	1985-86
73	v Sri Lanka at Auckland	2006-07
74	v Aust at Wellington	1981-82
74	v Pakistan at Sharjah	1989-90
94	v Aust at Christchurch	1989-90
97	v Aust at Faridabad	2003-04
103	v India at Chennai	2010-11
105	v Aust at Auckland	2005-06
108	v Pakistan at Wellington	1992-93
110	v Pakistan at Auckland	1993-94

The lowest totals against New Zealand are 69, by Kenya at Chennai in 2010-11, and 70, by Australia at Adelaide in 1985-86

Most sixes

151	CL Cairns
147	BB McCullum
96	LRPL Taylor
86	NJ Astle
84	CD McMillan
81	JDP Oram
68	SB Styris
63	SP Fleming
50	MJ Guptill
43	CZ Harris

Cairns also hit 2 for the World XI

Best strike rate

Runs per 100 balls   *Runs*

104.88	BL Cairns	987
99.43	IDS Smith	1055
89.98	BB McCullum	4952
89.72	JD Ryder	1100
86.61	JDP Oram	2434
85.16	NL McCullum	769
83.76	CL Cairns	4881
82.79	MJ Guptill	2555
81.66	LRPL Taylor	3755
81.44	DL Vettori	2058

Qualification: 500 runs

Most economical bowlers

Runs per over   *Wkts*

3.30	RJ Hadlee	158
3.57	EJ Chatfield	140
3.76	GR Larsen	113
4.06	BL Cairns	89
4.11	DL Vettori	276
4.14	W Watson	74
4.17	DN Patel	45
4.17	JV Coney	54
4.28	SE Bond	147
4.28	CZ Harris	203

Qualification: 2000 balls bowled

New Zealand's one-day international results

	Played	Won	Lost	Tied	No result	% win
v Australia	125	34	85	0	6	28.57
v Bangladesh	21	16	5	0	0	76.19
v England	77	38	33	2	4	53.42
v India	88	37	46	0	5	44.57
v Pakistan	89	35	51	1	2	40.80
v South Africa	58	20	34	0	4	37.03
v Sri Lanka	79	36	37	1	5	49.32
v West Indies	56	21	28	0	7	42.85
v Zimbabwe	35	25	8	1	1	75.00
v others (see below)	13	13	0	0	0	100.00
TOTAL	**641**	**275**	**327**	**5**	**34**	**45.71**

Other teams: Canada (P3, W3), East Africa (P1, W1), Ireland (P2, W2), Kenya (P2, W2), Netherlands (P1, W1), Scotland (P2, W2), United Arab Emirates (P1, W1), United States of America (P1, W1).

PAKISTAN
Test Match Records

Most appearances

124	Javed Miandad	
119	Inzamam-ul-Haq	
104	Wasim Akram	
103	Salim Malik	
90	Mohammad Yousuf	
88	Imran Khan	
87	Waqar Younis	
84	Younis Khan	
81	Wasim Bari	
78	Zaheer Abbas	

Inzamam-ul-Haq also played one Test for the World XI

Most runs

		Avge
8832	Javed Miandad	52.57
8829	Inzamam-ul-Haq	50.16
7530	Mohammad Yousuf	52.29
7058	Younis Khan	51.89
5768	Salim Malik	43.69
5062	Zaheer Abbas	44.79
4114	Mudassar Nazar	38.09
4052	Saeed Anwar	45.52
3931	Majid Khan	38.92
3915	Hanif Mohammad	43.98

Mohammad Yousuf was known as Yousuf Youhana until September 2005

Most wickets

		Avge
414	Wasim Akram	23.62
373	Waqar Younis	23.56
362	Imran Khan	22.81
261	Danish Kaneria	34.79
236	Abdul Qadir	32.80
208	Saqlain Mushtaq	29.83
185	Mushtaq Ahmed	32.97
178	Shoaib Akhtar	25.69
177	Sarfraz Nawaz	32.75
171	Iqbal Qasim	28.11

Six further bowlers have taken 100 wickets

Highest scores

337	Hanif Mohammad	v WI at Bridgetown	1957-58
329	Inzamam-ul-Haq	v NZ at Lahore	2001-02
313	Younis Khan	v Sri Lanka at Karachi	2008-09
280*	Javed Miandad	v India at Hyderabad	1982-83
274	Zaheer Abbas	v Eng at Birmingham	1971
271	Javed Miandad	v NZ at Auckland	1988-89
267	Younis Khan	v India at Bangalore	2004-05
260	Javed Miandad	v England at The Oval	1987
257*	Wasim Akram	v Zim at Sheikhupura	1996-97
240	Zaheer Abbas	v England at The Oval	1974

Hanif batted for 970 minutes, a Test record. Wasim Akram's innings included 12 sixes, a record for any Test innings

Best innings bowling

9-56	Abdul Qadir	v England at Lahore	1987-88
9-86	Sarfraz Nawaz	v Australia at Melbourne	1978-79
8-58	Imran Khan	v Sri Lanka at Lahore	1981-82
8-60	Imran Khan	v India at Karachi	1982-83
8-69	Sikander Bakht	v India at Delhi	1979-80
8-164	Saqlain Mushtaq	v England at Lahore	2000-01
7-40	Imran Khan	v England at Leeds	1987
7-42	Fazal Mahmood	v India at Lucknow	1952-53
7-49	Iqbal Qasim	v Australia at Karachi	1979-80
7-52	Intikhab Alam	v NZ at Dunedin	1972-73
7-52	Imran Khan	v Eng at Birmingham	1982

Wasim Akram took five or more wickets in a Test innings on 25 occasions, Imran Khan 23, Waqar Younis 22

Record wicket partnerships

1st	298	Aamer Sohail (160) and Ijaz Ahmed (151)	v West Indies at Karachi	1997-98
2nd	291	Zaheer Abbas (274) and Mushtaq Mohammad (100)	v England at Birmingham	1971
3rd	451	Mudassar Nazar (231) and Javed Miandad (280*)	v India at Hyderabad	1982-83
4th	350	Mushtaq Mohammad (201) and Asif Iqbal (175)	v New Zealand at Dunedin	1972-73
5th	281	Javed Miandad (163) and Asif Iqbal (166)	v New Zealand at Lahore	1976-77
6th	269	Mohammad Yousuf (223) and Kamran Akmal (154)	v England at Lahore	2005-06
7th	308	Waqar Hasan (189) and Imtiaz Ahmed (209)	v New Zealand at Lahore	1955-56
8th	313	Wasim Akram (257*) and Saqlain Mushtaq (79)	v Zimbabwe at Sheikhupura	1996-97
9th	190	Asif Iqbal (146) and Intikhab Alam (51)	v England at The Oval	1967
10th	151	Azhar Mahmood (128*) and Mushtaq Ahmed (59)	v South Africa at Rawalpindi	1997-98

Figures to 17.09.13. Updated records can be found at www.cricinfo.com/ci/engine/records

Test Match Records — PAKISTAN

Most catches

Fielders

93	Javed Miandad	
92	Younis Khan	
81	Inzamam-ul-Haq	
65	Majid Khan	
65	Mohammad Yousuf	
65	Salim Malik	

Most dismissals

Wicketkeepers — Ct/St

228	Wasim Bari	201/27
206	Kamran Akmal	184/22
147	Moin Khan	127/20
130	Rashid Latif	119/11
104	Salim Yousuf	91/13

Highest team totals

765-6d	v Sri Lanka at Karachi	2008-09
708	v England at The Oval	1987
699-5	v India at Lahore	1989-90
679-7d	v India at Lahore	2005-06
674-6	v India at Faisalabad	1984-85
657-8d	v West Indies at Bridgetown	1957-58
652	v India at Faisalabad	1982-83
643	v New Zealand at Lahore	2001-02
636-8d	v England at Lahore	2005-06
624	v Australia at Adelaide	1983-84

Pakistan have made four other scores of 600 or more, and one of 599-7d

Lowest team totals

Completed innings

49	v SA at Jo'burg	2012-13
53*	v Australia at Sharjah†	2002-03
59	v Australia at Sharjah†	2002-03
62	v Australia at Perth	1981-82
72	v Australia at Perth	2004-05
72	v England at Birmingham	2010
74	v England at Lord's	2010
77*	v West Indies at Lahore	1986-87
80	v England at Nottingham	2010
87	v England at Lord's	1954

* One batsman retired hurt or absent hurt.
† Same match

Best match bowling

14-116	Imran Khan	v Sri Lanka at Lahore	1981-82
13-101	Abdul Qadir	v England at Lahore	1987-88
13-114	Fazal Mahmood	v Australia at Karachi	1956-57
13-135	Waqar Younis	v Zimbabwe at Karachi	1993-94
12-94	Fazal Mahmood	v India at Lucknow	1952-53
12-94	Danish Kaneria	v Bangladesh at Multan	2001-02
12-99	Fazal Mahmood	v England at The Oval	1954
12-100	Fazal Mahmood	v West Indies at Dacca	1958-59
12-130	Waqar Younis	v NZ at Faisalabad	1990-91
12-165	Imran Khan	v Australia at Sydney	1976-77

Imran Khan took ten or more wickets in a match six times, Abdul Qadir, Waqar Younis and Wasim Akram five each

Hat-tricks

Wasim Akram	v Sri Lanka at Lahore	1998-99
Wasim Akram	v Sri Lanka at Dhaka	1998-99
Abdul Razzaq	v Sri Lanka at Galle	1999-2000
Mohammad Sami	v Sri Lanka at Lahore	2001-02

Wasim Akram's hat-tricks came in successive matches: he also took Pakistan's first two hat-tricks in one-day internationals.

RS Kaluwitharana was the first victim in both Wasim Akram's first hat-trick and in Abdul Razzaq's

Pakistan's Test match results

	Played	Won	Lost	Drawn	Tied	% win
v Australia	57	12	28	17	0	21.05
v Bangladesh	8	8	0	0	0	100.00
v England	74	16	22	36	0	21.62
v India	59	12	9	38	0	20.33
v New Zealand	50	23	7	20	0	46.00
v South Africa	21	3	11	7	0	14.28
v Sri Lanka	43	16	10	17	0	37.20
v West Indies	46	16	15	15	0	34.78
v Zimbabwe	17	10	3	4	0	58.82
TOTAL	375	116	105	154	0	30.93

Figures to 17.09.13. Updated records can be found at www.cricinfo.com/ci/engine/records

PAKISTAN — One-day International Records

Most appearances

375	Inzamam-ul-Haq
357	Shahid Afridi
356	Wasim Akram
283	Salim Malik
281	Mohammad Yousuf
262	Waqar Younis
261	Abdul Razzaq
253	Younis Khan
250	Ijaz Ahmed
247	Saeed Anwar

Javed Miandad (233), Moin Khan (219) and Shoaib Malik (216) also played in more than 200 ODIs

Most runs

		Avge
11701	Inzamam-ul-Haq	39.53
9554	Mohammad Yousuf	42.08
8824	Saeed Anwar	39.21
7381	Javed Miandad	41.70
7323	Shahid Afridi	23.77
7170	Salim Malik	32.88
7014	Younis Khan	31.88
6564	Ijaz Ahmed	32.33
5841	Rameez Raja	32.09
5490	Shoaib Malik	32.67

Abdul Razzaq (5031) and Aamer Sohail (4780) also scored more than 4000 runs

Most wickets

		Avge
502	Wasim Akram	23.52
416	Waqar Younis	23.84
357	Shahid Afridi	33.96
288	Saqlain Mushtaq	21.78
268	Abdul Razzaq	31.53
241	Shoaib Akhtar	24.70
182	Aqib Javed	31.43
182	Imran Khan	26.61
161	Umar Gul	28.59
161	Mushtaq Ahmed	33.29

Eight further bowlers have taken 100 wickets for Pakistan ODIs

Highest scores

194	Saeed Anwar	v India at Chennai	1996-97
160	Imran Nazir	v Zimbabwe at Kingston	2006-07
144	Younis Khan	v Hong Kong at Colombo	2004
143	Shoaib Malik	v India at Colombo	2004
141*	Mohammad Yousuf	v Zim at Bulawayo	2002-03
140	Saeed Anwar	v India at Dhaka	1997-98
139*	Ijaz Ahmed	v India at Lahore	1997-98
139*	Mohammad Hafeez	v Zimbabwe at Harare	2011
137*	Inzamam-ul-Haq	v N Zealand at Sharjah	1993-94
137	Ijaz Ahmed	v England at Sharjah	1998-99

Saeed Anwar scored 20 centuries, Mohammad Yousuf 15, Ijaz Ahmed and Inzamam-ul-Haq 10

Best innings bowling

7-12	Shahid Afridi	v W Indies at Providence	2013
7-36	Waqar Younis	v England at Leeds	2001
7-37	Aqib Javed	v India at Sharjah	1991-92
6-14	Imran Khan	v India at Sharjah	1984-85
6-16	Shoaib Akhtar	v New Zealand at Karachi	2001-02
6-18	Azhar Mahmood	v W Indies at Sharjah	1999-2000
6-26	Waqar Younis	v Sri Lanka at Sharjah	1989-90
6-27	Naved-ul-Hasan	v India at Jamshedpur	2004-05
6-30	Waqar Younis	v N Zealand at Auckland	1993-94
6-35	Abdul Razzaq	v Bangladesh at Dhaka	2001-02

Waqar Younis took five or more wickets 13 times (the ODI record), Shahid Afridi 9, Saqlain Mushtaq and Wasim Akram 6

Record wicket partnerships

1st	228*	Mohammad Hafeez (139*) and Imran Farhat (75*)	v Zimbabwe at Harare	2011
2nd	263	Aamer Sohail (134) and Inzamam-ul-Haq (137*)	v New Zealand at Sharjah	1993-94
3rd	230	Saeed Anwar (140) and Ijaz Ahmed (117)	v India at Dhaka	1997-98
4th	206	Shoaib Malik (128) and Mohammad Yousuf (87)	v India at Centurion	2009-10
5th	176	Younis Khan (89) and Umar Akmal (102*)	v Sri Lanka at Colombo	2009
6th	144	Imran Khan (102*) and Shahid Mahboob (77)	v Sri Lanka at Leeds	1983
7th	124	Mohammad Yousuf (91*) and Rashid Latif (66)	v Australia at Cardiff	2001
8th	100	Fawad Alam (63*) and Sohail Tanvir (59)	v Hong Kong at Karachi	2008
9th	73	Shoaib Malik (52*) and Mohammad Sami (46)	v South Africa at Centurion	2006-07
10th	103	Mohammad Aamer (73*) and Saeed Ajmal (33)	v New Zealand at Abu Dhabi	2009-10

*Figures to 17.09.13. Updated records can be found at **www.cricinfo.com/ci/engine/records***

One-day International Records — PAKISTAN

Most catches

Fielders

126	Younis Khan	
115	Shahid Afridi	
113	Inzamam-ul-Haq	
90	Ijaz Ahmed	
88	Wasim Akram	

Most dismissals

Wicketkeepers — Ct/St

287	Moin Khan	214/73
220	Rashid Latif	182/38
187	Kamran Akmal	156/31
103	Salim Yousuf	81/22
62	Wasim Bari	52/10

Highest team totals

385-7	v Bangladesh at Dambulla	2010
371-9	v Sri Lanka at Nairobi	1996-97
353-6	v England at Karachi	2005-06
351-4	v South Africa at Durban	2006-07
349	v Zimbabwe at Kingston	2006-07
347-5	v Zimbabwe at at Karachi	2007-08
344-5	v Zimbabwe at Bulawayo	2002-03
344-8	v India at Karachi	2003-04
343-5	v Hong Kong at Colombo	2004
338-5	v Sri Lanka at Swansea	1983

Pakistan have reached 300 on 45 further occasions

Lowest team totals

Completed innings

43	v W Indies at Cape Town	1992-93
71	v W Indies at Brisbane	1992-93
74	v England at Adelaide	1991-92
75	v Sri Lanka at Lahore	2008-09
81	v West Indies at Sydney	1992-93
85	v England at Manchester	1978
87	v India at Sharjah	1984-85
89	v S Africa at Mohali	2006-07
107	v S Africa at Cape Town	2006-07
108	v Australia at Nairobi	2002-03

Against India in 1984-85 Pakistan were chasing only 126 to win

Most sixes

315	Shahid Afridi
143	Inzamam-ul-Haq
124	Abdul Razzaq
121	Wasim Akram
97	Saeed Anwar
87	Ijaz Ahmed
87	Mohammad Yousuf
61	Moin Khan
61	Shoaib Malik
58	Misbah-ul-Haq

Afridi hit 2 other sixes in official ODIs

Best strike rate

Runs per 100 balls		Runs
114.65	Shahid Afridi	7323
89.60	Manzoor Elahi	741
88.33	Wasim Akram	3717
85.73	Umar Akmal	2176
84.80	Zaheer Abbas	2572
84.51	Naved-ul-Hasan	524
83.83	Kamran Akmal	3168
81.67	Abdul Razzaq	5031
81.30	Moin Khan	3266
81.01	Imran Nazir	1895

Qualification: 500 runs

Most economical bowlers

Runs per over		Wkts
3.63	Sarfraz Nawaz	63
3.71	Akram Raza	38
3.89	Imran Khan	182
3.89	Wasim Akram	502
4.00	Mohammad Hafeez	104
4.06	Abdul Qadir	132
4.14	Arshad Khan	56
4.14	Tauseef Ahmed	55
4.17	Saeed Ajmal	146
4.24	Mudassar Nazar	111

Qualification: 2000 balls bowled

Pakistan's one-day international results

	Played	Won	Lost	Tied	No result	% win
v Australia	89	31	54	1	3	36.62
v Bangladesh	31	30	1	0	0	96.77
v England	72	28	42	0	2	40.00
v India	125	71	50	0	4	58.67
v New Zealand	89	51	35	1	2	59.19
v South Africa	63	20	42	0	1	32.25
v Sri Lanka	132	77	50	1	4	60.54
v West Indies	126	55	68	3	0	44.84
v Zimbabwe	47	42	3	1	1	92.39
v others (see below)	25	23	1	1	0	94.00
TOTAL	**799**	**428**	**346**	**8**	**17**	**55.24**

Other teams: Afghanistan (P1, W1), Canada (P2, W2), Hong Kong (P2, W2), Ireland (P5, W3, T1, L1), Kenya (P6, W6), Namibia (P1, W1), Netherlands (P3, W3), Scotland (P3, W3), United Arab Emirates (P2, W2).

SOUTH AFRICA *Test Match Records*

Most appearances

161	JH Kallis	
146	MV Boucher	
109	GC Smith	
108	SM Pollock	
101	G Kirsten	
101	M Ntini	
90	HH Gibbs	
85	AB de Villiers	
72	AA Donald	
70	HM Amla	
70	DJ Cullinan	

Kallis, Boucher and Smith all also played one Test for the World XI

Most runs

		Avge
13045	JH Kallis	55.98
8741	GC Smith	49.10
7289	G Kirsten	45.27
6364	AB de Villiers	50.50
6167	HH Gibbs	41.95
5785	HM Amla	52.11
5498	MV Boucher	30.54
4554	DJ Cullinan	44.21
3781	SM Pollock	32.31
3714	WJ Cronje	36.41

Kallis (83 runs), Smith (12) and Boucher (17) also played one Test for the World XI against Australia

Most wickets

		Avge
421	SM Pollock	23.11
390	M Ntini	28.82
332	DW Steyn	22.65
330	AA Donald	22.25
287	JH Kallis	32.41
175	M Morkel	29.97
170	HJ Tayfield	25.91
134	PR Adams	32.87
123	TL Goddard	26.22
123	A Nel	31.86

Four other bowlers have taken 100 wickets. Kallis also took one wicket for the World XI

Highest scores

311*	HM Amla	v England at The Oval	2012
278*	AB de Villiers	v Pakistan at Abu Dhabi	2010-11
277	GC Smith	v England at Birmingham	2003
275*	DJ Cullinan	v New Zealand at Auckland	1998-99
275	G Kirsten	v England at Durban	1999-2000
274	RG Pollock	v Australia at Durban	1969-70
259	GC Smith	v England at Lord's	2003
255*	DJ McGlew	v New Zealand at Wellington	1952-53
253*	HM Amla	v India at Nagpur	2009-10
236	EAB Rowan	v England at Leeds	1951

Smith's 277 and 259 were in consecutive matches

Best innings bowling

9-113	HJ Tayfield	v England at Johannesburg	1956-57
8-53	GB Lawrence	v N Zealand at Johannesburg	1961-62
8-64	L Klusener	v India at Calcutta	1996-97
8-69	HJ Tayfield	v England at Durban	1956-57
8-70	SJ Snooke	v England at Johannesburg	1905-06
8-71	AA Donald	v Zimbabwe at Harare	1995-96
7-23	HJ Tayfield	v Australia at Durban	1949-50
7-29	GF Bissett	v England at Durban	1927-28
7-29	KJ Abbott	v Pakistan at Centurion	2012-13
7-37	M Ntini	v W Indies at Port-of-Spain	2004-05

Klusener and Abbott were making their Test debuts

Record wicket partnerships

1st	415	ND McKenzie (226) and GC Smith (232)	v Bangladesh at Chittagong	2007-08
2nd	315*	HH Gibbs (211*) and JH Kallis (148*)	v New Zealand at Christchurch	1998-99
3rd	429*	JA Rudolph (222*) and HH Dippenaar (177*)	v Bangladesh at Chittagong	2002-03
4th	249	JH Kallis (177) and G Kirsten (137)	v West Indies at Durban	2003-04
5th	267	JH Kallis (147) and AG Prince (131)	v West Indies at St John's	2004-05
6th	271	AG Prince (162*) and MV Boucher (117)	v Bangladesh at Centurion	2008-09
7th	246	DJ McGlew (255*) and ARA Murray (109)	v New Zealand at Wellington	1952-53
8th	150	ND McKenzie (103) and SM Pollock (111)	v Sri Lanka at Centurion	2000-01
	150	G Kirsten (130) and M Zondeki (59)	v England at Leeds	2003
9th	195	MV Boucher (78) and PL Symcox (108)	v Pakistan at Johannesburg	1997-98
10th	107*	AB de Villiers (278*) and M Morkel (35*)	v Pakistan at Abu Dhabi	2010-11

Figures to 17.09.13. Updated records can be found at **www.cricinfo.com/ci/engine/records**

Test Match Records — SOUTH AFRICA

Most catches

Fielders

190	JH Kallis	
157	GC Smith	
94	HH Gibbs	
89	AB de Villiers	
83	G Kirsten	

Most dismissals

Wicketkeepers — Ct/St

553	MV Boucher	530/23
152	DJ Richardson	150/2
141	JHB Waite	124/17
56	DT Lindsay	54/2
55	AB de Villiers	53/2

Highest team totals

682-6d	v England at Lord's	2003
658-9d	v West Indies at Durban	2003-04
651	v Australia at Cape Town	2008-09
637-2d	v England at The Oval	2012
622-9d	v Australia at Durban	1969-70
621-5d	v New Zealand at Auckland	1998-99
620-4d	v India at Centurion	2010-11
620-7d	v Pakistan at Cape Town	2002-03
620	v Australia at Johannesburg	1966-67
604-6d	v West Indies at Centurion	2003-04

South Africa also scored 600-3d against Zimbabwe at Harare in 2001-02

Lowest team totals

Completed innings

30	v Eng at Port Elizabeth	1895-96
30	v Eng at Birmingham	1924
35	v Eng at Cape Town	1898-99
36	v Aust at Melbourne	1931-32
43	v Eng at Cape Town	1888-89
45	v Aust at Melbourne	1931-32
47	v Eng at Cape Town	1888-89
58	v England at Lord's	1912
72	v Eng at Johannesburg	1956-57
72	v Eng at Cape Town	1956-57

South Africa's lowest total since their return to Test cricket in 1991-92 is 84 against India at Johannesburg in 2006-07

Best match bowling

13-132	M Ntini	v W Indies at Port-of-Spain	2004-05
13-165	HJ Tayfield	v Australia at Melbourne	1952-53
13-192	HJ Tayfield	v England at Johannesburg	1956-57
12-127	SJ Snooke	v England at Johannesburg	1905-06
12-139	AA Donald	v India at Port Elizabeth	1992-93
12-181	AEE Vogler	v England at Johannesburg	1909-10
11-60	DW Steyn	v Pakistan at Jo'burg	2012-13
11-112	AE Hall	v England at Cape Town	1922-23
11-113	AA Donald	v Zimbabwe at Harare	1995-96
11-127	AA Donald	v England at Jo'burg	1999-2000

Hall was making his Test debut

Hat-tricks

GM Griffin	v England at Lord's	1960

Griffin achieved the feat in his second and final Test (he was no-balled for throwing in the same match).

GA Lohmann (for England at Port Elizabeth in 1895-96), TJ Matthews (twice in the same match for Australia at Manchester in 1912) and TWJ Goddard (for England at Johannesburg in 1938-39) have taken Test hat-tricks against South Africa

South Africa's Test match results

	Played	Won	Lost	Drawn	Tied	% win
v Australia	88	20	48	20	0	22.72
v Bangladesh	8	8	0	0	0	100.00
v England	141	31	56	54	0	21.98
v India	27	12	7	8	0	44.44
v New Zealand	40	23	4	13	0	57.50
v Pakistan	21	11	3	7	0	52.38
v Sri Lanka	20	10	5	5	0	50.00
v West Indies	25	16	3	6	0	64.00
v Zimbabwe	7	6	0	1	0	85.71
TOTAL	377	137	126	114	0	36.33

Figures to 17.09.13. Updated records can be found at www.cricinfo.com/ci/engine/records

SOUTH AFRICA One-day International Records

Most appearances

316	JH Kallis	
294	SM Pollock	
290	MV Boucher	
248	HH Gibbs	
245	JN Rhodes	
192	GC Smith	
188	WJ Cronje	
185	G Kirsten	
172	M Ntini	
171	L Klusener	

Kallis, Pollock, Boucher, Ntini and Smith also appeared in official ODIs for composite teams

Most runs

		Avge
11469	JH Kallis	46.06
8094	HH Gibbs	36.13
6942	GC Smith	38.78
6798	G Kirsten	40.95
5935	JN Rhodes	35.11
5667	AB de Villiers	49.71
5565	WJ Cronje	38.64
4523	MV Boucher	28.44
3860	DJ Cullinan	32.99
3675	HM Amla	54.85

Kallis (29 runs), Smith (0), de Villiers (150) and Boucher (163) also appeared in official ODIs for composite teams

Most wickets

		Avge
387	SM Pollock	24.31
272	AA Donald	21.78
266	JH Kallis	31.75
265	M Ntini	24.53
192	L Klusener	29.95
114	WJ Cronje	34.78
106	A Nel	27.68
100	CK Langeveldt	29.62
100	DW Steyn	29.24
95	N Boje	35.27
95	PS de Villiers	27.74
95	AJ Hall	26.47

Pollock, Ntini, Kallis and Boje also appeared in ODIs for composite teams

Highest scores

188*	G Kirsten	v UAE at Rawalpindi	1995-96
175	HH Gibbs	v Australia at Johannesburg	2005-06
169*	DJ Callaghan	v N Zealand at Verwoerdburg	1994-95
161	AC Hudson	v Netherlands at Rawalpindi	1995-96
153	HH Gibbs	v B'desh at Potchefstroom	2002-03
150*	JP Duminy	v Netherlands at Amstelveen	2013
150	HM Amla	v England at Southampton	2012
147*	MV Boucher	v Zimbabwe at Potchefstroom	2006-07
146	AB de Villiers	v West Indies at St George's	2006-07
143	HH Gibbs	v N Zealand at Johannesburg	2002-03

Gibbs has scored 21 one-day hundreds, Kallis 17, de Villiers 14, Kirsten 13, Amla 11 and Smith 10

Best bowling figures

6-22	M Ntini	v Australia at Cape Town	2005-06
6-23	AA Donald	v Kenya at Nairobi	1996-97
6-35	SM Pollock	v W Indies at East London	1998-99
6-49	L Klusener	v Sri Lanka at Lahore	1997-98
5-18	AJ Hall	v England at Bridgetown	2006-07
5-20	SM Pollock	v Eng at Johannesburg	1999-2000
5-21	L Klusener	v Kenya at Amstelveen	1999
5-21	N Boje	v Australia at Cape Town	2001-02
5-21	M Ntini	v Pakistan at Mohali	2006-07
5-23	SM Pollock	v Pakistan at Johannesburg	2006-07

Klusener has taken five wickets in an ODI innings six times, Pollock five and Ntini four

Record wicket partnerships

1st	235	G Kirsten (115) and HH Gibbs (111)	v India at Kochi	1999-2000
2nd	209	G Kirsten (124) and ND McKenzie (131*)	v Kenya at Cape Town	2001-02
3rd	238	HM Amla (122) and AB de Villiers (128)	v Pakistan at Johannesburg	2012-13
4th	232	DJ Cullinan (124) and JN Rhodes (121)	v Pakistan at Nairobi	1996-97
5th	183*	JH Kallis (109*) and JN Rhodes (94*)	v Pakistan at Durban	1997-98
6th	137	WJ Cronje (70*) and SM Pollock (75)	v Zimbabwe at Johannesburg	1996-97
7th	114	MV Boucher (68) and L Klusener (75*)	v India at Nagpur	1999-2000
8th	138*	JM Kemp (100*) and AJ Hall (56*)	v India at Cape Town	2006-07
9th	95	DA Miller (56*) and RK Kleinveldt (43)	v England at The Oval	2013
10th	67*	JA Morkel (23*) and M Ntini (42*)	v New Zealand at Napier	2003-04

Figures to 17.09.13. Updated records can be found at www.cricinfo.com/ci/engine/records

One-day International Records **SOUTH AFRICA**

Most catches

Fielders

125	JH Kallis	
108	HH Gibbs	
105	JN Rhodes	
104	SM Pollock	
103	GC Smith	

Most dismissals

Wicketkeepers   *Ct/St*

415	MV Boucher	394/21
165	DJ Richardson	148/17
84	AB de Villiers	81/3
9	SJ Palframan	9/0
8	MN van Wyk	7/1

Highest team totals

438-9	v Australia at Johannesburg	2005-06
418-5	v Zimbabwe at Potchefstroom	2006-07
399-6	v Zimbabwe at Benoni	2010-11
392-6	v Pakistan at Centurion	2006-07
365-2	v India at Ahmedabad	2009-10
363-3	v Zimbabwe at Bulawayo	2001-02
358-4	v Bangladesh at Benoni	2008-09
356-4	v West Indies at St George's	2006-07
354-3	v Kenya at Cape Town	2001-02
354-6	v England at Cape Town	2009-10

438-9 was the highest total in all ODIs at the time, and came from 49.5 overs; all the others above were scored in 50 overs, apart from 353-3 (40)

Lowest team totals

Completed innings

69	v Australia at Sydney	1993-94
83	v England at Nottingham	2008
101*	v Pakistan at Sharjah	1999-2000
106	v Australia at Sydney	2001-02
107	v England at Lord's	2003
107	v England at Lord's	2003
108	v NZ at Mumbai	2006-07
119	v Eng at Port Elizabeth	2009-10
123	v Aust at Wellington	1994-95
129	v Eng at East London	1995-96
129	v Aust at Centurion	2011-12

* One batsman retired hurt

Most sixes

136	JH Kallis
128	HH Gibbs
94	WJ Cronje
91	AB de Villiers
81	MV Boucher
76	L Klusener
55	SM Pollock
52	JM Kemp
47	JN Rhodes
44	GC Smith

de Villiers (4), Boucher (2), Pollock (3) and Kemp (1) and also hit sixes for the Africa XI

Best strike rate

Runs per 100 balls   *Runs*

101.33	JA Morkel	760
100.32	DA Miller	618
93.03	AB de Villiers	5667
91.19	HM Amla	3675
89.91	L Klusener	3576
89.29	N Boje	1410
88.79	F du Plessis	967
85.55	SM Pollock	3193
84.66	MV Boucher	4523
83.84	JP Duminy	2959

Qualification: 500 runs

Most economical bowlers

Runs per over   *Wkts*

3.57	PS de Villiers	95
3.65	SM Pollock	387
3.94	CR Matthews	79
4.15	AA Donald	272
4.15	PL Symcox	72
4.28	BM McMillan	70
4.44	WJ Cronje	114
4.50	RP Snell	44
4.51	N Boje	95
4.51	AJ Hall	95
4.51	M Ntini	265

Qualification: 2000 balls bowled

South Africa's one-day international results

	Played	Won	Lost	Tied	No result	% win
v Australia	80	36	41	3	0	46.87
v Bangladesh	14	13	1	0	0	92.85
v England	51	25	22	1	3	53.12
v India	67	40	25	0	2	61.53
v New Zealand	58	34	20	0	4	62.96
v Pakistan	63	42	20	0	1	67.74
v Sri Lanka	56	26	28	1	1	48.18
v West Indies	52	38	12	1	1	75.49
v Zimbabwe	32	29	2	0	1	93.54
v others (see below)	20	20	0	0	0	100.00
TOTAL	**493**	**303**	**171**	**6**	**13**	**63.75**

Other teams: Canada (P1, W1), Ireland (P3, W3), Kenya (P10, W10), Netherlands (P4, W4), Scotland (P1, W1), United Arab Emirates (P1, W1).

SRI LANKA — Test Match Records

Most appearances

138	DPMD Jayawardene	
132	M Muralitharan	
117	KC Sangakkara	
111	WPUJC Vaas	
110	ST Jayasuriya	
93	PA de Silva	
93	A Ranatunga	
90	MS Atapattu	
87	TM Dilshan	
83	HP Tillekeratne	

Ranatunga uniquely played in his country's first Test and their 100th

Most runs

		Avge
10806	DPMD Jayawardene	49.56
10486	KC Sangakkara	56.98
6973	ST Jayasuriya	40.07
6361	PA de Silva	42.97
5502	MS Atapattu	39.02
5492	TM Dilshan	40.98
5462	TT Samaraweera	48.76
5105	A Ranatunga	35.69
4545	HP Tillekeratne	42.87
3089	WPUJC Vaas	24.32

RS Mahanama (2576) and AP Gurusinha (2452) also scored 2000 runs

Most wickets

		Avge
795	M Muralitharan	22.67
355	WPUJC Vaas	29.58
200	HMRKB Herath	29.52
101	SL Malinga	33.15
100	CRD Fernando	37.84
98	ST Jayasuriya	34.34
85	GP Wickremasinghe	41.87
73	RJ Ratnayake	35.10
69	HDPK Dharmasena	42.31
64	BAW Mendis	34.20
64	DNT Zoysa	33.70

Muralitharan also took 5 for the World XI

Highest scores

374	DPMD Jayawardene	v SA at Colombo	2006
340	ST Jayasuriya	v India at Colombo	1997-98
287	KC Sangakkara	v SA at Colombo	2006
275	DPMD Jayawardene	v Ind at Ahmedabad	2009-10
270	KC Sangakkara	v Zim at Bulawayo	2003-04
267	PA de Silva	v NZ at Wellington	1990-91
253	ST Jayasuriya	v Pak at Faisalabad	2004-05
249	MS Atapattu	v Zim at Bulawayo	2003-04
242	DPMD Jayawardene	v India at Colombo	1998-99
240	DPMD Jayawardene	v Pak at Karachi	2008-09

Sangakkara has made 33 Test centuries, Jayawardene 31, de Silva 20, Atapattu and TM Dilshan 16

Best innings bowling

9-51	M Muralitharan	v Zimbabwe at Kandy	2001-02
9-65	M Muralitharan	v England at The Oval	1998
8-46	M Muralitharan	v West Indies at Kandy	2005
8-70	M Muralitharan	v England at Nottingham	2006
8-83	JR Ratnayeke	v Pakistan at Sialkot	1985-86
8-87	M Muralitharan	v India at Colombo	2001-02
7-46	M Muralitharan	v England at Galle	2003-04
7-71	WPUJC Vaas	v West Indies at Colombo	2001-02
7-84	M Muralitharan	v South Africa at Galle	2000-01
7-89	HMRKB Herath	v Bangladesh at Colombo	2012-13

Muralitharan took five or more wickets in an innings a record 67 times

Record wicket partnerships

1st	335	MS Atapattu (207*) and ST Jayasuriya (188)	v Pakistan at Kandy	2000
2nd	576	ST Jayasuriya (340) and RS Mahanama (225)	v India at Colombo	1997-98
3rd	624	KC Sangakkara (287) and DPMD Jayawardene (374)	v South Africa at Colombo	2006
4th	437	DPMD Jayawardene (240) and TT Samaraweera (231)	v Pakistan at Karachi	2008-09
5th	280	TT Samaraweera (138) and TM Dilshan (168)	v Bangladesh at Colombo	2005-06
6th	351	DPMD Jayawardene (275) and HAPW Jayawardene (154*)	v India at Ahmedabad	2009-10
7th	223*	HAPW Jayawardene (120*) and WPUJC Vaas (100*)	v Bangladesh at Colombo	2007
8th	170	DPMD Jayawardene (237) and WPUJC Vaas (69)	v South Africa at Galle	2004-05
9th	118	TT Samaraweera (83) and BAW Mendis (78)	v India at Colombo	2010
10th	79	WPUJC Vaas (68*) and M Muralitharan (43)	v Australia at Kandy	2003-04

Figures to 17.09.13. Updated records can be found at **www.cricinfo.com/ci/engine/records**

Test Match Records — SRI LANKA

Most catches

Fielders
194	DPMD Jayawardene	
89	HP Tillekeratne	
78	ST Jayasuriya	
77	TM Dilshan	
70	M Muralitharan	

Highest team totals

952-6d	v India at Colombo	1997-98
760-7d	v India at Ahmedabad	2009-10
756-5d	v South Africa at Colombo	2006
713-3d	v Zimbabwe at Bulawayo	2003-04
644-7d	v Pakistan at Karachi	2008-09
642-4d	v India at Colombo	2010
628-8d	v England at Colombo	2003-04
627-9d	v West Indies at Colombo	2001-02
610-6d	v India at Colombo	2001-02
606	v Pakistan at Lahore	2008-09

952-6d is the highest total in all Tests. In all Sri Lanka have reached 500 on 28 occasions

Lowest team totals

Completed innings
71	v Pakistan at Kandy	1994-95
73*	v Pakistan at Kandy	2005-06
81	v England at Colombo	2000-01
82	v India at Chandigarh	1990-91
82	v England at Cardiff	2011
93	v NZ at Wellington	1982-83
95	v S Africa at Cape Town	2000-01
97	v N Zealand at Kandy	1983-84
97	v Australia at Darwin	2004
101	v Pakistan at Kandy	1985-86

* One batsman absent hurt

Most dismissals

Wicketkeepers — Ct/St
151	KC Sangakkara	131/20
129	HAPW Jayawardene	97/32
119	RS Kaluwitharana	93/26
35	HP Tillekeratne	33/2
34	SAR Silva	33/1

Best match bowling

16-220	M Muralitharan	v England at The Oval	1998
14-191	WPUJC Vaas	v West Indies at Colombo	2001-02
13-115	M Muralitharan	v Zimbabwe at Kandy	2001-02
13-171	M Muralitharan	v South Africa at Galle	2000
12-82	M Muralitharan	v Bangladesh at Kandy	2007
12-117	M Muralitharan	v Zimbabwe at Kandy	1997-98
12-157	HMRKB Herath	v Bangladesh at Colombo	2012-13
12-171	HMRKB Herath	v England at Galle	2011-12
12-225	M Muralitharan	v South Africa at Colombo	2006
11-93	M Muralitharan	v England at Galle	2003-04

Muralitharan took ten or more wickets in a match a record 22 times; the only others to do it for Sri Lanka are Herath (3), Vaas (2), UDU Chandana and BAW Mendis

Hat-tricks

DNT Zoysa	v Zimbabwe at Harare	1999-2000

He dismissed TR Gripper, MW Goodwin and NC Johnson with the first three balls of his first over, the second of the match.

Four hat-tricks have been taken against Sri Lanka in Tests, all of them for Pakistan: two by Wasim Akram (in successive Tests in the Asian Test Championship at Lahore and Dhaka in 1998-99), Abdul Razzaq (at Galle in 2000-01) and Mohammad Sami (at Lahore in 2001-02)

Sri Lanka's Test match results

	Played	Won	Lost	Drawn	Tied	% win
v Australia	26	1	17	8	0	3.84
v Bangladesh	14	13	0	1	0	92.85
v England	26	7	10	9	0	26.92
v India	35	6	14	15	0	17.14
v New Zealand	28	8	10	10	0	28.57
v Pakistan	43	10	16	17	0	23.25
v South Africa	20	5	10	5	0	25.00
v West Indies	15	6	3	6	0	40.00
v Zimbabwe	15	10	0	5	0	66.66
TOTAL	**222**	**66**	**80**	**76**	**0**	**29.72**

Figures to 17.09.13. Updated records can be found at www.cricinfo.com/ci/engine/records

SRI LANKA — *One-day International Records*

Most appearances

441	ST Jayasuriya	
399	DPMD Jayawardene	
347	KC Sangakkara	
343	M Muralitharan	
321	WPUJC Vaas	
308	PA de Silva	
269	A Ranatunga	
268	MS Atapattu	
267	TM Dilshan	
213	RS Mahanama	

HP Tillekeratne also played 200 ODIs

Most runs

		Avge
13664	ST Jayasuriya	32.51
11539	KC Sangakkara	39.92
11085	DPMD Jayawardene	32.99
9284	PA de Silva	34.90
8529	MS Atapattu	37.57
7643	TM Dilshan	37.46
7456	A Ranatunga	35.84
5218	WU Tharanga	34.10
5162	RS Mahanama	29.49
3950	RP Arnold	35.26

AP Gurusinha (3902), HP Tillekeratne (3789) and RS Kaluwitharana (3711) also scored 3000 runs

Most wickets

		Avge
523	M Muralitharan	23.07
399	WPUJC Vaas	27.45
320	ST Jayasuriya	36.67
235	SL Malinga	26.53
183	CRD Fernando	30.66
154	KMDN Kulasekara	32.86
151	UDU Chandana	31.72
138	HDPK Dharmasena	36.21
133	MF Maharoof	26.80
109	BAW Mendis	20.82
109	GP Wickremasinghe	39.64

DNT Zoysa (108) and PA de Silva (106) also took 100 wickets

Highest scores

189	ST Jayasuriya	v India at Sharjah	2000-01
174*	WU Tharanga	v India at Kingston	2013
169	KC Sangakkara	v South Africa at Colombo	2013
160*	TM Dilshan	v India at Hobart	2011-12
160	TM Dilshan	v India at Rajkot	2009-10
157	ST Jayasuriya	v Netherlands at Amstelveen	2006
152	ST Jayasuriya	v England at Leeds	2006
151*	ST Jayasuriya	v India at Mumbai	1996-97
145	PA de Silva	v Kenya at Kandy	1995-96
144	TM Dilshan	v Zimbabwe at Pallekele	2010-11
144	DPMD J'dene	v England at Leeds	2011

Jayasuriya scored 28 centuries, Dilshan 17, Sangakkara 16, Jayawardene 15 and Tharanga 13

Best bowling figures

8-19	WPUJC Vaas	v Zimbabwe at Colombo	2001-02
7-30	M Muralitharan	v India at Sharjah	2000-01
6-13	BAW Mendis	v India at Karachi	2008
6-14	MF Maharoof	v West Indies at Mumbai	2006-07
6-20	AD Mathews	v India at Colombo	2008-09
6-25	WPUJC Vaas	v B'desh at P'maritzburg	2002-03
6-27	CRD Fernando	v England at Colombo	2007-08
6-29	ST Jayasuriya	v England at Moratuwa	1992-93
6-29	BAW Mendis	v Zimbabwe at Harare	2008-09
6-38	SL Malinga	v Kenya at Colombo	2010-11

Vaas's 8-19 are the best bowling figures in all ODIs. In his 6-25 Vaas took a hat-trick with the first three balls of the match, and four wickets in all in the first over

Record wicket partnerships

1st	286	WU Tharanga (109) and ST Jayasuriya (152)	v England at Leeds	2006
2nd	200	TM Dilshan (160*) and KC Sangakkara (105)	v India at Hobart	2011-12
3rd	226	MS Atapattu (102*) and DPMD Jayawardene (128)	v India at Sharjah	2000-01
4th	171*	RS Mahanama (94*) and A Ranatunga (87*)	v West Indies at Lahore	1997-98
5th	166	ST Jayasuriya (189) and RP Arnold (52*)	v India at Sharjah	2000-01
6th	159	LPC Silva (67) and CK Kapugedera (95)	v West Indies at Port-of-Spain	2007-08
7th	126*	DPMD Jayawardene (94*) and UDU Chandana (44*)	v India at Dambulla	2005-06
8th	91	HDPK Dharmasena (51*) and DK Liyanage (43)	v West Indies at Port-of-Spain	1996-97
9th	132	AD Mathews (77*) and SL Malinga (56)	v Australia at Melbourne	2010-11
10th	51	RP Arnold (103) and KSC de Silva (2*)	v Zimbabwe at Bulawayo	1999-2000

Figures to 17.09.13. Updated records can be found at www.cricinfo.com/ci/engine/records

One-day International Records — SRI LANKA

Most catches

Fielders

195	DPMD Jayawardene	
128	M Muralitharan	
123	ST Jayasuriya	
109	RS Mahanama	
96	TM Dilshan	

Most dismissals

Wicketkeepers — Ct/St

410	KC Sangakkara	328/82
206	RS Kaluwitharana	131/75
45	HP Tillekeratne	39/6
34	DSBP Kuruppu	26/8
30	RG de Alwis	27/3

Highest team totals

443-9	v Netherlands at Amstelveen	2006
411-8	v India at Rajkot	2009-10
398-5	v Kenya at Kandy	1995-96
357-9	v Bangladesh at Lahore	2008
349-9	v Pakistan at Singapore	1995-96
348-1	v India at Kingston	2013
343-5	v Australia at Sydney	2002-03
339-4	v Pakistan at Mohali	1996-97
332-7	v Canada at Hambantota	2010-11
332-8	v Bangladesh at Karachi	2008

Sri Lanka scored 324-2 in 37.3 overs against England at Leeds in 2006

Lowest team totals

Completed innings

43	v S Africa at Paarl	2011-12
55	v W Indies at Sharjah	1986-87
78*	v Pakistan at Sharjah	2001-02
86	v W Indies at Manchester	1975
91	v Australia at Adelaide	1984-85
96	v India at Sharjah	1983-84
96	v India at Port-of-Spain	2013
98	v S Africa at Colombo	1993-94
98	v India at Sharjah	1998-99
99	v England at Perth	1998-99

* One batsman absent hurt

Most sixes

268	ST Jayasuriya
102	PA de Silva
65	KC Sangakkara
64	A Ranatunga
62	DPMD Jayawardene
46	TM Dilshan
42	AP Gurusinha
28	WU Tharanga
27	CK Kapugedera
26	KMDN Kulasekara
26	AD Mathews

Jayasuriya also hit 2 for the Asia XI

Best strike rate

Runs per 100 balls — Runs

109.56	NLTC Perera	630
91.25	ST Jayasuriya	13364
86.80	RJ Ratnayake	612
86.15	TM Dilshan	7643
84.44	MF Maharoof	1042
82.18	AD Mathews	2048
81.69	KMDN Kulasekara	1004
81.13	PA de Silva	9284
78.04	DPMD Jayawardene	11085
77.90	A Ranatunga	7456

Qualification: 500 runs

Most economical bowlers

Runs per over — Wkts

3.92	M Muralitharan	523
4.18	WPUJC Vaas	399
4.18	SD Anurasiri	32
4.19	HMRKB Herath	51
4.27	HDPK Dharmasena	138
4.29	VB John	34
4.29	CPH Ramanayake	68
4.40	BAW Mendis	109
4.50	DS de Silva	32
4.50	RS Kalpage	73

Qualification: 2000 balls bowled

Sri Lanka's one-day international results

	Played	Won	Lost	Tied	No result	% win
v Australia	90	31	55	0	4	36.04
v Bangladesh	33	28	4	0	1	87.50
v England	51	25	26	0	0	49.01
v India	143	53	78	1	11	40.53
v New Zealand	79	37	36	1	5	50.67
v Pakistan	132	50	77	1	4	39.45
v South Africa	56	28	26	1	1	51.81
v West Indies	51	21	27	0	3	43.75
v Zimbabwe	47	39	7	0	1	84.78
v others (see below)	16	15	1	0	0	93.75
TOTAL	**698**	**327**	**337**	**4**	**30**	**49.25**

Other teams: Bermuda (P1, W1), Canada (P2, W2), Ireland (P1, W1), Kenya (P6, W5, L1), Netherlands (P3, W3), Scotland (P1, W1), United Arab Emirates (P2, W2).

WEST INDIES — *Test Match Records*

Most appearances

148	S Chanderpaul	
132	CA Walsh	
130	BC Lara	
121	IVA Richards	
116	DL Haynes	
110	CH Lloyd	
108	CG Greenidge	
102	CL Hooper	
98	CEL Ambrose	
97	CH Gayle	

GS Sobers (next on the list with 93 caps) played 85 successive Tests between 1954-55 and 1971-72

Most runs

		Avge
11912	BC Lara	53.17
10830	S Chanderpaul	57.81
8540	IVA Richards	50.23
8032	GS Sobers	57.78
7558	CG Greenidge	44.72
7515	CH Lloyd	46.67
7487	DL Haynes	42.29
6836	CH Gayle	42.45
6227	RB Kanhai	47.53
5949	RB Richardson	44.39

Greenidge and Haynes put on 6482 runs together, the Test record by any pair of opening batsmen

Most wickets

		Avge
519	CA Walsh	24.44
405	CEL Ambrose	20.99
376	MD Marshall	20.94
309	LR Gibbs	29.09
259	J Garner	20.97
249	MA Holding	23.68
235	GS Sobers	34.03
202	AME Roberts	25.61
192	WW Hall	26.38
165	FH Edwards	37.87

In all 18 West Indians have reached 100 Test wickets

Highest scores

400*	BC Lara	v England at St John's	2003-04
375	BC Lara	v England at St John's	1993-94
365*	GS Sobers	v Pakistan at Kingston	1957-58
333	CH Gayle	v Sri Lanka at Galle	2010-11
317	CH Gayle	v South Africa at St John's	2004-05
302	LG Rowe	v England at Bridgetown	1973-74
291	IVA Richards	v England at The Oval	1976
291	RR Sarwan	v England at Bridgetown	2008-09
277	BC Lara	v Australia at Sydney	1992-93
270*	GA Headley	v England at Kingston	1934-35

Lara scored 34 Test centuries, S Chanderpaul 28, Sobers 26, Richards 24, CG Greenidge and CH Lloyd 19

Best innings bowling

9-95	JM Noreiga	v India at Port-of-Spain	1970-71
8-29	CEH Croft	v Pakistan at Port-of-Spain	1976-77
8-38	LR Gibbs	v India at Bridgetown	1961-62
8-45	CEL Ambrose	v England at Bridgetown	1989-90
8-92	MA Holding	v England at The Oval	1976
8-104	AL Valentine	v England at Manchester	1950
7-22	MD Marshall	v England at Manchester	1988
7-25	CEL Ambrose	v Australia at Perth	1992-93
7-37	CA Walsh	v New Zealand at Wellington	1994-95
7-49	S Ramadhin	v England at Birmingham	1957

Valentine was playing in his first Test, Croft and Noreiga in their second

Record wicket partnerships

1st	298	CG Greenidge (149) and DL Haynes (167)	v England at St John's	1989-90
2nd	446	CC Hunte (260) and GS Sobers (365*)	v Pakistan at Kingston	1957-58
3rd	338	ED Weekes (206) and FMM Worrell (167)	v England at Port-of-Spain	1953-54
4th	399	GS Sobers (226) and FMM Worrell (197*)	v England at Bridgetown	1959-60
5th	322	BC Lara (213) and JC Adams (94)	v Australia at Kingston	1998-99
6th	282*	BC Lara (400*) and RD Jacobs (107*)	v England at St John's	2003-04
7th	347	DS Atkinson (219) and CC Depeiaza (122)	v Australia at Bridgetown	1954-55
8th	148	JC Adams (101*) and FA Rose (69)	v Zimbabwe at Kingston	1999-2000
9th	161	CH Lloyd (161*) and AME Roberts (68)	v India at Calcutta	1983-84
10th	143	D Ramdin (107*) and TL Best (95)	v England at Birmingham	2012

Figures to 17.09.13. Updated records can be found at **www.cricinfo.com/ci/engine/records**

Test Match Records — WEST INDIES

Most catches

Fielders
164	BC Lara	
122	IVA Richards	
115	CL Hooper	
109	GS Sobers	
96	CG Greenidge	

Most dismissals

Wicketkeepers		Ct/St
270	PJL Dujon	265/5
219	RD Jacobs	207/12
189	DL Murray	181/8
150	D Ramdin	147/3
101	JR Murray	98/3

Highest team totals

790-3d	v Pakistan at Kingston	1957-58
751-5d	v England at St John's	2003-04
749-9d	v England at Bridgetown	2008-09
747	v South Africa at St John's	2004-05
692-8d	v England at The Oval	1995
687-8d	v England at The Oval	1976
681-8d	v England at Port-of-Spain	1953-54
660-5d	v New Zealand at Wellington	1994-95
652-8d	v England at Lord's	1973
648-9d	v Bangladesh at Khulne	2012-13

West Indies have passed 600 in Tests on ten further occasions, seven of them coming against India

Lowest team totals

Completed innings
47	v England at Kingston	2003-04
51	v Aust at Port-of-Spain	1998-99
53	v Pakistan at Faisalabad	1986-87
54	v England at Lord's	2000
61	v England at Leeds	2000
76	v Pakistan at Dacca	1958-59
77	v NZ at Auckland	1955-56
78	v Australia at Sydney	1951-52
82	v Australia at Brisbane	2000-01
86*	v England at The Oval	1957

One batsman absent hurt. West Indies have been dismissed for less than 100 on seven further occasions

Best match bowling

14-149	MA Holding	v England at The Oval	1976
13-55	CA Walsh	v N Zealand at Wellington	1994-95
12-121	AME Roberts	v India at Madras	1974-75
11-84	CEL Ambrose	v England at Port-of-Spain	1993-94
11-89	MD Marshall	v India at Port-of-Spain	1988-89
11-107	MA Holding	v Australia at Melbourne	1981-82
11-120	MD Marshall	v N Zealand at Bridgetown	1984-85
11-126	WW Hall	v India at Kanpur	1958-59
11-134	CD Collymore	v Pakistan at Kingston	2004-05
11-147	KD Boyce	v England at The Oval	1973

Marshall took ten or more wickets in a Test four times, Ambrose and Walsh three

Hat-tricks

WW Hall	v Pakistan at Lahore	1958-59

The first Test hat-trick not for England or Australia

LR Gibbs	v Australia at Adelaide	1960-61

Gibbs had taken three wickets in four balls in the previous Test, at Sydney

CA Walsh	v Australia at Brisbane	1988-89

The first Test hat-trick to be split over two innings

JJC Lawson	v Australia at Bridgetown	2002-03

Also split over two innings

West Indies' Test match results

	Played	Won	Lost	Drawn	Tied	% win
v Australia	111	32	54	24	1	28.82
v Bangladesh	10	6	2	2	0	60.00
v England	148	53	45	50	0	35.81
v India	88	30	14	44	0	34.09
v New Zealand	39	12	9	18	0	30.76
v Pakistan	46	15	16	15	0	32.60
v South Africa	25	3	16	6	0	12.00
v Sri Lanka	15	3	6	6	0	20.00
v Zimbabwe	8	6	0	2	0	75.00
TOTAL	490	160	162	167	1	32.65

Figures to 17.09.13. Updated records can be found at www.cricinfo.com/ci/engine/records

WEST INDIES *One-day International Records*

Most appearances

295	BC Lara	
268	S Chanderpaul	
251	CH Gayle	
238	DL Haynes	
227	CL Hooper	
224	RB Richardson	
205	CA Walsh	
187	IVA Richards	
181	RR Sarwan	
176	CEL Ambrose	

27 West Indians have played more than 100 ODIs. Lara and Gayle also played for the World XI

Most runs

		Avge
10348	BC Lara	40.90
8778	S Chanderpaul	41.60
8688	CH Gayle	37.93
8648	DL Haynes	41.37
6721	IVA Richards	47.00
6248	RB Richardson	33.41
5804	RR Sarwan	42.67
5761	CL Hooper	35.34
5134	CG Greenidge	45.03
3799	MN Samuels	31.13

Gayle has scored 21 ODI hundreds, Lara 19, Haynes 17, Greenidge, Richards and Chanderpaul 11

Most wickets

		Avge
227	CA Walsh	30.47
225	CEL Ambrose	24.12
193	CL Hooper	36.05
173	DJ Bravo	30.13
157	CH Gayle	35.01
157	MD Marshall	26.96
146	J Garner	18.84
142	MA Holding	21.36
130	M Dillon	32.44
118	IR Bishop	26.50
118	IVA Richards	35.83

WKM Benjamin and RA Harper both took exactly 100 wickets

Highest scores

189*	IVA Richards	v England at Manchester	1984
181	IVA Richards	v Sri Lanka at Karachi	1987-88
169	BC Lara	v Sri Lanka at Sharjah	1995-96
157*	XM Marshall	v Canada at King City	2008-09
156	BC Lara	v Pakistan at Adelaide	2004-05
153*	IVA Richards	v Australia at Melbourne	1979-80
153*	CH Gayle	v Zimbabwe at Bulawayo	2003-04
153	BC Lara	v Pakistan at Sharjah	1993-94
152*	DL Haynes	v India at Georgetown	1988-89
152*	CH Gayle	v S Africa at Johannesburg	2003-04
152	CH Gayle	v Kenya at Nairobi	2001-02

S Chanderpaul scored 150 v SA at East London in 1998-99

Best bowling figures

7-51	WW Davis	v Australia at Leeds	1983
6-15	CEH Croft	v England at Kingstown	1980-81
6-22	FH Edwards	v Zimbabwe at Harare	2003-04
6-27	KAJ Roach	v Netherlands at Delhi	2010-11
6-29	BP Patterson	v India at Nagpur	1987-88
6-41	IVA Richards	v India at Delhi	1989-90
6-43	DJ Bravo	v Zim at St George's	2012-13
6-50	AH Gray	v Aust at Port-of-Spain	1990-91
5-1	CA Walsh	v Sri Lanka at Sharjah	1986-87
5-17	CEL Ambrose	v Australia at Melbourne	1988-89

Edwards's feat was in his first ODI: he also took 5-36 on his Test debut

Record wicket partnerships

1st	200*	SC Williams (78*) and S Chanderpaul (109*)	v India at Bridgetown	1996-97
2nd	221	CG Greenidge (115) and IVA Richards (149)	v India at Jamshedpur	1983-84
3rd	195*	CG Greenidge (105*) and HA Gomes (75*)	v Zimbabwe at Worcester	1983
4th	226	S Chanderpaul (150) and CL Hooper (108)	v South Africa at East London	1998-99
5th	154	CL Hooper (112*) and S Chanderpaul (67)	v Pakistan at Sharjah	2001-02
6th	154	RB Richardson (122) and PJL Dujon (53)	v Pakistan at Sharjah	1991-92
7th	115	PJL Dujon (57*) and MD Marshall (66)	v Pakistan at Gujranwala	1986-87
8th	101	AD Russell (41) and DJG Sammy (84)	v Australia at Gros Islet	2011-12
9th	77	RR Sarwan (65) and IDR Bradshaw (37)	v New Zealand at Christchurch	2005-06
10th	106*	IVA Richards (189*) and MA Holding (12*)	v England at Manchester	1984

Figures to 17.09.13. Updated records can be found at **www.cricinfo.com/ci/engine/records**

One-day International Records — WEST INDIES

Most catches

Fielders

120	CL Hooper	
117	BC Lara	
107	CH Gayle	
100	IVA Richards	
75	RB Richardson	

Most dismissals

Wicketkeepers Ct/St

204	PJL Dujon	183/21
189	RD Jacobs	160/29
137	D Ramdin	131/6
68	CO Browne	59/9
51	CS Baugh	39/12
51	JR Murray	44/7

Highest team totals

360-4	v Sri Lanka at Karachi	1987-88
347-6	v Zimbabwe at Bulawayo	2003-04
339-4	v Pakistan at Adelaide	2004-05
337-4	v Zimbabwe at St George's	2012-13
333-6	v Zimbabwe at Georgetown	2005-06
333-7	v Sri Lanka at Sharjah	1995-96
333-8	v India at Jamshedpur	1983-84
330-8	v Netherlands at Delhi	2010-11
324-4	v India at Ahmedabad	2002-03
324-8	v India at Nagpur	2006-07

All these totals came from 50 overs except the 333-8 at Jamshedpur (45)

Lowest team totals

Completed innings

54	v S Africa at Cape Town	2003-04
61	v B'desh at Chittagong	2011-12
70	v Australia at Perth	2012-13
80	v Sri Lanka at Mumbai	2006-07
87	v Australia at Sydney	1992-93
91	v Zimbabwe at Sydney	2000-01
93	v Kenya at Pune	1995-96
98	v Pakistan at Providence	2013
103	v Pak at Melbourne	1996-97
110	v Australia at Manchester	1999

The 87 was in a match reduced to 30 overs: Australia made 101-9

Most sixes

203	CH Gayle	
133	BC Lara	
126	IVA Richards	
87	KA Pollard	
85	S Chanderpaul	
81	CG Greenidge	
75	RL Powell	
67	MN Samuels	
65	CL Hooper	
61	DJG Sammy	

XM Marshall holds the West Indian record for sixes in an innings (12)

Best strike rate

Runs per 100 balls Runs

119.34	AD Russell	660
99.09	DJG Sammy	1313
96.66	RL Powell	2085
93.78	DR Smith	1102
93.54	KA Pollard	1869
90.20	IVA Richards	6721
84.19	CH Gayle	8688
81.44	J Charles	764
81.22	CH Lloyd	1977
80.77	DJ Bravo	2495

Qualification: 500 runs

Most economical bowlers

Runs per over Wkts

3.09	J Garner	146
3.32	MA Holding	142
3.40	AME Roberts	87
3.48	CEL Ambrose	225
3.53	MD Marshall	157
3.83	CA Walsh	227
3.97	RA Harper	100
4.00	CE Cuffy	41
4.09	EAE Baptiste	36
4.13	SP Narine	60

Qualification: 2000 balls bowled

West Indies' one-day international results

	Played	Won	Lost	Tied	No result	% win
v Australia	135	59	70	3	3	45.83
v Bangladesh	25	16	7	0	2	69.56
v England	85	41	40	0	4	50.61
v India	109	58	48	1	2	54.67
v New Zealand	56	28	21	0	7	57.14
v Pakistan	126	68	55	3	0	55.15
v South Africa	52	12	38	1	1	24.50
v Sri Lanka	51	27	21	0	3	56.25
v Zimbabwe	44	34	9	0	1	79.06
v others (see below)	19	17	1	0	1	89.47
TOTAL	**702**	**360**	**310**	**8**	**24**	**53.68**

Other teams: Bermuda (P1, W1), Canada (P4, W4), Ireland (P4, W3, NR1), Kenya (P6, W5, L1), Netherlands (P2, W2), Scotland (P2, W2).

ZIMBABWE *Test Match Records*

Most appearances

67	GW Flower	
65	HH Streak	
63	A Flower	
60	ADR Campbell	
46	GJ Whittall	
37	SV Carlisle	
30	HK Olonga	
29	DD Ebrahim	
28	T Taibu	
27	CB Wishart	

Zimbabwe played no Test cricket between September 2005 and August 2011

Most runs

		Avge
4794	A Flower	51.54
3457	GW Flower	29.54
2858	ADR Campbell	27.21
2207	GJ Whittall	29.42
1990	HH Streak	22.35
1615	SV Carlisle	26.91
1546	T Taibu	30.31
1464	DL Houghton	43.05
1414	MW Goodwin	42.84
1292	H Masakadza	26.91

BRM Taylor (1260), DD Ebrahim (1225), CB Wishart (1098) and GJ Rennie (1023) also reached 1000 runs

Most wickets

		Avge
216	HH Streak	28.14
80	RW Price	36.06
70	PA Strang	36.02
68	HK Olonga	38.52
56	BC Strang	39.33
53	AM Blignaut	37.05
51	GJ Whittall	40.94
32	M Mbangwa	31.43
30	DH Brain	30.50
30	KM Jarvis	31.73

EA Brandes took 26 wickets, and GW Flower, TJ Friend and AG Huckle all took 25

Highest scores

266	DL Houghton	v Sri Lanka at Bulawayo	1994-95
232*	A Flower	v India at Nagpur	2000-01
203*	GJ Whittall	v New Zealand at Bulawayo	1997-98
201*	GW Flower	v Pakistan at Harare	1994-95
199*	A Flower	v South Africa at Harare	2001-02
188*	GJ Whittall	v New Zealand at Harare	2000-01
183*	A Flower	v India at Delhi	2000-01
171	BRM Taylor	v Bangladesh at Harare	2012-13
166*	MW Goodwin	v Pakistan at Bulawayo	1997-98
163*	TMK Mawoyo	v Pakistan at Bulawayo	2011

Andy Flower scored 12 Test centuries, Grant Flower 6, Houghton, Taylor and Whittall 4

Best innings bowling

8-109	PA Strang	v New Zealand at Bulawayo	2000-01
6-59	DT Hondo	v Bangladesh at Dhaka	2004-05
6-73	RW Price	v West Indies at Harare	2003-04
6-73	HH Streak	v India at Harare	2005-06
6-87	HH Streak	v England at Lord's	2000
6-90	HH Streak	v Pakistan at Harare	1994-95
6-109	AG Huckle	v New Zealand at Bulawayo	1997-98
6-121	RW Price	v Australia at Sydney	2003-04
5-27	HH Streak	v WI at Port-of-Spain	1999-2000
5-31	TJ Friend	v Bangladesh at Dhaka	2001-02

AJ Traicos took 5-86 in Zimbabwe's inaugural Test, against India in 1992-93: he was 45, and had played three Tests for South Africa 22 years previously

Record wicket partnerships

1st	164	DD Ebrahim (71) and ADR Campbell (103)	v West Indies at Bulawayo	2001
2nd	135	MH Dekker (68*) and ADR Campbell (75)	v Pakistan at Rawalpindi	1993-94
3rd	194	ADR Campbell (99) and DL Houghton (142)	v Sri Lanka at Harare	1994-95
4th	269	GW Flower (201*) and A Flower (156)	v Pakistan at Harare	1994-95
5th	277*	MW Goodwin (166*) and A Flower (100*)	v Pakistan at Bulawayo	1997-98
6th	165	DL Houghton (121) and A Flower (59)	v India at Harare	1992-93
7th	154	HH Streak (83*) and AM Blignaut (92)	v West Indies at Harare	2001
8th	168	HH Streak (127*) and AM Blignaut (91)	v West Indies at Harare	2003-04
9th	87	PA Strang (106*) and BC Strang (42)	v Pakistan at Sheikhupura	1996-97
10th	97*	A Flower (183*) and HK Olonga (11*)	v India at Delhi	2000-01

Figures to 17.09.13. Updated records can be found at **www.cricinfo.com/ci/engine/records**

Test Match Records — ZIMBABWE

Most catches

Fielders
- 60 ADR Campbell
- 43 GW Flower
- 34 SV Carlisle
- 19 GJ Whittall
- 17 DL Houghton/ HH Streak/BRM Taylor

Most dismissals

Wicketkeepers		Ct/St
151	A Flower	151/9
60	T Taibu	55/5
16	WR James	16/0
14	R Mutumbami	12/2
5	RW Chakabva	5/0

Highest team totals

563-9d	v West Indies at Harare	2001
544-4d	v Pakistan at Harare	1994-95
542-7d	v Bangladesh at Chittagong	2001-02
507-9d	v West Indies at Harare	2003-04
503-6	v India at Nagpur	2000-01
462-9d	v Sri Lanka at Bulawayo	1994-95
461	v New Zealand at Bulawayo	1997-98
457	v Bangladesh at Bulawayo	2000-01
456	v India at Harare	1992-93
441	v Bangladesh at Harare	2003-04

Zimbabwe's 456 in 1992-93 is the highest by any country in their first Test match

Lowest team totals

Completed innings

51	v N Zealand at Napier	2011-12
54	v SA at Cape Town	2004-05
59	v N Zealand at Harare	2005-06
63	v WI at Port-of-Spain	1999-2000
79	v Sri Lanka at Galle	2001-02
83	v England at Lord's	2000
94	v Eng at Chester-le-Street	2003
99	v N Zealand at Harare	2005-06
102	v S Africa at Harare	1999-2000
102	v WI at Kingston	1999-2000
102	v Sri Lanka at Harare	2003-04

At Harare in 2005-06 and Napier in 2011-12 Zimbabwe were bowled out twice on the same day by New Zealand

Best match bowling

11-255	AG Huckle	v N Zealand at Bulawayo	1997-98
10-158	PA Strang	v N Zealand at Bulawayo	2000-01
10-161	RW Price	v West Indies at Harare	2003-04
9-72	HH Streak	v WI at Port-of-Spain	1999-2000
9-105	HH Streak	v Pakistan at Harare	1994-95
9-235	RW Price	v W Indies at Bulawayo	2003-04
8-104	GW Flower	v Pakistan at Chittagong	2001-02
8-105	HH Streak	v Pakistan at Harare	1994-95
8-110	AM Blignaut	v Bangladesh at Bulawayo	2000-01
8-114	HH Streak	v Pakistan at Rawalpindi	1993-94

Blignaut was playing in his first Test, Huckle in his second

Hat-tricks

AM Blignaut	v Bangladesh at Harare	2003-04

Blignaut dismissed Hannan Sarkar, Mohammad Ashraful and Mushfiqur Rahman to reduce Bangladesh to 14-5.

The only Test hat-trick against Zimbabwe was taken by DNT Zoysa for Sri Lanka at Harare in 1999-2000, when he removed TR Gripper, MW Goodwin and NC Johnson with the first three balls he bowled, in the second over of the match

Zimbabwe's Test match results

	Played	Won	Lost	Drawn	Tied	% win
v Australia	3	0	3	0	0	0.00
v Bangladesh	11	6	2	3	0	54.54
v England	6	0	3	3	0	0.00
v India	11	2	7	2	0	18.18
v New Zealand	15	0	9	6	0	0.00
v Pakistan	17	3	10	4	0	17.64
v South Africa	7	0	6	1	0	0.00
v Sri Lanka	15	0	10	5	0	0.00
v West Indies	8	0	6	2	0	0.00
TOTAL	93	11	56	26	0	11.82

Figures to 17.09.13. Updated records can be found at www.cricinfo.com/ci/engine/records

ZIMBABWE

One-day International Records

Most appearances

221	GW Flower	
213	A Flower	
188	ADR Campbell	
187	HH Streak	
151	P Utseya	
150	E Chigumbura	
150	T Taibu	
147	GJ Whittall	
146	BRM Taylor	
129	H Masakadza	

S Matsikenyeri played in 112 ODIs, SV Carlisle 111, V Sibanda 109 and RW Price 102

Most runs

			Avge
6786	A Flower		35.34
6571	GW Flower		33.52
5185	ADR Campbell		30.50
4414	BRM Taylor		33.69
3429	H Masakadza		27.43
3393	T Taibu		29.25
2947	E Chigumbura		24.15
2901	HH Streak		28.44
2740	SV Carlisle		27.67
2705	GJ Whittall		22.54

V Sibanda (2626) and S Matsikenyeri (2205) also scored more than 2000 runs

Most wickets

			Avge
237	HH Streak		29.81
119	P Utseya		47.82
104	GW Flower		40.62
100	RW Price		35.75
96	PA Strang		33.05
89	E Chigumbura		41.14
88	GJ Whittall		39.55
75	GB Brent		37.01
70	EA Brandes		32.37
70	CB Mpofu		38.41

Brandes took Zimbabwe's only ODI hat-trick, against England at Harare in 1996-97

Highest scores

194*	CK Coventry	v Bangladesh at Bulawayo		2009
178*	H Masakadza	v Kenya at Harare		2009-10
172*	CB Wishart	v Namibia at Harare		2002-03
156	H Masakadza	v Kenya at Harare		2009-10
145*	BRM Taylor	v S Africa at Bloemfontein		2010-11
145	A Flower	v India at Colombo		2002-03
142*	GW Flower	v Bangladesh at Bulawayo		2000-01
142*	A Flower	v England at Harare		2001-02
142	DL Houghton	v New Zealand at Hyderabad		1987-88
140	GW Flower	v Kenya at Dhaka		1998-99

ADR Campbell made seven ODI centuries, GW Flower and BRM Taylor six, A Flower and NC Johnson four

Best bowling figures

6-19	HK Olonga	v England at Cape Town	1999-2000
6-20	BC Strang	v Bangladesh at Nairobi	1997-98
6-28	HK Olonga	v Kenya at Bulawayo	2002-03
6-46	AG Cremer	v Kenya at Harare	2009-10
6-52	CB Mpofu	v Kenya at Nairobi	2008-09
5-20	BV Vitori	v Bangladesh at Harare	2011
5-21	PA Strang	v Kenya at Patna	1995-96
5-22	PA Strang	v Kenya at Dhaka	1998-99
5-28	EA Brandes	v England at Harare	1996-97
5-30	BV Vitori	v Bangladesh at Harare	2011

Vitori took five wickets in each of his first two ODIs, a unique feat

Record wicket partnerships

1st	167	V Sibanda (96) and H Masakadza (80)	v West Indies at Bulawayo	2007-08
2nd	150	GW Flower (78) and GJ Rennie (76)	v Kenya at Nairobi	1997-98
3rd	181	T Taibu (98) and CR Ervine (85)	v Canada at Nagpur	2010-11
4th	202	SV Carlisle (109) and SM Ervine (100)	v India at Adelaide	2003-04
5th	186*	MW Goodwin (112*) and GW Flower (96*)	v West Indies at Chester-le-Street	2000
6th	188	T Taibu (103*) and S Matsikenyeri (86)	v South Africa at Benoni	2009-10
7th	130	A Flower (142*) and HH Streak (56)	v England at Harare	2001-02
8th	117	DL Houghton (142) and IP Butchart (54)	v New Zealand at Hyderabad	1987-88
9th	55	KM Curran (62) and PWE Rawson (19)	v West Indies at Birmingham	1983
10th	60	SW Masakadza (45*) and IA Nicolson (14)	v Ireland at Harare	2010-11

Figures to 17.09.13. Updated records can be found at www.cricinfo.com/ci/engine/records

One-day International Records — ZIMBABWE

Most catches

Fielders

86	GW Flower	
74	ADR Campbell	
52	H Masakadza	
46	E Chigumbura	
46	P Utseya	

Most dismissals

Wicketkeepers — Ct/St

165	A Flower	133/32
145	T Taibu	112/33
81	BRM Taylor	62/19
12	DL Houghton	10/2
10	F Mutizwa	8/2

Highest team totals

351-7	v Kenya at Mombasa	2008-09
340-2	v Namibia at Harare	2002-03
338-7	v Bermuda at Port-of-Spain	2005-06
329-3	v Kenya at Harare	2009-10
329-9	v New Zealand at Bulawayo	2011-12
325-6	v Kenya at Dhaka	1998-99
323-7	v Bangladesh at Bulawayo	2009
313-4	v Kenya at Harare	2009-10
312-4	v Sri Lanka at New Plymouth	1991-92
312-8	v Bangladesh at Bulawayo	2009

Zimbabwe have made ten further totals of 300 or more

Lowest team totals

Completed innings

35	v Sri Lanka at Harare	2003-04
38	v Sri Lanka at Colombo	2001-02
44	v Bang at Chittagong	2009-10
65	v India at Harare	2005-06
67	v Sri Lanka at Harare	2008-09
69	v Kenya at Harare	2005-06
80	v Sri Lanka at Mirpur	2008-09
85	v WI at Ahmedabad	2006-07
92	v England at Bristol	2003
94	v Pakistan at Sharjah	1996-97

Zimbabwe have also been bowled out for 99 twice

Most sixes

83	E Chigumbura	
59	BRM Taylor	
48	HH Streak	
46	H Masakadza	
44	ADR Campbell	
37	GW Flower	
32	T Taibu	
30	V Sibanda	
28	SV Carlisle	
28	CK Coventry	

Coventry hit seven in one innings

Best strike rate

Runs per 100 balls — Runs

106.28	AM Blignaut	626
88.37	CK Coventry	821
85.53	SM Ervine	698
82.11	E Chigumbura	2947
77.65	CR Ervine	702
76.83	SC Williams	1483
76.52	MN Waller	753
75.94	CN Evans	764
75.69	TJ Friend	548
74.59	A Flower	6786

Qualification: 500 runs

Most economical bowlers

Runs per over — Wkts

3.88	AJ Traicos	19
3.99	RW Price	100
4.13	BC Strang	46
4.34	P Utseya	119
4.37	PA Strang	96
4.37	AR Whittall	45
4.40	EC Rainsford	45
4.50	HH Streak	237
4.52	AH Shah	18
4.64	GW Flower	104

Qualification: 1000 balls bowled

Zimbabwe's one-day international results

	Played	Won	Lost	Tied	No result	% win
v Australia	28	1	26	0	1	3.70
v Bangladesh	59	28	31	0	0	47.45
v England	30	8	21	0	1	27.58
v India	56	10	44	2	0	19.64
v New Zealand	35	8	25	1	1	25.00
v Pakistan	47	3	42	1	1	7.60
v South Africa	32	2	29	0	1	6.45
v Sri Lanka	47	7	39	0	1	15.21
v West Indies	44	9	34	0	1	20.93
v others (see below)	43	34	6	1	2	79.06
TOTAL	**421**	**110**	**297**	**5**	**9**	**27.30**

Other teams: Bermuda (P2, W2), Canada (P2, W2), Ireland (P5, W3, L1, T1), Kenya (P32, W25, L5, NR 2), Namibia (P1, W1), Netherlands (P1, W1).

INTERNATIONAL SCHEDULE 2013-14

	Tests	ODIs	T20Is
October 2013			
Bangladesh v New Zealand	2	3	1
India v Australia	–	7	1
Pakistan v South Africa in UAE	2	5	2
Zimbabwe v Sri Lanka	2	3	–
November 2013			
Australia v England	5	5	3
India v West Indies	2	3	–
Sri Lanka v New Zealand	–	3	1
December 2013			
New Zealand v West Indies	3	5	2
Pakistan v Sri Lanka in UAE	3	5	2
South Africa v India	3	5	2
February 2014			
Bangladesh v Sri Lanka	2	–	–
New Zealand v India	3	5	1
South Africa v Australia	3	–	3
March 2014			
ICC World Twenty20 in Bangladesh	–	–	27
Bangladesh tri-series (also Pakistan, Sri Lanka)	–	7	–
West Indies v England	–	3	3
May 2014			
England v Sri Lanka	2	5	1
West Indies V New Zealand	3	5	2
June 2014			
Bangladesh v India	–	3	–
England v India	5	5	1
Zimbabwe v Australia	–	3	–
July 2014			
West Indies v Bangladesh	2	3	1
Zimbabwe v South Africa	2	3	1
October 2014			
Bangladesh v Zimbabwe	2	–	–
Bangladesh tri-series (also Sri Lanka, Zimbabwe)	–	7	–
India v West Indies	3	5	1
Pakistan v Australia	3	–	–
November 2014			
Australia v South Africa	–	5	3
Pakistan v New Zealand	3	3	1
Sri Lanka v England	–	5	2
December 2014			
Australia v India	4	–	–
New Zealand v Sri Lanka	2	5	1
Pakistan v Zimbabwe	2	3	2
South Africa v West Indies	3	5	2

Details subject to change. Some tours may continue into the month(s) after the one shown above